# *The Power of* Positive Thinking

and

# *The Amazing Results of* Positive Thinking

*Norman Vincent Peale*

**A Fireside Book**
Published by Simon & Schuster
New York London Toronto Sydney

FIRESIDE
Rockefeller Center
1230 Avenue of the Americas
New York, NY 10020



This Fireside Edition 2005

FIRESIDE and colophon are registered trademarks
of Simon & Schuster, Inc.

For information regarding special discounts for bulk purchases,
please contact Simon & Schuster Special Sales at 1-800-456-6798
or business@simonandschuster.com.

Manufactured in the United States of America

10 9 8 7 6 5 4 3 2

Library of Congress Cataloging-in-Publication Data is available.

ISBN-13: 978-0-7432-9215-3
ISBN-10: 0-7432-9215-4

These titles were originally published individually.

Acknowledgment is made to Sermon Publications, Inc., for permission to
reprint certain excerpts from "Self-Improvement Handbook," "What's
Your Trouble?" and the "How Card" series by Norman Vincent Peale.

# CONTENTS

# *The Power of* Positive Thinking

Dedicated
to my brothers
Robert Clifford Peale, M.D., F.I.C.S
and
The Reverend Leonard Delaney Peale
Effective Helpers of Mankind

# CONTENTS

# PREFACE

At the time I wrote this book it never occurred to me that more than two million copies would be sold in various hardcover editions and that it would one day attract a vast new readership through a paperback edition such as this. Frankly, however, my gratitude for this event is not from the viewpoint of books sold, but in terms of the many persons to whom I have been privileged to suggest a simple, workable philosophy of living.

The dynamic laws which the book teaches were learned the hard way by trial and error in my personal search for a way of life. But I found in them an answer to my own problems and, believe me, I am the most difficult person with whom I have worked. The book is my effort to share my spiritual experience, for if it helped me, I felt it might also be of help to others.

In formulating this simple philosophy of life I found my own answers in the teachings of Jesus Christ. I have merely tried to describe those truths in the language and thought forms understandable to present day people. The way of life to which this book is a witness is very wonderful. It is not easy. Indeed, it often is hard, but it is full of joy and hope and victory.

I well recall the day I sat down to begin writing the book. I knew that the best work required more ability than I possessed and therefore I needed help that only God could give. My wife and I have the policy of taking God into working partnership in all our problems and activities. So we had a very earnest session of prayer, asking for guidance, and we put the project into God's hands. When the manuscript was ready for the publisher Mrs. Peale and I again prayed, dedicating the manuscript. We asked only that it might help people to live more effective lives. When the first book of these two million copies came from the press to us it was again a spiritual moment. We thanked God for His help and dedicated the book once more.

The book was written for the plain people of this world, of whom certainly I am one. I was born and reared in humble Midwestern circumstances in a dedicated Christian home. The everyday people of this land are my own kind whom I know and love and believe in with great faith. When anyone of them lets God have charge of his life the power and glory are amazingly demonstrated.

The book is written with deep concern for the pain, difficulty and struggle of human existence. It teaches the cultivation of peace of mind, not as an escape from life into protected quiescence, but as a power center out of which comes driving energy for constructive personal and social living. It teaches positive thinking, not as a means to fame, riches or power, but as the practical application of faith to overcome defeat and accomplish worthwhile creative values in life. It teaches a hard, disciplinary way of life, but one which offers great joy to the person who achieves victory over himself and the difficult circumstances of the world.

To all who have written me about the joyous victory they have had through practicing the spiritual techniques of this book and to those who will yet have such experience may I say how happy I am for all that is happening to them as they live by dynamic spiritual formulas.

I wish finally to express deep appreciation to my publishers for their never-failing support, co-operation and friendship. I have never worked with finer people than my cherished friends at Prentice-Hall. I look forward with great pleasure to my association with Fawcett Publications. May God continue to use this book in human helpfulness.

NORMAN VINCENT PEALE

# INTRODUCTION

## *What This Book Can Do for You*

THIS BOOK IS WRITTEN to suggest techniques and to give examples which demonstrate that you do not need to be defeated by anything, that you can have peace of mind, improved health, and a never-ceasing flow of energy. In short, that your life can be full of joy and satisfaction. Of this I have no doubt at all for I have watched countless persons learn and apply a system of simple procedures that has brought about the foregoing benefits in their lives. These assertions, which may appear extravagant, are based on bonafide demonstrations in actual human experience.

Altogether too many people are defeated by the everyday problems of life. They go struggling, perhaps even whining, through their days with a sense of dull resentment at what they consider the "bad breaks" life has given them. In a sense there may be such a thing as "the breaks" in this life, but there is also a spirit and method by which we can control and even determine those breaks. It is a pity that people should let themselves be defeated by the problems, cares, and difficulties of human existence, and it is also quite unnecessary.

In saying this I certainly do not ignore or minimize the hardships and tragedies of the world, but neither do I allow them to dominate. You can permit obstacles to control your mind to the point where they are uppermost and thus become the dominating factors in your thought pattern. By learning how to cast them from the mind, by refusing to become mentally subservient to them, and by channeling spiritual power through your thoughts you can rise above obstacles which ordinarily might defeat you. By methods I shall outline, obstacles are simply not permitted to destroy your happiness and well-being. You need be defeated only if you are willing to be. This book teaches you how to "will" not to be.

The purpose of this book is a very direct and simple one. It makes no pretense to literary excellence nor does it seek to demonstrate any unusual scholarship on my part. This is simply a practical, direct-action, personal-improvement manual. It is written with the sole objective of helping the reader achieve a happy, satisfying, and worthwhile life. I thoroughly and enthusiastically believe in certain demonstrated and effective principles which, when practiced, produce a victorious life. My aim is to set them forth in this volume in a logical, simple, and understandable manner so that the reader feeling a sense of need, may learn a practical method by which he can build for himself, with God's help, the kind of life he deeply desires.

If you read this book thoughtfully, carefully absorbing its teachings, and if you will sincerely and persistently practice the principles and formulas set forth herein, you can experience an amazing improvement within yourself. By using the techniques outlined here you can modify or change the circumstances in which you now live, assuming control over them rather than continuing to be directed by them. Your relations with other people will improve. You will become a more popular, esteemed, and well-liked individual. By mastering these principles, you will enjoy a delightful new sense of well-being. You may attain a degree of health not hitherto known by you and experience a new and keen pleasure in living. You will become a person of greater usefulness and will wield an expanded influence.

How can I be so certain that the practice of these principles will produce such results? The answer is simply that for many years in the Marble Collegiate Church of New York City we have taught a system of creative living based on spiritual techniques, carefully noting its operation in the lives of hundreds of people. It is no speculative series of extravagant assertions that I make, for these principles have worked so efficiently over so long a period of time that they are now firmly established as documented and demonstrable truth. The system outlined is a perfected and amazing method of successful living.

In my writings, including several books, in my regular weekly newspaper column in nearly one hundred dailies, in my national radio program over seventeen years, in our magazine, *Guide-*

*posts*, and in lectures in scores of cities, I have taught these same scientific yet simple principles of achievement, health, and happiness. Hundreds have read, listened, and practiced, and the results are invariably the same: new life, new power, increased efficiency, greater happiness.

Because so many have requested that these principles be put into book form, the better to be studied and practiced, I am publishing this new volume under the title, *The Power of Positive Thinking*. I need not point out that the powerful principles contained herein are not my invention but are given to us by the greatest Teacher who ever lived and who still lives. This book teaches applied Christianity; a simple yet scientific system of practical techniques of successful living that works.

NORMAN VINCENT PEALE

# 1

# *Believe in Yourself*

BELIEVE IN YOURSELF! Have faith in your abilities! Without a humble but reasonable confidence in your own powers you cannot be successful or happy. But with sound self-confidence you can succeed. A sense of inferiority and inadequacy interferes with the attainment of your hopes, but self-confidence leads to self-realization and successful achievement. Because of the importance of this mental attitude, this book will help you believe in yourself and release your inner powers.

It is appalling to realize the number of pathetic people who are hampered and made miserable by the malady popularly called the inferiority complex. But you need not suffer from this trouble. When proper steps are taken, it can be overcome. You can develop creative faith in yourself—faith that is justified.

After speaking to a convention of businessmen in a city auditorium, I was on the stage greeting people when a man approached me and with a peculiar intensity of manner asked, "May I talk with you about a matter of desperate importance to me?"

I asked him to remain until the others had gone, then we went backstage and sat down.

"I'm in this town to handle the most important business deal of my life," he explained. "If I succeed, it means everything to me. If I fail, I'm done for."

I suggested that he relax a little, that nothing was quite that final. If he succeeded, that was fine. If he didn't, well, tomorrow was another day.

"I have a terrible disbelief in myself," he said dejectedly. "I have no confidence. I just don't believe I can put it over. I am very discouraged and depressed. In fact," he lamented, "I'm just about sunk. Here I am, forty years old. Why is it that all my life I have been tormented by inferiority feelings, by lack of confidence, by self-doubt? I listened to your speech tonight in which you talked about the power of positive thinking, and I want to ask how I can get some faith in myself."

"There are two steps to take," I replied. "First, it is important to discover why you have these feelings of no power. That requires analysis and will take time. We must approach the maladies of our emotional life as a physician probes to find something wrong physically. This cannot be done immediately, certainly not in our brief interview tonight, and it may require treatment to reach a permanent solution. But to pull you through this immediate problem I shall give you a formula which will work if you use it.

"As you walk down the street tonight I suggest that you repeat certain words which I shall give you. Say them over several times after you get into bed. When you awaken tomorrow, repeat them three times before arising. On the way to your important appointment say them three additional times. Do this with an attitude of faith and you will receive sufficient strength and ability to deal with this problem. Later, if you wish, we can go into an analysis of your basic problem, but whatever we come up with following that study, the formula which I am now going to give you can be a large factor in the eventual cure."

Following is the affirmation which I gave him—"I can do all things through Christ which strengtheneth me." (Philippians 4:13) He was unfamiliar with these words so I wrote them on a card and had him read them over three times aloud.

"Now, follow that prescription, and I am sure things will come out all right."

He pulled himself up, stood quietly for a moment, then said with considerable feeling, "O.K., Doctor. O.K."

I watched him square his shoulders and walk out into the night. He seemed a pathetic figure, and yet the way he carried himself as he disappeared showed that faith was already at work in his mind.

Subsequently he reported that this simple formula "did wonders" for him and added, "It seems incredible that a few words from the Bible could do so much for a person."

This man later had a study made of the reasons for his inferiority attitudes. They were cleared away by scientific counseling and by the application of religious faith. He was taught how to have faith; was given certain specific instructions to follow (these are given later in this chapter). Gradually he attained a strong, steady, reasonable confidence. He never ceases to express amazement at the way in which things now flow toward rather than away from him. His personality has taken on a positive, not negative, character so that he no longer repels success, but, on the contrary, draws it to him. He now has an authentic confidence in his own powers.

There are various causes of inferiority feelings, and not a few stem from childhood.

An executive consulted me about a young man whom he wished to advance in his company. "But," he explained, "he cannot be trusted with important secret information and I'm sorry, for otherwise I would make him my administrative assistant. He has all the other necessary qualifications, but he talks too much, and without meaning to do so divulges matters of a private and important nature."

Upon analysis I found that he "talked too much" simply because of an inferiority feeling. To compensate for it he succumbed to the temptation of parading his knowledge.

He associated with men who were rather well to do, all of whom had attended college and belonged to a fraternity. But this boy was reared in poverty, had not been a college man or fraternity member. Thus he felt himself inferior to his associates in education and social background. To build himself up with his associates and to enhance his self-esteem, his subconscious mind, which always seeks to provide a compensatory mechanism, supplied him with a means for raising his ego.

He was on "the inside" in the industry, and accompanied his superior to conferences where he met outstanding men and listened to important private conversations. He reported just enough of his "inside information" to cause his associates to regard him with admiration and envy. This served to elevate his self-esteem and satisfy his desire for recognition.

When the employer became aware of the cause of this personality trait, being a kindly and understanding man, he pointed out to the young man the opportunities in business to which his abilities could lead him. He also described how his inferiority feelings caused his unreliability in confidential matters. This self-knowledge, together with a sincere practicing of the techniques of faith and prayer, made him a valuable asset to his company. His real powers were released.

I can perhaps illustrate the manner in which many youngsters acquire an inferiority complex through the use of a personal reference. As a small boy I was painfully thin. I had lots of energy, was on a track team, was healthy and hard as nails, but thin. And that bothered me because I didn't want to be thin. I wanted to be fat. I was called "skinny," but I didn't want to be called "skinny." I wanted to be called "fat." I longed to be hard-boiled and tough and fat. I did everything to get fat. I drank cod-liver oil, consumed vast numbers of milk shakes, ate thousands of chocolate sundaes with whipped cream and nuts, cakes and pies innumerable, but they did not affect me in the slightest. I stayed thin and lay awake nights thinking and agonizing about it. I kept on trying to get heavy until I was about thirty, when all of a sudden did I get heavy? I bulged at the seams. Then I became self-conscious because I was so fat, and finally had to take off forty pounds with equal agony to get myself down to respectable size.

In the second place (to conclude this personal analysis which I give only because it may help others by showing how this malady works), I was a minister's son and was constantly reminded of that fact. Everybody else could do everything, but if I did even the slightest little thing—"Ah, you are a preacher's son." So I didn't want to be a preacher's son, for preachers' sons are supposed to be nice and namby-pamby. I wanted to be known as a hard-boiled fellow. Perhaps that is why preachers' sons get their reputation for being a little difficult, because they rebel against having to carry the banner of the church all the time. I vowed there was one thing I would never do, and that was to become a preacher.

Also, I came of a family practically every member of which was a performer in public, a platform speaker, and that was the last thing I wanted to be. They used to make me get up in public to make speeches when it scared me to death, even filled me with terror. That was years ago, but the twinge of it comes to me every now and then when I walk onto a platform. I had to use every known device to develop confidence in what powers the good Lord gave me.

I found the solution of this problem in the simple techniques of faith taught in the Bible. These principles are scientific and sound and can heal any personality of the pain of inferiority feelings.

Their use can enable the sufferer to find and release the powers which have been inhibited by a feeling of inadequacy.

Such are some of the sources of the inferiority complex which erect power barriers in our personalities. It is some emotional violence done to us in childhood, or the consequences of certain circumstances, or something we did to ourselves. This malady arises out of the misty past in the dim recesses of our personalities.

Perhaps you had an older brother who was a brilliant student. He got A's in school; you made only C's, and you never heard the last of it. So you believed that you could never succeed in life as he could. He got A's and you got C's, so you reasoned that you were consigned to getting C's all your life. Apparently you never realized that some of those who failed to get high grades in school have been the greatest successes outside of school. Just because somebody gets an A in college doesn't make him the greatest man in the United States, because maybe his A's will stop when he gets his diploma, and the fellow who got C's in school will go on later to get the real A's in life.

The greatest secret for eliminating the inferiority complex, which is another term for deep and profound self-doubt, is to fill your mind to overflowing with faith. Develop a tremendous faith in God and that will give you a humble yet soundly realistic faith in yourself.

The acquiring of dynamic faith is accomplished by prayer, lots of prayer, by reading and mentally absorbing the Bible and by practicing its faith techniques. In another chapter I deal with specific formulas of prayer, but I want to point out here that the type of prayer that produces the quality of faith required to eliminate inferiority is of a particular nature. Surface skimming, formalistic and perfunctory prayer is not sufficiently powerful.

A wonderful colored woman, a cook in the home of friends of mine in Texas, was asked how she so completely mastered her troubles. She answered that ordinary problems could be met by ordinary prayers, but that "when a big trouble comes along, you have to pray deep prayers."

One of my most inspiring friends was the late Harlowe B. Andrews of Syracuse, New York, one of the best businessmen and competent spiritual experts I ever knew. He said the trouble with most prayers is that they aren't big enough. "To get anywhere with faith," said he, "learn to pray big prayers. God will rate you according to the size of your prayers." Doubtless he was right, for the Scriptures say, "According to your faith be it unto you." (Matthew 9:29) So the bigger your problem, the bigger your prayer should be.

Roland Hayes, the singer, quoted his grandfather to me, a man whose education was not equal to that of his grandson, but whose native wisdom was obviously sound. He said, "The trouble with lots of prayers is they ain't got no suction." Drive your prayers deep into your doubts, fears, inferiorities. Pray deep, big prayers that have plenty of suction and you will come up with powerful and vital faith.

Go to a competent spiritual adviser and let him teach you how to have faith. The ability to possess and utilize faith and gain the release of powers it provides are skills and, like any skills, must be studied and practiced to gain perfection.

At the conclusion of this chapter are listed ten suggestions for overcoming your inferiority pattern and for developing faith. Practice these rules diligently and they will aid you in developing confidence in yourself by dissipating your feelings of inferiority, however deeply imbedded.

At this point, however, I wish to indicate that to build up feelings of self-confidence the practice of suggesting confidence concepts to your mind is very effective. If your mind is obsessed by thoughts of insecurity and inadequacy it is, of course, due to the fact that such ideas have dominated your thinking over a long period of time. Another and more positive pattern of ideas must be given the mind, and that is accomplished by repetitive suggestion or confidence ideas. In the busy activities of daily existence thought disciplining is required if you are to re-educate the mind and make of it a power-producing plant. It is possible, even in the midst of your daily work, to drive confident thoughts into consciousness. Let me tell you about one man who did so by the use of a unique method.

One icy winter morning he called for me at a hotel in a Midwestern city to take me about thirty-five miles to another town to fill a lecture engagement. We got into his car and started off at a rather high rate of speed on the slippery road. He was going a little faster than I thought reasonable, and I reminded him that we had plenty of time and suggested that we take it easy.

"Don't let my driving worry you," he replied. "I used to be filled with all kinds of insecurities myself, but I got over them. I was afraid of everything. I feared an automobile trip or an airplane flight; and if any of my family went away I worried until they returned. I always went around with a feeling that something was going to happen, and it made my life miserable. I was saturated with inferiority and lacked confidence. This state of mind reflected itself in my business and I wasn't doing very well. But I hit upon a wonderful plan which knocked all these insecurity feelings out of my mind, and now I live with a feeling of confidence, not only in myself but in life generally."

This was the "wonderful plan." He pointed to two clips fastened on the instrument panel of the car just below the windshield and, reaching into the glove compartment, took out a pack of small cards. He selected one and slipped it beneath the clip. It read, "If ye have faith . . . nothing shall be impossible unto you." (Matthew 17:20) He removed that one, shuffled expertly through the cards with one hand as he drove, selected another, and placed it under the clip. This one read, "If God be for us, who can be against us?" (Romans 8:31)

"I'm a traveling salesman," he explained, "and I drive around all day calling on my customers. I have discovered that while a man drives he thinks all kinds of thoughts. If his pattern of thought is negative, he will think many negative thoughts during the day and that, of course, is bad for him; but that is the way I used to be. I used to drive around all day between calls thinking fear and defeat thoughts, and incidentally that is one reason my sales were down. But since I have been using these cards as I drive and committing the words to memory, I have learned to think differently. The old insecurities that used to haunt me are just about all gone, and instead of thinking fear thoughts of defeat and ineffectiveness, I think thoughts of faith and courage. It is really wonderful the way this method has changed me. It has helped in my business, too, for how can one expect to make a sale if he drives up to a customer's place of business thinking he is not going to make a sale?"

This plan used by my friend is a very wise one. By filling his mind with affirmations of the presence, support, and help of God, he had actually changed his thought processes. He put an end to the domination of his long-held sense of insecurity. His potential powers were set free.

We build up the feeling of insecurity or security by how we think. If in our thoughts we constantly fix attention upon sinister expectations of dire events that might happen, the result will be constantly to feel insecure. And what is even more serious is the tendency to create, by the power of thought, the very condition we fear. This salesman actually created positive results by vital thoughts of courage and confidence through the process of placing the cards before him in his car. His powers, curiously inhibited by a defeat psychology, now flowed out of a personality in which creative attitudes had been stimulated.

Lack of self-confidence apparently is one of the great problems besetting people today. In a university a survey was made of six hundred students in psychology courses. The students were asked to state their most difficult personal problem. Seventy-five per cent listed lack of confidence. It can safely be assumed that the same large proportion is true of the population generally. Everywhere you encounter people who are inwardly afraid, who shrink from life, who suffer from a deep sense of inadequacy and insecurity, who doubt their own powers. Deep within themselves they mistrust their ability to meet responsibilities or to grasp opportunities. Always they are beset by the vague and sinister fear that something is not going to be quite right. They do not believe that they have it in them to be what they want to be, and so they try to make themselves content with something less than that of which they are capable. Thousands upon thousands go crawling through life on their hands and knees, defeated and afraid. And in most cases such frustration of power is unnecessary.

The blows of life, the accumulation of difficulties, the multiplication of problems tend to sap energy and leave you spent and discouraged. In such a condition the true status of your power is often obscured, and a person yields to a discouragement that is not justified by the facts. It is vitally essential to re-appraise your personality assets. When done in an attitude of reasonableness, this evaluation will convince you that you are less defeated than you think you are.

For example, a man fifty-two years of age consulted me. He was in great despondency. He revealed utter despair. He said he "was all through." He informed me that everything he had built up over his lifetime had been swept away.

"Everything?" I asked.

"Everything," he repeated. He was through, he reiterated. "I have nothing left at all. Everything is gone. There is no hope, and I am too old to start all over again. I have lost all faith."

Naturally I felt sympathetic toward him, but it was evident that his chief trouble was the fact that dark shadows of hopelessness had entered his mind and discolored his outlook, distorting it. Behind this twisted thinking his true powers had retreated, leaving him without force.

"So," I said, "suppose we take a piece of paper and write down the values you have left."

"There's no use," he sighed. "I haven't a single thing left. I thought I told you that."

I said, "Let's just see anyway." Then asked, "Is your wife still with you?"

"Why, yes, of course, and she is wonderful. We have been married for thirty years. She would never leave me no matter how bad things are."

"All right, let us put that down—your wife is still with you and she will never leave you no matter what happens. How about your children? Got any children?"

"Yes," he replied, "I have three and they are certainly wonderful. I have been touched by the way they have come to me and said, 'Dad, we love you, and we'll stand by you.' "

"Well, then," I said, "that is number two—three children who love you and who will stand by you. Got any friends?" I asked.

"Yes," he said, "I really have some fine friends. I must admit they have been pretty decent. They have come around and said they would like to help me, but what can they do? They can't do anything."

"That is number three—you have some friends who would like to help you and who hold you in esteem. How about your integrity? Have you done anything wrong?"

"My integrity is all right," he replied. "I have always tried to do the right thing and my conscience is clear."

"All right," I said, "we will put that down as number four—integrity. How about your health?"

"My health is all right," he answered. "I have had very few sick days and I guess I am in pretty good shape physically."

"So let's put down as number five—good physical health. How about the United States? Do you think it's still doing business and is the land of opportunity?"

"Yes," he said. "It is the only country in the world I would want to live in."

"That is number six—you live in the United States, land of opportunity, and you are glad to be here." Then I asked, "How about your religious faith? Do you believe in God and that God will help you?"

"Yes," he said. "I do not think I could have gotten through this at all if I hadn't had some help from God."

"Now," I said, "let's list the assets we have figured out:

"1. A wonderful wife—married for thirty years.

"2. Three devoted children who will stand by you.

"3. Friends who will help you and who hold you in esteem.

"4. Integrity—nothing to be ashamed of.

"5. Good physical health.

"6. Live in the United States, the greatest country in the world.

"7. Have religious faith."

I shoved it across the table at him. "Take a look at that. I guess you have quite a total of assets. I thought you told me everything had been swept away."

He grinned ashamedly. "I guess I didn't think of those things. I never thought of it that way. Perhaps things aren't so bad at that," he said pensively. "Maybe I can start all over again if I can just get some confidence, if I can get the feel of some power within me."

Well, he got it, and he did start all over again. But he did so only when he changed his viewpoint, his mental attitude. Faith swept away his doubts, and more than enough power to overcome all his difficulties emerged from within him.

This incident illustrates a profound truth which is expressed in a very important statement made by the famous psychiatrist, Dr. Karl Menninger. He said, "Attitudes are more important than facts." That is worth repeating until its truth grips you. Any fact facing us, however difficult, even seemingly hopeless, is not so important as our attitude toward that fact. How you think about a fact may defeat you before you ever do anything about it.

You may permit a fact to overwhelm you mentally before you start to deal with it actually. On the other hand, a confident and optimistic thought pattern can modify or overcome the fact altogether.

I know a man who is a tremendous asset to his organization, not because of any extraordinary ability, but because he invariably demonstrates a triumphant thought pattern. Perhaps his associates view a proposition pessimistically, so he employs what he calls "the vacuum-cleaner method." That is, by a series of questions he "sucks the dust" out of his associates' minds; he draws out their negative attitudes. Then quietly he suggests positive ideas concerning the proposition until a new set of attitudes gives them a new concept of the facts.

They often comment upon how different facts appear when this man "goes to work on them." It's the confidence attitude that makes the difference, nor does this rule out objectivity in an appraisal of facts. The inferiority complex victim sees all facts through discolored attitudes. The secret of correction is simply to gain a normal view, and that is always slanted on the positive side.

So if you feel that you are defeated and have lost confidence in your ability to win, sit down, take a piece of paper and make a list, not of the factors that are against you, but of those that are for you. If you or I or anybody think constantly of the forces that seem to be against us, we will build them up into a power far beyond that which is justified. They will assume a formidable strength which they do not actually possess. But if, on the contrary, you mentally visualize and affirm and reaffirm your assets and keep your thoughts on them, emphasizing them to the fullest extent, you will rise out of any difficulty regardless of what it may be. Your inner powers will reassert themselves and, with the help of God, lift you from defeat to victory.

One of the most powerful concepts, one which is a sure cure for lack of confidence, is the thought that God is actually with you and helping you. This is one of the simplest teachings in religion, namely, that Almighty God will be your companion, will stand by you, help you, and see you through. No other idea is so powerful in developing self-confidence as this simple belief when practiced. To practice it simply affirm "God is with me; God is helping me; God is guiding me." Spend several minutes each day visualizing His presence. Then practice believing that affirmation. Go about your business on the assumption that what you have affirmed and visualized is true. Affirm it, visualize it, believe it, and it will actualize itself. The release of power which this procedure stimulates will astonish you.

Feelings of confidence depend upon the type of thoughts that habitually occupy your mind. Think defeat and you are bound to feel defeated. But practice thinking confident thoughts, make it a dominating habit, and you will develop such a strong sense of capacity that regardless of what difficulties arise you will be able to overcome them. Feelings of confidence actually induce increased strength. Basil King once said, "Be bold, and mighty forces will come to your aid." Experience proves the truth of this. You will feel these mighty forces aiding you as your increasing faith reconditions your attitudes.

Emerson declared a tremendous truth, "They conquer who believe they can." And he added, "Do the thing you fear and the death of fear is certain." Practice confidence and faith and your fears and insecurities will soon have no power over you.

Once when Stonewall Jackson planned a daring attack, one of his generals fearfully objected, saying, "I am afraid of this" or "I fear that . . ." Putting his hand on his timorous subordinate's shoulder, Jackson said, "General, never take counsel of your fears."

The secret is to fill your mind with thoughts of faith, confidence, and security. This will force out or expel all thoughts of doubt, all lack of confidence. To one man who for a long time had been haunted by insecurities and fears I suggested that he read through the Bible underlining in red pencil every statement it contains relative to courage and confidence. He also committed them to memory, in effect cramming his mind full of the healthiest, happiest, most powerful thoughts in the world. These dynamic thoughts changed him from cringing hopelessness to a man of compelling force. The change in him in a few weeks was remarkable. From almost complete defeat he became a confident and inspiring personality. He now radiates courage and magnetism. He regained confidence in himself and his own powers by a simple process of thought conditioning.

To sum up—what can you do *now* to build up your self-confidence? Following are ten simple, workable rules for overcoming inadequacy attitudes and learning to practice faith. Thousands have used these rules, reporting successful results. Undertake this program and you, too, will build up confidence in your powers. You, too, will have a new feeling of power.

1. Formulate and stamp indelibly on your mind a mental picture of yourself as succeeding. Hold this picture tenaciously. Never permit it to fade. Your mind will seek to develop this picture. Never think of yourself as failing; never doubt the reality of the mental image. That is most dangerous, for the mind always tries to complete what it pictures. So *always* picture "success" no matter how badly things seem to be going at the moment.

2. Whenever a negative thought concerning your personal powers comes to mind, deliberately voice a positive thought to cancel it out.

3. Do not built up obstacles in your imagination. Depreciate every so-called obstacle. Minimize them. Difficulties must be studied and efficiently dealt with to be eliminated, but they must be seen for only what they are. They must not be inflated by fear thoughts.

4. Do not be awestruck by other people and try to copy them. Nobody can be you as efficiently as YOU can. Remember also that most people, despite their confident appearance and demeanor, are often as scared as you are and as doubtful of themselves.

5. Ten times a day repeat these dynamic words, "If God be *for* us, who can be *against* us?" (Romans 8:31) (Stop reading and repeat them NOW slowly and confidently.)

6. Get a competent counselor to help you understand why you do what you do. Learn the origin of your inferiority and self-doubt feelings which often begin in childhood. Self-knowledge leads to a cure.

7. Ten times each day practice the following affirmation, repeating it out loud if possible. "I can do all things through Christ which strengtheneth me." (Philippians 4:13) Repeat those words NOW. That magic statement is the most powerful antidote on earth to inferiority thoughts.

8. Make a true estimate of your own ability, then raise it 10 per cent. Do not become egotistical, but develop a wholesome self-respect. Believe in your own God-released powers.

9. Put yourself in God's hands. To do that simply state, "I am in God's hands." Then believe you are NOW receiving all the power you need. "Feel" it flowing into you. Affirm that "the kingdom of God is within you" (Luke 17:21) in the form of adequate power to meet life's demands.

10. Remind yourself that God is with you and nothing can defeat you. Believe that you *now* RECEIVE power from him.

# 2

# A Peaceful Mind Generates Power

AT BREAKFAST IN A HOTEL dining room three of us fell to discussing how well we had slept the night before, a truly momentous topic. One man complained of a sleepless night. He had tossed and turned and was about as exhausted as when he retired. "Guess I'd better stop listening to the news before going to bed," he observed. "I tuned in last night and sure got an ear full of trouble."

That is quite a phrase, "an ear full of trouble." Little wonder he had a disturbed night. "Maybe the coffee I drank before retiring had something to do with it," he mused.

The other man spoke up, "As for me, I had a grand night. I got my news from the evening paper and from an early broadcast and had a chance to digest it before I went to sleep. Of course," he continued, "I used my go-to-sleep plan which never fails to work."

I prodded him for his plan, which he explained as follows: "When I was a boy, my father, a farmer, had the habit of gathering the family in the parlor at bedtime and he read to us out of the Bible. I can hear him yet. In fact, every time I hear those Bible verses I always seem to hear them in the tone of my father's voice. After prayers I would go up to my room and sleep like a top. But when I left home I got away from the Bible reading and prayer habit.

"I must admit that for years practically the only time I ever prayed was when I got into a jam. But some months ago my wife and I, having a number of difficult problems, decided we would try it again. We found it a very helpful practice, so now every night before going to bed she and I together read the Bible and have a little session of prayer. I don't know what there is about it, but I have been sleeping better and things have improved all down the line. In fact, I find it so helpful that even out on the road, as I am now, I still read the Bible and pray. Last night I got into bed and read the 23rd Psalm. I read it out loud and it did me a lot of good."

He turned to the other man and said, "I didn't go to bed with an ear full of trouble. I went to sleep with a mind full of peace."

Well, there are two cryptic phrases for you—"an ear full of trouble" and "a mind full of peace." Which do you choose?

The essence of the secret lies in a change of mental attitude. One must learn to live on a different thought basis, and even though thought change requires effort, it is much easier than to continue living as you are. The life of strain is difficult. The life of inner peace, being harmonious and without stress, is the easiest type of existence. The chief struggle then in gaining mental peace is the effort of revamping your thinking to the relaxed attitude of acceptance of God's gift of peace.

As an illustration of taking a relaxed attitude and therefore receiving peace, I always think of an experience in a certain city where I lectured one evening. Prior to going on the platform I was sitting backstage going over my speech when a man approached and wanted to discuss a personal problem.

I informed him that at the moment it was impossible to talk as I was just about to be introduced, and asked him to wait. While speaking I noticed him in the wings nervously pacing up and down, but afterward he was nowhere about. However, he had given me his card, which indicated that he was a man of considerable influence in that city.

Back at my hotel, although it was late, I was still troubled by this man so I telephoned him. He was surprised at my call and explained that he did not wait because obviously I was busy. "I just wanted you to pray with me," he said. "I thought if you would pray with me, perhaps I could get some peace."

"There is nothing to prevent us from praying together on the telephone right now," I said.

Somewhat in surprise, he replied, "I have never heard of praying on the telephone."

"Why not?" I asked. "A telephone is simply a gadget of communication. You are some blocks from me, but by means of the telephone we are together. Besides," I continued, "the Lord is with each of us. He is at both ends of this line and in between. He is with you and He is with me."

"All right," he conceded. "I'd like to have you pray for me."

So I closed my eyes and prayed for the man over the telephone, and I prayed just as though we were in the same room. He could hear and the Lord could hear. When I finished I suggested, "Won't you pray?" There was no response. Then at the other end of the line I heard sobbing and finally, "I can't talk," he said.

"Go on and cry for a minute or two and then pray," I suggested. "Simply tell the Lord everything that is bothering you. I assume this is a private line, but if not, and if anybody is listening, it won't matter. As far as anyone is concerned, we are just a couple of voices. Nobody would know it is you and I."

Thus encouraged, he started to pray, hesitantly at first, and then with great impetuosity he poured out his heart, and it was filled with hate, frustration, failure—a mass of it. Finally he prayed plaintively, "Dear Jesus, I have a lot of nerve to ask you to do anything for me, because I never did anything for you. I guess you know what a no-account I am, even though I put on a big front. I am sick of all this, dear Jesus. Please help me."

So I prayed again, and asked the Lord to answer his prayer, then said, "Lord, at the other end of the telephone wire, place your hand on my friend and give him peace. Help him now to yield himself and accept your gift of peace." Then I stopped, and there was a rather long pause, and I shall never forget the tone in his voice as I heard him say, "I shall always remember this experience, and I want you to know that for the first time in months I feel clean inside and happy and peaceful." This man employed a simple technique for having a peaceful mind. He emptied his mind and he received peace as a gift from God.

As a physician said, "Many of my patients have nothing wrong with them except their thoughts. So I have a favorite prescription that I write for some. but it is not a prescription that you can fill at a drugstore. The prescription I write is a verse from the Bible, 'Romans 12:2.' I do not write out that verse for my patients. I make them look it up and it reads: '. . . be ye transformed by the renewing of your mind . . .' To be happier and healthier they need a renewing of their minds, that is, a change in the pattern of their thoughts. When they 'take' this prescription, they actually achieve a mind full of peace. That helps to produce health and well-being."

A primary method for gaining a mind full of peace is to practice emptying the mind. This will be emphasized in another chapter, but I mention it here to underscore the importance of a frequent mental catharsis. I recommend a mind-emptying at least twice a day, more often if necessary. Definitely practice emptying your mind of fears, hates, insecurities, regrets, and guilt feelings. The mere fact that you consciously make this effort to empty your mind tends to give relief. Haven't you experienced a sense of release when you have been able to pour out to somebody whom you can trust worrisome matters that lay heavy upon the heart? As a pastor I have often observed how much it means to people to have someone to whom they can truly and in confidence tell everything troubling their minds.

I conducted a religious service on board the *S.S. Lurline* on a recent voyage to Honolulu. In the course of my talk I suggested that people who were carrying worries in their minds might go to the stern of the vessel and imaginatively take such anxious thought out of the mind, drop it overboard, and watch it disappear in the wake of the ship. It seems an almost childlike suggestion, but a man came to me later that day and said, "I did as you suggested and am amazed at the relief it has given me. During this voyage," he said, "every evening at sunset I am going to drop all my worries overboard until I develop the psychology of casting them entirely out of my consciousness. Every day I shall watch them disappear in the great ocean of time. Doesn't the Bible say something about 'forgetting those things that are behind'?"

The man to whom this suggestion appealed is not an impractical sentimentalist. On the contrary, he is a person of extraordinary mental stature, an outstanding leader in his field.

Of course, emptying the mind is not enough. When the mind is emptied, something is bound to enter. The mind cannot long remain a vacuum. You cannot go around permanently with an empty mind. I admit that some people seem to accomplish that feat, but by and large it is necessary to refill the emptied mind or the old, unhappy thoughts which you have cast out will come sneaking in again.

To prevent that happening, immediately start filling your mind with creative and healthy thoughts. Then when the old fears, hates, and worries that have haunted you for so long try to edge back in, they will in effect find a sign on the door of your mind reading "occupied." They may struggle for admission, for having lived in your mind for a long time, they feel at home there. But the new and healthy thoughts which you have taken in will now be stronger and better fortified, and therefore able to repulse them. Presently the old thoughts will give up altogether and leave you alone. You will permanently enjoy a mind full of peace.

At intervals during the day practice thinking a carefully selected series of peaceful thoughts. Let mental pictures of the most peaceful scenes you have ever witnessed pass across your mind, as, for example, some beautiful valley filled with the hush of evening time, as the shadows lengthen and the sun sinks to rest. Or recall the silvery light of the moon falling upon rippling waters, or remember the sea washing gently upon soft shores of sand. Such peaceful thought images will work upon your mind as a healing medicine. So now and then during every day allow motion pictures of peace slowly to cross your mind.

Practice the technique of suggestive articulation, that is, repeat audibly some peaceful words. Words have profound suggestive power, and there is healing in the very saying of them. Utter a series of panicky words and your mind will immediately go into a mild state of nervousness. You will perhaps feel a sinking in the pit of your stomach that will affect your entire physical mechanism. If, on the contrary, you speak peaceful, quieting words, your mind will react in a peaceful manner. Use such a word as "tranquillity." Repeat that word slowly several times. *Tranquillity* is one of the most beautiful and melodic of all English words, and the mere saying of it tends to induce a tranquil state.

Another healing word is "serenity." Picturize serenity as you say it. Repeat it slowly and in the mood of which the word is a symbol. Words such as these have a healing potency when used in this manner.

It is also helpful to use lines from poetry or passages from the Scriptures. A man of my acquiantance who achieved a remarkable peace of mind has the habit of writing on cards unusual quotations expressing peacefulness. He carries one of the cards in his wallet at all times, referring to it frequently until each quotation is committed to memory. He says that each such idea dropped into the subconscious "lubricates" his mind with peace. A peaceful concept is indeed oil on troubled thoughts. One of the quotations which he used is from a sixteenth-century mystic, "Let nothing disturb you. Let nothing frighten you. Everything passes away except God. God alone is sufficient."

The words of the Bible have a particularly strong therapeutic value. Drop them into your mind, allowing them to "dissolve" in consciousness, and they will spread a healing balm over your entire mental structure. This is one of the simplest processes to perform and also one of the most effective in attaining peace of mind.

A salesman told me of an incident that took place in a Midwestern hotel room. He was one of a group of businessmen having a conference. One man was very much on edge. He was snappy, argumentative, high-strung. Everyone present knew him quite well and realized he was under great nervous pressure. But finally his irritating attitudes began to get on everybody's nerves. Presently this nervous individual opened his traveling bag, took out a big bottle of brackish-looking medicine, and poured himself a large dose. Asked what this medicine was, he growled, "Oh, it's something for nerves. I feel like I'm going to break in pieces. The pressure I'm under makes me wonder if I am going to crack up. I try not to show it, but I suppose even you fellows have observed that I'm nervous. This medicine was recommended and I've swallowed several bottles of it, but I don't seem to get any better."

The other men laughed, then one said in a kindly manner, "Bill, I don't know anything about that medicine you are taking. Maybe it's all right. It probably is, but I can give you some medicine for those nerves that will do you more good than that. I know, because it cured me, and I was worse off than you are."

"What is this medicine?" snapped the other.

The other man reached into his bag and pulled out a book. "This book will do the job, and I really mean it. I suppose you think it strange that I carry a Bible around in my bag, but I don't care who knows it. I am not a bit ashamed of it. I have been carrying this Bible in my bag for the past two years, and I have marked places in it that help keep my mind at peace. It works for me, and I think it can do something for you too. Why not give it a trial?"

The others were listening with interest to this unusual speech.

The nervous man had sunk low in his chair. Seeing that he was making an impression, the speaker continued, "I had a peculiar experience in a hotel one night which got me into the habit of reading the Bible. I was getting into a pretty tense state. I was out on a business trip and late one afternoon came up to my room terribly nervous. I tried to write some letters, but couldn't get my mind on them. I paced up and down the room, tried to read the paper, but that annoyed me, so I decided to go down and get a drink—anything to get away from myself.

"While standing by the dresser, my eye happened to fall upon a Bible lying there. I had seen many such Bibles in hotel rooms, but had never read any of them. However, something impelled me, and I opened the book to one of the Psalms and started to read it. I remember that I read that one standing up, then sat down and read another. I was interested but certainly surprised at myself—me reading the Bible! It was a laugh, but I kept on reading.

"Soon I came to the 23rd Psalm. I had learned that one as a boy in Sunday school and was surprised that I still knew most of it by heart. I tried saying it over, especially that line where it says, 'He leadeth me beside the still waters; he restoreth my soul.' I liked that line. It sort of got me. I sat there repeating it over and over—and the next thing I knew I woke up.

"Apparently I had dropped off to sleep and slept soundly. I slept only about fifteen minutes, but upon awakening was as refreshed and rested as if I'd had a good night's sleep. I can remember yet the wonderful feeling of complete refreshment. Then I realized that I felt peaceful, and said to myself, 'Isn't it strange? What is wrong with me that I have missed something as wonderful as this?'

"So after that experience," he said, "I bought a Bible, a little one I could put in my bag, and I've been carrying it ever since. I honestly like to read it, and I am not nearly so nervous as I used to be. So," he added, "try that, Bill, and see if it doesn't work."

Bill did try it, and he kept on trying it. He reported that it was a bit strange and difficult for him at first, and he read the Bible on the sly when nobody was around. He didn't want to be thought holy or pious. But now he says he brings it out on trains and planes or "any old place" and reads it, and it "does him a world of good."

"I no longer need to take nerve medicine," he declared.

This scheme must have worked in Bill's case, for he is easy to get along with now. His emotions are under control. These two men found that getting peace of mind isn't complicated. You merely feed your mind with thoughts that cause it to be peaceful. To have a mind full of peace merely fill it full of peace. It's as simple as that.

There are other practical ways by which you can develop serenity and quiet attitudes. One way is through your conversation. Depending upon the words we use and the tone in which we use them, we can talk ourselves into being nervous, high-strung, and upset. We can talk ourselves into either negative or positive results. By our speech we can also achieve quiet reactions. Talk peaceful to be peaceful.

In a group when the conversation takes a trend that is upsetting, try injecting peaceful ideas into the talk. Note how it counteracts the nervous tensions. Conversation filled with expressions of unhappy expectation, at breakfast, for example, often sets the tone of the day. Little wonder things turn out according to the unhappy specifications. Negative conversation adversely affects circumstances. Certainly talk of a tense and nervous nature enhances inner agitation.

On the contrary, start each day by affirming peaceful, contented, and happy attitudes and your days will tend to be pleasant and successful. Such attitudes are active and definite factors in creating satisfactory conditions. Watch your manner of speech then if you wish to develop a peaceful state of mind.

It is important to eliminate from conversations all negative ideas, for they tend to produce tension and annoyance inwardly. For example, when you are with a group of people at luncheon, do not comment that the "Communists will soon take over the country." In the first place, Communists are not going to take over the country, and by so asserting you create a depressing reaction in the minds of others. It undoubtedly affects digestion adversely. The depressing remark colors the attitude of all present, and everyone goes away with a perhaps slight but definite feeling of annoyance. They also carry away with then a mild but definite feeling that something is wrong with everything. There are times when we must face these harsh questions and deal with them objectively and vigorously, and no one has more contempt for Communism than I have, but as a general thing to have peace of mind, fill your personal and group conversations with positive, happy, optimistic, satisfying expressions.

The words we speak have a direct and definite effect upon our thoughts. Thoughts create words, for words are the vehicles of ideas. But words also affect thoughts and help to condition if not to create attitudes. In fact, what often passes for thinking starts with talk. Therefore if the average conversation is scrutinized and disciplined to be sure that it contains peaceful expressions, the result will be peaceful ideas and ultimately, therefore, a peaceful mind.

Another effective technique in developing a peaceful mind is the daily practice of silence. Everyone should insist upon not less than a quarter of an hour of absolute quiet every twenty-four hours. Go alone into the quietest place available to you and sit or lie down for fifteen minutes and practice the art of silence. Do not talk to anyone. Do not write. Do not read. Think as little as possible. Throw your mind into neutral. Conceive of your mind as quiescent, inactive. This will not be easy at first because thoughts are stirring up your mind, but practice will increase your efficiency. Conceive of your mind as the surface of a body of water and see how nearly quiet you can make it, so that there is not a ripple. When you have attained a quiescent state, then begin to listen for the deeper sounds of harmony and beauty and of God that are to be found in the essence of silence.

Americans unfortunately are not skilled in this practice, which is a pity, for as Thomas Carlyle said, "Silence is the element in which great things fashion themselves." This generation of Americans has missed something that our forefathers knew and which helped to condition their character—and that is the silence of the great forest or of the far-reaching plains.

Perhaps our lack of inner peace is due to some extent to the effect of noise upon the nervous system of modern people. Scientific experiments show that noise in the place where we work, live, or sleep reduces efficiency to a noticeable degree. Contrary to popular belief, it is doubtful if we ever completely adjust our physical, mental, or nervous mechanisms to noise. No matter how familiar a repeated sound becomes, it never passes unheard by the subconscious. Automobile horns, the roar of airplanes, and other strident noises actually result in physical activity during sleep. Impulses transmitted to and through the nerves by these sounds cause muscular movements which detract from real rest. If the reaction is sufficiently severe, it partakes of the nature of shock.

On the contrary, silence is a healing, soothing, healthy practice. Starr Daily says, "No man or woman of my acquaintance who knows how to practice silence and does it has ever been sick to my knowledge. I have noticed that my own afflictions come upon me when I do not balance expression with relaxation." Starr Daily closely associates silence with spiritual healing. The sense of rest that results from a practice of complete silence is a therapy of utmost value.

In the circumstances of modern life, with its acceleration of pace, the practice of silence is admittedly not so simple as it was in the days of our forefathers. A vast number of noise-producing gadgets exist that they did not know, and our daily program is more hectic. Space has been annihilated in the modern world, and apparently we are also attempting to annihilate the factor of time. It is only rarely possible for an individual to walk in deep woods or sit by the sea or meditate on a mountaintop or on the deck of a vessel in the midst of the ocean. But when we do have such experiences, we can print on the mind the picture of the silent place and the feel of the moment and return to it in memory to live it over again just as truly as when we were actually in that scene. In fact, when you return to it in memory the mind tends to remove any unpleasant factors present in the actual situation. The memory visit is often an improvement over the actual for the mind tends to reproduce only the beauty in the remembered scene.

For example, as I write these words, I am on a balcony of one of the most beautiful hotels in the world, the Royal Hawaiian on the famed and romantic Waikiki Beach in Honolulu, Hawaii. I am looking into a garden filled with graceful palm trees, swaying in the balmy breeze. The air is laden with the aroma of exotic flowers. Hibiscus, of which on these islands there are two thousand varieties, fill the garden. Outside my windows are papaya trees laden with ripening fruit. The brilliant color of the royal poinciana, the flame of the forest trees, adds to the glamor of the scene; and the acacia trees are hung heavily with their exquisite white flowers.

The incredible blue ocean surrounding these islands stretches away to the horizon. The white waves are surging in, and the

Hawaiians and my fellow visitors are riding gracefully on surfboards and outrigger canoes. Altogether it is a scene of entrancing beauty. It has an indescribably healing effect upon me as I sit here writing about the power generated in a peaceful mind. The insistent responsibilities under which I ordinarily live seem so far away. Though I am in Hawaii to give a series of lectures and to write this book, nevertheless the peace with which this place is filled envelops me. Yet I realize that when I have returned to my home in New York, five thousand miles away, I shall only then truly savor the exquisite joy of the beauty which I now behold. It will become enshrined in memory as a prized retreat to which my mind can go in the busy days that lie ahead. Often, when far from this idyllic place, I shall return in memory to find peace along the palm-lined, foam-washed beach at Waikiki.

Fill your mind with all peaceful experiences possible, then make planned and deliberate excursions to them in memory. You must learn that the easiest way to an easy mind is to create an easy mind. This is done by practice, by the application of some such simple principles as outlined here. The mind quickly responds to teaching and discipline. You can make the mind give you back anything you want, but remember the mind can give back only what it was first given. Saturate your thoughts with peaceful experiences, peaceful words and ideas, and ultimately you will have a storehouse of peace-producing experiences to which you may turn for refreshment and renewal of your spirit. It will be a vast source of power.

I spent a night with a friend who has a very lovely home. We had breakfast in a unique and interesting dining room. The four walls are painted in a beautiful mural picturing the countryside in which my host was reared as a boy. It is a panorama of rolling hills, gentle valleys, and singing streams, the latter clean and sun speckled, and babbling over rocks. Winding roads meander through pleasant meadows. Little houses dot the landscape. In a central position is a white church surmounted by a tall steeple.

As we breakfasted my host talked of this region of his youth, pointing out various points of interest in the painting around the wall. Then he said, "Often as I sit in this dining room I go from point to point in my memory and relive other days. I recall, for example, walking up that lane as a boy with bare feet, and I can remember yet how the clean dust felt between my toes. I remember fishing in that trout stream on many a summer afternoon and coasting down those hills in the wintertime.

"There is the church I attended as a boy." He grinned and said, "I sat through many a long sermon in that church but gratefully recall to mind the kindliness of the people and the sincerity of their lives. I can sit here and look at that church and think of the hymns I heard there with my mother and father as we sat together in the pew. They are long buried in that cemetery alongside the church, but in memory I go and stand by their graves and hear them speak to me as in days gone by. I get very tired and sometimes am nervous and tense. It helps to sit here and go back to the days when I had an untroubled mind, when life was new and fresh. It does something for me. It gives me peace."

Perhaps we all cannot have such murals on the dining-room walls, but you can put them around the wall of your mind: pictures of the most beautiful experiences of your life. Spend time among the thoughts which these pictures suggest. No matter how busy you may be or what responsibilities you carry, this simple, rather unique practice, having proved successful in many instances, may have a beneficial effect upon you. It is an easily practiced, easy way to a peaceful mind.

There is a factor in the matter of inner peace which must be stated because of its importance. Frequently I find that people who are lacking in inner peace are victims of a self-punishment mechanism. At some time in their experience they have committed a sin and the sense of guilt haunts them. They have sincerely sought Divine forgiveness, and the good Lord will always forgive anyone who asks Him and who means it. However, there is a curious quirk within the human mind whereby sometimes an individual will not forgive himself.

He feels that he deserves punishment and therefore is constantly anticipating that punishment. As a result he lives in a constant apprehension that something is going to happen. In order to find peace under these circumstances he must increase the intensity of his activity. He feels that hard work will give him some release from his sense of guilt. A physician told me that in his practice a number of cases of nervous breakdown were traceable to a sense of guilt for which the patient had unconsciously attempted to compensate by hectic overwork. The patient attributed his breakdown not to the sense of guilt, but to his overworked condition. "But," said the physician, "these men need not have broken down from overwork if first the sense of guilt had been fully released." Peace of mind under such circumstances is available by yielding the guilt as well as the tension it produces to the healing therapy of Christ.

At a resort hotel where I had gone for a few days of quiet writing I encountered a man from New York whom I knew slightly. He was a high-pressured, hard-driving, and exceedingly nervous business executive. He was sitting in the sun in a deck chair. At his invitation I sat down and chatted with him.

"I'm glad to see you relaxing in this beautiful spot," I commented.

He replied nervously, "I haven't any business being here. I've so much work to do at home. I'm under terrible pressure. Things have got me down, I'm nervous and can't sleep. I'm jumpy. My wife insisted that I come down here for a week. The doctors say there's nothing wrong with me if I just get to thinking right and relax. But how in the world do you do that?" he challenged. Then he gave me a piteous look. "Doctor," he said, "I would give anything if I could be peaceful and quiet. It's what I want more than anything in this world."

We talked a bit, and it came out in the conversation that he was always worrying that something sinister was going to happen. For years he had anticipated some dire event, living in constant apprehension about "something happening" to his wife or his children or his home.

It was not difficult to analyze his case. His insecurity arose from a double source—from childhood insecurities and from later guilty experiences. His mother had always felt that "something was going to happen," and he had absorbed her anxiety feelings. Later he committed some sins, and his subconscious mind insisted upon self-punishment. He became victim to the mechanism of self-punishment. As a result of this unhappy combination I found him this day in a highly inflamed state of nervous reaction.

Finishing our conversation, I stood beside his chair a moment. There was no one near, so I rather hesitantly suggested, "Would you by any chance like me to pray with you?" He nodded, and I put my hand on his shoulder and prayed, "Dear Jesus, as You healed people in the long ago and gave them peace, heal this man now. Give him fully of Thy forgiveness. Help him to forgive himself. Separate him from all his sins and let him know that You do not hold them against him. Set him free from them. Then let Thy peace flow into his mind, and into his soul, and into his body."

He looked up at me with a strange look on his face and then turned away, for there were tears in his eyes and he didn't want me to see them. We were both a bit embarrassed, and I left him. Months later I met him, and he said, "Something happened to me down there that day when you prayed for me. I felt a strange sense of quietness and peace, and," he added, "healing."

He goes to church regularly now and he reads the Bible every day of his life. He follows the laws of God and he has lots of driving force. He is a healthy, happy man, for he has peace in his heart and mind.

# 3

# *How to Have Constant Energy*

A MAJOR-LEAGUE baseball pitcher once pitched a game when the temperature was over one hundred degrees. He lost several pounds as a result of the afternoon's exertion. At one stage of the game his energy sagged. His method for restoring his ebbing strength was unique. He simply repeated a passage from the Old Testament—"But they that wait upon the Lord shall renew their strength; they shall mount up with wings as eagles; they shall run, and not be weary; and they shall walk, and not faint." (Isaiah 40:31)

Frank Hiller, the pitcher who had this experience, told me that reciting this verse on the pitcher's mound actually gave him a renewal of strength so that he was able to complete the game with energy to spare. He explained the technique by saying, "I passed a powerful energy-producing thought through my mind."

How we think we feel has a definite effect on how we actually feel physically. If your mind tells you that you are tired, the body mechanism, the nerves, and the muscles accept the fact. If your mind is intensely interested, you can keep on at an activity indefinitely. Religion functions through our thoughts, in fact, it is a system of thought discipline. By supplying attitudes of faith to the mind it can increase energy. It helps you to accomplish prodigious activity by suggesting that you have ample support and resources of power.

A friend in Connecticut, an energetic man, full of vitality and vigor, says that he goes to church regularly to "get his batteries recharged." His concept is sound. God *is* the source of all energy—energy in the universe, atomic energy, electrical energy, and spiritual energy; indeed every form of energy derives from the Creator. The Bible emphasizes this point when it says, "He giveth power to the faint; and to them that have no might he increaseth strength." (Isaiah 40:29)

In another statement the Bible describes the energizing and re-energizing process: ". . . in Him we live (that is, have vitality), and move (have dynamic energy), and have our being (attain completeness)." (Acts 17:28)

Contact with God establishes within us a flow of the same type of energy that re-creates the world and that renews springtime every year. When in spiritual contact with God through our thought processes, the Divine energy flows through the personality, automatically renewing the original creative act. When contact with the Divine energy is broken, the personality gradually becomes depleted in body, mind, and spirit. An electric clock connected with an outlet does not run down and will continue indefinitely to keep accurate time. Unplug it, and the clock stops. It has lost contact with the power flowing through the universe. In general this process is operative in human experience though in a less mechanical manner.

A number of years ago I attended a lecture at which a speaker asserted before a large audience that he had not been tired in thirty years. He explained that thirty years before he had passed through a spiritual experience in which by self-surrender he had made contact with Divine power. From then on he possessed sufficient energy for all of his activities, and these were prodigious. He so obviously illustrated his teachings that everyone in that vast audience was profoundly impressed.

To me it was a revelation of the fact that in our consciousness we can tap a reservoir of boundless power as a result of which it is not necessary to suffer depletion of energy. For years I have studied and experimented with the ideas which this speaker outlined and which others have expounded and demonstrated, and it is my conviction that the principles of Christianity scientifically utilized can develop an uninterrupted and continuous flow of energy into the human mind and body.

These findings were corroborated by a prominent physician with whom I was discussing a certain man whom we both know. This man, whose responsibilities are very heavy, works from morning until night without interruption, but always seems able to assume new obligations. He has the knack of handling his work easily and with efficiency.

I commented to the physician that I hoped this man was not setting a dangerous pace that might possibly lead to a breakdown.

The physician shook his head. "No," he replied, "as his physician I do not think there is any danger of a crack-up, and the reason is that he is a thoroughly well-organized individual with no energy leaks in his make-up. He operates a well-regulated machine. He handles things with easy power and carries burdens without strain. He never wastes an ounce of energy, but every effort is applied with maximum force."

"How do you account for this efficiency, this seemingly boundless energy?" I asked.

The physician studied for a moment. "The answer is that he is a normal individual, emotionally well integrated, and, what is more important, he is a soundly religious person. From his religion he has learned how to avoid drainage of power. His religion is a workable and useful mechanism for preventing energy leaks. It is not hard work that drains off energy but emotional upheaval, and this man is entirely free from that."

Increasingly people are realizing that the maintenance of a sound spiritual life is important in enjoying energy and personality force.

The body is designed to produce all needed energy over an amazingly long period of time. If the individual takes reasonable care of his body from the standpoint of proper diet, exercise, sleep, no physical abuse, the body will produce and maintain astonishing energy and sustain itself in good health. If he gives similar attention to a well-balanced emotional life, energy will be conserved. But if he allows energy leaks caused by hereditary or self-imposed emotional reaction of a debilitating nature, he will be lacking in vital force. The natural state of the individual when body, mind, and spirit work harmoniously is that of a continuous replacement of necessary energy.

Mrs. Thomas A. Edison, with whom I often discussed the habits and characteristics of her famous husband, the world's greatest inventive wizard, told me that it was Mr. Edison's custom to come into the house from his laboratory after many hours of labor and lie down on his old couch. She said he would fall asleep as naturally as a child, in perfect relaxation, sinking into a deep and untroubled slumber. After three or four, or sometimes five hours he would become instantly wide awake, completely refreshed, and eager to return to his work.

Mrs. Edison, in answer to my request that she analyze her

husband's ability to rest in a manner so natural and complete, said, "He was nature's man," by which she meant that he was completely in harmony with nature and with God. In him there were no obsessions, no disorganizations, no conflicts, no mental quirks, no emotional instability. He worked until he needed to sleep, then he slept soundly and arose and returned to his work. He lived for many years, and was in many respects the most creative mind ever to appear on the American continent. He drew his energy from emotional self-mastery, the ability to relax completely. His amazingly harmonious relationship with the universe caused nature to reveal to him its inscrutable secrets.

Every great personality I have ever known, and I have known many, who has demonstrated the capacity for prodigious work has been a person in tune with the Infinite. Every such person seems in harmony with nature and in contact with the Divine energy. They have not necessarily been pious people, but invariably they have been extraordinarily well organized from an emotional and psychological point of view. It is fear, resentment, the projection of parental faults upon people when they are children, inner conflicts and obsessions that throw off balance the finely equated nature, thus causing undue expenditure of natural force.

The longer I live the more I am convinced that neither age nor circumstance needs to deprive us of energy and vitality. We are at last awakening to the close relationship between religion and health. We are beginning to comprehend a basic truth hitherto neglected, that our physical condition is determined very largely by our emotional condition, and our emotional life is profoundly regulated by our thought life.

All through its pages, the Bible talks about vitality and force and life. The supreme over-all word of the Bible is life, and life means vitality—to be filled with energy. Jesus stated the key expression, ". . . I am come that they might have life, and that they might have it more abundantly." (John 10:10) This does not rule out pain or suffering or difficulty, but the clear implication is that if a person practices the creative and re-creative principles of Christianity he can live with power and energy.

The practice of the above-mentioned principles will serve to bring a person into the proper tempo of living. Our energies are destroyed because of the high tempo, the abnormal pace at which we go. The conservation of energy depends upon getting your personality speed synchronized with the rate of God's movement. God is in you. If you are going at one rate and God at another, you are tearing yourself apart. "Though the mills of God grind slowly, yet they grind exceeding small." The mills of most of us grind very rapidly, and so they grind poorly. When we become attuned to God's rhythm we develop a normal tempo within ourselves and energy flows freely.

The hectic habits of this age have many disastrous effects. A friend of mine commented upon an observation made by her aged father. He said that in early days when a young man came courting in the evening he sat with his intended in the parlor. Time in those days was measured by the deliberate, ponderous strokes of the grandfather clock, which has a very long pendulum. It seemed to say, "There—is—plenty—of—time. There—is—plenty—of—time. There—is—plenty—of—time." But modern clocks, having a shorter pendulum with a swifter stroke, seem to say, "Time to get busy! Time to get busy! Time to get busy! Time to get busy!"

Everything is speeded up, and for that reason many people are tired. The solution is to get into the time synchronization of Almighty God. One way to do this is by going out some warm day and lying down on the earth. Get your ear close down to the ground and listen. You will hear all manner of sounds. You will hear the sound of the wind in the trees and the murmur of insects, and you will discover presently that there is in all these sounds a well-regulated tempo. You cannot get that tempo by listening to traffic in the city streets, for it is lost in the confusion of sound. You can get it in church where you hear the word of God and the great hymns. Truth vibrates to God's tempo in a church. But you can also find it in a factory if you have a mind to.

A friend of mine, an industrialist in a large plant in Ohio, told me that the best workmen in his plant are those who get into harmony with the rhythm of the machine on which they are working. He declares that if a worker will work in harmony with the rhythm of his machine he will not be tired at the end of the day. He points out that the machine is an assembling of parts according to the law of God. When you love a machine and get to know it, you will be aware that it has a rhythm. It is one with the rhythm of the body, of the nerves, of the soul. It is in God's rhythm, and you can work with that machine and not get tired if you are in harmony with it. There is a rhythm of the stove, a rhythm of the typewriter, a rhythm of the office, a rhythm of an automobile, a rhythm of your job. So to avoid tiredness and to have energy, feel your way into the essential rhythm of Almighty God and all His works.

To accomplish this, relax physically. Then conceive of your mind as likewise relaxing. Follow this mentally by visualizing the soul as becoming quiescent, then pray as follows: "Dear God, You are the source of all energy. You are the source of the energy in the sun, in the atom, in all flesh, in the bloodstream, in the mind. I hereby draw energy from You as from an illimitable source." Then practice believing that you receive energy. Keep in tune with the Infinite.

Of course many people are tired simply because they are not interested in anything. Nothing ever moves them deeply. To some people it makes no difference what's going on or how things go. Their personal concerns are superior even to all crises in human history. Nothing makes any real difference to them except their own little worries, their desires, and their hates. They wear themselves out stewing around about a lot of inconsequential things that amount to nothing. So they become tired. They even become sick. The surest way not to become tired is to lose yourself in something in which you have a profound conviction.

A famous statesman who made seven speeches in one day was still boundless in energy.

"Why are you not tired after making seven speeches?" I asked.

"Because," he said, "I believe absolutely in everything I said in those speeches. I am enthusiastic about my convictions."

That's the secret. He was on fire for something. He was pouring himself out, and you never lose energy and vitality in so doing. You only lose energy when life becomes dull in your mind. Your mind gets bored and therefore tired doing nothing. You don't have to be tired. Get interested in something. Get absolutely enthralled in something. Throw yourself into it with abandon. Get out of yourself. Be somebody. Do something. Don't sit around moaning about things, reading the papers, and saying, "Why don't they do something?" The man who is out doing something isn't tired. If you're not getting into good causes, no wonder you're tired. You're disintegrating. You're deteriorating. You're dying on the vine. The more you lose yourself in something bigger than yourself, the more energy you will have. You don't have time to think about yourself and get bogged down in your emotional difficulties.

To live with constant energy it is important to get your emotional faults corrected. You will never have full energy until you do.

The late Knute Rockne, one of the greatest football coaches this country ever produced, said that a football player cannot have sufficient energy unless his emotions are under spiritual control. In fact, he went so far as to say that he would not have a man on his team who did not have a genuinely friendly feeling for every fellow player. "I have to get the most energy out of a man," he said, "and have discovered that it cannot be done if he hates another man. Hate blocks his energy and he isn't up to par until he eliminates it and develops a friendly feeling." People who lack energy are disorganized to one degree or another by their deep, fundamental emotional and psychological conflicts. Sometimes the results of this disorganization are extreme, but healing is ever possible.

In a Midwestern city I was asked to talk with a man, formerly a very active citizen of that community, who had suffered an acute decline in vitality. It was thought by his associates that he had had a stroke. This impression was given by the shuffling manner in which he moved, by an extraordinary lethargic attitude, and by his complete detachment of himself from the activities to which he had formerly given a large portion of his time. He sat despondently in his chair hour after hour, and often he would weep. He exhibited many of the symptoms of a nervous breakdown.

I arranged to see him in my hotel room at a certain hour. My door was open and through it I could see the elevator. I chanced to be looking in that direction when the elevator door opened and this man came shuffling down the hall. It seemed that at any moment he would topple over, and he gave every evidence of scarcely being able to negotiate the distance. I asked him to be seated and engaged him in conversation, which conversation was rather fruitless, for it revealed little enlightenment because of his tendency to complain about his condition and his inability to give thoughtful consideration to my questions. This was apparently due to his enormous self-pity.

When I asked him if he would like to be well, he looked up at me in the most intense and pathetic manner. His desperation was revealed by his answer which was that he would give anything in the world if he could regain the energy and the interest in life which he formerly enjoyed.

I began to draw out of him certain facts regarding his life and experience. These were all of a very intimate nature and many of them so deeply imbedded in his consciousness that it was with the utmost difficulty that his personality yielded them up. They had to do with old infantile attitudes, fears that stemmed from earliest days, most of them deriving from the mother-child relationship. Not a few guilt situations appeared. It seemed that over the course of the years these factors had accumulated like drifting sand across the channel of a river. The flow of power was gradually decreased so that an insufficient amount of energy was passing through. The man's mind was in such a complete state of retreating that a process of reasoning and enlightenment seemed quite impossible.

I sought for guidance and found myself, quite to my surprise, standing beside him and placing my hand upon his head. I prayed, asking God to heal the man. I suddenly became aware of what seemed to be the passing of power through my hand which rested upon his head. I hasten to add that there is no healing power in my hand, but now and then a human being is used as a channel, and it was evidently so in this instance, for presently the man looked up with an expression of the utmost happiness and peace and he said simply, "He was here. He touched me. I feel entirely different."

From this time on his improvement was pronounced, and at the present time he is practically his old self again, except for the fact that he now possesses a quiet and serene confidence which was not present previously. Apparently the clogged channel in his personality through which the passage of power had been impeded was opened by an act of faith and the free flow of energy was renewed.

The facts suggested by this incident are that such healings do take place and that a gradual accumulation of psychological factors can cut off the flow of energy. The further fact is stressed that these same factors are susceptible to the power of faith to disintegrate them and thus reopen the channel of Divine human energy within an individual.

The effect of guilt and fear feelings on energy is widely recognized by all authorities having to do with the problems of human nature. The quantity of vital force required to give the personality relief from either guilt or fear or a combination of each is so great that often only a fraction of energy remains for the discharge of the functions of living. Energy drainage occasioned by fear and guilt is of such an amount as to leave little power to be applied to a person's job. The result is that he tires quickly. Not being able to meet the full requirements of his responsibility, he retreats into an apathetic, dull, listless condition and is indeed even ready to give up and fall back sleepily in a state of enervation.

A businessman was referred to me by a psychiatrist whom the patient had been consulting. It appeared that the patient, generally regarded as quite morally strict and upright, had become involved with a married woman. He had attempted to break off this relationship but was encountering resistance from his partner in infidelity, although he had earnestly besought her to abandon their practice and allow him to return to his former state of respectability.

She had threatened him with the possibility that she might enlighten her husband concerning these escapades if he insisted in his desire to cease the relationship. The patient recognized the fact that if the husband became apprised of the situation, it would result in disgrace for him in his community. He happened to be a prominent citizen and prized his high standing.

As a result of his fear of exposure and a sense of guilt he had been unable to sleep or rest. And since this had gone on for two or three months he was in a very serious slump in energy and did not possess the vitality to perform his job efficiently. Inasmuch as some important matters were pending, the situation was serious.

When the psychiatrist suggested that he see me, a clergyman, because of his inability to sleep, he remonstrated by saying there was no way in which a clergyman could correct the condition which caused his sleeplessness, but, on the contrary, he felt that a medical doctor might supply effective medication.

When he stated his attitude to me I simply asked him how he expected to sleep when he had two very annoying and unpleasant bedfellows with whom he was attempting to sleep.

"Bedfellows?" he asked in surprise. "I have no bedfellows."

"Oh, yes, you have," I said, "and there is nobody in this world who can sleep with those two, one on either side."

"What do you mean?" he asked.

I said, "You are trying to sleep every night between fear on one side and guilt on the other, and you are attempting an impossible feat. It makes no difference how many sleeping pills you take, and you admit you have taken many such pills, but they have had no effect upon you. The reason they do not affect you is that they cannot reach the deeper levels of your mind where this sleeplessness originates and which is siphoning off your energy. You must eradicate fear and guilt before you will ever be able to sleep and regain your strength."

We dealt with the fear which was of exposure by the simple expedient of getting him ready in mind to face whatever might ensue as a result of doing the right thing, which was of course to break off the relationship regardless of consequences. I assured him that whatever he did that was right would turn out right. One never does wrong by doing right. I urged him to put the matter in God's hands and simply do the right thing, leaving the outcome to God.

He did that, not without trepidation, but with considerable sincerity just the same. The woman, either through shrewdness or some expression of her own better nature or through the more doubtful expedient of transferring her affections elsewhere, released him.

The guilt was handled by seeking God's forgiveness. When this is sincerely sought it is never denied, and our patient found surcease and relief. It was astonishing how when this double weight was lifted from his mind his personality once again began to function normally. He was able to sleep. He found peace and renewal of strength. Energy quickly returned. A wiser and thankful man, he became able to carry on his normal activities.

A not infrequent case of diminishing energy is staleness. The pressure, monotony, and unceasing continuity of responsibilities dull the freshness of mind which a person must have to approach his work successfully. As an athlete goes stale so does the individual, whatever his occupation, tend to come upon dry and arid periods. During such a condition of mind the expenditure of greater energy is required to do with difficulty what one formerly did with comparative ease. As a result the vital powers are hard put to it to supply the force required, and the individual often loses his grip and power.

A solution for this state of mind was employed by a prominent business leader, president of the board of trustees of a certain university. A professor who had formerly been outstanding and extraordinarily popular had begun to slip in teaching ability and in the power to interest students. It was the verdict of the students as well as the private opinion of the trustees that this teacher must either recover his former capacity to teach with interest and enthusiasm or it would be necessary to replace him. This latter expedient was entertained with hesitancy for the reason that there still remained a normal expectancy of several active years before he reached the age of retirement.

The businessman above referred to asked the professor to come to his office and announced to him that the board of trustees was giving him a six months' leave of absence with all expenses paid and with full salary. There was only one stipulation, and that was that he go away to a place of rest and give himself over to gaining a complete renewal of strength and energy.

The businessman invited him to use a cabin which he himself owned in a wilderness setting and made the curious suggestion that he take no books except one book, the Bible. He suggested that the professor's daily program be walking, fishing, and some manual work in the garden; that he read the Bible every day for such a period as would enable him to read the Book through three times in the six months. He further suggested that he memorize as many passages as possible for the purpose of saturating his mind with the great words and ideas which the Book contains.

The businessman said, "I believe that if you spend six months outdoors chopping wood, digging in the soil, reading the Bible, and fishing in the deep lakes you will become a new man."

The professor agreed to this unique proposal. His adjustment to this radically different mode of life was an easier one than he or anyone who knew him expected. In fact, he was surprised to find that he actually liked it. After he became conditioned to active outdoor living he discovered that it had an immense appeal for him. He missed his intellectual associates and his reading for a while, but forced back upon the Bible, his only book, he became immersed in it, and to his amazement found, as he put it, "a library within itself." In its pages he found faith and peace and power. In six months he was a new man.

The businessman now tells me that this professor has become, as he puts it, "a person of compelling power." Staleness passed away, the old-time energy returned, power surged back, zest for living was renewed.

# 4

# *Try Prayer Power*

IN A BUSINESS OFFICE high above the city streets two men were having a serious conversation. One, heavily troubled by a business and personal crisis, paced the floor restlessly, then sat dejectedly, head in hand, a picture of despair. He had come to the other for advice, since he was considered a man of great understanding. Together they had explored the problem from every angle but seemingly without result, which only served to deepen the troubled man's discouragement. "I guess no power on earth can save me," he sighed.

The other reflected for a moment, then spoke rather diffidently. "I wouldn't look at it that way. I believe you are wrong in saying there is no power that can save you. Personally, I have found that there is an answer to every problem. There is a power that can help you." Then slowly he asked, "Why not try prayer power?"

Somewhat surprised, the discouraged man said, "Of course I believe in prayer, but perhaps I do not know how to pray. You speak of it as something practical that fits a business problem. I never thought of it that way but I'm willing to try prayer if you will show me how."

He did apply practical prayer techniques and in due course got his answer. Matters ultimately turned out satisfactorily. That is not to say he did not have difficulties. In fact, he had rather a hard time of it but ultimately he worked out of this trouble. Now he believes in prayer power so enthusiastically that I recently heard him say, "Every problem can be solved and solved right if you pray."

Experts in physical health and well-being often utilize prayer in their therapy. Disability, tension, and kindred troubles may result from a lack of inner harmony. It is remarkable how prayer restores the harmonious functioning of body and soul. A friend of mine, a physiotherapist, told a nervous man to whom he was giving a massage, "God works through my fingers as I seek to relax your physical body, which is the temple of your soul. While I work on your outward being, I want you to pray for God's relaxation inwardly." It was a new idea to the patient, but he happened to be in a receptive mood and he tried passing some peace thoughts through his mind. He was amazed at the relaxing effect this had on him.

Jack Smith, operator of a health club, which is patronized by many outstanding people, believes in the therapy of prayer and uses it. He was at one time a prize fighter, then a truck driver, later a taxi driver, and finally opened his health club. He says that while he probes his patrons for physical flabbiness he also probes for spiritual flabbiness because, he declares, "You can't get a man physically healthy until you get him spiritually healthy."

One day Walter Huston, the actor, sat by Jack Smith's desk. He noted a big sign on the wall on which were penciled the following letters: A P R P B W P R A A. In surprise Huston asked, "What do those letters mean?"

Smith laughed and said, "They stand for 'Affirmative Prayers Release Powers By Which Positive Results Are Accomplished.' "

Huston's jaw dropped in astonishment. "Well, I never expected to hear anything like that in a health club."

"I use methods like that," said Smith, "to make people curious so they will ask what those letters mean. That gives me an opportunity to tell them that I believe affirmative prayers always get results."

Jack Smith, who helps men to keep physically fit, believes that prayer is as important, if not more important, than exercise, steam baths, and a rubdown. It is a vital part of the power-releasing process.

People are doing more praying today than formerly because they find that it adds to personal efficiency. Prayer helps them to tap forces and to utilize strength not otherwise available.

A famous psychologist says, "Prayer is the greatest power available to the individual in solving his personal problems. Its power astonishes me."

Prayer power is a manifestation of energy. Just as there exist scientific techniques for the release of atomic energy, so are there scientific procedures for the release of spiritual energy through the mechanism of prayer. Exciting demonstrations of this energizing force are evident.

Prayer power seems able even to normalize the aging process, obviating or limiting infirmity and deterioration. You need not lose your basic energy or vital power or become weak and listless merely as a result of accumulating years. It is not necessary to allow your spirit to sag or grow stale or dull. Prayer can freshen you up every evening and send you out renewed each morning. You can receive guidance in problems if prayer is allowed to permeate your subconscious, the seat of the forces which determines whether you take right or wrong actions. Prayer has the power to keep your reactions correct and sound. Prayer driven deeply into your subconscious can remake you. It releases and keeps power flowing freely.

If you have not experienced this power, perhaps you need to learn new techniques of prayer. It is well to study prayer from an efficiency point of view. Usually the emphasis is entirely religious though no cleavage exists between the two concepts. Scientific spiritual practice rules out stereotyped procedure even as it does in general science. If you have been praying in a certain manner, even if it has brought you blessings, which it doubtless has, perhaps you can pray even more profitably by varying the pattern and by experimenting with fresh prayer formulas. Get new insights; practice new skills to attain greatest results.

It is important to realize that you are dealing with the most tremendous power in the world when you pray. You would not use an old-fashioned kerosene lamp for illumination. You want the most up-to-date lighting devices. New and fresh spiritual techniques are being constantly discovered by men and women of spiritual genius. It is advisable to experiment with prayer power according to such methods as prove sound and effective. If this sounds new and strangely scientific, bear in mind that the secret of prayer is to find the process that will most effectively open your mind humbly to God. Any method through which you can stimulate the power of God to flow into your mind is legitimate and usable.

An illustration of a scientific use of prayer is the experience of two famous industrialists, whose names would be known to many readers were I permitted to mention them, who had a conference about a business and technical matter. One might think that these men would approach such a problem on a purely technical basis, and they did that and more; they also prayed about it. But they did not get a successful result. Therefore they called in a country preacher, an old friend of one of them, because, as they explained, the Bible prayer formula is, "Where two or three are gathered together in my name, there am I in the midst of them." (Matthew 18:20) They also pointed to a further formula, namely, "If two of you shall agree on earth as touching any thing that they shall ask, it shall be done for them of my Father which is in heaven." (Matthew 18:19)

Being schooled in scientific practice, they believe that in dealing with prayer as a phenomenon they should scrupulously follow the formulas outlined in the Bible which they described as the textbook of spiritual science. The proper method for employing a science is to use the accepted formulas outlined in the textbook of that science. They reasoned that if the Bible provides that two or three should be gathered together, perhaps the reason they were not succeeding was that they needed a third party.

Therefore the three men prayed, and to guard against error in the process they also brought to bear on the problem various other Biblical techniques such as those suggested in the statements: "According to your faith be it unto you." (Matthew 9:29) "What things soever ye desire, when ye pray, believe that ye receive them, and ye shall have them." (Mark 11:24)

After several thoroughgoing sessions of prayer the three men together affirmed that they had received the answer. The outcome was entirely satisfactory. Subsequent results indicated that Divine guidance was actually obtained.

These men are great enough scientists not to require precise explanation of the operation of these spiritual laws any more than in the case of naturalistic laws but are content with the fact that the law does operate when "proper" techniques are employed.

"While we cannot explain it," they said, "the fact remains that we were baffled by our problem and we tried prayer according to the formulas in the New Testament. That method worked and we got a beautiful result." They did add that it seemed to them that faith and harmony are important factors in the prayer process.

A man opened a small business in New York City a number of years ago, his first establishment being, as he characterized it, "a little hole in the wall." He had one employee. In a few years they moved into a larger room and then into extensive quarters. It became a very successful operation.

This man's method of business as he described it was "to fill the little hole in the wall with optimistic prayers and thoughts." He declared that hard work, positive thinking, fair dealing, right treatment of people, and the proper kind of praying always get results. This man, who has a creative and unique mind, worked out his own simple formula for solving his problems and overcoming his difficulties through prayer power. It is a curious formula but I have practiced it and personally know that it works. I have suggested it to many people who also found real value in its use. It is recommended to you.

The formula is (1) PRAYERIZE, (2) PICTURIZE, (3) ACTUALIZE.

By "prayerize" my friend meant a daily system of creative prayer. When a problem arose he talked it over with God very simply and directly in prayer. Moreover, he did not talk with God as to some vast and far-off shadowy being but conceived of God as being with him in his office, in his home, on the street, in his automobile, always near by as a partner, as a close associate. He took seriously the Biblical injunction to "pray without ceasing." He interpreted it as meaning that he should go about every day discussing with God in a natural, normal manner the questions that had to be decided and dealt with. The Presence came finally to dominate his conscious and ultimately his unconscious thinking. He "prayerized" his daily life. He prayed as he walked or drove his car or performed other everyday activities. He filled his daily life full of prayer—that is, he lived by prayer. He did not often kneel to offer his prayers but would, for example, say to God as to a close associate, "What will I do about this, Lord?" or "Give me a fresh insight on this, Lord." He prayerized his mind and so prayerized his activities.

The second point in his formula of creative prayer is to "picturize." The basic factor in physics is force. The basic factor in psychology is the realizable wish. The man who assumes success tends already to have success. People who assume failure tend to have failure. When either failure or success is picturized it strongly tends to actualize in terms equivalent to the mental image pictured.

To assure something worth while happening, first pray about it and test it according to God's will; then print a picture of it on your mind as happening, holding the picture firmly in consciousness. Continue to surrender the picture to God's will—that is to say, put the matter in God's hands—and follow God's guidance. Work hard and intelligently, thus doing your part to achieve success in the matter. Practice believing and continue to hold the picturization firmly in your thoughts. Do this and you will be astonished at the strange ways in which the picturization comes to pass. In this manner the picture "actualizes." That which you have "prayerized" and "picturized" "actualizes" according to the pattern of your basic realizable wish when conditioned by invoking God's power upon it, and if, moreover, you give fully of yourself to its realization.

I have personally practiced this three-point prayer method and find great power in it. It has been suggested to others who have likewise reported that it released creative power into their experience.

For example, a woman discovered that her husband was drifting from her. Theirs had been a happy marriage, but the wife had become preoccupied in social affairs and the husband had gotten busy in his work. Before they knew it, the close, old-time companionship was lost. One day she discovered his interest in another woman. She lost her head and became hysterical. She consulted her minister, who adroitly turned the conversation to herself. She admitted being a careless homemaker and that she had also become self-centered, sharp-tongued, and nagging.

She then confessed that she had never felt herself the equal of her husband. She had a profound sense of inferiority regarding him, feeling unable to maintain equality with him socially and intellectually. So she retreated into an antagonistic attitude that manifested itself in petulance and criticism.

The minister saw that the woman had more talent, ability, and charm than she was revealing. He suggested that she create an image or picture of herself as capable and attractive. He whimsically told her that "God runs a beauty parlor" and that faith techniques could put beauty on a person's face and charm and ease in her manner. He gave her instruction in how to pray and how spiritually to "picturize." He also advised her to hold a mental image of the restoration of the old-time companionship, to visualize the goodness in her husband, and to picture a restored harmony between the two of them. She was to hold this picture with faith. In this manner he prepared her for a most interesting personal victory.

About this time her husband informed her that he wanted a divorce. She had conquered herself to the extent of being able to receive this request with calmness. She simply replied that she was willing if he wanted it, but suggested a deferral of the decision for ninety days on the ground that divorce is so final. "If at the end of ninety days you still feel that you want a divorce, I will co-operate with you." She said this calmly. He gave her a quizzical look, for he had expected an outburst.

Night after night he went out, and night after night she sat at home, but she pictured him as seated in his old chair. He was not in the chair, but she painted an image of him there comfortably reading as in the old days. She visualized him puttering around the house, painting and fixing things as he had formerly done. She even pictured him drying the dishes as he did when they were first married. She visualized the two of them playing golf together and taking hikes as they once did.

She maintained this picture with steady faith, and one night there he actually sat in his old chair. She looked twice to be sure that it was the reality rather than the picturization, but perhaps a picturization is a reality, for at any rate the actual man was there. Occasionally he would be gone but more and more nights he sat in his chair. Then he began to read to her as in the old days. Then one sunny Saturday afternoon he asked, "What do you say to a game of golf?"

The days went by pleasantly until she realized that the ninetieth day had arrived, so that evening she said quietly, "Bill, this is the ninetieth day."

"What do you mean," he asked, puzzled, "the ninetieth day?"

"Why, don't you remember? We agreed to wait ninety days to settle that divorce matter and this is the day."

He looked at her for a moment, then hidden behind his paper turned a page, saying, "Don't be silly. I couldn't possibly get along without you. Where did you ever get the idea I was going to leave you?"

The formula proved a powerful mechanism. She prayerized, she picturized, and the sought-for result was actualized. Prayer power solved her problem and his as well.

I have known many people who have successfully applied this technique not only to personal affairs but to business matters as well. When sincerely and intelligently brought into situations, the results have been so excellent that this must be regarded as an extraordinarily efficient method of prayer. People who take this method seriously and actually use it get astonishing results.

At an industrial convention banquet I was seated at the speaker's table next to a man who, though a bit on the rough side, was very likable. He may have felt a bit cramped by his proximity to a preacher, which obviously wasn't his usual company. During the dinner he used a number of theological words, but they were not put together in a theological manner. After each outburst he apologized, but I advised him that I had heard all those words before.

He told me he had been a church attendant as a boy but "had gotten away from it." He gave me that old story which I have heard all my life and which even now people will get off as something entirely new, viz., "When I was a boy my father made me go to Sunday school and church and crammed religion down my throat. So when I got away from home I couldn't take it any more and have seldom been to church since."

This man then observed that "perhaps he should start going to church since he was getting old." I commented that he would be lucky to find a seat. This surprised him for he "did not think anybody went to church any more." I told him that more people attend church each week than frequent any other institution in the country. This rather bowled him over.

He was head of a medium-sized business and he fell to telling me how much money his firm took in last year. I told him I knew quite a few churches whose take exceeded that. This really hit him in the solar plexus, and I noted his respect for the church mounting by leaps and bounds. I told him about the thousands of religious books that are sold, more than any other type of book. "Maybe you fellows in the church are on the ball at that," he slangily remarked.

At this moment another man came up to our table and enthusiastically told me that "something wonderful" had happened to him. He said he had been very depressed, for things hadn't been going well with him. He decided to get away for a week or so and on this vacation read one of my books[1] in which practical faith techniques are outlined. He said this brought him the first satisfaction and peace he had felt. It encouraged him as to his own possibilities. He began to believe that the answer to his trouble was practical religion.

"So," he said, "I began to practice the spiritual principles presented in your book. I began to believe and affirm that with God's help the objectives I was endeavoring to accomplish could be achieved. A feeling came over me that everything was going to be all right, and from then on nothing could upset me. I absolutely knew it was going to be O.K. So I began to sleep better and feel better. I felt as if I had taken a tonic. My new understanding and practice of spiritual techniques were the turning point."

When he left us, my table companion, who had listened in on this recital, said, "I never heard anything like that before. That fellow talks about religion as happy and workable. It was never presented to me that way. He also gives the impression that religion is almost a science, that you can use it to improve your health and do better in your job. I never thought of religion in that connection."

Then he added, "But do you know what struck me? It was the look on that guy's face."

Now the curious fact is that when my table companion made that statement a semblance of the same look was on his own face. For the first time he was getting the idea that religious faith is not something piously stuffy but is a scientific procedure for successful living. He was observing at firsthand the practical working of prayer power in personal experience.

Personally, I believe that prayer is a sending out of vibrations from one person to another and to God. All of the universe is in vibration. There are vibrations in the molecules of a table. The air is filled with vibrations. The reaction between human beings is also in vibration. When you send out a prayer for another person, you employ the force inherent in a spiritual universe. You transport from yourself to the other person a sense of love, helpfulness, support—a sympathetic, powerful understanding—and in

[1]*A Guide to Confident Living.* Prentice-Hall, Inc., 1948.

this process you awaken vibrations in the universe through which God brings to pass the good objectives prayed for. Experiment with this principle and you will know its amazing results.

For example, I have a habit, which I often use, of praying for people as I pass them. I remember being on a train traveling through West Virginia when I had a curious thought. I saw a man standing on a station platform, then the train moved on and he passed from sight. It occurred to me that I was seeing him for the first and last time. His life and mine touched lightly for just a fraction of an instant. He went his way and I went mine. I wondered how his life would turn out.

Then I prayed for that man, sending out an affirmative prayer that his life would be filled with blessings. Then I began praying for other people I saw as the train passed. I prayed for a man plowing in the field and asked the Lord to help him and give him a good crop. I saw a mother hanging up clothes, and that line of freshly washed garments told me she had a large family. A glimpse of her face and the way in which she handled the clothes of the children told me she was a happy woman. I prayed for her, that she would have a happy life, that her husband would always be true to her and that she would be true to him. I prayed that they might be a religious family and that the children would grow up strong, honorable young people.

In one station I saw a man leaning half asleep against a wall, and I prayed that he would wake up and get off relief and amount to something.

Then we stopped at a station, and there was a lovable little kid, one pants leg longer than the other, shirt open at the neck, wearing a too-big sweater, hair tousled, face dirty. He was sucking a lollipop and working hard on it. I prayed for him, and as the train started to move he looked up at me and gave me the most wonderful smile. I knew my prayer had caught him, and I waved to him, and he waved back at me. I shall never see that boy again in all likelihood, but our lives touched. It had been a cloudy day up to that point, but suddenly the sun came out and I think there was a light in the boy's heart, for it was revealed on his face. I know that my heart felt happy. I am sure it was because the power of God was moving in a circuit through me, to the boy and back to God; and we were all under the spell of prayer power.

One of the important functions of prayer is as a stimulus to creative ideas. Within the mind are all of the resources needed for successful living. Ideas are present in consciousness which, when released and given scope together with proper implementation, can lead to the successful operation of any project or undertaking. When the New Testament says, "The kingdom of God is within you," (Luke 17:21) it is informing us that God our Creator has laid up within our minds and personalities all the potential powers and ability we need for constructive living. It remains for us to tap and develop these powers.

For example, a man of my acquaintance is connected with a business where he is the chief of four executives. At regular intervals these men have what they call an "idea session," the purpose of which is to tap all the creative ideas lurking in the minds of any of the four. For this session they use a room without telephones, buzzers, or other usual office equipment. The double window is fully insulated so that street noises are for the most part eliminated.

Before starting the session the group spends ten minutes in silent prayer and meditation. They conceive of God as creatively working in their minds. Each in his own way silently prays, affirming that God is about to release from his mind the proper ideas needed in the business.

Following the quiet period all start talking, pouring out ideas that have come to their minds. Memos of the ideas are written upon cards and thrown on the table. No one is permitted to criticize any idea at this particular juncture for argument might stop the flow of creative thought. The cards are gathered up and each one is evaluated at a later session; but this is the idea-tapping session, stimulated by prayer power.

When this practice was inaugurated a high percentage of the ideas suggested proved to be without particular value, but as the sessions continued the percentage of good ideas increased. Now many of the best suggestions which have later demonstrated their practical value were evolved in the "idea session."

As one of the executives explained, "We have come up with insights that not only show on our balance sheet but we have also gained a new feeling of confidence. Moreover, there is a deeper feeling of fellowship among the four of us and this has spread to others in the organization."

Where is the old-fashioned businessman who says that religion is theoretical and has no place in business? Today any successful and competent businessman will employ the latest and best-tested methods in production, distribution, and administration, and many are discovering that one of the greatest of all efficiency methods is prayer power.

Alert people everywhere are finding that by trying prayer power they feel better, work better, do better, sleep better, are better.

My friend Grove Patterson, editor of the Toledo *Blade*, is a man of remarkable vigor. He says that his energy results, in part at least, from his methods of prayer. For example, he likes to fall asleep while praying, for he believes that his subconscious is most relaxed at that time. It is in the subconscious that our life is largely governed. If you drop a prayer into the subconscious at the moment of its greatest relaxation, the prayer has a powerful effect. Mr. Patterson chuckled as he said, "Once it worried me because I would fall asleep while praying. Now I actually try to have it so."

Many unique methods of prayer have come to my attention, but one of the most effective is that advocated by Frank Laubach in his excellent book, *Prayer, the Mightiest Power in the World.* I regard this as one of the most practical books on prayer, for it outlines fresh prayer techniques that work. Dr. Laubach believes that actual power is generated by prayer. One of his methods is to walk down the street and "shoot" prayers at people. He calls this type of praying, "flash prayers." He bombards passers-by with prayers, sending out thoughts of good will and love. He says that people passing him on the street as he "shoots" prayers at them often turn around and look at him and smile. They feel the emanation of a power like electrical energy.

In a bus he "shoots" prayers at his fellow passengers. Once he was sitting behind a man who seemed to be very gloomy. He had noticed when he entered the bus that the man had a scowl on his face. He began to send out toward him prayers of good will and faith, conceiving of these prayers as surrounding him and driving into his mind. Suddenly the man began to stroke the back of his head, and when he left the bus the scowl was gone and a smile had replaced it. Dr. Laubach believes that he has often changed the entire atmosphere of a car or bus full of people by the process of "swishing love and prayers all around the place."

In a Pullman club car a half-intoxicated man was quite boorish and rude, talking in an overbearing manner and generally making himself obnoxious. I felt that everyone in the car took a dislike to him. Halfway down the car from him I determined to try Frank Laubach's method. So I started to pray for him, meanwhile visualizing his better self and sending out thoughts of good will toward him. Presently, for no seemingly apparent reason, the man turned in my direction, gave me a most disarming smile, and raised his hand in the gesture of salute. His attitude changed and he became quiet. I have every reason to believe that the prayer thoughts effectively reached out toward him.

It is my practice before making a speech to any audience to pray for the people present and to send out thoughts of love and good will toward them. Sometimes I select out of the audience one or two people who seem to be either depressed or even antagonistic and send my prayer thoughts and good-will attitude specifically toward them. Recently addressing a Chamber of Commerce annual dinner in a southwestern city, I noted a man in the audience who seemed to be scowling at me. It was altogether possible that his facial expression was not in any way related to me, but he seemed antagonistic. Before starting to speak I prayed for him and "shot" a series of prayers and good-will thoughts in his direction. As I spoke, I continued to do this.

When the meeting was over, while shaking hands with those around me, suddenly my hand was caught in a tremendous clasp and I was looking into the face of the man. He was smiling broadly. "Frankly I did not like you when I came to this meeting," he said. "I do not like preachers and saw no reason for having you, a minister, as speaker at our Chamber of Commerce dinner. I was hoping that your speech would not be successful. However, as you spoke something seemed to touch me. I feel like a new person. I had a strange sense of peace—and doggone it, I like you!"

It was not my speech that had this effect. It was the emanation of prayer power. In our brains we have about two billion little storage batteries. The human brain can send off power by thoughts and prayers. The human body's magnetic power has actually been tested. We have thousands of little sending stations, and when these are turned up by prayer it is possible for a tremendous power to flow through a person and to pass between human beings. We can send off power by prayer which acts as both a sending and receiving station.

There was a man, an alcoholic, with whom I had been working. He had been "dry" (as the Alcoholics Anonymous term it) for about six months. He was on a business trip, and one Tuesday afternoon about four o'clock I had a strong impression that he was in trouble. This man dominated my thoughts. I felt something drawing me so I dropped everything and started praying for him. I prayed for about a half-hour, then the impression seemed to let up and I discontinued my prayers.

A few days later he telephoned me. "I have been in Boston all week," he said, "and I want you to know I'm still 'dry,' but early in the week I had a very hard time."

"Was it on Tuesday at four o'clock?" I asked.

Astonished, he replied, "Why, yes, how did you know? Who told you?"

"Nobody told me," I replied. "That is, no human told me." I described my feelings concerning him on Tuesday at four o'clock and told about praying for him for half an hour.

He was astounded, and explained, "I was at the hotel and stopped in front of the bar. I had a terrible struggle with myself. I thought of you, for I needed help badly right then, and I started to pray."

Those prayers starting out from him reached me, and I began to pray for him. Both of us joining in prayer completed the circuit and reached God, and the man got his answer in the form of strength to meet the crisis. And what did he do?

He went to a drugstore, bought a box of candy, and ate all of it without stopping. That pulled him through, he declared—"prayer and candy."

A young married woman admitted she was filled with hates, jealousy, and resentment toward neighbors and friends. She was also very apprehensive, always worrying about her children, whether they would be sick or get into an accident or fail in school. Her life was a pathetic mixture of dissatisfaction, fear, hate, and unhappiness. I asked her if she ever prayed. She said, "Only when I get so up against it that I am just desperate; but I must admit that prayer doesn't mean anything to me, so I don't pray very often."

I suggested that the practice of real prayer could change her life and gave her some instructions in sending out love thoughts instead of hate thoughts and confidence thoughts instead of fear thoughts. I suggested that every day at the time for the children to come home from school she pray, and make her prayers an affirmation of God's protective goodness. Doubtful at first, she became one of the most enthusiastic advocates and practicers of prayer I have ever known. She avidly reads books and pamphlets and practices every effective prayer-power technique. This procedure revamped her life as is illustrated by the following letter which she wrote me recently:

"I feel that my husband and I have both made wonderful progress in the last few weeks. My greatest progress dates from the night you told me that 'every day is a good day if you pray.' I began to put into practice the idea of affirming that this would be a good day the minute I woke up in the morning, and *I can positively say that I have not had a bad or upsetting day since that time*. The amazing thing is that my days actually haven't been any smoother or any more free from petty annoyances than they ever were, but they just don't seem to have the power to upset me any more. Every night I begin my prayers by listing all the things for which I am grateful, little things that happened during the day which added to the happiness of my day. I know that this habit has geared my mind to pick out the nice things and forget the unpleasant ones. The fact that for six weeks I have not had a single bad day and have refused to get downhearted with anyone is really marvelous to me."

She discovered amazing power in trying prayer power.

You can do the same. Following are ten rules for getting effective results from prayer:

1. Set aside a few minutes every day. Do not say anything. Simply practice thinking about God. This will make your mind spiritually receptive.

2. Then pray orally, using simple, natural words. Tell God anything that is on your mind. Do not think you must use stereotyped pious phrases. Talk to God in your own language. He understands it.

3. Pray as you go about the business of the day, on the subway or bus or at your desk. Utilize minute prayers by closing your

eyes to shut out the world and concentrating briefly on God's presence. The more you do this every day the nearer you will feel God's presence.

4. Do not always ask when you pray, but instead affirm that God's blessings are being given, and spend most of your prayers giving thanks.

5. Pray with the belief that sincere prayers can reach out and surround your loved ones with God's love and protection.

6. Never use a negative thought in prayer. Only positive thoughts get results.

7. Always express willingness to accept God's will. Ask for what you want, but be willing to take what God gives you. It may be better than what you ask for.

8. Practice the attitude of putting everything in God's hands. Ask for the ability to do your best and to leave the results confidently to God.

9. Pray for people you do not like or who have mistreated you. Resentment is blockade number one of spiritual power.

10. Make a list of people for whom to pray. The more you pray for other people, especially those not connected with you, the more prayer results will come back to you.

# 5

# *How to Create Your Own Happiness*

WHO DECIDES WHETHER you shall be happy or unhappy? The answer—you do!

A television celebrity had as a guest on his program an aged man. And he was a very rare old man indeed. His remarks were entirely unpremeditated and of course absolutely unrehearsed. They simply bubbled up out of a personality that was radiant and happy. And whenever he said anything, it was so naïve, so apt, that the audience roared with laughter. They loved him. The celebrity was impressed, and enjoyed it with the others.

Finally he asked the old man why he was so happy. "You must have a wonderful secret of happiness," he suggested.

"No," replied the old man, "I haven't any great secret. It's just as plain as the nose on your face. When I get up in the morning," he explained, "I have two choices—either to be happy or to be unhappy, and what do you think I do? I just choose to be happy, and that's all there is to it."

That may seem an oversimplification, and it may appear that the old man was superficial, but I recall that Abraham Lincoln, whom nobody could accuse of being superficial, said that people were just about as happy as they made up their minds to be. You can be unhappy if you want to be. It is the easiest thing in the world to accomplish. Just choose unhappiness. Go around telling yourself that things aren't going well, that nothing is satisfactory, and you can be quite sure of being unhappy. But say to yourself, "Things are going nicely. Life is good. I choose happiness," and you can be quite certain of having your choice.

Children are more expert in happiness than adults. The adult who can carry the spirit of a child into middle and old age is a genius, for he will preserve the truly happy spirit with which God endowed the young. The subtlety of Jesus Christ is remarkable, for He tells us that the way to live in this world is to have the childlike heart and mind. In other words, never get old or dull or jaded in spirit. Don't become super-sophisticated.

My little daughter Elizabeth, aged nine, has the answer to happiness. One day I asked her, "Are you happy, honey?"

"Sure I'm happy," she replied.

"Are you always happy?" I asked.

"Sure," she answered, "I'm always happy."

"What makes you happy?" I asked her.

"Why, I don't know," she said, "I'm just happy."

"There must be something that makes you happy," I urged.

"Well," she said, "I'll tell you what it is. My playmates, they make me happy. I like them. My school makes me happy. I like to go to school. (I didn't say anything, but she never got that from me.) I like my teachers. And I like to go to church. I like Sunday school and my Sunday-school teacher. I love my sister Margaret and my brother John. I love my mother and father. They take care of me when I'm sick, and they love me and are good to me."

That is Elizabeth's formula for happiness, and it seems to me that it's all there—her playmates (that's her associates), her school (the place where she works), her church and Sunday school (where she worships), her sister, brother, mother, and father (that means the home circle where love is found). There you have happiness in a nutshell, and the happiest time of your life is in relation to those factors.

A group of boys and girls were asked to list the things that made them happiest. Their answers were rather touching. Here is the boys' list: "A swallow flying; looking into deep, clear water; water being cut at the bow of a boat; a fast train rushing; a builder's crane lifting something heavy; my dog's eyes."

And here is what the girls said made them happy: "Street lights on the river; red roofs in the trees; smoke rising from a chimney; red velvet; the moon in the clouds." There is something in the beautiful essence of the universe that is expressed, though only half-articulated, by these things. To become a happy person have a clean soul, eyes that see romance in the commonplace, a child's heart, and spiritual simplicity.

Many of us manufacture our own unhappiness. Of course not all unhappiness is self-created, for social conditions are responsible for not a few of our woes. Yet it is a fact that to a large extent by our thoughts and attitudes we distill out of the ingredients of life either happiness or unhappiness for ourselves.

"Four people out of five are not so happy as they can be," declares an eminent authority, and he adds, "Unhappiness is the most common state of mind." Whether human happiness strikes as low a level as this, I would hesitate to say, but I do find more people living unhappy lives than I would care to compute. Since a fundamental desire of every human being is for that state of existence called happiness, something should be done about it. Happiness is achievable and the process for obtaining it is not complicated. Anyone who desires it, who wills it, and who learns and applies the right formula may become a happy person.

In a railroad dining car I sat across from a husband and wife, strangers to me. The lady was expensively dressed, as the furs, diamonds, and costume which she wore indicated. But she was having a most unpleasant time with herself. Rather loudly she proclaimed that the car was dingy and drafty, the service abominable, and the food most unpalatable. She complained and fretted about everything.

Her husband, on the contrary, was a genial, affable, easygoing man who obviously had the capacity to take things as they came. I thought he seemed a bit embarrassed by his wife's critical attitude and somewhat disappointed, too, as he was taking her on this trip for pleasure.

To change the conversation he asked what business I was in, and then said that he was a lawyer. Then he made a big mistake, for with a grin he added, "My wife is in the manufacturing business."

This was surprising, for she did not seem to be the industrial or executive type, so I asked, "What does she manufacture?"

"Unhappiness," he replied. "She manufactures her own unhappiness."

Despite the icy coolness that settled upon the table following this ill-advised observation, I was grateful for his remark, for it describes exactly what so many people do—"They manufacture their own unhappiness."

It is a pity, too, for there are so many problems created by life itself that dilute our happiness that it is indeed most foolish to distill further unhappiness within your own mind. How foolish to manufacture personal unhappiness to add to all the other difficulties over which you have little or no control!

Rather than to emphasize the manner in which people manufacture their own unhappiness, let us proceed to the formula for putting an end to this misery-producing process. Suffice it to say that we manufacture our unhappiness by thinking unhappy thoughts, by the attitudes which we habitually take, such as the negative feeling that everything is going to turn out badly, or that other people are getting what they do not deserve and we are failing to get what we do deserve.

Our unhappiness is further distilled by saturating the consciousness with feelings of resentment, ill will, and hate. The unhappiness-producing process always makes important use of the ingredients of fear and worry. Each of these matters is dealt with elsewhere in this book. We merely want to make the point at the present time and stress it forcefully that a very large proportion of the unhappiness of the average individual is self-manufactured. How, then, may we proceed to produce not unhappiness but happiness?

An incident from one of my railroad journeys may suggest an answer. One morning in an old-style Pullman car approximately a half-dozen of us were shaving in the men's lounge. As always in such close and crowded quarters after a night on the train, this group of strangers was not disposed to be gay, and there was little conversation and that little was mostly mumbled.

Then a man came in wearing on his face a broad smile. He greeted us all with a cheery good morning, but received rather unenthusiastic grunts in return. As he went about his shaving he was humming, probably quite unconsciously, a gay little tune. It got a bit on the nerves of some of the men. Finally one said rather sarcastically, "You certainly seem to be happy this morning! Why all the cheer?"

"Yes," the man answered, "as a matter of fact, I am happy. I do feel cheerful." Then he added, "I make it a habit to be happy."

That is all that was said, but I am sure that each man in that lounge left the train with those interesting words in mind, "I make it a habit to be happy."

The statement is really very profound, for our happiness or unhappiness depends to an important degree upon the habit of mind we cultivate. That collection of wise sayings, the book of Proverbs, tells us that ". . . he that is of a merry heart hath a continual feast." (Proverbs 15:15) In other words, cultivate the merry heart; that is, develop the happiness habit, and life will become a continual feast, which is to say you can enjoy life every day. Out of the happiness habit comes a happy life. And because we can cultivate a habit, we therefore have the power to create our own happiness.

The happiness habit is developed by simply practicing happy thinking. Make a mental list of happy thoughts and pass them through your mind several times every day. If an unhappiness thought should enter your mind, immediately stop, consciously eject it, and substitute a happiness thought. Every morning before arising, lie relaxed in bed and deliberately drop happy thoughts into your conscious mind. Let a series of pictures pass across your mind of each happy experience you expect to have during the day. Savor their joy. Such thoughts will help cause events to turn out that way. Do not affirm that things will not go well that day. By merely saying that, you can actually help to make it so. You will draw to yourself every factor, large and small, that will contribute to unhappy conditions. As a result, you will find yourself asking, "Why does everything go badly for me? What is the matter with everything?"

The reason can be directly traced to the manner in which you begin the day in your thoughts.

Tomorrow try this plan instead. When you arise, say out loud three times this one sentence, "This is the day which the Lord hath made; we will rejoice and be glad in it." (Psalm 118:24) Only personalize it and say, "I will rejoice and be glad in it." Repeat it in a strong, clear voice and with positive tone and emphasis. The statement, of course, is from the Bible and it is a good cure for unhappiness. If you repeat that one sentence three times before breakfast and meditate on the meaning of the words you will change the character of the day by starting off with a happiness psychology.

While dressing or shaving or getting breakfast, say aloud a few such remarks as the following, "I believe this is going to be a wonderful day. I believe I can successfully handle all problems that will arise today. I feel good physically, mentally, emotionally. It is wonderful to be alive. I am grateful for all that I have had, for all that I now have, and for all that I shall have. Things aren't going to fall apart. God is here and He is with me and He will see me through. I thank God for every good thing."

I once knew an unhappy sort of fellow who always said to his wife at breakfast, "This is going to be another tough day." He didn't really think so, but he had a mental quirk whereby if he said it was going to be a tough day, it might turn out pretty well. But things really started going badly with him, which was not surprising, for if you visualize and affirm an unhappy outcome, you tend thereby to create just that type of condition. So affirm happy outcomes at the start of every day, and you will be surprised at how often things will turn out so.

But it is not sufficient to apply to the mind even such an important affirmation therapy as I have just suggested unless throughout the day you also base your actions and attitudes upon fundamental principles of happy living.

One of the most simple and basic of such principles is that of human love and good will. It is amazing what happiness a sincere expression of compassion and tenderness will induce.

My friend Dr. Samuel Shoemaker once wrote a moving story about a mutual friend, Ralston Young, famous as Redcap No. 42 in the Grand Central Station in New York. He carries bags for a living, but his real job is living the spirit of Christ as a redcap in one of the world's greatest railway stations. As he carries a man's suitcase, he tries to share a little Christian fellowship with him. He carefully watches a customer to see if there is any way in which he can give him more courage and hope. He is very skillful in the way he goes about it too.

One day, for example, he was asked to take a little old lady to her train. She was in a wheel chair, so he took her down on the elevator. As he wheeled her into the elevator he noticed that there were tears in her eyes. Ralston Young stood there as the elevator descended, closed his eyes, and asked the Lord how he could help her, and the Lord gave him an idea. As he wheeled her off the elevator, he said with a smile, "Ma'am, if you don't mind my saying so, that is a mighty pretty hat you are wearing."

She looked up at him and said, "Thank you."

"And I might add," he said, "that sure is a pretty dress you have on. I like it so much."

Being a woman, this appealed to her, and despite the fact that she was not feeling well, she brightened up and asked, "Why in the world did you say those nice things to me? It is very thoughtful of you."

"Well," he said, "I saw how unhappy you were. I saw that you were crying, and I just asked the Lord how I could help you. The Lord said, 'Speak to her about her hat.' The mention of the dress," he added, "was my own idea." Ralston Young and the Lord together knew how to get a woman's mind off her troubles.

"Don't you feel well?" he then asked.

"No," she replied. "I am constantly in pain. I am never free from it. Sometimes I think I can't stand it. Do you, by any chance, know what it means to be in pain all the time?"

Ralston had an answer. "Yes, ma'am, I do, for I lost an eye, and it hurt like a hot iron day and night."

"But," she said, "you seem to be happy now. How did you accomplish it?"

By this time he had her in her seat in the train, and he said, "Just by prayer, ma'am, just by prayer."

Softly she asked, "Does prayer, just prayer, take your pain away?"

"Well," answered Ralston, "perhaps it doesn't always take it away. I can't say that it does, but it always helps to overcome it so it doesn't seem like it hurts so much. Just keep on prayin', ma'am, and I'll pray for you too."

Her tears were dried now, and she looked up at him with a lovely smile, took him by the hand, and said, "You've done me so much good."

A year passed, and one night in Grand Central Station Ralston Young was paged to come to the Information booth. A young woman was there who said, "I bring you a message from the dead. Before she died my mother told me to find you and to tell you how much you helped her last year when you took her to the train in her wheel chair. She will always remember you, even in eternity. She will remember you, for you were so kind and loving and understanding." Then the young woman burst into tears and sobbed in her grief.

Ralston stood quietly watching her. Then he said, "Don't cry, missy, don't cry. You shouldn't cry. Give a prayer of thanksgiving."

Surprised, the girl said, "Why should I give a prayer of thanksgiving?"

"Because," said Ralston, "many people have become orphans much younger than you. You had your mother for a long, long time, and besides you still have her. You will see her again. She is near to you now and she always will be near to you. Maybe," he said, "she is right with us now—the two of us, as we talk."

The sobs ended and the tears dried. Ralston's kindness had the same effect on the daughter as it had had on the mother. In this huge station, with thousands of people passing by, the two of them felt the presence of one who inspired this wonderful redcap to go around this way spreading love.

"Where love is," said Tolstoy, "God is," and, we might add, where God and love are, there is happiness. So a practical principle in creating happiness is to practice love.

A genuinely happy man is a friend of mine, H. C. Mattern, who, with his equally happy wife, Mary, travels throughout the country in the course of his work. Mr. Mattern carries a unique business card on the reverse side of which is stated the philosophy which has brought happiness to him and his wife and to hundreds of others who have been so fortunate as to feel the impact of their personalities.

The card reads as follows: "The way to happiness: keep your heart free from hate, your mind from worry. Live simply, expect little, give much. Fill your life with love. Scatter sunshine. Forget self, think of others. Do as you would be done by. Try this for a week and you will be surprised."

As you read these words you may say, "There is nothing new in that." Indeed, there is something new in it if you have never tried it. When you start to practice it you will find it the newest, freshest, most astonishing method of happy and successful living you have ever used. What is the value of having known these principles all your life if you have never made use of them? Such inefficiency in living is tragic. For a man to have lived in poverty when all the time right on his doorstep is gold indicates an unintelligent approach to life. This simple philosophy is the way to happiness. Practice these principles for just one week, as Mr. Mattern suggests, and if it has not brought you the beginnings of real happiness, then your unhappiness is very deep seated indeed.

Of course in order to give power to these principles of happiness and make them work it is necessary to support them with a dynamic quality of mind. You are not likely to secure effective results even with spiritual principles without spiritual power. When one experiences a dynamic spiritual change inwardly, success with happiness-producing ideas becomes extraordinarily easy. If you begin to use spiritual principles, however awkwardly, you will gradually experience spiritual power inwardly. I can assure you that this will give you the greatest surge of happiness you have ever known. It will stay with you, too, as long as you live a God-centered life.

In my travels about the country I have been encountering an increasing number of genuinely happy individuals. These are persons who have been practicing the techniques described in this book and which I have presented in other volumes and in other writings and talks and which other writers and speakers have likewise been giving to receptive people. It is astonishing how people can become inoculated with happiness through an inner experience of spiritual change. People of all types everywhere are having this experience today. In fact, it has become one of the most popular phenomena of our times, and if it continues to develop and expand, the person who has not had a spiritual experience will soon be considered old-fashioned and behind the times. Nowadays it is smart to be spiritually alive. It is old-fogyism to be ignorant of that happiness-producing transformation which people everywhere are enjoying at this time.

Recently, after finishing a lecture in a certain city, a big, strapping, fine-looking man came up to me. He slapped me on the shoulder with such force that it almost bowled me over.

"Doctor," he said in a booming voice, "how about coming out with the gang? We are having a big party at the Smiths' house, and we would like you to come along. It's going to be a whale of a shindig and you ought to get in on it." So ran his racy invitation.

Well, obviously this didn't sound like a proper party for a preacher, and I was hesitant. I was afraid I might cramp everyone's style, so I began to make excuses.

"Oh, forget it," my friend told me. "Don't worry, this is your kind of party. You will be surprised. Come on along. You will get the kick of your life out of it."

So I yielded and went along with my buoyant and racy friend and he was certainly one of the most infectious personalities I had encountered in quite a while. Soon we came to a big house set back among trees with a wide, sweeping driveway up to the front door. From the noise issuing from the open windows there was no question but that quite a party was in progress, and I wondered what I was getting myself into. My host, with a great shout, dragged me into the room, and we had quite a handshaking time, and he introduced me to a large group of gay and exuberant people. They were a happy, joyous lot of folk.

I looked around for a bar, but there wasn't any. All that was being served was coffee, fruit juice, ginger ale, sandwiches, and ice cream, but there was lots of those.

"These people must have stopped somewhere before coming here," I remarked to my friend.

He was shocked, and said, "Stopped somewhere? Why, you don't understand. These people have got the spirit all right, but not the kind of 'spirit' you are thinking about. I am surprised at you," he said. "Don't you realize what makes this crowd so happy? They have been renewed spiritually. They have got something. They have been set free from themselves. They have found God as a living, vital, honest-to-goodness reality. Yes," he said, "they have got spirit all right, but it isn't the kind that you get out of a bottle. They have got spirit in their hearts."

Then I saw what he meant. This wasn't a crowd of sad-faced, stodgy people. They were the leaders of that town—businessmen, lawyers, doctors, teachers, society people, and a lot of simpler folk besides, and they were having a wonderful time at this party—talking about God, and they were doing it in the most natural manner imaginable. They were telling one another about the changes that had occurred in their lives through revitalized spiritual power.

Those who have the naïve notion that you can't laugh and be gay when you are religious should have been in on that party.

Well, I went away from that party with a Bible verse running through my mind, "In him was life; and the life was the light of men." (John 1:4) That was the light I saw on the faces of those happy people. An inner light was reflected outwardly on their faces, and it came from an effervescent spiritual something that they had taken into themselves. Life means vitality, and these people obviously were getting their vitality from God. They had found the power that creates happiness.

This is no isolated incident. I venture the assertion that in your own community, if you will look around for them, you will find lots of people just like those described above. If you don't find them in your own home town, come to the Marble Collegiate Church in New York City and you will find them by the score.

But you can get the same spirit by reading this book if you practice the simple principles set forth.

As you read this book believe what you read, because it is true; then start working on the practical suggestions the book contains and you, too, will have the spiritual experience that produces this quality of happiness. I know this is so, because many of those to whom I have referred and shall refer in later chapters got their vital new life in the same way. Then, having been changed inwardly, you will begin to create out of yourself not unhappiness, but a happiness of such quality and character that you will wonder if you are living in the same world. As a matter of fact it won't be the same world because you are not the same, and what you are determines the world in which you live, so as you change, your world changes also.

If happiness is determined by our thoughts it is necessary to drive off the thoughts which make for depression and discouragement. This can be done first by simply determining to do it; second, by utilizing an easily employed technique which I suggested to a businessman. I met him at a luncheon and have seldom heard such gloom as he got off. His conversation would have been ultra-depressing had I permitted it to affect me. It reeked with pessimism. To hear him talk you would think everything was headed for ruin. Of course the man was tired. Accumulated problems had swamped his mind which was seeking release in retreat from a world which was too much for his depleted energy. His principal trouble was in his depressed thought pattern. He needed an infusion of light and faith.

So rather boldly I said, "If you want to feel better and stop being miserable, I can give you something that will fix you up."

"What can you do?" he snorted. "Are you a miracle worker?"

"No," I replied, "but I can put you in touch with a miracle worker who will drain off that unhappiness of yours and give you a new slant on life. I mean that," I concluded, as we separated.

Apparently he became curious, for he got in touch with me later and I gave him a little book of mine called *Thought Conditioners*.[1] It contains forty health and happiness producing thoughts. Inasmuch as it is a pocket-sized booklet, I suggested

[1]*Thought Conditioners*, published by Sermon Publications, Inc., Distribution Office, Pawling, New York.

that he carry it for easy consultation and that he drop one of the suggested thoughts in his mind every day for forty days. I further suggested that he commit each thought to memory, thus allowing it to dissolve in consciousness, and that he visualize this healthy thought sending a quieting and healing influence through his mind. I assured him that if he would follow this plan, these healthy thoughts would drive off the diseased thoughts that were sapping his joy, energy, and creative ability.

The idea at first impressed him as being a bit queer and he had his doubts, but he followed directions. After about three weeks he called me on the telephone and shouted, "Boy, this sure works! It is wonderful. I have snapped out of it, and I wouldn't have believed it possible."

He remains "snapped out of it" and is a genuinely happy person. This pleasant condition resulted because he became skilled in the power to create his own happiness. He later commented that his first mental hurdle was honestly to face the fact that while his unhappiness made him miserable, yet he was at home in self-pity and self-punishment thoughts. He knew that these sick thoughts were the cause of his trouble, but he shrank from the effort required to desire change sufficiently to actually go about changing. But when he began systematically to insert healthy spiritual thoughts into his mind as directed, he began first to want new life, then to realize the thrilling fact that he could have it, then the even more amazing fact that he was getting it. The result was that after some three weeks of a self-improvement process new happiness "burst" upon him.

Everywhere in this country today are groups of people who have found the happy way. If we can have even one such group in every city, town, and hamlet in America, we can change the life of this country within a very short time. And what kind of group do we mean? Let me explain.

I was speaking in a Western city and returned to my hotel room rather late. I wanted to get a little sleep, for I was to be up at five-thirty next morning to catch a plane. As I was preparing for bed, the telephone rang, and a lady said, "There are about fifty of us at my house waiting for you."

I explained that I could not come due to the early hour of my departure in the morning.

"Oh," she said, "two men are on their way to get you. We have been praying for you, and we want you to come and pray with us before you leave the city."

I am glad I went, though I had very little sleep that night.

The men who came for me were a couple of alcoholics who had been healed by the power of faith. They were two of the happiest, most lovable fellows you can imagine.

The home to which they took me was packed. People were sitting on the stairways, on the tables, on the floor. One man was even perched on the grand piano. And what were they doing? They were having a prayer meeting. They told me that sixty such prayer groups were going on in that city all the time.

I was never in such a meeting. They were anything but a stuffy group. They were a released, happy crowd of real people. I found myself strangely moved. The spirit in that room was tremendous in its lifting force. The group would burst into song, and I never heard such singing. The room was filled with a wonderful spirit of laughter.

Then a woman stood up. I saw that she had braces on her legs, and she said, "They told me I would never walk again. Do you want to see me walk?" And she walked up and down the room.

"What did it?" I asked.

"Jesus," she replied simply.

Then another fine-looking girl said, "Did you ever see a victim of the narcotics habit? Well, I was one and I was healed." There she sat, a beautiful, modest, charming young woman and she, too, said, "Jesus did it."

Then a couple who had drifted apart told me that they had been brought together and they were happier than ever before.

"How did it come about?" I asked. And their reply was, "Jesus did it."

A man said he had been a victim of alcohol, that he had dragged his family down until they were living in abject poverty and he was a complete failure. And now as he stood before me he was a strong, healthy personality. I started to ask how, but he nodded and said, "Jesus did it."

Then they burst into another song, and then someone dimmed the lights and we all held hands around in a great circle. I had a feeling as though I had hold of an electric wire. Power was flowing around that room. Without any question I was the least spiritually developed person in that group. I knew in that moment that

Jesus Christ was right there in that house and those people had found Him. They had been touched by His power. He had given them new life. This life bubbled up in an irrepressible effervescence.

This is the secret of happiness. All else is secondary. Get this experience and you've got real, unalloyed happiness, the best the world offers. Don't miss it whatever you do in this life, for this is it.

# 6

## *Stop Fuming and Fretting*

MANY PEOPLE MAKE life unnecessarily difficult for themselves by dissipating power and energy through fuming and fretting.

Do you ever "fume" and "fret"? Here is a picture of yourself if you do. The word "fume" means to boil up, to blow off, to emit vapor, to be agitated, to be distraught, to seethe. The word "fret" is equally descriptive. It is reminiscent of a sick child in the night, a petulant half-cry, half-whine. It ceases, only to begin again. It has an irritating, annoying, penetrating quality. To fret is a childish term, but it describes the emotional reaction of many adults.

The Bible advises us to "Fret not thyself . . ." (Psalm 37:1) This is sound advice for the people of our time. We need to stop fuming and fretting and get peaceful if we are to have power to live effectively. And how do we go about doing so?

A first step is to reduce your pace or at least the tempo of your pace. We do not realize how accelerated the rate of our lives has become, or the speed at which we are driving ourselves. Many people are destroying their physical bodies by this pace, but what is even more tragic, they are tearing their minds and souls to shreds as well. It is possible for a person to live a quiet existence physically and yet maintain a high tempo emotionally. Even an invalid can live at too high a pace from that standpoint. The character of our thoughts determines pace. When the mind goes rushing on pell-mell from one feverish attitude to another it becomes feverish and the result is a state bordering on petulance. The pace of modern life must be reduced if we are not to suffer profoundly from its debilitating over-stimulation and super-excitement. This over-stimulation produces toxic poisons in the body and creates emotional illness. It produces fatigue and a sense of frustration so that we fume and fret about everything from our personal troubles to the state of the nation and the world. If the effect of this emotional disquiet is so pronounced physically, what must its effect be on that deep inner essence of the personality known as the soul?

It is impossible to have peace of soul if the pace is so feverishly accelerated. God won't go that fast. He will not endeavor to keep up with you. He says in effect, "Go ahead if you must with this foolish pace and when you are worn out I will offer my healing. But I can make your life so rich if you will slow down now and live and move and have your being in me." God moves imperturbably, slowly, and with perfect organization. The only wise rate at which to live is God's rate. God gets things done and they are done right and He does them without hurry. He neither fumes nor frets. He is peaceful and therefore efficient. This same peace is offered to us—"Peace I leave with you, my peace I give unto you . . ." (John 14:27)

In a sense this is a pathetic generation, especially in the great cities because of the effect of nervous tension, synthetic excitement, and noise; but the malady extends into the country districts also, for the air waves transmit tension.

I was amused by an old lady who, in talking about this matter, said, "Life is so daily." That remark certainly spoke volumes about the pressure, responsibilities, and tension of daily life. Its persistent, insistent demand upon us is provocative of pressure.

One wonders whether this generation of Americans is not so accustomed to tension that many are in the unhappy state of not being comfortable without it. The deep quietness of woods and valleys so well known to our forefathers is an unaccustomed state to them. The tempo of their lives is such that in many instances they have an incapacity to draw upon the sources of peace and quietness which the physical world offers.

One summer afternoon my wife and I went for a long walk in the woods. We were stopping at the beautiful Lake Mohonk Mountain House which is set in one of the finest natural parks in America, 7,500 acres of virgin mountainside in the middle of which is a lake lying like a gem in the forest. The word *mohonk* means "lake in the sky." Aeons ago some giant upheaval of the earth cast up these sheer cliffs. You come out of the deep woods onto some noble promontory and rest your eyes on great valleys set among hills, rock-ribbed and ancient as the sun. These woods, mountains, and valleys constitute what ought to be a sure retreat from every confusion of this world.

On this afternoon as we walked there was a mixture of summer showers and sunlit hours. We were drenched and started to fret about it a bit because it took the press out of our clothes. Then we told each other that it doesn't hurt a human being to get drenched with clean rain water, that the rain feels cool and fresh on one's face, and that you can always sit in the sun and dry yourself out. We walked under the trees and talked and then fell silent.

We were listening, listening deeply to the quietness. In a strict sense, the woods are never still. There is tremendous activity always in process, but nature makes no strident noises regardless of the vastness of its operation. Nature's sounds are quiet, harmonious.

On this beautiful afternoon, nature was laying its hand of healing quietness upon us, and we could actually feel the tension being drawn off.

Just as we were falling under this spell, the faint sounds of what passes for music came to us. It was nervous, high-strung music of the jitterbug variety. Presently through the woods came three young people, two young women and a young man, and the latter was lugging a portable radio.

They were three young city people out for a walk in the woods and tragically enough were bringing their noise along with them. They were nice young folk, too, for they stopped and we had a pleasant talk with them. It occurred to me to ask them to turn that thing off and listen to the music of the woods, but I didn't feel it was my business to instruct them, and finally they went on their way.

We commented on the loss they were incurring, that they could pass through this peacefulness and not give ear to the music that is as old as the world, harmony and melody the like of which man has never equaled: the song of the wind through the trees, the sweet notes of birds singing their hearts out, the whole background of the music of the spheres.

This is still to be found in America in our woods and great plains, in our valleys, in our mountain majesties, and where the ocean foams on soft shores of sand. We should avail ourselves of its healing. Remember the words of Jesus, "Come ye yourselves apart into a desert place, and rest awhile." (Mark 6:31) Even as I write these words and give you this good advice, I recall instances where it has been necessary to remind myself to practice the same truth, which emphasizes that we must everlastingly discipline ourselves to quietness if we expect its benefits in our lives.

One autumn day Mrs. Peale and I took a trip into Massachusetts to see our son John at Deerfield Academy. We told him we would arrive at 11 A.M., and we pride ourselves on the good old American custom of promptness. Therefore, being a bit behind schedule, we were driving at breakneck speed through the autumnal landscape. My wife said, "Norman, did you see that radiant hillside?"

"What hillside?" I asked.

"It just went by on the other side," she explained. "Look at that beautiful tree."

"What tree?" I was already a mile past it.

"This is one of the most glorious days I have ever seen," my wife said. "How could you possibly imagine such amazing colors as these New England hillsides in October? In fact," she said, "it makes me happy inside."

That remark of hers so impressed me that I stopped the car and went back a quarter of a mile to a lake backed by towering hills dressed in autumn colors. We sat and looked and meditated. God with His genius and skill had painted that scene in the varied colors which He alone can mix. In the still waters of the lake lay a reflected vision of His glory, for the hillside was unforgettably pictured in that mirrorlike pond.

For quite a while we sat without a word until finally my wife broke the silence by the only appropriate statement that one could make, "He leadeth me beside the still waters." (Psalm 23:2) We arrived at Deerfield at eleven, but we were not tired. In fact, we were deeply refreshed.

To help reduce this tension which seems to dominate our people everywhere, you can start by reducing your own pace. To do that you will need to slow down, quiet down. Do not fume. Do not fret. Practice being peaceful. Practice "the peace of God which passeth all understanding." (Philippians 4:7) Then note the quiet power sense that wells up within you.

A friend of mine who was compelled to take an enforced rest as a result of "pressure" wrote me, "Many lessons have been learned during this enforced retreat. Now I know better than before that in the quiet we become aware of His presence. Life can get muddled. But 'muddied water,' says Lao-tse, 'let stand, will become clear.' "

A physician gave some rather whimsical advice to a patient, an aggressive, go-getter type of businessman. Excitedly he told the doctor what an enormous amount of work he had to do and that he had to get it done right away quick or else.

"I take my brief case home every night and it's packed with work," he said with nervous inflection.

"Why do you take work home with you at night?" the doctor asked quietly.

"I have to get it done," he fumed.

"Cannot someone else do it, or help you with it?" asked the doctor.

"No," the man snapped. "I am the only one who can do it. It must be done just right, and I alone can do it as it must be done, and it has to be done quickly. Everything depends upon me."

"If I write you a prescription, will you follow it?" asked the doctor.

This, believe it or not, was the prescription. His patient was to take off two hours every working day and go for a long walk. Then he was to take off a half-day a week and spend that half-day in a cemetery.

In astonishment the patient demanded, "Why should I spend a half-day in a cemetery?"

"Because," answered the doctor, "I want you to wander around and look at the gravestones of men who are there permanently. I want you to meditate on the fact that many of them are there because they thought even as you do, that the whole world rested on their shoulders. Meditate on the solemn fact that when you get there permanently the world will go on just the same and, as important as you are, others will be able to do the work you are now doing. I suggest that you sit on one of those tombstones and repeat this statement, '. . . a thousand years in Thy sight are but as yesterday when it is past, and as a watch in the night.' " (Psalm 90:4)

The patient got the idea. He slowed his pace. He learned to delegate authority. He achieved a proper sense of his own importance. He stopped fuming and fretting. He got peaceful. And, it might be added, he does better work. He is developing a more competent organization and he admits that his business is in better condition.

A prominent manufacturer was afflicted with tension, in fact, he was in a very high-strung frame of mind. As he himself described it, "he leapt out of bed every morning and immediately got himself into high gear. He was in such a rush and dither that he 'made his breakfast on soft-boiled eggs because they slid down fast.' " This hectic pace left him fagged and worn at about midday. He sank into bed every night exhausted.

It so happens that his home is situated in a grove of trees. Very early one morning, unable to sleep, he arose and sat by the window. He became interested in watching a bird emerge from his night's sleep. He noticed that a bird sleeps with his head under his wing, the feathers pulled all around himself. When he awakened, he pulled his bill out from under his feathers, took a sleepy look around, stretched one leg to its full length, meanwhile stretching the wing over the leg until it spread out like a fan. He pulled the leg and wing back and then repeated the same process with the other leg and wing, whereupon he put his head down in his feathers again for a delicious little cat nap (only in this case a bird nap), then the head came out again. This time the bird looked around eagerly, threw his head back, gave his wings and legs two more big stretches, then he sent up a song, a thrilling, melodic song of praise to the day, wherewith he hopped down off the limb, got himself a drink of cold water, and started looking for food.

My high-strung friend said to himself, "If that's the way the birds get up, sort of slow and easy like, why wouldn't it be a good method for me to start the day that way?" He actually went through the same performance, even to singing, and noticed that the song was an especially beneficial factor, that it was a releasing mechanism.

"I can't sing," he chuckled, "but I practiced sitting quietly in a chair and singing. Mostly I sang hymns and happy songs. Imagine, me singing, but I did. My wife thought I was bereft of my senses. The only thing I had on the bird was that I did a little praying, too, then, like the bird, I felt like some food, and I wanted a good breakfast—bacon and eggs. And I took my time eating it. After that I went to work in a released frame of mind. It surely did start me off for the day minus the tension, and it helped me go through the day in a peaceful and relaxed manner."

A former member of a championship university crew told me that their shrewd crew coach often reminded them, "To win this or any race, row slowly." He pointed out that rapid rowing tends to break the stroke and when the stroke is broken it is with the greatest difficulty that a crew recovers the rhythm necessary to win. Meanwhile other crews pass the disorganized group. It is indeed wise advise—"To go fast, row slowly."

In order to row slowly or to work slowly and maintain the steady pace that wins, the victim of high tempo will do well to get the co-ordinating peace of God into his mind, his soul, and, it might be added, into his nerves and muscles also.

Have you ever considered the importance of having the peace of God in your muscles, in your joints? Perhaps your joints will not pain so much when they have the peace of God in them. Your muscles will work with correlation when the peace of God who created them governs their action. Speak to your muscles every day and to your joints and to your nerves, saying, "Fret not thyself." (Psalm 37:1) Relax on a couch or bed, think of each important muscle from head to feet, and say to each, "The peace of God is touching you." Then practice "feeling" that peace throughout your entire body. In due course your muscles and joints will take heed.

Slow down, for whatever you really want will be there when you get there if you work toward it without stress, without pressing. If, proceeding under God's guidance and in His smooth and unhurried tempo, it is not there, then it was not supposed to be there. If you miss it, perhaps you should have missed it. So definitely seek to develop a normal, natural, God-ordered pace. Practice and preserve mental quiet. Learn the art of letting go all nervous excitement. To do this, stop at intervals and affirm, "I now relinquish nervous excitement—it is flowing from me. I am at peace." Do not fume. Do not fret. Practice being peaceful.

To attain this efficient state of living, I recommend the practice of thinking peaceful thoughts. Every day we perform a series of acts designed to care for the body properly. We bathe, brush the teeth, take exercise. In similar fashion we should give time and planned effort to keeping the mind in a healthy state. One way to do this is to sit quietly and pass a series of peaceful thoughts through the mind. For example, pass through the thoughts the memory of a lofty mountain, a misty valley, a sun-speckled trout stream, silver moonlight on water.

At least once in every twenty-four hours, preferably in the busiest part of the day, deliberately stop whatever you are doing for ten or fifteen minutes and practice serenity.

There are times when it is essential resolutely to check our headlong pace, and it must be emphasized that the only way to stop is to stop.

I went to a certain city on a lecture date and was met at the train by a committee. I was rushed to a bookstore where I had an autographing party and then to another bookstore where another autographing party was held. Then they rushed me to a luncheon. After rushing through the luncheon I was rushed to a meeting. After the meeting I was rushed back to the hotel where I changed my clothes and was rushed to a reception where I met several hundred people and drank three glasses of fruit punch. Then I was rushed back to the hotel and told I had twenty minutes to dress for dinner. When I was getting dressed the telephone rang and somebody said, "Hurry, hurry, we must rush down to dinner."

Excitedly I chattered, "I will rush right down."

I rushed from the room and was so excited that I could scarcely get the key into the lock. Hastily I felt myself, to be sure that I was completely dressed, and rushed toward the elevator. All of a sudden I stopped. I was out of breath. I asked myself, "What is this all about? What is the meaning of this ceaseless rush? This is ridiculous!"

Then I declared independence, and said, "I do not care if I go to dinner. I do not care whether I make a talk. I do not have to go to this dinner and I do not have to make a speech." So deliberately and slowly I walked back to my room and took my time about unlocking the door. I telephoned the man downstairs and said, "If you want to eat, go ahead. If you want to save a place for me, I will be down after a while, but I am not going to rush any more."

So I removed my coat, sat down, took off my shoes, put my feet up on the table, and just sat. Then I opened the Bible and very slowly read aloud the 121st Psalm, "I will lift up mine eyes unto the hills from whence cometh my help." I closed the book and had a little talk with myself, saying, "Come on now, start living a slower and more relaxed life," and then I affirmed, "God is here and His peace is touching me.

"I do not need anything to eat," I reasoned. "I eat too much anyway. Besides, the dinner will probably not be very good, and if I am quiet now I will give a better speech at eight o'clock."

So I sat there resting and praying for fifteen minutes. I shall never forget the sense of peace and personal mastery I had when I walked out of that room. I had the glorious feeling of having overcome something, of having taken control of myself emotionally, and when I reached the dining room the others had just finished the first course. All I missed was the soup, which by general consent was no great loss.

This incident was an amazing experience of the healing presence of God. I gained these values by simply stopping, by quietly reading the Bible, by sincerely praying, and by thinking some peaceful thoughts for a few moments.

Physicians generally seem to feel that much physical trouble could be avoided or overcome by practicing the philosophy and methodology of not fuming or fretting.

A prominent citizen of New York told me that his doctor suggested that he come to our clinic at the church "because," said his physician, "you need to develop a calm philosophy of living. Your power resources are played out."

"My doctor says I am pushing myself to the limit. He tells me I'm too tense, too high-strung, that I fume and fret too much, and," he concluded, "my doctor declares the only sure cure is for me to develop what he calls a calm philosophy of living."

My visitor arose and paced the floor, then demanded, "But how in the world can I do that? It's a lot easier said than done."

Then this excited gentleman went on to say that his doctor had given him certain suggestions for developing this calm philosophy of living. The suggestions as outlined were indeed wise. "But then," he explained, "the doctor suggested that I see you people here at the church, for he feels that if I learn to use religious faith in a practical manner it will give me peace of mind and bring down my blood pressure. Then I will feel better physically. While I realize the doctor's prescription is sensible," he complained, "how can a man fifty years old, of a high-strung nature such as mine, suddenly change the habits of a lifetime and develop this so-called calm philosophy of living?"

That did indeed seem to be a problem, for he was a bundle of excitable and explosive nerves. He paced the floor, he thumped the table, his voice was high-pitched. He gave the impression of a thoroughly disturbed and baffled man. Obviously he was showing up at his worst, but he was clearly revealing the inner state of his personality, and the insight thus gained gave us a chance to help him through understanding him better.

As I listened to his words and observed his attitude, I again understood why Jesus Christ retains his remarkable hold on men. It is because He has the answer to such problems as this, and I proved that fact by suddenly changing the line of the conversation. Without any introductory words I began to recite certain Bible texts such as, "Come unto me, all ye that labor and are heavy laden, and I will give you rest." (Matthew 11:28) And again, "Peace I leave with you, my peace I give unto you: not as the world giveth, give I unto you. Let not your heart be troubled, neither let it be afraid." (John 14:27) And still again, "Thou wilt keep him in perfect peace, whose mind is stayed on thee." (Isaiah 26:3)

I recited these words slowly, deliberately, reflectively. As this reciting went on, I noticed that my visitor stopped being agitated. Quietness came over him and then we both sat in silence. It seemed that we sat so for several minutes. Perhaps it wasn't that long, but finally he took a deep breath.

"Why, that's funny," he said. "I feel a lot better. Isn't that queer? I guess it was those words that did it."

"No, not the words alone," I answered, "though they do have a remarkable effect upon the mind, but something deeper happened just then. He touched you a minute ago—the Physician with the healing touch. He was present in this room."

My visitor evidenced no surprise at this assertion, but eagerly and impetuously agreed—and conviction was written on his face. "That's right, He sure was. I felt Him. I see what you mean. Now I understand—Jesus Christ will help me develop a calm philosophy of living."

This man found what increasing thousands are presently discovering, that a simple faith in and practice of the principles and techniques of Christianity bring peace and quietness and therefore new power to body, mind, and spirit. It is the perfect antidote to fuming and to fretting. It helps a person to become peaceful and thus to tap new resources of strength.

Of course it was necessary to teach this man a new pattern of thinking and acting. This was done in part by suggesting literature written by experts in the field of spiritual culture. For example, we gave him lessons in the skill of church going. We showed him how to make church worship a therapy. He was instructed in the scientific use of prayer and relaxation. And as a result of this practice eventually he became a healthy man. Anyone willing to follow this program and sincerely put these principles into day-by-day practice can, I believe, develop inner peace and power. Many of these techniques are outlined in this book.

In attaining emotional control the daily practice of healing techniques is of first importance. Emotional control cannot be gained in any magical or easy way. You cannot develop it by merely reading a book, although that is often helpful. The only sure method is by working at it regularly, persistently, scientifically, and by developing creative faith.

I suggest that you begin with such a primary procedure as simply the practice of keeping physically still. Don't pace the floor. Don't wring your hands. Don't pound or shout or argue or walk up and down. Don't let yourself get worked up into a dither. In excitement one's physical movements become accentuated. Therefore begin at the simplest place, that is by ceasing physical movement. Stand still, sit down, lie down. Certainly keep the voice down to a low pitch.

In developing a calm control it is necessary to think calmness, for the body responds sensitively to the type of thoughts that pass through the mind. It is also true that the mind can be quieted by first making the body quiet. That is to say, a physical attitude can induce desired mental attitudes.

In a speech I related the following incident which occurred in a committee meeting I attended. A gentleman who heard me tell this story was greatly impressed by it and took its truth to heart. He tried the technique suggested and reports that it has been very effective in controlling his fuming and fretting.

I was in a meeting where a discussion was going on which finally became rather bitter. Tempers were becoming frayed and some of the participants were decidedly on edge. Sharp remarks were passed. Suddenly one man arose, deliberately took off his coat, opened his collar, and lay down upon a couch. All were astonished, and someone asked if he felt ill.

"No," he said, "I feel fine, but I am beginning to get mad, and I have learned that it is difficult to get mad lying down."

We all laughed, and the tension was broken. Then our whimsical friend went on to explain that he had "tried a little trick" with himself. He had a quick temper, and when he felt himself getting mad he found that he was clenching his fist and raising his voice, so he deliberately extended his fingers, not allowing them to form into a fist. In proportion to the rising of his tension or anger, he depressed his voice and talked in exaggerated low tones. "You cannot carry on an argument in a whisper," he said with a grin.

This principle can be effective in controlling emotional excitements, fretting, and tension, as many have discovered by experimentation. A beginning step, therefore, in achieving calmness is to discipline your physical reactions. You will be surprised at how quickly this can reduce the heat of your emotions, and when emotional heat is driven off, fuming and fretting subside. You will be amazed at the energy and power you will save. You will be much less tired.

It is, moreover, a good procedure to practice being phlegmatic or apathetic, even indifferent. To a certain extent even practice being sluggish. People thus constituted are less likely to emotional breaks. Highly organized individuals may do well to cultivate these reactions to a degree at least.

Naturally one does not want to lose the keen, sensitive responsiveness characteristic of the highly organized individual. But the practice of being phlegmatic tends to bring such a keyed-up personality to a balanced emotional position.

Following is a technique consisting of six points which I have personally found of great helpfulness in reducing the tendency to fume and fret. I have suggested its use to countless people who practice it and find it of great value:

1. Sit relaxed in a chair. Completely yield yourself to the chair. Starting with your toes and proceeding to the top of your head, conceive of every portion of the body as relaxing. Affirm relaxation by saying, "My toes are relaxed—my fingers—my facial muscles."

2. Think of your mind as the surface of a lake in a storm, tossed by waves and in tumult. But now the waves subside, and the surface of the lake is placid and unruffled.

3. Spend two or three minutes thinking of the most beautiful and peaceful scenes you have ever beheld, as, for example, a mountain at sunset, or a deep valley filled with the hush of early morning, or a woods at noonday, or moonlight upon rippling waters. In memory relive these scenes.

4. Repeat slowly, quietly, bringing out the melody in each, a series of words which express quietness and peace, as, for example, (a) tranquillity (say it very deliberately and in a tranquil manner); (b) serenity; (c) quietness. Think of other such words and repeat them.

5. Make a mental list of times in your life when you have been conscious of God's watchful care and recall how, when you were worried and anxious, He brought things out right and took care of you. Then recite aloud this line from an old hymn, "So long Thy power hath kept me, sure it STILL will lead me on."

6. Repeat the following, which has an amazing power to relax and quiet the mind: "Thou wilt keep him in perfect peace, whose mind is stayed on thee." (Isaiah 26:3) Repeat this several times during the day, whenever you have a fraction of a moment. Repeat it aloud if possible, so that by the end of the day you will have said it many times. Conceive of these words as active, vital substances permeating your mind, sending into every area of your

thinking a healing balm. This is the best-known medicine for taking tension from the mind.

As you work with the techniques suggested in this chapter, the tendency to fume and fret will gradually be modified. In direct proportion to your progress the power heretofore drawn off by this unhappy habit will be felt in your increased ability to meet life's responsibilities.

# 7

# Expect the Best and Get It

"WHY DOES MY boy fail in every job he gets?" asked a puzzled father about his thirty-year-old son.

It was indeed difficult to understand the failure of this young man, for seemingly he had everything. Of good family, his educational and business opportunities were beyond the average. Nevertheless, he had a tragic flair for failure. Everything he touched went wrong. He tried hard enough, yet somehow he missed success. Presently he found an answer, a curiously simple but potent answer. After practicing this newfound secret for a while he lost the flair for failure and acquired the touch of success. His personality began to focus, his powers to fuse.

Not long ago at luncheon I could not help admiring this dynamic man at the height of his power. "You amaze me," I commented. "A few years ago you were failing at everything. Now you have worked up an original idea into a fine business. You are a leader in your community. Please explain this remarkable change in you."

"Really it was quite simple," he replied. "I merely learned the magic of believing. I discovered that if you expect the worst you will get the worst, and if you expect the best you will get the best. It all happened through actually practicing a verse from the Bible."

"And what is that verse?"

" 'If thou canst believe, all things are possible to him that believeth.' (Mark 9:23) I was brought up in a religious home," he explained, "and heard that verse many times, but it never had any effect upon me. One day in your church I heard you emphasize those words in a talk. In a flash of insight I realized that the key I had missed was that my mind was not trained to believe, to think positively, to have faith in either God or myself. I followed your suggestion of putting myself in God's hands and practiced your outlined techniques of faith. I trained myself to think positively about everything. Along with that I try to live right." He smiled and said, "God and I struck up a partnership. When I adopted that policy, things began to change almost at once for me. I got into the habit of expecting the best, not the worst, and that is the way my affairs have turned out lately. I guess it's a kind of miracle, isn't it?" he asked as he concluded his fascinating story.

But it wasn't miraculous at all. Actually what had happened was that he had learned to use one of the most powerful laws in the world, a law recognized alike by psychology and religion, namely, change your mental habits to belief instead of disbelief. Learn to expect, not to doubt. In so doing you bring everything into the realm of possibility.

This does not mean that by believing you are necessarily going to get everything you want or think you want. Perhaps that would not be good for you. When you put your trust in God, He guides your mind so that you do not want things that are not good for you or that are inharmonious with God's will. But it does definitely mean that when you learn to believe, then that which has seemingly been impossible moves into the area of the possible. Every great thing at last becomes for you a possibility.

William James, the famous psychologist, said, "Our belief at the beginning of a doubtful undertaking is the one thing (now get that—*is the one thing*) that insures the successful outcome of your venture." To learn to believe is of primary importance. It is the basic factor of succeeding in any undertaking. When you expect the best, you release a magnetic force in your mind which by a law of attraction tends to bring the best to you. But if you expect the worst, you release from your mind the power of repulsion which tends to force the best from you. It is amazing how a sustained expectation of the best sets in motion forces which cause the best to materialize.

An interesting illustration of this fact was described some years ago by Hugh Fullerton, a famous sports writer of a bygone era. As a boy, Hugh Fullerton was my favorite writer of sports stories. One story which I have never forgotten concerned Josh O'Reilly, one-time manager of the San Antonio Club of the Texas league. O'Reilly had a roster of great players, seven of whom had been hitting over three hundred, and everybody thought his team would easily take the championship. But the club fell into a slump and lost seventeen of the first twenty games. The players simply couldn't hit anything, and each began to accuse the other of being a "jinx" to the team.

Playing the Dallas Club, a rather poor team that year, only one San Antonio player got a hit, and that, strangely enough, was the pitcher. O'Reilly's team was badly beaten that day. In the clubhouse after the game the players were a disconsolate lot. Josh O'Reilly knew that he had an aggregation of stars and he realized that their trouble was simply that they were thinking wrong. They didn't expect to get a hit. They didn't expect to win. They expected to be defeated. They were thinking not victory but defeat. Their mental pattern was not one of expectation but of doubt. This negative mental process inhibited them, froze their muscles, threw them off their timing, and there was no free flow of easy power through the team.

It so happened that a preacher named Schlater was popular in that neighborhood at that time. He claimed to be a faith healer and apparently was getting some astounding results. Throngs crowded to hear him and most everybody had confidence in him. Perhaps the fact that they did believe in his power enabled Schlater to achieve results.

O'Reilly asked each player to lend him his two best bats. Then he asked the members of the team to stay in the clubhouse until he returned. He put the bats in a wheelbarrow and went off with them. He was gone for an hour. He returned jubilantly to tell the players that Schlater, the preacher, had blessed the bats and that these bats now contained a power that could not be overcome. The players were astounded and delighted.

The next day they overwhelmed Dallas, getting 37 base hits and 20 runs. They hammered their way through the league to a championship, and Hugh Fullerton said that for years in the Southwest a player would pay a large sum for a "Schlater bat."

Regardless of Schlater's personal power, the fact remains that something tremendous happened in the minds of those ballplayers. Their thought pattern was changed. They began thinking in terms of expectation, not doubt. They expected not the worst, but the best. They expected hits, runs, victories, and they got them. They had the power to get what they wanted. There was no difference in the bats themselves, I am quite sure of that, but there was certainly a difference in the minds of the men who used them. Now they knew they could make hits. Now they knew they could get runs. Now they knew they could win. A new thought pattern changed the minds of those men so that the creative power of faith could operate.

Perhaps you have not been doing so well in the game of life. Perhaps you stand up to bat and cannot make a hit. You strike out time and again and your batting average is lamentably low. Let me give you a suggestion. I guarantee that it will work. The basis for my assurance is the fact that thousands of people have been trying it with very great results. Things will be very different for you if you give this method a real trial.

Start reading the New Testament and notice the number of times it refers to faith. Select a dozen of the strongest statements about faith, the ones that you like the best. Then memorize each one. Let these faith concepts drop into your conscious mind. Say them over and over again, especially just before going to sleep at night. By a process of spiritual osmosis they will sink from your conscious into your subconscious mind and in time will modify and reslant your basic thought pattern. This process will change you into a believer, into an expecter, and when you become such, you will in due course become an achiever. You will have new power to get what God and you decide you really want from life.

The most powerful force in human nature is the spiritual-power technique taught in the Bible. Very astutely the Bible emphasizes the method by which a person can make something of himself. Faith, belief, positive thinking, faith in God, faith in other people, faith in yourself, faith in life. This is the essence of the technique that teaches. "If thou canst believe," it says, "all things are possible to him that believeth." (Mark 9:23) "If ye have faith . . . nothing shall be impossible unto you." (Matthew 17:20) "According to your faith be it unto you." (Matthew 9:29) Believe—believe—so it drives home the truth that faith moves mountains.

Some skeptical person who has never learned this powerful law of the effect of right thinking may doubt my assertions regarding the amazing results which happen when this technique is employed.

Things become better when you expect the best instead of the worst, for the reason that being freed from self-doubt, you can put your whole self into your endeavor, and nothing can stand in the way of the man who focuses his entire self on a problem. When you approach a difficulty as a personal unity, the difficulty, which itself is a demonstration of disunity, tends to deteriorate.

When the entire concentration of all your force—physical, emotional, and spiritual—is brought to bear, the consolidation of these powers properly employed is quite irresistible.

Expecting the best means that you put your whole heart (i.e., the central essence of your personality) into what you want to accomplish. People are defeated in life not because of lack of ability, but for lack of wholeheartedness. They do not wholeheartedly expect to succeed. Their heart isn't in it, which is to say they themselves are not fully given. Results do not yield themselves to the person who refuses to give himself to the desired results.

A major key to success in this life, to attaining that which you deeply desire, is to be completely released and throw all there is of yourself into your job or any project in which you are engaged. In other words, whatever you are doing, give it all you've got. Give every bit of yourself. Hold nothing back. Life cannot deny itself to the person who gives life his all. But most people, unfortunately, don't do that. In fact, very few people do, and this is a tragic cause of failure, or, if not failure, it is the reason we only half attain.

A famous Canadian athletic coach, Ace Percival, says that most people, athletes as well as non-athletes, are "holdouts," that is to say, they are always keeping something in reserve. They do not invest themselves 100 percent in competition. Because of that fact they never achieve the highest of which they are capable.

Red Barber, famous baseball announcer, told me that he had known few athletes who completely give themselves.

Don't be a "holdout." Go all out. Do this, and life will not hold out on you.

A famous trapeze artist was instructing his students how to perform on the high trapeze bar. Finally, having given full explanations and instruction in this skill, he told them to demonstrate their ability.

One student, looking up at the insecure perch upon which he must perform, was suddenly filled with fear. He froze completely. He had a terrifying vision of himself falling to the ground. He couldn't move a muscle, so deep was his fright. "I can't do it! I can't do it!" he gasped.

The instructor put his arm around the boy's shoulder and said, "Son, you can do it, and I will tell you how." Then he made a statement which is of inestimable importance. It is one of the wisest remarks I have ever heard. He said, "Throw your heart over the bar and your body will follow."

Copy that one sentence. Write it on a card and put it in your pocket. Place it under the glass on your desk top. Tack it up on your wall. Stick it in your shaving mirror. Better still, write it on your mind, you who really want to do something with life. It's packed with power, that sentence. "Throw your heart over the bar and your body will follow."

Heart is the symbol of creative activity. Fire the heart with where you want to go and what you want to be. Get it so deeply fixed in your unconscious that you will not take no for an answer, then your entire personality will follow where your heart leads. "Throw your heart over the bar" means to throw your faith over your difficulty, throw your affirmation over every barrier, throw your visualization over your obstacles. In other words, throw the spiritual essence of you over the bar and your material self will follow in the victory groove thus pioneered by your faith-inspired mind. Expect the best, not the worst, and you will attain your heart's desire. It is what is in the heart of you, either good or bad, strong or weak, that finally comes to you. Emerson said, "Beware of what you want for you will get it."

That this philosophy is of practical value is illustrated by the experience of a young woman whom I interviewed a number of years ago. She made an appointment to see me in my office at two o'clock on a certain afternoon. Being quite busy that day, I had gotten a little behind schedule, and it was about five minutes after two when I walked into the conference room where she was waiting. It was obvious that she was displeased for her lips were pressed firmly together.

"It's five minutes after two, and we had an appointment at 2 P.M.," she said. "I always admire promptness."

"So do I. I always believe in being prompt, and I hope you will forgive me for my unavoidable delay," I said with a smile.

But she was not in a smiling mood, for she said crisply, "I have a very important problem to present to you and I want an answer, and I expect an answer." Then she shot out at me: "I might as well put it to you bluntly. I want to get married."

"Well," I replied, "that is a perfectly normal desire and I should like to help you."

"I want to know why I can't get married," she continued. "Every time I form a friendship with a man, the next thing I know he fades out of the picture and another chance is gone by, and," she added, speaking frankly, "I am not getting any younger. You conduct a personal-problem clinic to study people and you have had some experience, and I am putting my problem right up to you. Tell me, why can't I get married?"

I studied her to see if she was the kind of person to whom one could speak frankly, for certain things had to be said if she really meant business. Finally I decided that she was of big enough caliber to take the medicine that would be required if she was to correct her personality difficulties, so I said, "Well, now, let's analyze the situation. Obviously you have a good mind and a fine personality, and, if I may say so, you are a very handsome lady."

All of these things were true. I congratulated her in every way that I honestly could, but then I said, "I think that I see your difficulty and it is this. You took me to task because I was five minutes late for our appointment. You were really quite severe with me. Has it ever occurred to you that your attitude represents a pretty serious fault? I think a husband would have a very difficult time if you checked him up that closely all the time. In fact, you would so dominate him that, even if you did marry, your marital life would be unsatisfactory. Love cannot live under domination."

Then I said, "You have a very firm way of pressing your lips together which indicates a domineering attitude. The average male, I might as well tell you, does not like to be dominated, at least so that he knows it." Then I added, "I think you would be a very attractive person if you got those too-firm lines out of your face. You must have a little softness, a little tenderness, and those lines are too firm to be soft." Then I observed her dress, which was obviously quite expensive, but she didn't wear it very well, and so I said, "This may be a bit out of my line, and I hope you won't mind, but perhaps you could get that dress to hang a little better." I know my description was awkward, but she was a good sport about it and laughed right out loud.

She said, "You certainly don't use style phraseology, but I get the idea."

Then I suggested, "Perhaps it might help to get your hair fixed up a little. It's a little—floaty. Then you might also add a little sweet-smelling perfume—just a whiff of it. But the really important thing is to get a new attitude that will change the lines on your face and give you that indefinable quality known as spiritual joy. This I am certain will release charm and loveliness in you."

"Well," she burst out, "never did I expect to get this combination of advice in a minister's office."

"No," I chuckled, "I suppose not, but nowadays we have to cover the whole field in a human problem."

Then I told her about an old professor of mine at Ohio Wesleyan University, "Rolly" Walker, who said, "God runs a beauty parlor." He explained that some girls when they came to college were very pretty, but when they came back to visit the campus thirty years later their beauty had faded. The moonlight-and-roses loveliness of their youth did not last. On the other hand, other girls came to college who were very plain, but when they returned thirty years later they were beautiful women. "What made the difference?" he asked. "The latter had the beauty of an inner spiritual life written on their faces," and then he added, "God runs a beauty parlor."

Well, this young lady thought about what I told her for a few minutes and then she said, "There's a lot of truth in what you say. I'll try it."

Here is where her strong personality proved effective, for she did try it.

A number of years went by and I had forgotten her. Then in a certain city, after making a speech, a very lovely-looking lady with a fine-looking man and a little boy about ten years of age came up to me. The lady asked smilingly, "Well, how do you think it hangs?"

"How do I think what hangs?" I asked, puzzled.

"My dress," she said. "Do you think it hangs right?"

Bewildered, I said, "Yes, I think it hangs all right, but just why do you ask?"

"Don't you know me?" she asked.

"I see a great many people in my life," I said. "Frankly, no, I don't think I have ever seen you before."

Then she reminded me of our talk of years ago which I have described.

"Meet my husband and my little boy. What you told me was absolutely true," she said very earnestly. "I was the most frustrated, unhappy individual imaginable when I came to see you, but I put into practice the principles you suggested. I really did, and they worked."

Her husband then spoke up and said, "There was never a sweeter person in the world than Mary here," and I must say that she looked the part. She had evidently visited "God's beauty parlor."

Not only did she experience a softening and mellowing of her inner spirit, but she properly used a great quality which she possessed, namely, the driving force to get what she wanted. This led her to the point where she was willing to change herself so that her dreams could be realized. She had that quality of mind whereby she took herself in hand, she applied the spiritual techniques, and she had a profound and yet simple faith that what her heart told her she wanted could be obtained by the proper creative and positive procedures.

So the formula is to know what you want, test it to see if it is a right thing, change yourself in such a manner that it will naturally come to you, and always have faith. With the creative force of belief you stimulate that particular gathering together of circumstances which brings your cherished wish to pass.

Students of modern dynamic thought are realizing more and more the practical value of the ideas and teachings of Jesus, especially such truths as the dictum, "According to your faith, be it unto you." (Matthew 9:29) According to your faith in yourself, according to your faith in your job, according to your faith in God, this far will you get and no further. If you believe in your job and in yourself and in the opportunities of your country, and if you believe in God and will work hard and study and put yourself into it—in other words, if you "throw your heart over the bar," you can swing up to any high place to which you want to take your life and your service and your achievement. Whenever you have a bar, that is to say a barrier, in front of you, stop, close your eyes, visualize everything that is above the bar and nothing that is below it, then imaginatively throw "your heart" over that bar and see yourself as being given lifting power to rise above it. Believe that you are experiencing this upthrust of force. You will be amazed at the lifting force you will receive. If in the depth of your mind you visualize the best and employ the powers of faith and energy, you will get the best.

Naturally in this process of achieving the best it is important to know where you want to go in life. You can reach your goal, your best dreams can come true, you can get where you want to go only if you know what your goal is. Your expectation must have a clearly defined objective. Lots of people get nowhere simply because they do not know where they want to go. They have no clear-cut, precisely defined purpose. You cannot expect the best if you think aimlessly.

A young man of twenty-six consulted me because he was dissatisfied with his job. He was ambitious to fill a bigger niche in life and wanted to know how to improve his circumstances. His motive seemed unselfish and entirely worth while.

"Well, where do you want to go?" I asked.

"I just don't know exactly," he said hesitantly. "I have never given it any thought. I only know I want to go somewhere other than where I am."

"What can you do best?" I then asked. "What are your strong points?"

"I don't know," he responded. "I never thought that over either."

"But what would you like to do if you had your choice? What do you really want to do?" I insisted.

"I just can't say," he replied dully. "I don't really know what I would like to do. I never thought it over. Guess I ought to figure that one out too."

"Now, look here," I said, "you want to go somewhere from where you are, but you don't know where you want to go. You don't know what you can do or what you would like to do. You will have to get your ideas organized before you can expect to start getting anywhere."

That is the failure point with many people. They never get anywhere because they have only a hazy idea where they want to go, what they want to do. No objective leads to no end.

We made a thorough analysis, testing this young man's capabilities, and found some assets of personality he did not know he possessed. But it was necessary to supply a dynamic to move him forward, so we taught him the techniques of practical faith. Today he is on the way to achievement.

Now he knows where he wants to go and how to get there. He knows what the best is and he expects to attain it and he will—nothing can stop him.

I asked an outstanding newspaper editor, an inspiring personality, "How did you get to be the editor of this important paper?"

"I wanted to be," he replied simply.

"Is that all there is to it?" I asked. "You wanted to be and so there you are."

"Well, that may not be all of it, but that was a large part of the process," he explained. "I believe that if you want to get somewhere, you must decide definitely where you want to be or what you want to accomplish. Be sure it is a right objective, then photograph this objective on your mind and hold it there. Work hard, believe in it, and the thought will become so powerful that it will tend to assure success. There is a deep tendency," he declared, "to become what your mind pictures, provided you hold the mental picture strongly enough and if the objective is sound."

So saying, the editor pulled a well-worn card from his wallet and said, "I repeat this quotation every day of my life. It has become my dominating thought."

I copied it and am giving it to you: "A man who is self-reliant, positive, optimistic, and undertakes his work with the assurance of success magnetizes his condition. He draws to himself the creative powers of the universe."

It is indeed a fact that the person who thinks with positive self-reliance and optimism does magnetize his condition and releases power to attain his goal. So expect the best at all times. Never think of the worst. Drop it out of your thought, relegate it. Let there be no thought in your mind that the worst will happen. Avoid entertaining the concept of the worst, for whatever you take into your mind can grow there. Therefore take the best into your mind and only that. Nurture it, concentrate on it, emphasize it, visualize it, prayerize it, surround it with faith. Make it your obsession. Expect the best, and spiritually creative mind power aided by God power will produce the best.

It may be that as you read this book you are down to what you think is the worst and you may remark that no amount of thinking will affect your situation. The answer to that objection is that it simply isn't so. Even if you may be down to the worst, the best is potentially within you. You have only to find it, release it, and rise up with it. This requires courage and character, to be sure, but the main requirement is faith. Cultivate faith and you will have the necessary courage and character.

A woman was compelled by adversity to go into sales work, a type of activity for which she had no training. She undertook to demonstrate vacuum cleaners from house to house. She took a negative attitude toward herself and her work. She "just didn't believe she could do this job." She "knew" she was going to fail. She feared to approach a house even though she came for a requested demonstration. She believed that she could not make the sale. As a result, as is not surprising, she failed in a high percentage of her interviews.

One day she chanced to call upon a woman who evidenced consideration beyond the average. To this customer the saleswoman poured out her tale of defeat and powerlessness. The other woman listened patiently, then said quietly, "If you expect failure, you will get failure, but if you expect to succeed, I am sure you will succeed." And she added, "I will give you a formula which I believe will help you. It will restyle your thinking, give you new confidence, and help you to accomplish your goals. Repeat this formula before every call. Believe in it and then marvel at what it will do for you. This is it. 'If God be for us, who can be against us?' (Romans 8:31) But change it by personalizing it so that you say, 'If God be for *me*, who can be against *me*?' If God be for me, then I know that with God's help I can sell vacuum cleaners. God realizes that you want security and support for your little children and yourself, and by practicing the method I suggest you will be given power to get what you want."

She learned to utilize this formula. She approached each house expecting to make a sale, affirming and picturizing positive, not negative, results. As the saleswoman employed this principle she presently acquired new courage, new faith, and deeper confidence in her own ability. Now she declares, "God helps me sell vacuum cleaners," and who can dispute it?

It is a well-defined and authentic principle that what the mind profoundly expects it tends to receive. Perhaps this is true because what you really expect is what you actually want. Unless you really want something sufficiently to create an atmosphere of positive factors by your dynamic desire, it is likely to elude you. "If with all your heart"—that is the secret. "If with all your heart," that is to say, if with the full complement of your personality, you reach out creatively toward your heart's desire, your reach will not be in vain.

Let me give you four words as a formulation of a great law—*faith power works wonders*. Those four words are packed with dynamic and creative force. Hold them in your conscious mind. Let them sink into the unconscious and they can help you to overcome any difficulty. Hold them in your thoughts, say them over and over again. Say them until your mind accepts them, until you believe them—*faith power works wonders*.

I have no doubt about the effectiveness of this concept, for I have seen it work so often that my enthusiasm for faith power is absolutely boundless.

You can overcome any obstacle. You can achieve the most tremendous things by faith power. And how do you develop faith power? The answer is: to saturate your mind with the great words of the Bible. If you will spend one hour a day reading the Bible and committing its great passages to memory, thus allowing them to recondition your personality, the change in you and in your experience will be little short of miraculous.

Just one section of the Bible will accomplish this for you. The eleventh chapter of Mark is enough. You will find the secret in the following words, and this is one of the greatest formulas the Book contains: "Have faith in God (that's positive, isn't it?) for verily I say unto you, that whosoever shall say unto *this* mountain (that's specific) be thou removed (that is, stand aside) and be thou cast into the sea (that means out of sight—anything you threw into the sea is gone for good. The *Titanic* lies at the bottom of the sea. And the sea bottom is lined with ships. Cast your opposition called a "mountain" into the sea) and shall not doubt in his heart (Why does this statement use the word heart: Because it means you are not to doubt in your subconscious, in the inner essence of you. It isn't so superficial as a doubt in the conscious mind. That is a normal, intelligent questioning. It's a deep fundamental doubt that is to be avoided) but shall believe that those things which he saith shall come to pass, he shall have whatsoever he saith." (Mark 11:22-23)

This is not some theory that I have thought up. It is taught by the most reliable book known to man. Generation after generation, no matter what develops in the way of knowledge and science, the Bible is read by more people than any other book. Humanity rightly has more confidence in it than any other document ever written, and the Bible tells us that faith power works wonders.

The reason, however, that great things do not happen to some people is that they are not specific in their application of faith power. We are told, "Ye shall say to *this* mountain." That is to say, do not address your efforts to the entire mountain range of all your difficulties, but attack one thing that may be defeating you at the moment. Be specific. Take them one by one.

If there is something you want, how do you go about getting it? In the first place, ask yourself, "Should I want it?" Test that question very honestly in prayer to be sure you should want it and whether you should have it. If you can answer that question in the affirmative, then ask God for it and don't be backward in asking Him. And if God, having more insight, believes that you shouldn't have it, you needn't worry—He won't give it to you. But if it is a right thing, ask Him for it, and when you ask, do not doubt in your heart. Be specific.

The validity of this law was impressed upon me by something that a friend of mine, a Midwestern businessman, told me. This man is a big, extrovertish, outgoing, lovable gentleman, a truly great Christian. He teaches the largest Bible class in his state. In the town where he lives he is Mr. "Town" himself. He is head of a plant employing forty thousand people.

His office desk is full of religious literature. He even has some of my sermons and pamphlets there. In his plant, one of the biggest in the United States, he manufactures refrigerators.

He is one of those whole-souled, rugged individuals who has the capacity to have faith. He believes that God is right there in his office with him.

My friend said, "Preach a big faith—not any little old watered-down faith. Don't be afraid that faith isn't scientific enough. I am a scientist," he said. "I use science in my business every day, and I use the Bible every day. The Bible will work. Everything in the Bible works if you believe in it."

When he was made general manager of this plant it was whispered around town, "Now that Mr. —— is general manager, we'll have to bring our Bibles to work with us." After a few days he called into his office some of the men who were making this remark. He uses language they understand, and he said, "I hear you guys are going around town saying that now I am general manager, you will have to bring your Bibles to work with you."

"Oh, we didn't mean that," they said in embarrassment.

He said, "Well, you know, that's a —— good idea, but I don't want you to come lugging them under your arms. Bring them here in your hearts and in your minds. If you come with a spirit of good will and faith in your hearts and minds, believe me, we'll do business.

"So," he said, "the kind of faith to have is the specific kind, the kind that moves this particular mountain."

Suddenly he said to me, "Did you ever have a toe bother you?"

I was rather astonished by that, but before I could answer he said, "I had a toe that bothered me and I took it to the doctors here in town, and they are wonderful doctors, and they said there wasn't anything wrong with the toe that they could see. But they were wrong, because it hurt. So I went out and got a book on anatomy and read up on toes. It is really a simple construction. There's nothing but a few muscles and ligaments and a bony structure. It seemed that anybody who knows anything about a toe could fix it, but I couldn't get anybody to fix that toe, and it hurt me all the time. So I sat down one day and took a look at that toe. Then I said, 'Lord, I'm sending this toe right back to the plant. You made that toe. I make refrigerators and I know all there is to know about a refrigerator. When we sell a refrigerator, we guarantee the customer service. If his refrigerator doesn't work right and if our service agents can't fix it, he brings it back to the plant and we fix it, because we know how.' So I said, 'Lord, you made this toe. You manufactured it, and your service agents, the doctors, don't seem to know how to get it working right, and if you don't mind, Lord, I would like to have it fixed up as soon as possible, because it's bothering me.' "

"How is the toe now?" I asked.

"Perfect," he replied.

Perhaps this is a foolish kind of story, and I laughed when he told it, but I almost cried, too, for I saw a wonderful look on that man's face as he related that incident of a specific prayer.

Be specific. Ask God for any right thing, but as a little child, don't doubt. Doubt closes the power flow. Faith opens it. The power of faith is so tremendous that there is nothing that Almighty God cannot do for us, with us, or through us if we let Him channel His power through our minds.

So roll those words around on your tongue. Say them over and over again until they lodge deeply in your mind, until they get down into your heart, until they take possession of the essence of you: ". . . whosoever shall say unto this mountain, be thou removed, and be thou cast into the sea, and shall not doubt in his heart, but shall believe that those things which he saith shall come to pass, he shall have whatsoever he saith." (Mark 11:23)

I suggested these principles some months ago to an old friend of mine, a man who perpetually expects the worst. Up to the time of our discussion, never did I hear him say anything other than that things would not turn out right. He took this negative attitude toward every project or problem. He expressed vigorous disbelief in the principles outlined in this chapter and offered to make a test to prove that I am wrong in my conclusions. He is an honest man, and he faithfully tried these principles in connection with several matters and actually kept a score card. He did this for six months. He volunteered the information at the end of that period that 85 per cent of the matters under investigation had turned out satisfactorily.

"I am now convinced," he said, "although I wouldn't have believed it possible, but it is evidently a fact, that if you expect the best, you are given some strange kind of power to create conditions that produce the desired results. From now on I am changing my mental attitude and shall expect the best, not the worst. My test indicates that this is not theory, but a scientific way to meet life's situations."

I might add that even the high percentage he attained can be raised with practice, and of course practice in the art of expectation is as essential as practice on a musical instrument or with a golf club. Nobody ever mastered any skill except through intensive, persistent, and intelligent practice. Also it should be noted that my friend approached this experiment at first in a spirit of doubt which would tend adversely to affect his earlier results.

Every day as you confront the problems of life, I suggest that you affirm as follows: "I believe God gives me power to attain what I really want."

Never mention the worst. Never think of it. Drop it out of your consciousness. At least ten times every day affirm, "I expect the best and with God's help will attain the best."

In so doing your thoughts will turn toward the best and become conditioned to its realization. This practice will bring all of your powers to focus upon the attainment of the best. It will bring the best to you.

# 8

# *I Don't Believe in Defeat*

IF YOU ARE thinking thoughts of defeat, I urge you to rid yourself of such thoughts, for as you think defeat you tend to get it. Adopt the "I don't believe in defeat" attitude.

I want to tell you about some people who have put this philosophy into effect with excellent results and shall explain the techniques and formulas which they used so successfully. If you read these incidents carefully and thoughtfully and believe as they did and think positively and put these techniques into operation, you too, can overcome defeats which at the present moment may seem inevitable.

I hope you are not like an "obstacle man" of whom I was told. He was called an obstacle man because, regardless of whatever suggestion was advanced, his mind instantly went to all possible obstacles in connection with it, but he met his match and learned a lesson which helped to change his negative attitude. It came about in the following manner.

The directors of his firm had a project under consideration which involved considerable expense and some definite hazards as well as success possibilities. In the discussions regarding this venture the obstacle man would invariably say, and always with a scholarly air (invariably this type acts wise, probably a cover-up for inner doubt feelings), "Now just a moment. Let's consider the obstacles involved."

Another man, who said very little but who was respected by his associates for his ability and achievements and for a certain indomitable quality which characterized him, presently spoke up and asked, "Why do you constantly emphasize the obstacles in this proposition instead of the possibilities?"

"Because," replied the obstacle man, "to be intelligent one must always be realistic, and it is a fact that there are certain definite obstacles in connection with this project. What attitude would you take toward these obstacles, may I ask?"

The other man unhesitatingly replied, "What attitude would I take toward these obstacles? Why, I would just remove them, that's all, and then I would forget them."

"But," said the obstacle man, "that is easier said than done. You say you would remove them and then you would forget them. May I ask if you have any technique for removing obstacles and for forgetting them that the rest of us have never discovered?"

A slow smile came over the face of the other man as he said, "Son, I have spent my entire life removing obstacles and I never yet saw one that could not be removed provided you had enough faith and guts and were willing to work. Since you want to know how it's done, I will show you."

He then reached into his pocket and took out his wallet. Under the isinglass window was a card on which were written some words. He shoved the wallet across the table and said, "There, son, read that. That is my formula, and don't give me the song and dance that it won't work either. I know better from experience."

The obstacle man picked up the wallet and with a strange look on his face read the words to himself.

"Read them out loud," urged the owner of the wallet.

This is what he read in a slow, dubious voice, "I can do all things through Christ which strengtheneth me." (Philippians 4:13)

The owner of the wallet put it back in his pocket and said, "I have lived a long time and have faced a lot of difficulties in my time, but there is power in those words—actual power—and with them you can remove any obstacle."

He said this with confidence and everybody knew he meant it. This positiveness, together with the facts of his experience which were known to all, for he was a remarkable man who had overcome many odds, and because of the further fact that he was not in any sense "holier than thou," made his words convincing to the men around the table. At any rate, there was no more negative talk. The project was put into operation and, despite difficulties and risks, turned out successfully.

The technique used by this man is based on the primary fact about an obstacle which is—don't be afraid of it. Practice believing that God is with you and that in combination with Him you have the power to handle it.

So the first thing to do about an obstacle is simply to stand up to it and not complain about it or whine under it but forthrightly attack it. Don't go crawling through life on your hands and knees half-defeated. Stand up to your obstacles and do something about them. You will find that they haven't half the strength you think they have.

A friend in England sent me a book by Winston Churchill entitled *Maxims and Reflections*. In this book Churchill tells of the British General Tudor, who commanded a division of the British Fifth Army which faced the great German assault in March 1918. The odds were heavily against him, but General Tudor knew how to meet an apparently immovable and undefeatable obstacle. His method was simple. He merely stood and let the obstacle break on him and he, in turn, broke the obstacle.

Here is what Churchill said about General Tudor. This is a very great sentence and it is filled with power: "The impression I had of Tudor was of an iron peg, hammered into the frozen ground, immovable."

General Tudor knew how to stand up to an obstacle. Just stand up to it, that's all, and don't give way under it, and it will finally break. You will break it. Something has to break, and it won't be you, it will be the obstacle.

You can do this when you have faith, faith in God and faith in yourself. Faith is the chief quality you need. It is enough. In fact, it is more than enough.

Use that formula which the businessman suggested and you will develop this brand of powerful faith in God and in yourself. You will learn to know yourself, your own ability, your power to do things. To the degree to which your attitude shifts from negative to positive the mastery touch will come to you. Then, with assurance, you can say to yourself under any and all circumstances and mean it, "I don't believe in defeat."

Take the story of Gonzales, who won the national tennis championship a few years ago in a grueling battle. He had been practically unknown, and because of wet weather he had not been able to perfect his game prior to the tournament. The sports writer of a metropolitan newspaper in analyzing Gonzales said that there were certain defects in his techniques, and gave it as his opinion that probably greater champions had played on the courts, however, he credited Gonzales with a marvelous serve and a skillful volley. But the factor that won the championship, said the writer, was his staying power and the further fact that "he was never defeated by the discouraging vicissitudes of the game."

That is one of the most subtle lines I have ever read in any sports story—"He was never defeated by the discouraging vicissitudes of the game."

It means, does it not, that when the game seemed to go against him he did not let discouragement creep in nor negative thoughts dominate and thus lose the power needed to win. This mental and spiritual quality made that man a champion. He was able to face obstacles, to stand up to them and overcome them.

Faith supplies staying power. It contains dynamic to keep one going when the going is hard. Anybody can keep going when the going is good, but some extra ingredient is needed to enable you to keep fighting when it seems that everything is against you. It is a great secret, that of never being "defeated by the discouraging vicissitudes of the game."

You may counter, "But you don't know my circumstances. I am in a different situation than anybody else and I am as far down as a human being can get."

In that case you are fortunate, for if you are as far down as you can get there is no further down you can go. There is only one direction you can take from this position, and that is up. So your situation is quite encouraging. However, I caution you not to take the attitude that you are in a situation in which nobody has ever been before. There is no such situation.

Practically speaking, there are only a few human stories and they have all been enacted previously. This is a fact that you must never forget—there are people who have overcome every conceivable difficult situation, even the one in which you now find yourself and which to you seems utterly hopeless. So did it seem to some others, but they found an out, a way up, a path over, a pass through.

One of the most inspiring illustrations of this act is the story of Amos Parrish who twice every year brings together hundreds of leading department-store executives and style experts in two huge clinics held in the Grand Ballroom of the Waldorf-Astoria Hotel in New York City. At these clinics Mr. Parrish gives advice to the merchants and their associates on business trends, on merchandise, on selling methods, and other matters important to the conduct of their business. Having attended a number of the clinics, however, I am convinced that the greatest values Mr. Parrish transmits to his customers are courage and positive thinking, a deep belief in themselves, and the confidence that they can overcome all difficulties.

He seems a living example of the philosophy which he teaches. As a boy he was sickly. Moreover, he stuttered. He was sensitive and a victim of an inferiority complex. It was thought that he would not live because of his weakened physical condition, but one day Amos Parrish had a spiritual experience. Faith dawned in his mind, and from then on he knew that with the help of God and the utilization of his own powers he could achieve.

He developed a unique idea of service to businessmen, and so highly do they rate it that they are willing to pay large fees to attend a two-day session twice a year under the business wisdom and inspiration of Amos Parrish. To me it is a moving experience to sit with that big crowd in a hotel ballroom and listen to "A. P.," as he is affectionately called, talk positive thinking to those important businessmen and women.

Sometimes he has the greatest difficulty with his stuttering, but he is never discouraged. He refers to it frankly and with a sense of humor. One day, for example, he was trying to say the word Cadillac. He tried several times and was unable to get it out, and finally did so with a powerful effort. Then he commented, "I can't even say C-C-C-Cadillac, let alone buy one." The audience roared with laughter, but I noted that they looked up at him with affection written on their faces. Everyone leaves a meeting at which he speaks with the conviction that they, too, can turn their obstacles into assets.

Again I repeat, there is no difficulty you cannot overcome. A wise and philosophical Negro man once said to me, when asked how he overcame his difficulties, "How do I get through a trouble? Well, first I try to go around it, and if I can't go around it, I try to get under it, and if I can't get under it, I try to go over it, and if I can't get over it, I just plow right through it." Then he added, "God and I plow right through it."

Take seriously that formula of a businessman given earlier in this chapter. Stop reading for a moment and repeat it over to yourself five times, and each time you say it conclude with this affirmation, "I believe that." Here is the formula again, "I can do all things through Christ which strengtheneth me." (Philippians 4:13) Say that five times every day and it will release indomitable power in your mind.

Your subconscious, which always resents any change, may say to you, "You don't believe any such thing." But remember that your subconscious mind in a sense is one of the greatest liars in existence. It concurs in and sends back to you your own errors about your abilities. You have created the negative attitude in your subconscious and it gives this error back to you. So just turn on your subconscious and say to it, "Now look here, I do believe that. I insist upon believing it." If you talk to your subconscious mind with that positiveness, in due course it will be convinced. One reason is because you are now feeding it positive thoughts. In other words, you are at last telling the truth to your subconscious. After a while your subconscious mind will begin to send back the truth to you, the truth being that with the help of Jesus Christ there isn't any obstacle you cannot overcome.

An effective method for making your subconscious positive in character is to eliminate certain expressions of thought and speech which we may call the "little negatives." These so-called "little negatives" clutter up the average person's conversation, and while each one is seemingly unimportant in itself, the total effect of these attitudes is to condition the mind negatively. When this thought of "little negatives" first occurred to me, I began to analyze my own conversational habits and was shocked by what I found. I discovered that I was making such statements as, "I'm afraid I'll be late," or "I wonder if I'll have a flat tire," or "I don't think I can do that," or "I'll never get through this job. There's so much to do." If something turned out badly, I might say, "Oh, that's just what I expected." Or, again, I might observe a few clouds in the sky and would gloomily state, "I knew it was going to rain."

These are "little negatives" to be sure, and a big thought is of course more powerful than a little one, but it must never be forgotten that "mighty oaks from little acorns grow," and if a mass of "little negatives" clutter up your conversation, they are bound to seep into your mind. It is surprising how they accumulate in force, and presently, before you know it, they will grow into "big negatives." So I determined to go to work on the "little negatives" and root them out of my conversation. I found that the best way to eliminate them was deliberately to say a positive word about everything. When you keep asserting that things are going to work out well, that you can do the job, that you will not have a flat tire, that you will get there on time, by talking up good results you invoke the law of positive effects and good results occur. Things do turn out well.

On a roadside billboard I saw an advertisement of a certain brand of motor oil. The slogan read, "A clean engine always delivers power." So will a mind free of negatives produce positives, that is to say, a clean mind will deliver power. Therefore flush out your thoughts, give yourself a clean mental engine, remembering that a clean mind, even as a clean engine, always delivers power.

So to overcome your obstacles and live the "I don't believe in defeat" philosophy, cultivate a positive-idea pattern deeply in your consciousness. What we do with obstacles is directly determined by our mental attitude. Most of our obstacles, as a matter of fact, are mental in character.

"Ah," you may object, "mine are not mental, mine are real."

Perhaps so, but your attitude toward them is mental. The only possible way you can have an attitude is by the mental process, and what you think about your obstacles largely determines what you do about them. Form the mental attitude that you cannot remove an obstacle and you will not remove it, not if you think you can't. But get the idea firmly fixed that the obstacle is not so great as you previously considered it to be. Hold the idea that it is removable, and however faintly you entertain this positive thought, from the very moment you begin to think in this manner, the process is inaugurated which will lead to its ultimate removal.

If you have been long defeated by a difficulty, it is probably because you have told yourself for weeks, months, and even for years that there is nothing you can do about it. You have so emphasized your inability to yourself that your mind gradually accepted the conclusion upon which you have insisted, and when your mind is convinced, you are convinced, for as you think so are you.

But, on the contrary, when you employ this new and creative concept, "I can do all things through Christ," then you develop a new mental slant. Emphasize and re-emphasize that positive attitude and you will finally convince your own consciousness that you can do something about difficulties. When at last your mind becomes convinced, astonishing results will begin to happen. Of a sudden you discover that you have the power you would never acknowledge.

I played golf with a man who was not only an excellent golfer but a philosopher as well. As we went around the golf course the game itself drew out of him certain gems of wisdom for one of which I shall ever be grateful.

I hit a ball into the rough, into some high grass. When we came up to my ball I said in some dismay, "Now just look at that. I certainly am in the rough. I have a bad lie. It is going to be tough getting out of here."

My friend grinned and said, "Didn't I read something about positive thinking in your books?"

Sheepishly I acknowledged that such was the case.

"I wouldn't think negatively about that lie of yours," he said. "Do you think you could get a good hit if this ball were lying out on the fairway on the short grass?"

I said I thought so.

"Well," he continued, "why do you think you could do better out there than here?"

"Because," I replied, "the grass is cut short on the fairway and the ball can get away better."

Then he did a curious thing. "Let's get down on our hands and knees," he suggested, "and examine the situation. Let's see just how this ball does lie."

So we got down on our hands and knees, and he said, "Observe that the relative height of the ball here is about the same as it would be on the fairway, the only difference being that you have about five or six inches of grass above the ball."

Then he did an even more whimsical thing. "Notice the quality and character of this grass," he said. He pulled off a blade and handed it to me. "Chew it," he said.

I chewed, and he asked, "Isn't that tender?"

"Why, yes," I replied. "It certainly does seem to be tender grass."

"Well," he continued, "an easy swing of your number-five iron will cut through that grass almost like a knife." And then he gave me this sentence which I am going to remember as long as I live, and I hope you will also.

"The rough is only mental. In other words," he continued, "it is rough because you think it is. In your mind you have decided that here is an obstacle which will cause you difficulty. The power to overcome this obstacle is in your mind. If you visualize yourself lifting that ball out of the rough, believing you can do it, your mind will transfer flexibility, rhythm, and power to your muscles and you will handle that club in such a manner that the ball will rise right out of there in a beautiful shot. All you need to do is to keep your eye on that ball and tell yourself that you are going to lift it out of that grass with a lovely stroke. Let the stiffness and tension go out of you. Hit it with exhilaration and power. Remember, the rough is only mental."

To this day I remember the thrill, the sense of power and delight I had in the clean shot that dropped the ball to the edge of the green.

That is a very great fact to remember in connection with difficult problems—"the rough is only mental."

Your obstacles are present all right. They are not fanciful, but they are not actually so difficult as they seem. Your mental attitude is the most important factor. Believe that Almighty God has put in you the power to lift yourself out of the rough by keeping your eye firmly fixed on the source of your power. Affirm to yourself that through this power you can do anything you have to do. Believe that this power is taking the tension out of you, that this power is flowing through you. Believe this, and a sense of victory will come.

Now take another look at that obstacle that has been bothering you. You will find that it isn't so formidable as you thought. Say to yourself, "The rough is only mental. I think victory—I get victory." Remember that formula. Write it on a piece of paper, put it in your wallet, stick it up on your mirror where you shave each morning, put it over the kitchen sink, put it on your dressing table and on your desk—keep looking at it until its truth drives into the depths of your consciousness, until it permeates your whole mental attitude, until it becomes a positive obsession—"I can do all things through Christ which strengtheneth me."

What may seem to be a difficult proposition is, as I have

pointed out, hard or easy in proportion to how we think about it. It may be said that three men vitally affected the thought processes of Americans—Emerson, Thoreau, and William James. Analyze the American mind even to this late date and it is evident that the teachings of these three philosophers combined to create that particular genius of the American who is not defeated by obstacles and who accomplishes "impossibles" with amazing efficiency.

A fundamental doctrine of Emerson is that the human personality can be touched with Divine power and thus greatness can be released from it. William James pointed out that the greatest factor in any undertaking is one's belief about it. Thoreau told us that the secret of achievement is to hold a picture of a successful outcome in mind.

Still another wise American was Thomas Jefferson, who, like Franklin, set for his guidance a series of rules. Franklin had thirteen daily rules; Jefferson only ten. One of Jefferson's rules was this, and I think it is priceless, "Always take hold of things by the smooth handle." That is, go at a job or at your difficulty by the use of a method that will encounter the least resistance. Resistance causes friction in mechanics, therefore it is necessary in mechanics to overcome or reduce friction. The negative attitude is a friction approach. That is why negativism develops such great resistance. The positive approach is the "smooth handle" technique. It is in harmony with the flow of the universe. It not only encounters less resistance, but actually stimulates assistance forces. It is remarkable how from early life until the end of your earthly existence the application of this philosophy will enable you to attain successful results in areas where otherwise you would be defeated.

For example, a woman sent her fifteen-year-old son to us. She said she wanted him "straightened out." It annoyed her to no end that her boy could never get over 70 in any of his studies. "This boy has a great mind potentially," she declared proudly.

"How do you know he has a great mind?" I asked.

"Because he is my son," she said. "I graduated from college *magna cum laude*."

The boy came in very glumly, so I asked, "What's the matter, son?"

"I don't know. My mother sent me to see you."

"Well," I commented, "You don't seem to be burning with enthusiasm. Your mother says you get only 70's."

"Yes," he said, "that's all I get, and," he added, "that isn't the worst of it. I've even received less than that."

"Do you think you have a good mind, son?" I asked.

"My mother says I have. I don't know—I think I'm awful dumb. Dr. Peale," he said earnestly, "I study the stuff. At home I read it over once and then close the book and try to remember it. I repeat this process about three times, and then I think that if three times doesn't get it into my head how am I ever going to get it into my head? And then I go to school thinking maybe I have it, and the teacher calls on me to say something, and I stand up and can't remember a thing. Then," he said, "examinations come along and I sit there and just get hot and cold all over and I can't think of the answers. I don't know why," he continued. "I know that my mother was a great scholar. I guess I just haven't got it in me."

This negative thought pattern combined with the inferiority feeling stimulated by his mother's attitude was of course overwhelming him. He froze up in his mind. His mother had never told him to go to school and study for the wonder and glory of learning knowledge. She was not wise enough to encourage him to compete with himself rather than with others. And she was constantly insisting that he duplicate her success in scholarship. Little wonder that under this pressure he froze mentally.

I gave him some suggestions that proved helpful. "Before you read your lessons, pause a moment and pray in this manner, 'Lord, I know I have a good mind and that I can get my work.' Then get yourself relaxed and read the book without strain. Imagine you are reading a story. Do not read it twice unless you wish. Simply believe that you got it on the first reading. Visualize the material as soaking in and germinating. Then next morning, as you go to school, say to yourself, 'I have a wonderful mother. She is very pretty and sweet, but she must have been an old bookworm to get those high marks. And who wants to be an old bookworm anyway? I don't want to become magna cum nothing. I only want to get through school creditably.'

"In class, when the teacher calls on you, quickly pray before answering. Then believe the Lord will at that moment help your mind to deliver. When an examination is given, affirm in prayer that God is releasing your mind and that the right answers are given you."

The boy followed these ideas, and what marks do you think he got the following semester? Ninety! I am sure that this boy, having discovered the amazing workability of the "I don't believe in defeat philosophy," will employ the amazing power of positive thinking in all the affairs of his life.

I could use so many illustrations of the manner in which men's lives have been revamped by these procedures that this book would grow to unwieldy size. Moreover, these are incidents and experiences out of everyday life that are in no way theoretical, but are entirely practical. My mail is literally filled with testimonials sent by people who, having heard or read accounts I have told of victorious life experiences, have felt moved to relate similar occurrences in their own lives.

Such a letter came from a gentleman who tells about his father as follows. I know several people who have used the plan in this letter with amazing results.

"My father was a traveling salesman. One time he sold furniture, another time hardware, sometimes it was leather goods. He changed his line every year.

"I would hear him telling Mother that this was his last trip in stationery or in bed lamps or whatever it was he was selling at the moment. Next year everything would be different; we would be on Easy Street. He had a chance to go with a firm that had a product that sold itself. It was always the same. My father never had a product that sold. He was always tense, always afraid of himself, always whistling in the dark.

"Then one day a fellow salesman gave Father a copy of a little three-sentence prayer. He was told to repeat it just before calling on a customer. Father tried it, and the results were almost miraculous. He sold 85 per cent of all calls made during the first week, and every week thereafter the results were wonderful. Some weeks the percentage ran as high as 95, and Father had sixteen weeks in which he sold every customer called on.

"Father gave this prayer to several other salesmen, and in each case it brought astounding results.

"The prayer my father used is as follows:

'I believe I am always divinely guided.

I believe I will always take the right turn of the road.

I believe God will always make a way where there is no way.' "

The head of a small firm who had a great many difficulties in establishing his business told me that he was immeasurably helped by a technique which he invented. He had trouble, he said, with the tendency to "blow up" a small difficulty into a seemingly insurmountable obstacle. He knew that he was approaching his problems in a defeatist attitude, and had common sense enough to realize that these obstacles were not so difficult as he made them appear to be. As he told the story, I wondered if he did not have that curious psychological difficulty known as the will to fail.

He employed a device which reconditioned his mental attitude and after a time had a noticeable effect on his business. He simply placed a large wire basket on his office desk. The following words were printed on a card and wired to this basket, "With God all things are possible." Whenever a problem came up which the old mechanism of defeat began to develop into a big difficulty, he threw the paper pertaining to it into the basket marked "With God all things are possible" and let it rest there for a day or two. "It is queer how each matter when I took it out of that basket again didn't seem difficult at all," he reported.

In this act he dramatized the mental attitude of putting the problem in God's hands. As a result he received power to handle the problem normally and therefore successfully.

As you finish this chapter please say the following line aloud: "I don't believe in defeat." Continue to affirm that until the idea dominates your subconscious attitudes.

# 9

# How to Break the Worry Habit

YOU DO NOT need to be a victim of worry. Reduced to its simplest form, what is worry? It is simply an unhealthy and destructive mental habit. You were not born with the worry habit. You acquired it. And because you can change any habit and any acquired attitude, you can cast worry from your mind. Since aggressive, direct action is essential in the elimination process, there is just one proper time to begin an effective attack on worry, and that is now. So let us start breaking your worry habit at once.

Why should we take the worry problem this seriously? The reason is clearly stated by Dr. Smiley Blanton, eminent psychiatrist, "Anxiety is the great modern plague."

A famous psychologist asserts that "fear is the most disintegrating enemy of human personality," and a prominent physician declares that "worry is the most subtle and destructive of all human diseases." Another physician tells us that thousands of people are ill because of "dammed-up anxiety." These sufferers have been unable to expel their anxieties which have turned inward on the personality, causing many forms of ill-health. The destructive quality of worry is indicated by the fact that the word itself is derived from an old Anglo-Saxon word meaning "to choke." If someone were to put his fingers around your throat and press hard, cutting off the flow of vital power, it would be a dramatic demonstration of what you do to yourself by long-held and habitual worry.

We are told that worry is not infrequently a factor in arthritis. Physicians who have analyzed the causes of this prevalent disease assert that the following factors, at least some of them, are nearly always present in arthritic cases: financial disaster, frustration, tension, apprehension, loneliness, grief, long-held ill will, and habitual worry.

A clinic staff is said to have made a study of one hundred seventy-six American executives of the average age of forty-four years and discovered that one half had high blood pressure, heart disease, or ulcers. It was notable in every case of those thus afflicted that worry was a prominent factor.

The worrier, so it seems, is not likely to live as long as the person who learns to overcome his worries. The *Rotarian* magazine carried an article entitled "How Long Can You Live?" The author says that the waistline is the measure of your life line. The article also declares that if you want to live long, observe the following rules: (1) Keep calm. (2) Go to church. (3) Eliminate worry.

A survey shows that church members live longer than non-church members (better join the church if you don't want to die young). Married people, according to the article, live longer than single people. Perhaps this is because a married couple can divide the worry. When you are single, you have to do it all alone.

A scientific expert on length of life made a study of some 450 people who lived to be one hundred years of age. He found that these people lived long and contented lives for the following reasons: (1) They kept busy. (2) They used moderation in all things. (3) They ate lightly and simply. (4) They got a great deal of fun out of life. (5) They were early to bed and early up. (6) They were free from worry and fear, especially fear of death. (7) They had serene minds and faith in God.

Haven't you often heard a person say, "I am almost sick with worry," and then add with a laugh, "But I guess worry never really makes you ill." But that is where he is wrong. Worry can make you ill.

Dr. George W. Crile, famous American surgeon, said, "We fear not only in our minds but in our hearts, brains, and viscera, that whatever the cause of fear and worry, the effect can always be noted in the cells, tissues, and organs of the body."

Dr. Stanley Cobb, neurologist, says that worry is intimately connected with the symptoms of rheumatoid arthritis.

A doctor recently stated that there is an epidemic of fear and worry in this country. "All doctors," he declared, "are having cases of illness which are brought on directly by fear, and aggravated by worry and a feeling of insecurity."

But do not be discouraged, for you can overcome your worries.

There is a remedy that will bring you sure relief. It can help you break the worry habit. And the first step to take in breaking it is simply to believe that you can. Whatever you believe you can do, you can do, with God's help.

Here, then, is a practical procedure which will help to eliminate abnormal worry from your experience.

Practice emptying the mind daily. This should be done preferably before retiring at night to avoid the retention by the consciousness of worries while you sleep. During sleep, thoughts tend to sink more deeply into the subconscious. The last five minutes before going to sleep are of extraordinary importance, for in that brief period the mind is most receptive to suggestion. It tends to absorb the last ideas that are entertained in waking consciousness.

This process of mind drainage is important in overcoming worry, for fear thoughts, unless drained off, can clog the mind and impede the flow of mental and spiritual power. But such thoughts can be emptied from the mind and will not accumulate if they are eliminated daily. To drain them, utilize a process of creative imagination. Conceive of yourself as actually emptying your mind of all anxiety and fear. Picture all worry thoughts as flowing out as you would let water flow from a basin by removing the stopper. Repeat the following affirmation during this visualization: "With God's help I am now emptying my mind of all anxiety, all fear, all sense of insecurity." Repeat this slowly five times, then add, "I believe that my mind is now emptied of all anxiety, all fear, all sense of insecurity." Repeat that statement five times, meanwhile holding a mental picture of your mind as being emptied of these concepts. Then thank God for thus freeing you from fear. Then go to sleep.

In starting the curative process the foregoing method should be utilized in midmorning and midafternoon as well as at bedtime. Go into some quiet place for five minutes for this purpose. Faithfully perform this process and you will soon note beneficial results.

The procedure may be further strengthened by imaginatively thinking of yourself as reaching into your mind and one by one removing your worries. A small child possesses an imaginative skill superior to that of adults. A child responds to the game of kissing away a hurt or throwing away a fear. This simple process works for the child because in his mind he believes that that is actually the end of it. The dramatic act is a fact for him and so it proves to be the end of the matter. Visualize your fears as being drained out of your mind and the visualization will in due course be actualized.

Imagination is a source of fear, but imagination may also be the cure of fear. "Imagineering" is the use of mental images to build factual results, and it is an astonishingly effective procedure. Imagination is not simply the use of fancy. The word imagination derives from the idea of imaging. That is to say, you form an image either of fear or of release from fear. What you "image" (imagine) may ultimately become a fact if held mentally with sufficient faith.

Therefore hold an image of yourself as delivered from worry and the drainage process will in time eliminate abnormal fear from your thoughts. However, it is not enough to empty the mind, for the mind will not long remain empty. It must be occupied by something. It cannot continue in a state of vacuum. Therefore, upon emptying the mind, practice refilling it. Fill it with thoughts of faith, hope, courage, expectancy. Say aloud such affirmations as the following: "God is now filling my mind with courage, with peace, with calm assurance. God is now protecting me from all harm. God is now protecting my loved ones from all harm. God is now guiding me to right decisions. God will see me through this situation."

A half-dozen times each day crowd your mind with such thoughts as these until the mind is overflowing with them. In due course these thoughts of faith will crowd out worry. Fear is the most powerful of all thoughts with one exception, and that one exception is faith. Faith can always overcome fear. Faith is the one power against which fear cannot stand. Day by day, as you fill your mind with faith, there will ultimately be no room left for fear. This is the one great fact that no one should forget. Master faith and you will automatically master fear.

So the process is—empty the mind and cauterize it with God's grace, then practice filling your mind with faith and you will break the worry habit.

Fill your mind with faith and in due course the accumulation of faith will crowd out fear. It will not be of much value merely to read this suggestion unless you practice it. And the time to begin practicing it is now while you think of it and while you are convinced that the number-one procedure in breaking the worry habit is to drain the mind daily of fear and fill the mind daily with faith. It is just as simple as that. Learn to be a practicer of faith until you become an expert in faith. Then fear cannot live in you.

The importance of freeing your mind of fear cannot be overemphasized. Fear something over a long period of time and there is a real possibility that by fearing you may actually help bring it to pass. The Bible contains a line which is one of the most terrible statements ever made—terrible in its truth: "For the thing which I greatly feared is come upon me . . ." (Job 3:25) Of course it will, for if you fear something continuously you tend to create conditions in your mind propitious to the development of that which you fear. An atmosphere is encouraged in which it can take root and grow. You tend to draw it to yourself.

But do not be alarmed. The Bible also constantly reiterates another great truth, "That which I have greatly believed has come upon me." It does not make that statement in so many words, and yet again and again and still again the Bible tells us that if we have faith "nothing is impossible" unto us, and "according to your faith be it done unto you." So if you shift your mind from fear to faith you will stop creating the object of your fear and will, instead, actualize the object of your faith. Surround your mind with healthy thoughts, thoughts of faith, and not fear, and you will produce faith results instead of fear results.

Strategy must be used in the campaign against the worry habit. A frontal attack on the main body of worry with the expectation of conquering it may prove difficult. Perhaps a more adroit plan is to conquer the outer fortifications one by one, gradually closing in on the main position.

To change the figure, it might be well to snip off the little worries on the farthest branches of your fear. Then work back and finally destroy the main trunk of worry.

At my farm it was necessary to take down a large tree, much to my regret. Cutting down a great old tree is fraught with sadness. Men came with a motor-driven saw and I expected them to start by cutting through the main trunk near the ground. Instead, they put up ladders and began snipping off the small branches, then the larger ones, and finally the top of the tree. Then all that remained was the huge central trunk, and in a few moments my tree lay neatly stacked as though it had not spent fifty years in growing.

"If we had cut the tree at the ground before trimming off the branches, it would have broken nearby trees in falling. It is easier to handle a tree the smaller you can make it," so explained the tree man.

The vast tree of worry which over long years has grown up in your personality can best be handled by making it as small as possible. Thus it is advisable to snip off the little worries and expressions of worry. For example, reduce the number of worry words in your conversation. Words may be the result of worry, but they also create worry. When a worry thought comes to mind, immediately remove it with a faith thought and expression. For example: "I'm worried that I will miss the train." Then start early enough to be sure you get there on time. The less worrying you do, the more likely you are to start promptly, for the uncluttered mind is systematic and is able to regulate time.

As you snip off these small worries you will gradually cut back to the main trunk of worry. Then with your developed greater power you will be able to eliminate basic worry, i.e., the worry habit, from your life.

My friend Dr. Daniel A. Poling gives a valuable suggestion. He says that every morning before he arises he repeats these two words, "I believe," three times. Thus at the day's beginning he conditions his mind to faith, and it never leaves him. His mind accepts the conviction that by faith he is going to overcome his problems and difficulties during the day. He starts the day with creative positive thoughts in his mind. He "believes," and it is very difficult to hold back the man who believes.

I related Dr. Poling's "I believe" technique in a radio talk and had a letter from a woman who told me that she had not been very faithful to her religion which happened to be the Jewish faith. She said their home was filled with contention, bickering, worry, and unhappiness. Her husband, she declared, "drank far too much for his own good" and sat around all day doing no work. He weakly complained that he couldn't find a job. This woman's mother-in-law lived with her and the latter "whined and complained of her aches and pains all the while."

This woman said that Dr. Poling's method impressed her and she decided to try it herself. So the next morning upon awakening she affirmed, "I believe, I believe, I believe." In her letter she excitedly reported, "It has been only ten days since I started this plan and my husband came home last night and told me he had a job paying $80 a week. And he also says that he is going to quit drinking. I believe he means it. What is even more wonderful, my mother-in-law has practically stopped complaining of her aches and pains. It is almost as if a miracle has happened in this house. My worries seem to have just about disappeared."

That does indeed seem almost magical, and yet that miracle happens every day to people who shift over from negative fear thoughts to positive faith thoughts and attitudes.

My good friend, the late Howard Chandler Christy, the artist, had many a sound anti-worry technique. Scarcely ever have I known a man so filled with the joy and delight of life. He had an indomitable quality, and his happiness was infectious.

My church has a policy of having the minister's portrait painted sometime during his pastorate. This portrait hangs in the minister's home until his death, when it reverts to the church and is placed in a gallery along with pictures of his predecessors. It is usually the policy of the Board of Elders and Deacons to have a portrait painted when in their wise judgment the minister is at the height of his good looks (mine was painted several years ago).

While sitting for Mr. Christy, I asked, "Howard, don't you ever worry?"

He laughed. "No, not on your life. I don't believe in it."

"Well," I commented, "that is quite a simple reason for not worrying. In fact, it seems to me too simple—you just don't believe in it, therefore you don't do it. Haven't you ever worried?" I asked.

He replied, "Well, yes, I tried it once. I noticed that everybody else seemed to worry and I figured I must be missing something, so one day I made up my mind to try it. I set aside a day and said, 'That is to be my worry day.' I decided I would investigate this worry business and do some worrying just to see what it was like.

"The night before the day came I went to bed early to get a good night's sleep to be rested up to do a good job of worrying the next day. In the morning I got up, ate a good breakfast—for you can't worry successfully on an empty stomach—and then decided to get to my worrying. Well, I tried my best to worry until along about noon, but I just couldn't make heads nor tails of it. It didn't make sense to me, so I just gave it up."

He laughed one of those infectious laughs of his.

"But," I said, "you must have some other method of overcoming worry." He did indeed, and it is perhaps the best method of all.

"Every morning I spend fifteen minutes filling my mind full of God," he said. "When your mind is full of God, there is no room for worry. I fill my mind full of God every day and I have the time of my life all day long."

Howard Christy was a great artist with a brush, but he was an equally great artist with life because he was able to take a great truth and simplify it down to its basic fact, namely, that only that comes out of the mind which originally you put into the mind. Fill the mind with thoughts of God rather than with thoughts of fear, and you will get back thoughts of faith and courage.

Worry is a destructive process of occupying the mind with thoughts contrary to God's love and care. Basically that is all worry is. The cure is to fill the mind with thoughts of God's power, His protection, and His goodness. So spend fifteen minutes daily filling your mind full of God. Cram your mind full of the "I believe philosophy," and you will have no mental room left to accommodate thoughts of worry and lack of faith.

Many people fail to overcome such troubles as worry because, unlike Howard Christy, they allow the problem to seem complicated and do not attack it with some simple technique. It is surprising how our most difficult personal problems often yield to an uncomplicated methodology. This is due to the fact that it is not enough to know what to do about difficulties. We must also know how to do that which should be done.

The secret is to work out a method of attack and keep working at it. There is value in doing something that dramatizes to our own minds that an effective counterattack is in process. In so doing we bring spiritual forces to bear upon the problem in a manner both understandable and usable.

One of the best illustrations of this technique strategy against worry was a scheme developed by a businessman. He was a tremendous worrier. In fact he was fast getting himself into a bad state of nerves and ill-health. His particular form of worry was that he was always doubtful as to whether he had done or said the right thing. He was always rehashing his decisions and getting himself unnerved about them. He was a post-mortem expert. He is an exceptionally intelligent man, in fact a graduate of two universities, in both instances with honors. I suggested that he ought to work out some simple method that would help him to drop the day when it was over and go ahead into the future and forget it. I explained the gripping effectiveness of simple, dramatized spiritual truth.

It is always true that the greatest minds have the best ability to be simple, that is, they have the capacity to work out some simple plans for putting profound truths into operation, and this man did that in connection with his worries. I noticed that he was improving and commented on it.

"Oh, yes," he said, "I finally got the secret and it has worked amazingly well." He said that if I would drop into his office sometime toward the close of the day he would show me how he had broken the worry habit. He telephoned me one day and asked me to have dinner that evening. I met him at his office at closing time. He explained that he had broken his worry habit by working out "a little ritual" that he performed every night before leaving his office. And it was very unique. It made a lasting impression upon me.

We picked up our hats and coats and started toward the door. By the door of his office stood a wastebasket and above it on the wall was a calendar. It was not one of those calendars where you see a week or a month, or three months, it was a one-day calendar. You could see only one date at a time, and that date was in large print. He said, "Now I will perform my evening ritual, the one that has helped me break the worry habit."

He reached up and tore off the calendar page for that particular day. He rolled it into a small ball and I watched with fascination as his fingers slowly opened and he dropped that "day" into the wastebasket. Then he closed his eyes and his lips moved, and I knew that he was praying, so was respectfully silent. Upon finishing his prayer he said aloud, "Amen. O.K., the day is over. Come on, let's go out and enjoy ourselves."

As we walked down the street I asked, "Would you mind telling me what you said in that prayer?"

He laughed and said, "I don't think it is your kind of prayer." But I persisted, and he said, "Well, I pray something like this: 'Lord, you gave me this day. I didn't ask for it, but I was glad to have it. I did the best I could with it and you helped me, and I thank you. I made some mistakes. That was when I didn't follow your advice, and I am sorry about that. Forgive me. But I had some victories and some successes, too, and I am grateful for your guidance. But now, Lord, mistakes or successes, victories or defeats, the day is over and I'm through with it, so I'm giving it back to you. Amen.' "

Perhaps that isn't an orthodox prayer, but it certainly proved to be an effective one. He dramatized the finishing of the day and he set his face to the future, expecting to do better the next day. He co-operated with God's method. When the day is over, God blacks it out by bringing down the curtain of night. By this method this man's past mistakes and failures, his sins of omission and commission gradually lost their hold on him. He was released from the worries that accumulated from his yesterdays. In this technique this man was practicing one of the most effective anti-worry formulas, which is described in these words, ". . . but this one thing I do, forgetting those things which are behind, and reaching forth unto those things which are before, I press toward the mark for the prize of the high calling of God in Christ Jesus." (Philippians 3:13-14)

Other practical anti-worry techniques may suggest themselves to you, and I should like to hear of those which after careful use prove effective. I believe that all of us who are interested in self-improvement are fellow students in God's great spiritual laboratory. Together we work out practical methods of successful living. People from everywhere are kind enough to write me about their methods and the results attained. I try to be helpful in making tested methods available to others through books, sermons, newspaper columns, radio, television, and other media. In this manner there can be developed a great many people who have the know-how for overcoming not only worry but other personal problems as well.

To conclude this chapter in a manner designed to help you go to work now to break the worry habit, I list a ten-point worry-breaking formula.

1. Say to yourself, "Worry is just a very bad mental habit. And I can change any habit with God's help."

2. You became a worrier by practicing worry. You can become free of worry by practicing the opposite and stronger habit of faith. With all the strength and perseverance you can command, start practicing faith.

3. How do you practice faith? First thing every morning before you arise say out loud, "I believe," three times.

4. Pray, using this formula, "I place this day, my life, my loved ones, my work in the Lord's hands. There is no harm in the Lord's hands, only good. Whatever happens, whatever results, if I am in the Lord's hands it is the Lord's will and it is good."

5. Practice saying something positive concerning everything about which you have been talking negatively. Talk positively. For example, don't say, "This is going to be a terrible day." Instead, affirm, "This is going to be a glorious day." Don't say, "I'll never be able to do that." Instead, affirm, "With God's help I will do that."

6. Never participate in a worry conversation. Shoot an injection of faith into all your conversations. A group of people talking pessimistically can infect every person in the group with negativism. But by talking things up rather than down you can drive off that depressing atmosphere and make everyone feel hopeful and happy.

7. One reason you are a worrier is that your mind is literally saturated with apprehension thoughts, defeat thoughts, gloomy thoughts. To counteract, mark every passage in the Bible that speaks of faith, hope, happiness, glory, radiance. Commit each to memory. Say them over and over again until these creative thoughts saturate your subconscious mind. Then the subconscious will return to you what you have given it, namely, optimism, not worry.

8. Cultivate friendships with hopeful people. Surround yourself with friends who think positive, faith-producing thoughts and who contribute to a creative atmosphere. This will keep you restimulated with faith attitudes.

9. See how many people you can help to cure their own worry

habit. In helping another to overcome worry you get greater power over it within yourself.

10. Every day of your life conceive of yourself as living in partnership and companionship with Jesus Christ. If He actually walked by your side, would you be worried or afraid? Well, then, say to yourself, "He is with me." Affirm aloud, "I am with you always." Then change it to say, "He is with me now." Repeat that affirmation three times every day.

# 10

# *Power to Solve Personal Problems*

I WANT TO tell you about some fortunate people who found the right solution to their problems.

They followed a simple but highly practical plan and in each case the outcome was a happy and successful one. These people are in no sense different than you. They had the same problems and difficulties that you have, but they found a formula which helped them to get the right answers to the difficult questions facing them. This same formula applied by you can get similar results.

First, let me tell you the story of a husband and wife, longtime friends of mine. For years Bill, the husband, worked hard until he finally reached the rung next to the top of the ladder in his company. He was in line for the presidency of the firm and felt certain that upon retirement of the president he would be advanced to that position. There was no apparent reason why his ambition should not be realized, for by ability, training, and experience he was qualified. Besides, he had been led to believe he was to be chosen.

However, when the appointment was made he was bypassed. A man was brought in from the outside to fill the post.

I arrived in his city just after the blow had fallen. The wife, Mary, was in an especially vindictive state of mind. At dinner she bitterly outlined all that she would "like to tell them." The intense disappointment, humiliation, frustration, focused in a burning anger which she poured out to her husband and me.

Bill, on the contrary, was quiet. Obviously hurt, disappointed, and bewildered, he took it courageously. Being essentially a gentle person, it was not surprising that he failed to become angry or violent in his reaction. Mary wanted him to resign immediately. She urged him to "tell them off and tell them plenty, then quit."

He seemed disinclined to take this action, saying perhaps it was for the best and he would go along with the new man and help him in any way that he could.

That attitude admittedly might be difficult, but he had worked for the company for so long that he would not be happy elsewhere, and, besides, he felt that in the secondary position the company could continue to use him.

The wife then turned to me and asked what I would do. I told her that I would, like herself, undoubtedly feel disappointed and hurt, but that I would try not to allow hate to creep in, for animosity not only corrodes the soul, but disorganizes thought processes as well.

I suggested that what we needed was Divine guidance, a wisdom beyond ourselves in this situation. There was such an emotional content in the problem that we might possibly be incapable of thinking the matter through objectively and rationally.

I suggested, therefore, that we have a few minutes of quietness, no one saying anything, that we sit quietly in an attitude of fellowship and prayer, turning our thoughts to the One who said, "Where two or three are gathered together in my name, there am I in the midst of them." (Matthew 18:20) I pointed out that there were three of us, and if we sought to achieve the spirit of being gathered in "His" name, He would also be present to quiet us and show us what to do.

It was not easy for the wife to accommodate herself to the mood suggested, but basically she was an intelligent, high-type person, and she joined in the plan.

Presently, after a few quiet minutes, I suggested that we join hands, and even though we were in a public restaurant I would quietly offer a prayer. In the prayer I asked for guidance. I requested peace of mind for Bill and Mary, and I went a step further and even asked God's blessing upon the new appointee. I also prayed that Bill would be able to fit in with the new administration and give more effective service than before.

After the prayer we sat silent for a time, then with a sigh the wife said, "Yes, I guess that is the way to do it. When I knew you were coming to dinner with us I feared that you would tell us to take a Christian position on this. Frankly, I didn't feel like doing that. I was boiling inwardly, but of course I realize that the right answer to this problem is to be found through that approach. I will try it faithfully, as difficult as it may be." She smiled wanly, but the animus was gone.

From time to time I checked with my friends, and found that while everything was not entirely as they desired, they gradually became fairly contented under the new arrangement. They were able to overcome their disappointment and ill will.

Bill even confided to me that he liked the new man and in a way enjoyed working with him. He told me that the new president often called him in for consultation and seemed to lean on him.

Mary was nice to the president's wife, and in fact they went to the fullest extent to be co-operative.

Two years passed. One day I arrived in their city and telephoned them.

"Oh, I am so excited I can hardly speak," Mary said.

I commented that anything that could put her in that state must be of unusual importance.

Ignoring this remark, she cried, "Oh, the most wonderful thing has happened. Mr. So-and-So," naming the president, "has been selected by another company at a big promotion for a special job which will take him out of our organization into a much better position and"—she posed the question—"guess what? Bill has just been notified that he is now president of this company. Come over right away and let the three of us give thanks together."

Later, as we sat together, Bill said, "Do you know, I am beginning to realize that Christianity isn't theoretical after all. We have solved a problem according to well-defined spiritually scientific principles. I shudder to think," he said, "of the terrible mistake we would have made had we not gone at this problem according to the formula contained in the teachings of Jesus.

"Who in the world," he asked, "is responsible for the silly idea that Christianity is impractical? Never again will I let a problem come up without attacking it in just the way the three of us solved this one."

Well, several years have passed, and Mary and Bill have had other problems, and to each of them they have applied this same technique, invariably with good results. By the "put it in God's hands" method they have learned to solve their problems right.

Another effective technique in problem solving is the simple device of conceiving of God as a partner. One of the basic truths taught by the Bible is that God is with us. In fact, Christianity begins with that concept, for when Jesus Christ was born He was called Immanuel, meaning "God with us."

Christianity teaches that in all the difficulties, problems, and circumstances of this life God is close by. We can talk to Him, lean upon Him, get help from Him, and have the inestimable benefit of His interest, support, and help. Practically everybody believes in a general way that this is true, and many have experienced the reality of this faith.

In getting correct solutions to your problems, however, it is necessary to go a step further than believing this, for one must actually practice the idea of presence. Practice believing that God is as real and actual as your wife, or your business partner, or your closest friend. Practice talking matters over with Him; believe that He hears and gives thought to your problem. Assume that He impresses upon your mind through consciousness the proper ideas and insights necessary to solve your problems. Definitely believe that in these solutions there will be no error, but that you will be guided to actions according to truth which results in right outcomes.

A businessman stopped me one day following a Rotary Club meeting in a Western city at which I had made a speech. He told me that something he had read in one of my newspaper columns had, as he put it, "completely revolutionized his attitude and saved his business."

Naturally I was interested and pleased that any little thing I had said would bring about such a splendid result.

"I had been having quite a difficult time in my business," he said. "In fact, it was beginning to be a very serious question as to whether I could save my business. A series of unfortunate circumstances together with market conditions, regulatory procedures, and dislocations to the economy of the country generally affected my line profoundly. I read this article of yours in which you advanced the idea of taking God in as a partner. I think you used the phrase, 'effect a merger with God.'

"When I first read that it seemed to me a rather 'cracked-brain idea.' How could a man on earth, a human being, take God as a partner? Besides, I had always thought of God as a vast being, so much bigger than man that I was like an insect in His sight, and yet you were saying that I should take Him as a partner. The idea seemed preposterous. Then a friend gave me one of your books and I found similar ideas scattered all through it. You told actual life stories about people who followed this advice. They all seemed to be sensible people, but still I was unconvinced. I always had the idea that ministers are idealistic theorists, that they know nothing about business and practical affairs. So I sort of 'wrote you off,' " he said with a smile.

"However, a funny thing happened one day. I went to my office so depressed that I actually thought perhaps the best thing for me to do would be to blow my brains out and get away from all these problems which seemed completely to floor me. Then into my mind came this idea of taking God as a partner. I shut the door, sat in my chair, and put my head on my arms on the desk. I might as well confess to you that I hadn't prayed more than a dozen times in as many years. However, I certainly did pray on this occasion. I told the Lord that I had heard this idea about taking Him in as a partner, that I wasn't actually sure what it meant, or how one did it. I told Him I was sunk, that I couldn't get any ideas except panicky ones, that I was baffled, bewildered, and very discouraged. I said, 'Lord, I can't offer You much in the way of a partnership, but please join with me and help me. I don't know how You can help me, but I want to be helped. So I now put my business, myself, my family, and my future in Your hands. Whatever You say goes. I don't even know how You are going to tell me what to do, but I am ready to hear and will follow Your advice if You will make it clear.'

"Well," he continued, "that was the prayer. After I finished praying I sat at my desk. I guess I expected something miraculous to happen, but nothing did. However, I did suddenly feel quiet and rested. I actually had a feeling of peacefulness. Nothing out of the ordinary occurred that day nor that night, but next day when I went to my office I had a brighter and happier feeling than usual. I began to feel confident that things would turn out right. It was hard to explain why I felt that way. Nothing was any different. In fact, you might even say things were a shade worse, but I was different, at least a little different.

"This feeling of peacefulness stayed with me and I began to feel better. I kept praying each day and talked to God as I would to a partner. They were not church prayers—just plain man-to-man talk. Then one day in my office, all of a sudden an idea popped up in my mind. It was like toast popping up in a toaster. I said to myself, 'Well, what do you know about that?' for it was something that had never occurred to me, but I knew instantly that it was just the method to follow. Why I had never thought of it before I haven't the slightest idea. My mind was too tied up, I guess. I hadn't been functioning mentally.

"I immediately followed the hunch." Then he stopped. "No, it was no hunch, it was my partner talking to me. I immediately put this idea into operation and things began to roll. New ideas began to flow out of my mind, and despite conditions I began to get the business back on an even keel. Now the general situation has improved considerably, and I'm out of the woods."

Then he said, "I don't know anything about preaching or about writing the kind of books you write, or any books for that matter, but let me tell you this—whenever you get a chance to talk to businessmen tell them that if they will take God as a partner in their business they will get more good ideas than they can ever use, and they can turn those ideas into assets. I don't merely mean money," he said, "although a way to get a good return on your investment, I believe, is to get God-guided ideas. But tell them that the God-partnership method is the way to get their problems solved right."

This incident is just one of many similar demonstrations of the law of Divine-human relationship working itself out in practical affairs. I cannot emphasize too strongly the effectiveness of this technique of problem solving. It has produced amazing results in the many cases coming under my observation.

In the very necessary business of solving personal problems, it is important, first of all, to realize that the power to solve them correctly is inherent within you. Second, it is necessary to work out and actualize a plan. Spiritual and emotional planlessness is a definite reason for the failure of many people to meet their personal problems successfully.

A business executive told me that he puts his dependence upon the "emergency powers of the human brain." It is his theory, and a sound one, that a human being possesses extra powers that may be tapped and utilized under emergency situations. In the ordinary conduct of day-by-day living, these emergency powers lie dormant, but under extraordinary circumstances the personality is able, when called upon, to deliver extra power if needed.

A person who develops a working faith does not allow these powers to lie dormant, but in proportion to his faith brings many of them into play in connection with normal activity. This explains why some people demonstrate greater force than others in daily requirements and in a crisis. They have made it a habit normally to draw upon powers that would otherwise be ignored except in some dramatic necessity.

When a difficult situation arises, do you know how to meet it? Have you any clearly defined plan for solving unusually difficult problems as they develop? Many people proceed on a hit-or-miss method, and, sadly enough, most frequently they miss. I cannot urge too strongly the importance of a planned use of your greater powers in meeting problems.

In addition to the method of two or three praying together in the "surrender of God" technique and that of establishing a partnership with God and the importance of a plan to tap and utilize emergency inner powers, there is still another tremendous technique—that of practicing faith attitudes. I read the Bible for years before it ever dawned on me that it was trying to tell me that if I would have faith—and really have it—that I could overcome all of my difficulties, meet every situation, rise above every defeat, and solve all of the perplexing problems of my life. The day that realization dawned on me was one of the greatest, if not the greatest, of my life. Undoubtedly many people will read this book who have never gotten the faith idea of living. But I hope you will get it now, for the faith technique is without question one of the most powerful truths in the world having to do with the successful conduct of human life.

Throughout the Bible the truth is emphasized again and again that "If ye have faith as a grain of mustard seed . . . nothing shall be impossible unto you." (Matthew 17:20) The Bible means this absolutely, factually, completely, and literally. It isn't an illusion, it isn't a fantasy. It is not an illustration, nor a symbol, nor a metaphor, but the absolute fact—"Faith, even as a grain of mustard seed," will solve your problems, any of your problems, all of your problems, if you believe it and practice it. "According to your faith, be it unto you." (Matthew 9:29) The requirement is faith, and directly in proportion to the faith that you have and use will you get results. Little faith gives you little results, medium faith gives you medium results, great faith gives you great results. But in the generosity of Almighty God, if you have only the faith symbolized by a grain of mustard seed, it will do amazing things in solving your problems.

For example, let me tell you the thrilling story of my friends Maurice and Mary Alice Flint. I became acquainted with them when a previous book of mine, *A Guide to Confident Living*, was condensed in *Liberty* magazine. Maurice Flint at that time was failing, and failing badly. Not only was he failing in his job, but as a person as well. He was filled with fear and resentment and was one of the most negative persons I have ever encountered. He was endowed with a nice personality and at heart was a wonderful fellow, but he had simply messed life up as he himself admitted.

He read the condensation of the book in which is emphasized the idea of "mustard-seed faith." At this time he was living in Philadelphia with his family, a wife and two sons. He telephoned my church in New York, but for some reason did not make contact with my secretary. I mention this to show his already changing mental attitude for normally he would never have called the second time, because it was his pathetic habit to give up everything after a feeble effort, but in this instance he persevered until he got through and secured the information relative to the time of church services. The next Sunday he drove from Philadelphia to New York with his family to attend church, which he continued to do even in the most inclement weather.

In an interview later he told me his life story in full detail and asked if I thought he could ever make anything of himself. The problems of money, of situations, of debts, of the future, and primarily of himself were so complicated and he was so overwhelmed with difficulty that he regarded the situation as completely hopeless.

I assured him that if he would get himself personally straightened out and get his mental attitudes attuned to God's pattern of thought, and if he would learn and utilize the technique of faith, all of his problems could be solved.

One attitude that both he and his wife had to clear out of their minds was that of resentment. They were dully mad at everybody and acutely so at some. They were in their present unhappy condition, so they reasoned in their diseased thoughts, not because of any failure on their part but because of "dirty deals" other people had given them. They actually used to lie in bed at night telling each other what they would like to say to other people by way of insult. In this unhealthy atmosphere they tried to find sleep and rest, but with no successful result.

Maurice Flint really took to the faith idea. It gripped him as nothing ever had. His reactions were weak, of course, for his will power was disorganized. At first he was unable to think with any power or force due to his long habit of negativism, but he held on tenaciously, even desperately, to the idea that if you have "faith as a grain of mustard seed, nothing is impossible." With what force he did have he absorbed faith. Of course, his capacity to have faith gradually increased as he practiced it.

One night he went into the kitchen where his wife was washing dishes. He said, "The faith idea is comparatively easy on Sunday in church, but I can't hold it. It fades. I was thinking that if I could carry a mustard seed in my pocket, I could feel it when I began to weaken and that would help me to have faith." He then asked his wife, "Do we have any of those mustard seeds, or are they just something mentioned in the Bible? Are there mustard seeds today?"

She laughed and said, "I have some right here in a pickle jar."

She fished one out and gave it to him. "Don't you know, Maurice," Mary Alice said, "that you don't need an actual mustard seed. That is only the symbol of an idea."

"I don't know about that," he replied. "It says mustard seed in the Bible and that's what I want. Maybe I need the symbol to get faith."

He looked at it in the palm of his hand and said wonderingly, "Is that all the faith I need—just a small amount like this tiny grain of mustard seed?" He held it for a while and then put it in his pocket, saying, "If I can just get my fingers on that during the day, it will keep me working on this faith idea." But the seed was so small he lost it, and he would go back to the pickle jar for another one, only to lose it also. One day when another seed became lost in his pocket, the idea came to him, Why couldn't he put the grain of mustard seed in a plastic ball? He could carry this ball in his pocket or put it on his watch chain always to remind him that if he had "faith as a grain of mustard seed, nothing would be impossible unto him."

He consulted a supposed expert in plastics and asked how to insert a mustard seed in a plastic ball so there would be no bubble. The "expert" said it could not be done for the reason that it had never been done, which of course was no reason at all.

Flint had enough faith by this time to believe that if he had faith "even as a grain of mustard seed" he could put a mustard seed in a plastic sphere. He went to work, and kept at it for weeks, and finally succeeded. He made up several pieces of costume jewelry: necklace, bow pin, key chain, bracelet, and sent them to me. They were beautiful, and on each gleamed the translucent sphere with the mustard seed within. With each one was a card which bore the title, "Mustard Seed Remembrancer." The card also told how this piece of jewelry could be used; how the mustard seed would remind the wearer that "if he had faith, nothing was impossible."

He asked me if I thought these articles could be merchandised. I was no expert in such matters so I showed them to Grace Oursler, consulting editor of *Guideposts* magazine. She took the jewelry to our mutual friend, Mr. Walter Hoving, president of Bonwit Teller Department Store, one of the greatest executives in the country. He at once saw the possibilities in this project. Imagine my astonishment and delight when in the New York papers a few days later was a two-column advertisement reading, "Symbol of faith—a genuine mustard seed enclosed in sparkling glass makes a bracelet with real meaning." And in the advertisement was the Scripture passage, "If ye have faith as a grain of mustard seed . . . nothing shall be impossible unto you." (Matthew 17:20) These articles sold like hot cakes. Now hundreds of great department stores and shops throughout the country find difficulty keeping them in stock.

Mr. and Mrs. Flint have a factory in a Midwestern city producing Mustard Seed Remembrancers. Curious, isn't it—a failure goes to church and hears a text out of the Bible and creates a great business. Perhaps you had better listen more intently to the reading of the Bible and the sermon the next time you go to church. Perhaps you, too, will get an idea that will rebuild not only your life but your business as well.

Faith in this instance created a business for manufacturing and distributing a product that has helped and will help thousands upon thousands of people. So popular and effective is it that others have copied it, but the Flint Mustard Seed Remembrancer is the original. The story of the lives that have been changed by this little device is one of the most romantic spiritual stories of this generation. But the effect on Maurice and Mary Alice Flint—the transformation of their lives, the remaking of their characters, the releasing of their personalities—this is a thrilling demonstration of faith power. No longer are they negative—they are positive. No more are they defeated—they are victorious. They no longer hate. They have overcome resentment and their hearts are filled with love. They are new people with a new outlook and a new sense of power. They are two of the most inspiring people I ever knew.

Ask Maurice and Mary Alice Flint how to get a problem solved right. They will tell you—"Have faith—really have faith." And believe me, they know.

If as you read this story you have said to yourself negatively (and that is being negative), "The Flints were never so bad off as I am," let me tell you that I have scarcely ever seen anybody as badly off as were the Flints. And let me say further that regardless of however desperate your situation may be, if you will use the four techniques outlined in this chapter, as did the Flints, you, too, can get your problem solved right.

In this chapter I have tried to show various methods for solving a problem. Now I wish to give ten simple suggestions as a concrete technique to use generally in solving your problems:

1. Believe that for every problem there is a solution.

2. Keep calm. Tension blocks the flow of thought power. Your brain cannot operate efficiently under stress. Go at your problem easy-like.

3. Don't try to force an answer. Keep your mind relaxed so that the solution will open up and become clear.

4. Assemble all the facts impartially, impersonally, and judicially.

5. List these fact on paper. This clarifies your thinking, bringing the various elements into orderly system. You see as well as think. The problem becomes objective, not subjective.

6. Pray about your problem, affirming that God will flash illumination into your mind.

7. Believe in and seek God's guidance on the promise of the 73rd Psalm, "Thou wilt guide me by thy counsel."

8. Trust in the faculty of insight and intuition.

9. Go to church and let your subconscious work on the problem as you attune to the mood of worship. Creative spiritual thinking has amazing power to give "right" answers.

10. If you follow these steps faithfully, then the answer that develops in your mind, or comes to pass, is the right answer to your problem.

# 11

# *How to Use Faith in Healing*

IS RELIGIOUS FAITH a factor in healing? Important evidence indicates that it is. There was a time in my own experience when I was not convinced of this, but now I am, and that very definitely. I have seen too many evidences to believe otherwise.

We are learning that faith properly understood and applied is a powerful factor in overcoming disease and establishing health.

My conviction regarding this important question is shared by many medical men. Newspapers carried an account of the visit to this country of the famous Viennese surgeon, Dr. Hans Finsterer. I quote the newspaper story which was headed "Honor Surgeon 'Guided by God.' "

"A Viennese doctor, Dr. Hans Finsterer, who believes 'the unseen hand of God' helps make an operation successful, was selected by the International College of Surgeons for its highest honor, 'master of surgery.' He was cited for his work in abdominal surgery with the use of local anesthesia only.

"Finsterer, seventy-two-year-old professor at the University of Vienna, has performed more than 20,000 major operations, among them 8,000 gastric resections (removal of part or all of the stomach) using only local anesthesia. Finsterer said that although considerable progress has been made in medicine and surgery in the past few years 'all advances are not sufficient in themselves to insure a happy outcome in every operation. In many instances,' he said, 'in what appeared to be simple surgical procedures the patients died, and in some cases where the surgeon despaired of a patient there was recovery.

" 'Some of our colleagues attribute these things to unpredictable chance, while others are convinced that in those difficult cases their work has been aided by the unseen hand of God. Of late years, unfortunately, many patients and doctors have lost their conviction that all things depend on the providence of God.

" 'When we are once again convinced of the importance of God's help in our activities, and especially in the treatment of our patients, then true progress will have been accomplished in restoring the sick to health.' "

So concludes the account of a great surgeon who combines his science with faith.

I spoke at the national convention of an important industry. It was a large gathering of the leaders in an amazingly creative merchandising enterprise that has established this particular industry as a vital factor in American business life.

I was somewhat surprised when one of the leaders of this organization at the convention luncheon where the discussion centered around taxation, rising costs, and business problems, turned to me and asked, "Do you believe that faith can heal?"

"There are a good many well-authenticated examples on record of people who have been healed by faith," I answered. "Of course, I do not think we should depend on faith alone to heal a physical ailment. I believe in the combination of God and the doctor. This viewpoint takes advantage of medical science and the science of faith, and both are elements in the healing process."

"Let me tell you my story," the man continued. "A number of year ago I had a malady that was diagnosed as osteoma of the jaw, that is, a bone tumor on my jaw. The doctors told me it was practically incurable. You can imagine how that disturbed me. Desperately I sought for help. Although I had attended church with fair regularity, still I was not a particularly religious man. I scarcely ever read the Bible. One day, however, as I lay in my bed it occurred to me that I would like to read the Bible, and I asked my wife to bring one to me. She was very surprised, for I have never before made such a request.

"I began to read, and found consolation and comfort. I also became a bit more hopeful and less discouraged. I continued to read for extended periods every day. But that wasn't the chief result. I began to notice that the condition which had troubled me was growing less noticeable. At first I thought I imagined this, then I became convinced that some change was taking place in me.

"One day while reading the Bible I had a curious inward

feeling of warmth and great happiness. It is difficult to describe, and long ago I got over trying to explain the feeling. From that time on my improvement was more rapid. I went back to the doctors who had first diagnosed my case. They examined me carefully. They were obviously surprised and agreed that my condition had improved, but warned me that this was only a temporary respite. Later, however, upon further examination, it was determined that the symptoms of osteoma had disappeared entirely. Still the doctors told me it would probably start all over again. This did not disturb me, for in my heart I knew that I was healed."

"How long has it been since your healing?" I asked.

"Fourteen years," was the answer.

I studied this man. Strong, sturdy, healthy, he is one of the outstanding men in his industry. The incident was told to me in the factual way that a businessman would recount it. There was not the slightest indication of doubt in this man's mind. Indeed how could there be, for whereas he had been condemned to death, here he was alive and vigorous.

What did it? The skillful work of the physician plus! And what was the plus? Obviously the faith that heals.

The healing described by this gentleman is but one of many similar accounts, and so many of them are attested by competent medical evidence that it seems we must encourage people to make greater use of the amazing power of faith in healing. Sadly the healing element in faith has suffered neglect. I am certain that faith can and does work what we call "miracles" but which are, in truth, the operation of spiritually scientific laws.

There is a growing emphasis in present-day religious practice which is designed to help people find healing from the sicknesses of mind, heart, soul, and body. This is a return to the original practice of Christianity. Only in recent times have we tended to overlook the fact that for centuries religion carried on healing activities. The very word "pastor" derives from a word meaning "the cure of souls." In modern times, however, man made the false assumption that it is impossible to harmonize the teachings of the Bible with what is called "science" and so the healing emphasis of religion was abandoned almost entirely to materialistic science. Today, however, the close association of religion and health is increasingly recognized.

It is significant that the word "holiness" derives from a word meaning "wholeness" and the word "meditation," usually used in a religious sense, closely resembles the root meaning of the word "medication." The affinity of the two words is startlingly evident when we realize that sincere and practical meditation upon God and His truth acts as a medication for the soul and body.

Present-day medicine emphasizes psychosomatic factors in healing, thus recognizing the relationship of mental states to bodily health. Modern medical practice realizes and takes into consideration the close connection between how a man thinks and how he feels. Since religion deals with thought and feeling and basic attitudes, it is only natural that the science of faith should be important in the healing process.

Harold Sherman, author and playwright, was asked to revise an important radio presentation with the promise that he would be contracted as the permanent writer. After some months of work, he was dismissed and his material used without credit. This resulted in financial difficulty and humiliation. The injustice rankling in his mind developed into a growing bitterness against the radio executive who had broken faith with him. Mr. Sherman declares that this is the one time in his life when he had murder in his heart. His hatred made him subject to a physical affliction in the form of a mycosis, a fungus growth which attacked the membranes of his throat. The best medical attention was secured, but something in addition was required. When he gave up his hate and developed a feeling of forgiveness and understanding, the condition gradually corrected itself. WIth the aid of medical science and a new mental attitude, he was healed of his affliction.

A sensible and effective pattern for health and happiness is to utilize the skills and methods of medical science to the fullest possible extent and at the same time apply the wisdom, the experience, and the techniques of spiritual science. There is impressive evidence to support the belief that God works through both the practitioner of science, the doctor, and the practitioner of faith, the minister. Many physicians join in this point of view.

At a Rotary Club luncheon I sat at a table with nine other men, one of them a physician who had recently been discharged from military service and had resumed his civilian practice. He said, "Upon my return from the Army, I noticed a change in my patients' troubles. I found that a high percentage do not need medicine but better thought patterns. They are not sick in their bodies so much as they are sick in their thoughts and emotions. They are all mixed up with fear thoughts, inferiority feelings, guilt, and resentment. I found that in treating them I needed to be about as much a psychiatrist as a physician, and then I discovered that not even those therapies helped me fully to do my job. I became aware that in many cases the basic trouble with people was spiritual. So I found myself frequently quoting the Bible to them. Then I fell into the habit of 'prescribing' religious and inspirational books, especially those that give guidance in how to live."

Directing his statements to me, he said, "It's about time you ministers began to realize that in the healing of many people you, too, have a function to perform. Of course you are not going to overlap on the work of the physician any more than we shall intrude on your function, but we doctors need the co-operation of ministers in helping people find health and well-being."

I received a letter from a physician in an upstate New York town who said, "Sixty per cent of the people in this town are sick because they are maladjusted in their minds and in their souls. It is hard to realize that the modern soul is sick to such an extent that the physical organs pain. I suppose in time," continues the doctor, "that ministers, priests, and rabbis will understand this relationship."

This physician was kind enough to say that he prescribes my book, *A Guide to Confident Living*, and other similar books to his patients and that noteworthy results have been achieved thereby.

The manager of a Birmingham, Alabama, bookstore sent me a prescription form made out by a physician of that city to be filled not at a drugstore, but at her bookstore. He prescribes specific books for specific troubles.

Dr. Carl R. Ferris, formerly president of the Jackson County Medical Society of Kansas City, Missouri, with whom I had the pleasure of appearing on a joint health-and-happiness radio program, declared that in treating human ills the physical and spiritual are often so deeply interrelated that there is often no clearly defined dividing line between the two.

Years ago my friend, Dr. Clarence W. Lieb, pointed out to me the effect on health of spiritual and psychiatric problems, and through his wise guidance I began to see that fear and guilt, hate and resentment, problems with which I was dealing, were often closely connected with problems of health and physical well-being. So profoundly does Dr. Lieb believe in this therapy that he with Dr. Smiley Blanton inaugurated the religio-psychiatric clinic which for years has ministered to hundreds at the Marble Collegiate Church in New York.

The late Dr. William Seaman Bainbridge and I worked closely together in the relationship of religion and surgery, and we were able to bring health and new life to many.

Two of my medical friends in New York, Dr. Z. Taylor Bercovitz and Dr. Howard Westcott, have been of inestimable help in my pastoral work through their wisely scientific and yet deeply spiritual understanding of the ills of the body, mind, and soul as related to faith.

"We have discovered the psychosomatic cause of high blood pressure as some form of subtle, repressed fear—a fear of things that might happen, not of things that are," says Dr. Rebecca Beard. "They are largely fears of things in the future. In that sense, therefore, they are imaginary, for they may never happen at all. In the case of diabetes, it is grief or disappointment which we found uses up more energy than any other emotion, thereby exhausting the insulin which is manufactured by the pancreas cells until they are worn out.

"Here we find the emotions involved in the past—reliving the past and not being able to go forward into life. The medical world can give relief in disorders like these. They can give something that can lower the blood pressure when it is high, or raise it when it is low, but not permanently. They can give insulin which will burn up more sugar into energy and give the diabetic relief. These are definite aids, but they do not offer complete cure. No drug or vaccine has been discovered to protect us from our own emotional conflicts. A better understanding of our own emotional selves and a return to religious faith seem to form the combination that holds the greatest promise of permanent help to any of us.

"The answer," Dr. Beard concludes, "is in the healing teachings of Jesus."

Another efficient woman physician wrote me of her own development in combining the therapy of medicine and faith. "I became interested in your straightforward religious philosophy. I had been working at top speed and getting tense, irritable, and at times beset with old fears and guilts, in fact in need of a release from morbid tension. At a low moment early one morning I picked up your book and began to read it. This was the prescription that I needed. Here was God, the great Physician, with faith in Him as an antibiotic to kill the germs of fear and render useless the virus of guilt.

"I began to practice the good Christian principles outlined in your book. Gradually there came a release of tension and I felt relaxed and happier and I slept well. I quit taking vitamin and pep pills. Then," she adds, and this is what I want to emphasize, "I began to feel that I wanted to share this new experience with my patients, those who came to me with neuroses. I was surprised to find how many had read your book and others. The patient and I seemed to have a common ground to work on. It has been an enriching experience. To talk about a faith in God has become a natural and easy thing to do.

"As a doctor," she adds, "I have seen a number of miraculous recoveries due to Divine aid being given. In the past few weeks I have had an additional experience. My sister had to undergo a serious operation about three weeks ago. Following the operation she developed an intestinal obstruction. On her fifth day she was very critically ill, and as I left the hospital at noon I realized that she must take a turn for the better very soon or her hope of recovery would be slim. I was very worried, so I drove slowly around for about twenty minutes praying for a relief of this obstruction. (Everything that could be done medically was being taken care of.) I had not been home more than ten minutes when the phone rang and her nurse told me that the obstruction had relieved itself and that she had taken a definite turn for the better, and since that time she has recovered completely. Could I feel otherwise than that God's intervention had saved her life?"

So runs the letter of a successful practicing physician.

In the light of this viewpoint based on a strictly commonsense scientific attitude we may approach the phenomenon of healing through faith with credibility. If I did not believe sincerely that the faith factor in healing is sound I would certainly not develop the point of view contained in this chapter.

Over a period of time I have received from many readers and radio listeners as well as from my own parishioners accounts of healings in which the element of faith has been present. I have meticulously investigated many of these to satisfy my own mind as to their truthfulness. Also I wanted to be able to declare to the most cynical that here is a way of health, happiness, and successful living which is so buttressed by evidence that only the person who wants to remain ill because of some subconscious will-to-fail attitude will ignore his possibilities for health implied in these experiences.

The formula which these many incidents together present is briefly stated—the employment of all the resources of medical and psychological science combined with the resources of spiritual science. This is a combination of therapies that can surely bring health and well-being if it is the plan of God for the patient to live. Obviously for each of us there comes a time for this mortal life to end (life itself never ends, only the earthly phase of it).

We in the so-called old-line churches have, in my humble judgment, missed one of our greatest possible contributions by failing to point out with positiveness that there is a sound message of health in Christianity. Failing to find this emphasis in the church, groups, organizations, and other spiritual bodies have been created to supply this deficiency in Christian teaching. But there is no longer any valid reason why all the churches should not recognize that which is authenticated, namely, that there is healing in faith and more generally offer sound healing techniques to our people. Fortunately everywhere today throughout our religious organizations thoughtful, scientifically minded spiritual leaders are taking that extra step of faith based on the facts (and the Scripture) and are making available to the people as never before the formulas of the marvelous healing grace of Jesus Christ.

In all of the investigations I have made into successful cases of healing, there seem to be certain factors present. First, a complete willingness to surrender oneself into the hands of God. Second, a complete letting go of all error such as sin in any form and a desire to be cleansed in the soul. Third, belief and faith in the combined therapy of medical science in harmony with the healing power of God. Fourth, a sincere willingness to accept God's answer, whatever it may be, and no irritation or bitterness against His will. Fifth, a substantial, unquestioning faith that God can heal.

In all these healings there seems to be an emphasis upon warmth and light and a feeling of assurance that power has passed through. In practically every case that I have examined, in one form or another, the patient talks about a moment when there was warmth, heat, beauty, peace, joy, and a sense of release. Sometimes it has been a sudden experience; other times a more gradual unfolding of the conviction that the healing has occurred.

Always in my investigation of these matters I have waited for elapsed time to prove that the healing is permanent and those cases which I report are not based on any temporary improvement which might conceivably be the result of a momentary resurgence of strength.

For example, may I relate a healing experience written for me by a woman whose reliability and judgment I profoundly respect. Documentation in this case is thoroughgoing and scientifically impressive. This woman was told that an immediate operation was necessary to remove a growth which had been diagnosed as malignant.

I quote her exact words: "All precautionary treatments were taken, but the manifestations returned. As may be expected, I was terrified; I knew further hospital treatments were futile. There was no hope, so I turned to God for help. A very consecrated and spiritual child of God helped me by prayer to realize that the right knowledge of God and His healing Christ would help me too. I was most receptive to this kind of thinking, and placed myself in God's hands.

"I had asked for this help one morning, as usual, and spent the day going about my household duties, which were many at that time. I was preparing the evening meal, all alone in the kitchen. I was aware of an unusually bright light in the room and felt a pressure against my whole left side, as though a person were standing very close beside me. I had heard of healings; I knew prayers were being offered in my behalf, so I decided this must be the healing Christ who was with me.

"I decided to wait until morning, to be sure; if the symptoms of the trouble were gone, then I would know. By morning, the improvement was so noticeable, and I was so free in my mind, that I was certain, and reported to my friend that the healing had taken place.

"The memory of that healing and the presence of Christ are as fresh in my mind today as then. That was fifteen years ago, and my health steadily improved until I am in excellent condition now."

In many heart cases the therapy of faith (a quiet, serene faith in Jesus Christ) undoubtedly stimulates healing. People who experience "a heart attack" who thereupon thoroughly and completely practice faith in Christ's healing grace, observing at the same time the rules prescribed by their physicians, report remarkable recovery histories. Perhaps such a person may even gain a greater degree of health than previously for having learned his limitations and, realizing the excess strains he has been placing upon himself, now conserves his strength.

But more than that he has learned one of the greatest techniques of human well-being, that of surrendering himself to the recuperative power of God. This is done by consciously attaching himself to the creative process through mentally conceiving of re-creative forces as operating within himself. The patient opens his consciousness to the tides of vitality and re-creative energy inherent in the universe which have been barred from his life through tension, high pressure, and other departures from the laws of well-being.

An outstanding man suffered a heart attack about thirty-five years ago. He was told that he would never be able to work again. The orders were that he must spend much of his time in bed. He would likely be an invalid the remainder of his days, which days would be relatively few in number, so he was informed. It is doubtful whether such statements would be made to him in present-day medical practice. At any rate he listened to these dire prophecies about his future and considered them carefully.

One morning he awakened early and picked up his Bible and by chance (or was it chance?) opened it to the account of one of the healings of Jesus. He also read the statement, "Jesus Christ the same yesterday, and today and forever." (Hebrews 13:8) It occurred to him that if Jesus could and did heal people long ago, and that if He is the same as He was then, why couldn't He heal today? "Why cannot Jesus heal me?" he asked. Then faith welled up within him.

Therefore, with simple confidence, he asked the Lord to heal him. He seemed to hear Jesus say, "Believest thou that I can do this?" And his answer was, "Yes, Lord, I believe that You can."

He closed his eyes and "seemed to feel the touch of the healing Christ upon his heart." All that day he had a strange sense of rest. As the days passed he became convinced that there was a rising tide of strength within him. Finally one day he prayed, "Lord, if it is Your will, tomorrow morning I am going to get dressed, go outside, and within a few days I am going back to work. I put myself completely in Your care. If I should die tomorrow as a result of the increased activity, I want to thank You for all the wonderful days I have had. With You to help me, I shall start out tomorrow and You will be with me all day long. I believe I will have sufficient strength, but if I should die as a result of this effort, I will be with You in eternity, and all will be well in either case."

In this calm faith he increased his activities as the days passed. He followed this formula every day for the entire period of his active career, which numbered thirty years from the date of his heart attack. He retired at seventy-five. Few men I have known have been more vigorous in their undertakings or have made a greater contribution to human welfare. Always, however, he conserved his physical and nervous strength. It was invariably his habit to lie down and rest after lunch, and he never allowed himself to get under stress. He was early to bed and early up, always employing rigorous and disciplinary rules of living.

In all his activities there was an absence of worry, resentment, and tension. He worked hard but easily.

The doctors were right. Had he continued according to the debilitating habits of his earlier life he would probably have long since been dead or at least an invalid. The advice of the physicians brought him to the point where the healing work of Christ could be accomplished. Without the heart attack he would not have been mentally or spiritually ready for healing.

Another friend of mine, a prominent businessman, suffered a heart attack. For weeks he was confined to his bed, but presently returned to his important responsibilities where he now accomplishes all that he ever did previously, but with much less tension. He seems to possess a new power that he did not enjoy before. His recovery proceeded from a definite and scientific spiritual approach to his health problem. He had competent physicians and followed their directions explicitly, which is an important factor in such situations.

In addition to the program of medication and treatment, however, he worked out a spiritual healing formula. He outlined it as follows, writing from the hospital, "An intimate friend of mine, only twenty-five years old, was brought into the hospital with an attack similar to mine and died within four hours. Two acquaintances of mine have suffered a similar fate in rooms near by. It must be that I have work yet to do. So I shall return and apply myself to the tasks before me with the expectation of living longer and more abundantly than I might have done without this experience. The doctors were wonderful, the nurses grand, the hospital ideal."

He then proceeds to outline the technique of spiritual convalescence which he employed. The formula consists of three parts. "(1) During the first stages, when absolute rest was demanded, I heeded the admonition of the Psalmist, 'Be still and know that I am God.' " (Psalm 46:10) That is to say, he completely relaxed and rested in the hands of God. "(2) As the days grew brighter, I used the affirmation, 'Wait on the Lord: be of good courage, and he shall strengthen thine heart.' " (Psalm 27:14) The patient put his heart under the care of God and God placed His hand of healing upon his heart and renewed it. "(3) Finally with the return of strength came a new assurance and confidence to which I gave expression in the affirmation, 'I can do all things through Christ which strengtheneth me.' " (Philippians 4:13) In this he affirmed positively that strength was being conferred upon him and in so doing he received new power.

In this three-point formula this man found healing. The able ministrations of his physicians conserved and stimulated the healing forces of his physical being. The equally wise application of faith completed his recovery by stimulating the spiritual powers within his nature. The two therapies together draw upon the two great renewal forces within our life, one the recuperative power of the human body and the other the restorative forces resident within the mind. One responds to medical treatment, the other to faith treatment, and God presides in both areas. He made both body and mind and He established the processes of health and well-being governing both. ". . . In Him we live and move and have our being." (Acts 17:28)

In the prevention of sickness and in healing mind and body, do not fail to draw upon one of the greatest resources available to you—the faith that heals.

In the light of the principles outlined in this chapter, what can you do of a constructive nature when a loved one or you are ill? Following are eight practical suggestions:

1. Follow the advice of a prominent medical school head who said, "In sickness, send for your minister even as you send for your doctor." In other words, believe that spiritual forces as well as medical technique are important in healing.

2. Pray for the doctor. Realize that God uses trained human instrumentality to aid His healing powers. As one doctor has put it, "We treat the patient and God heals him." Pray, therefore, that the doctor may be an open channel of God's healing grace.

3. Whatever you do, do not become panicky or filled with fear, for if you do, you will send out negative thoughts and therefore destructive thoughts in the direction of your loved one when he requires positive and healing thoughts to assist him.

4. Remember that God does nothing except by law. Also remember that our little materialistic laws are only fragmentary revelations of the great power flowing through the universe. Spiritual law also governs illness. God has arranged two remedies for all illness. One is healing through natural laws applicable by science, and the other brings healing by spiritual law applicable through faith.

5. Completely surrender your loved one into the hands of God. By your faith you can place him in the flow of Divine power. There is healing there, but in order for it to be effective the patient must be completely released to the operation of God's will. This is difficult to understand and equally difficult to perform, but it is a fact that if the great desire for the loved one to live is matched with an equally great willingness to relinquish him to God, healing powers are amazingly set in motion.

6. It is also important that harmony prevail in the family, that is, a spiritual harmony. Remember the emphasis in the scripture, Matthew 18:19: "If two of you shall agree on earth as touching anything that they shall ask, it shall be done for them of my Father which is in heaven." Apparently disharmony and disease are akin.

7. Form a picture in your mind of the loved one as being well.

Visualize him in perfect health. Picture him as radiant with the love and goodness of God. The conscious mind may suggest sickness, even death, but nine tenths of your mind is in the subconscious. Let the picture of health sink into the subconscious and this powerful part of your mind will send forth radiant health energy. What we believe in the subconscious we usually get. Unless your faith controls the subconscious, you will never get any good thing, for the subconscious gives back only that which you real thought is. If the real thought is negative, the results will also be negative. If the real thought is positive, you will get positive and healing results.

8. Be perfectly natural. Ask God to heal your loved one. That is what you want with all your heart, so ask Him please to do it, but we suggest that you say PLEASE just once. Thereafter in your prayer, thank Him for His goodness. This affirmative faith will help to release deep spiritual power and also joy through reassurance of God's loving care. This joy will sustain you, and remember that joy itself possesses healing power.

# 12

# *When Vitality Sags, Try This Health Formula*

A WOMAN, SO I have heard, went into a drugstore and asked for a bottle of psychosomatic medicine.

Such medicine, of course, is not found on drugstore shelves for it does not come in pills or bottles. But there is a psychosomatic medicine just the same and many of us need it. It is a prescription compounded of prayer, faith, and dynamic spiritual thinking.

It has been variously computed that from 50 to 75 per cent of present-day people are ill because of the influence of improper mental states on their emotional and physical make-up. Therefore such a medicine is of great importance. Many people who are below par will find that there is a health formula which, in addition to the services of their physicians, can be of great value to them.

The manner in which spiritual and emotional treatment can restore declining vitality is illustrated by the sales manager referred to us by the head of a large company. This sales executive, formerly a man of outstanding efficiency and energetic driving power, experienced a serious decline both in ability and energy. He lost his creative skill. Previously his sales ideas had been unique and outstanding. It soon become noticeable to his associates that this sales manager was slipping badly. He was urged to consult a doctor, and the company sent him to Atlantic City for a rest and later to Florida for a second attempt at recovery. Neither of these vacations seemed to be productive of any definite improvement.

His physician, who knew about our religio-psychiatric clinic, recommended to the company president that this sales manager come to us for an interview. The president asked him to come, which he did, but he was rather indignant at being sent to a church.

"This is a pretty pass," he fumed, "when they send a business-man to a preacher. I suppose you are going to pray with me and read the Bible," he said irritably.

"I wouldn't be surprised," I answered, "for sometimes our trouble lies in an area where prayer and the therapy of the Bible can have an important effect."

He proved most sullen and unco-operative until finally I was forced to say to him, "I want to tell you bluntly that you had better co-operate with us or you're going to be fired."

"Who told you that?" he demanded.

"Your boss," I replied. "In fact, he says that unless we can straighten you out, as much as he regrets it, you are going to be through."

You never saw such a stunned expression on anybody's face. "What do you think I ought to do?" he stammered.

"Often," I replied, "a person gets into the state in which you find yourself because the mind is filled with fear, anxiety, tension, resentment, guilt, or a combination of all of them. When these emotional impediments accumulate to a certain weight, the personality cannot support them any longer and gives way. Normal sources of emotional, spiritual, and intellectual power become clogged up. So a person becomes bogged down by resentment, by fear, or by guilt. I do not know your trouble, but I would suggest that you think of me as a sympathetic friend with whom you can be absolutely confident, and that you tell me about yourself." I emphasized that it was important he conceal nothing and that he completely empty himself of whatever fears, resentments, or guilt feelings might be in his mind. "I assure you that our interview will be held in strictest confidence. All your company wants is to have you back, the same highly efficient person you were."

In due course the trouble came out. He had committed a series of sins and these had involved him in a complicated maze of lies. He was living in fear of exposure, and all in all it was a most pathetic mass of inner confusion. It came little short of mental filth.

It was rather difficult to get him to talk, for he was essentially a decent person and had a strong sense of shame. I told him that I understood his reticence, but that this operation had to be performed and that it could not be accomplished without a thorough mind-emptying.

When it was all over, I shall never forget the manner in which he reacted. Standing on his feet he began to stretch. He stood on tiptoes, reaching his fingers toward the ceiling, and then took a deep breath. "My," he said, "I feel good." It was a dramatic expression of release and relief. Then I suggested that he pray and ask God to forgive him and to fill him with peace and cleanness.

"Do you mean for me to pray aloud?" he asked dubiously. "I never did that in my life."

"Yes," I said, "it is a good practice and will strengthen you."

It was a simple prayer, and as best as I can recall it, this is what he said, "Dear Lord, I have been an unclean man and I am sorry for the wrong I have done. I have poured it all out to my friend here. I now ask You to forgive me and to fill me with peace. Also make me strong so that I will never repeat these actions. Help me to be clean again and better—lots better."

He went back to his office that very day. Nothing was ever said to him, and it did not need to be, for soon he got back into stride and is one of the best sales managers in his city today.

Later I met his president, who said, "I don't know what you did to Bill, but he is certainly a ball of fire."

"I did nothing. God did it," I replied.

"Yes," he said, "I understand. Anyway, he is the old-time Bill."

When this man's vitality sagged, he tried a health formula that restored him to normal efficiency. He "took" some psychosomatic medicine which cured him of an unhealthy spiritual and mental condition.

Dr. Franklin Ebaugh of the University of Colorado Medical School maintains that one third of all cases of illness in general hospitals are clearly organic in nature and onset, one third are a combination of emotional and organic, and one third are clearly emotional.

Dr. Flanders Dunbar, author of *Mind and Body*, says, "It is not a question of whether an illness is physical or emotional, but how much of each."

Every thoughtful person who has ever considered the matter realizes that the doctors are right when they tell us that resentment, hate, grudge, ill will, jealousy, vindictiveness, are attitudes which produce ill-health. Have a fit of anger and experience for yourself that sinking feeling in the pit of your stomach, that sense of stomach sickness. Chemical reactions in the body are set up by emotional outbursts that result in feelings of ill-health. Should these be continued either violently or in a simmering state over a period of time, the general condition of the body will deteriorate.

In speaking of a certain man whom we both knew a physician told me that the patient died of "grudgitis." The physician actually felt that the deceased passed away because of a long-held hatred. "He did his body such damage that his resistance was lowered," the doctor explained, "so that when a physical malady attacked him he did not possess the stamina or renewing force to overcome it. He had undermined himself physically by the malignancy of his ill will."

Dr. Charles Miner Cooper, San Francisco physician, in an article entitled, "Heart-to-Heart Advice About Heart Trouble," says, "You must curb your emotional reactions. When I tell you that I have known a patient's blood pressure to jump sixty points almost instantaneously in response to an outburst of anger, you can understand what strain such reactions can throw upon the heart." One who is "quick on the trigger," he wrote, is likely to blame someone else, impulsively, for a fault or mistake, when it would be wiser simply to avoid being so much disturbed by what is done and is therefore unavoidable. He quoted the great Scottish surgeon, John Hunter. Dr. Hunter had a heart condition himself, and a thorough understanding of the effect of strong emotion on his heart. He said that his life was at the mercy of anyone who could annoy him. And, in fact, his death resulted from a heart attack caused by a fit of anger when he forgot to discipline himself.

Dr. Cooper concludes, "Whenever a business problem starts to vex you or you begin to get angry, let yourself go limp all over. This will dissipate your mounting inner turmoil. Your heart asks that it be permanently housed in a lean, cheerful, placid man who will intelligently curb his physical, mental, and emotional activities."

So if you are under par I suggest that you do a very scrupulous job of self-analysis. Honestly ask yourself if you are harboring any ill will or resentment or grudges, and if so cast them out. Get rid of them without delay. They do not hurt anybody else. They do no harm to the person against whom you hold these feelings, but every day and every night of your life they are eating at you. Many people suffer poor health not because of what they eat but from what is eating them. Emotional ills turn in upon yourself, sapping your energy, reducing your efficiency, causing deterioration in your health. And of course they siphon off your happiness.

So we realize today the effect of thought patterns upon physical states. We realize that a person can make himself ill by resentment. We know he can develop various kinds of physiological symptoms because of a sense of guilt. Also one may show definite physical symptoms as a result of fear and anxiety. We know that healing has been accomplished when the thoughts are changed.

Recently a diagnostician told me of a young woman who was admitted to the hospital with a temperature of one hundred and two degrees. She had a definite case of rheumatoid arthritis; her joints were badly swollen.

In order to study the case thoroughly the doctor gave her no medication except a slight sedative to relieve the pain. After two days the young woman asked the doctor, "How long will I be in this condition, and how long must I remain in the hospital?"

"I think I must tell you," replied the physician, "that you will probably be in the hospital for about six months."

"You mean it will be six months before I can get married?" she demanded.

"I am sorry," he said, "but I cannot promise you anything better than that."

This conversation took place in the evening. The next morning the patient's temperature was normal and the swelling was gone from her joints. Unable to account for the change, the doctor observed her for a few days, then sent her home.

In a month she was back in the hospital in the same condition as before: temperature one hundred and two, joints swollen. Counseling disclosed that her father insisted that she marry a certain man who would be an asset to him in his business connections. The girl loved her father, wanted to do as he wished, but did not want to marry a man whom she did not love. So her subconscious mind came to her assistance and in effect gave her rheumatoid arthritis and a temperature.

The doctor explained to the father that if he forced this marriage his daughter could become an invalid. When told that she need not go through with the marriage, the girl's recovery was quick and permanent.

Do not get the idea that if you have arthritis you are married to the wrong person! This incident merely illustrates the profound effect of mental pain on physical conditions.

I was interested to read a statement by a psychologist that infants can "catch" fear and hatred from people around them more quickly than they can catch measles or other infectious diseases. The virus of fear may burrow deeply into their subconsciousness and remain there for a lifetime. "But," adds the psychologist, "fortunately infants can also catch love and goodness and faith and so grow up to become normal, healthy children and adults."

In an article in the *Ladies' Home Journal*, Constance J. Foster quotes Dr. Edward Weiss of Temple University Medical School in a speech to the American College of Physicians in which Dr. Weiss stated that chronic victims of pains and aches in the muscles and joints may be suffering from nursing a smoldering grudge against someone close to them. He added that such persons usually are totally unaware that they bear a chronic resentment.

"To clear up any possible misunderstanding," the author continues, "it is necessary to state emphatically that emotions and feelings are quite as real as germs and no less respectable. The resultant pain and suffering of diseases caused primarily by the emotions are no more imaginary than those caused by bacteria. In no case is the patient consciously to blame for developing the disease. Such persons are not suffering from any disease of the mind, but rather from a disorder of their feelings, often linked to a marital or parent-child problem."

In this same magazine article the story is told of a certain Mrs. X who came to the doctor's office complaining of a breaking out on her hands which was diagnosed as eczema. The doctor encouraged Mrs. X to talk about herself. It developed that she was a very rigid person. Her lips were thin and unyielding. She was also rheumatoid. The doctor sent Mrs. X to a psychiatrist who saw at once that there was some irritating situation in her life which she was translating outwardly in the form of a skin rash, thus taking out on her own person the urge to scratch some thing or person.

The doctor finally put it to her bluntly. "What is eating you?" he asked. "You're peeved at something, aren't you?"

"She stiffened up like a ramrod and marched right out of the office, so I knew I'd hit the target too closely for comfort. A few days later she came back. Due to the agony of the eczema, she was ready to let me help her even if it meant she had to give up a hate.

"It turned out to be a family row over a will with Mrs. X feeling she had been treated unfairly by a younger brother. When she got rid of the hostility, she got well, and when she made up the quarrel with her brother, within twenty-four hours the eczema vanished."

That there is even a relationship between emotional disturbance and the common cold is indicated by Dr. L. J. Saul of the University of Pennsylvania Medical School, who has made a study of this subject.

"Emotional disturbances are believed to affect the blood circulation in the linings of the nose and throat. They also affect glandular secretions. These factors make the mucous membranes more susceptible to attack by cold viruses or germ infection."

Dr. Edmund P. Fowler, Jr., of Columbia University's College of Physicians and Surgeons, stated, "There are colds which develop in medical students at the time of their examinations and colds which develop in many persons before or after a trip. Colds develop in housewives when they must care for a large family. And one often sees a cold develop in a patient when his mother-in-law comes to live in the house, and it often disappears when she leaves." (Dr. Fowler does not specify the effects on the mother-in-law of a daughter-in-law or son-in-law. Perhaps she has a cold also.)

One of the cases Dr. Fowler reports concerned a twenty-five-year-old salesgirl. When she visited his office her nose was stuffy, the lining was red and congested, and she suffered from a headache and a mild temperature. These symptoms had persisted for nearly two weeks. Questioning disclosed that they had started a few hours after a violent quarrel with her fiancé.

Local treatments cleared up the cold but the young woman was back in a few weeks with another attack. This time the trouble had started after an argument with the butcher. Again local treatments brought relief. But the girl continued to have recurring colds, and each time they were traced to a fit of anger. Finally Dr. Fowler was able to persuade the girl that her bad temper was at the root of her chronic cold symptoms. When she learned to lead a calmer existence, her sneezes and sniffles disappeared.

And yet people still think that when the Bible tells you not to hate or to get angry that it is "theoretical advice." The Bible is not theoretical. It is our greatest book of wisdom. It is filled with practical advice on living and on health. Anger, resentment, and guilt make you sick, modern physicians tell us, which proves once again that the most up-to-date book on personal well-being is the Holy Bible, neglected by so many or regarded by them as purely a religious book and certainly as one that is not practical. No wonder more copies are read than all other books. That is because in this book we discover not only what is wrong with us but how to correct it as well.

Dr. Fowler calls attention to the "emotional colds" suffered by children who feel insecure. He reports that many cases of chronic colds occur in children who come from broken homes. An older child often has recurring respiratory infection when a new baby is born because he feels neglected and jealous. A nine-year-old boy had an extremely dictatorial father and an indulgent mother. The conflict between the strictness of one parent and the lenience of the other obviously was disturbing to the child. He particularly feared punishment by his father. This boy suffered for several years from continuous coughs and sniffles. It was noted that the colds disappeared when he went to camp—away from his parents.

Since irritation, anger, hate, and resentment have such a powerful effect in producing ill-health, what is the antidote? Obviously it is to fill the mind with attitudes of good will, forgiveness, faith, love, and the spirit of imperturbability. And how is that accomplished? Following are some practical suggestions. They have been used successfully by many in counterattacking especially the emotion of anger. A consistent application of these suggestions can produce feelings of well-being:

1. Remember that anger is an emotion, and an emotion is always warm, even hot. Therefore to reduce an emotion, cool it. And how do you cool it? When a person gets angry, the fists tend to clench, the voice rises in stridency, muscles tense, the body becomes rigid. (Psychologically you are poised for fight, adrenaline shoots through the body.) This is the old caveman hangover in the nervous system. So deliberately oppose the heat of this emotion with coolness—freeze it out. Deliberately, by an act of will, keep your hands from clenching. Hold your fingers out straight. Deliberately reduce your tone; bring it down to a whisper. Remember that it is difficult to argue in a whisper. Slump in a chair, or even lie down if possible. It is very difficult to get mad lying down.

2. Say aloud to yourself, "Don't be a fool. This won't get me anywhere, so skip it." At that moment it may be a bit hard to pray, but try it anyway; at least conjure up a picture of Jesus Christ in your mind and try to think of Him mad just as you are. You can't do it, and the effort will serve to puncture your angry emotions.

3. One of the best techniques for cooling off anger was suggested by Mrs. Grace Oursler. She formerly employed the usual "count to ten" technique but happened to notice that the first ten words of the Lord's Prayer worked better. "Our Father who art in Heaven, hallowed be Thy name." When angry, say that ten times and your anger will lose its power over you.

4. Anger is a great term expressing the accumulated vehemence of a multitude of minor irritations. These irritations, each rather small in itself, having gathered force by reason of the one being added to the other, finally blaze forth in a fury that often leaves us abashed at ourselves. Therefore, make a list of everything that irritates you. No matter how inconsequential it may be or how silly each is, list it just the same. The purpose in doing this is to dry up the tiny rivulets that feed the great river of anger.

5. Make each separate irritation a special object of prayer. Get a victory over each, one at a time. Instead of attempting to destroy all of your anger, which as we have pointed out is a consolidated force, snip away by prayer each annoyance that feeds your anger. In this way you will weaken your anger to the point where presently you will gain control over it.

6. Train yourself so that every time you feel the surge of anger you say, "Is this really worth what it is doing to me emotionally? I will make a fool of myself. I will lose friends." In order to get the full effect of this technique, practice saying to yourself a few times every day, "It is never worth it to get worked up or mad about anything." Also affirm: "It isn't worth it to spend $1000 worth of emotion on a five-cent irritation."

7. When a hurt-feeling situation arises, get it straightened out as quickly as possible. Don't brood over it for a minute longer than you can help. Do something about it. Do not allow yourself to sulk or indulge in self-pity. Don't mope around with resentful thoughts. The minute your feelings are hurt, do just as when you hurt your finger. Immediately apply the cure. Unless you do so the situation can become distorted out of all proportion. So put some spiritual iodine on the hurt at once by saying a prayer of love and forgiveness.

8. Apply grievance drainage to your mind. That is, open your mind and let the grievance flow out. Go to someone you trust and pour it out to him until not a vestige of it remains within you. Then forget it.

9. Simply start praying for the person who has hurt your feelings. Continue this until you feel the malice fading away. Sometimes you may have to pray for quite a while to get that result. A man who tried this method told me that he kept account of the number of times he needed to pray until the grievance left and peace came. It was exactly sixty-four times. He literally prayed it out of his system. This is positively guaranteed to work.

10. Say this little prayer: "May the love of Christ fill my heart." Then add this line: "May the love of Christ for ——— (insert the other's name) flood my soul." Pray this, mean it (or ask to mean it), and you will get relief.

11. Actually take the advice of Jesus to forgive seventy times seven. To be literal, that means four hundred ninety times. Before you have forgiven a person that many times you will be free of resentment.

12. Finally, this wild, undisciplined, primitive urge in you which flames to the surface can be tamed only by allowing Jesus Christ to take control. Therefore, complete this lesson by saying to Jesus Christ, "Even as You can convert a person's morals, so now I ask You to convert my nerves. As You give power over the

sins of the flesh, so give me power over the sins of the disposition. Bring my temper under Your control. Give me Thy healing peace in my nervous system as well as in my soul." If you are beset by temper, repeat the above prayer three times every day. It might be advisable to print it on a card and put it on your desk, or above the kitchen sink, or in your pocketbook.

13

# *Inflow of New Thoughts Can Remake You*

ONE OF THE most important and powerful facts about you is expressed in the following statement by William James, who was one of the wisest men America has produced. William James said, "The greatest discovery of my generation *is that human beings can alter their lives by altering their attitudes of mind.*" As you think, so shall you be. So flush out all old, tired, worn-out thoughts. Fill your mind with fresh, new creative thoughts of faith, love, and goodness. By this process you can actually remake your life.

And where do you find such personality remaking thoughts?

I know a business executive, a modest man, but the type of individual who is never defeated. No problem, no setback, no opposition ever gets him down. He simply attacks each difficulty with an optimistic attitude and a sure confidence that it will work out right, and, in some strange way, it always does for him. He seems to have a magic touch on life—a touch that never fails.

Because of that impressive characteristic this man always interested me. I knew there was a definite explanation of his being this way and of course wanted to hear his story, but in view of his modesty and reticence it was not easy to persuade him to talk about himself.

One day when he was in the mood he told me his secret, an amazingly simple but effective secret. I was visiting his plant, a modern, up-to-date structure, much of it air-conditioned. Latest-type machinery and methods of production make it a factory of outstanding efficiency. Labor-management relations seem as nearly perfect as is possible among imperfect human beings. A spirit of good will pervades the entire organization.

His office is ultra-modernistically decorated and furnished with handsome desks, rugs, and paneled with exotic woods. The decorating scheme is five startling colors blended together pleasantly. All in all it is the last word, and then some.

Imagine, then, my surprise to see on his highly polished white mahogany desk an old battered copy of the Bible. It was the only old object in those ultra-modern rooms. I commented upon this seemingly strange inconsistency.

"That book," he replied, pointing to the Bible, "is the most up-to-date thing in this plant. Equipment wears out and furnishing styles change, but that book is so far ahead of us that it never gets out of date.

"When I went to college, my good Christian mother gave me that Bible with the suggestion that if I would read and practice its teachings, I would learn how to get through life successfully. But I thought she was just a nice old lady"—he chuckled—"at my age she seemed old—she wasn't really, and to humor her, I took the Bible, but for years practically never looked at it. I thought I didn't need it. Well," he continued slangily, "I was a dope. I was stupid. And I got my life in a terrible mess.

"Everything went wrong primarily because I was wrong. I was thinking wrong, acting wrong, doing wrong. I succeeded at nothing, failed at everything. Now I realize that my principal trouble was wrong thinking. I was negative, resentful, cocky, opinionated. Nobody could tell me anything. I thought I knew everything. I was filled with gripes at everybody. Little wonder nobody liked me. I certainly was a 'washout.' "

So ran his dismal story. "One night in going through some papers," he continued, "I came across the long-forgotten Bible. It brought up old memories and I started aimlessly to read it. Do you know it is strange how things happen; how in just a flashing moment of time everything becomes different. Well, as I read, a sentence leaped up at me, a sentence that changed my life—and when I say changed, I mean changed. From the minute I read that sentence everything has been different, tremendously different."

"What is this wonderful sentence?" I wanted to know, and he quoted it slowly, " 'The Lord is the strength of my life . . . in this will I be confident.' (Psalm 27:1, 3)

"I don't know why that one line affected me so," he went on, "but it did. I know now that I was weak and a failure because I had no faith, no confidence. I was very negative, a defeatist. Something happened inside my mind. I guess I had what they call a spiritual experience. My thought pattern shifted from negative to positive. I decided to put my faith in God and sincerely do my best, trying to follow the principles outlined in the Bible. As I did so I began to get hold of a new set of thoughts. I began to think differently. In time my old failure thoughts were flushed out by this new spiritual experience and an inflow of new thoughts gradually but actually remade me."

So concluded the story of this businessman. He altered his thinking, and the new thoughts which flowed in displaced the old thoughts which had been defeating him and his life was changed.

This incident illustrates an important fact about human nature: you can think your way to failure and unhappiness, but you can also think your way to success and happiness. The world in which you live is not primarily determined by outward conditions and circumstances but by thoughts that habitually occupy your mind. Remember the wise words of Marcus Aurelius, one of the great thinkers of antiquity, who said, "A man's life is what his thoughts make of it."

It has been said that the wisest man who ever lived in America was Ralph Waldo Emerson, the Sage of Concord. Emerson declared, "A man is what he thinks about all day long."

A famous psychologist says, "There is a deep tendency in human nature to become precisely like that which you habitually imagine yourself to be."

It has been said that thoughts are things, that they actually possess dynamic power. Judged by the power they exercise one can readily accept such an appraisal. You can actually think yourself into or out of situations. You can make yourself ill with your thoughts and by the same token you can make yourself well by the use of a different and healing type of thought. Think one way and you attract the conditions which that type of thinking indicates. Think another way and you can create an entirely different set of conditions. Conditions are created by thoughts far more powerfully than conditions create thoughts.

Think positively, for example, and you set in motion positive forces which bring positive results to pass. Positive thoughts create around yourself an atmosphere propitious to the development of positive outcomes. On the contrary, think negative thoughts and you create around yourself an atmosphere propitious to the development of negative results.

To change your circumstances, first start thinking differently. Do not passively accept unsatisfactory circumstances, but form a picture in your mind of circumstances as they should be. Hold that picture, develop it firmly in all details, believe in it, pray about it, work at it, and you can actualize it according to that mental image emphasized in your positive thinking.

This is one of the greatest laws in the universe. Fervently do I wish I had discovered it as a very young man. It dawned upon me much later in life and I have found it to be one of the greatest if not my greatest discovery, outside of my relationship to God. And in a deep sense this law is a factor in one's relationship with God because it channels God's power into personality.

This great law briefly and simply stated is that if you think in negative terms you will get negative results. If you think in positive terms you will achieve positive results. That is the simple fact which is at the basis of an astonishing law of prosperity and success. In three words: Believe and succeed.

I learned this law in a very interesting manner. Some years ago a group of us consisting of Lowell Thomas, Captain Eddie Rickenbacker, Branch Rickey, Raymond Thornburg, and others established an inspirational self-help magazine called *Guideposts*. This magazine has a double function: first, by relating stories of people who through their faith have overcome difficulties, it teaches techniques of victorious living, victory over fear, over circumstances, over obstacles, over resentment. It teaches faith over all manner of negativism.

Second, as a non-profit, non-sectarian, inter-faith publication it teaches the great fact that God is in the stream of history and that this nation was founded on belief in God and His laws.

The magazine reminds its readers that America is the first great nation in history to be established on a definitely religious premise and that unless we keep it so our freedoms will deteriorate.

Mr. Raymond Thornburg as publisher and I as editor in starting the magazine had no financial backing to underwrite it. It was begun on faith. In fact, its first offices were in rooms above a grocery store in the little village of Pawling, New York. There was a borrowed typewriter, a few rickety chairs, and that was all; all except a great idea and great faith. Slowly a subscription list of 25,000 developed. The future seemed promising. Suddenly one night fire broke out, and within an hour the publishing house was destroyed and with it the total list of subscribers. Foolishly no duplicate list had been made.

Lowell Thomas, loyal and efficient patron of *Guideposts* from the very start, mentioned this sad circumstance on his radio broadcast and as a result we soon had 30,000 subscribers, practically all the old ones and many new ones.

The subscription list rose to approximately 40,000, but costs increased even more rapidly. The magazine, which has always been sold for less than cost in order widely to disseminate the message, was more expensive than anticipated and we were faced with difficult financial problems. In fact, at one time it seemed almost impossible to keep it going.

At this juncture we called a meeting, and I'm sure you never attended a more pessimistic, negative, discouraging meeting. It dripped with pessimism. Where were we going to get the money to pay our bills? We figured out ways of robbing Peter to pay Paul. Complete discouragement filled our minds.

A woman had been invited to this meeting whom we all regarded most highly. But one reason she was included in this meeting was because, on a previous occasion, she had contributed $2,000 to help inaugurate *Guideposts* magazine. It was hoped that lightning might strike twice in the same place. But this time she gave us something of more value than money.

As this dismal meeting progressed she remained silent for a long time, but finally said, "I suppose you gentlemen would like me to make another financial contribution. I might as well put you out of your misery. I am not going to give you another cent."

This did not put us out of our misery. On the contrary, it put us deeper into our misery. "But," she continued, "I will give you something far more valuable than money."

This astonished us, for we could not possibly imagine anything of more value than money in the circumstances.

"I am going to give you an idea," she continued, "a creative idea."

"Well," we thought to ourselves unenthusiastically, "how can we pay our bills with an idea?"

Ah, but an idea is just what will help you pay bills. Every achievement in this world was first projected as a creative idea.

First the idea, then faith in it, then the means of implementing the idea. That is the way success proceeds.

"Now," she said, "here is the idea. What is your present trouble? It is that you *lack* everything. You *lack* money. You *lack* subscribers. You *lack* equipment. You *lack* ideas. You *lack* courage. Why do you *lack* all these requirements? Simply because you are thinking *lack*. If you think *lack* you create the conditions that produce a state of *lack*. By this constant mental emphasis upon what you *lack* you have frustrated the creative forces that can give impetus to the development of *Guideposts*. You have been working hard from the standpoint of doing many things, but you have failed to do the one all-important thing that will lend power to all your other efforts: you have not employed positive thinking. Instead, you have thought in terms of *lack*.

"To correct that situation—reverse the mental process and begin to think prosperity, achievement, success. This will require practice but it can be done quickly if you will demonstrate faith. The process is to visualize; that is, to see *Guideposts* in terms of successful achievement. Create a mental picture of *Guideposts* as a great magazine, sweeping the country. Visualize large numbers of subscribers, all eagerly reading this inspirational material and profiting thereby. Create a mental image of lives being changed by the philosophy of achievement which *Guideposts* teaches monthly in its issues.

"Do not hold mental pictures of difficulties and failures, but lift your mind above them and visualize powers and achievements. When you elevate your thoughts into the area of visualized attainment you look down on your problems rather than from below up at them and thus you get a much more encouraging view of them. Always come up over your problems. Never approach a problem from below.

"Now let me continue further," she said. "How many subscribers do you need at the moment to keep going?"

We thought quickly and said, "100,000." We had 40,000.

"All right," she said confidently, "that is not hard. That is easy. Visualize 100,000 people being creatively helped by this magazine and you will have them. In fact, the minute you can see them in your mind, you will have them."

She turned to me and said, "Norman, can you see 100,000

subscribers at this minute? Look out there, look ahead of you. In your mind's eye can you see them?"

I wasn't convinced as yet, and I said rather doubtfully, "Well, maybe so, but they seem pretty dim to me."

She was a little disappointed in me, I thought, as she asked, "Can't you imaginatively visualize 100,000 subscribers?"

I guess my imagination wasn't working very well because all I could see was the insufficient but actual 40,000.

Then she turned to my old friend Raymond Thornburg who has been blessed with a gloriously victorious personality, and she said, calling him by his nickname, "Pinky, can you visualize 100,000 subscribers?"

I rather doubted that Pinky would see them. He is a rubber manufacturer who gives his time freely from his own business to help advance this inspirational, non-profit magazine, and you would not ordinarily think that a rubber manufacturer would respond to this type of thinking. But he has the faculty of creative imagination. I noticed by the fascinated look on his face that she had him. He was gazing straight ahead with rather a look of wonder when she asked, "Do you see the 100,000 subscribers?"

"Yes," he cried with eagerness, "yes, I do see them."

Electrified, I demanded, "Where? Point them out to me."

Then I, too, began to visualize them.

"Now," continued our friend, "let us bow our heads and together thank God for giving us 100,000 subscribers."

Frankly I thought that was pushing the Lord rather hard, but it was justified by a verse in the Scriptures where it says, "And all things, whatsoever ye shall ask in prayer, believing, ye shall receive them." (Matthew 21:22) That means when you pray for something, at the same time visualize what you pray for. Believe that if it is God's will and is worth while, not selfishly sought after, but for human good, that it is at that moment given you.

If you have difficulty in following this reasoning, let me tell you that from that moment until the present writing *Guideposts* never lacked for anything. It has found wonderful friends and has had fine support. It has been able always to meet its bills, purchase needed equipment, finance itself, and as I write these words *Guideposts* is nearing the half million mark and more subscriptions are coming in regularly, sometimes as many as three or four thousand per day.

I recite this instance not for the purpose of advertising *Guideposts*, although I strongly recommend this magazine to all my readers, and if you would like to be a subscriber, write to *Guideposts*, Pawling, New York, for information. But I tell the story because I was awed by this experience, realizing that I had stumbled upon a law, a tremendous law of personal victory. I decided to apply it thereafter to my own problems and wherever I have done so can report a marvelous result. Wherever I have failed to do so, I have missed great results.

It is as simple as this—put your problem in God's hands. In your thoughts rise above the problem so that you look down upon it, not up at it. Test it according to God's will. That is, do not try to get success from something that is wrong. Be sure it is right morally, spiritually, and ethically. You can never get a right result from an error. If your thinking is wrong, it is wrong and not right and can never be right so long as it is wrong. If it is wrong in the essence it is bound to be wrong in the result.

Therefore be sure it is right, then hold it up in God's name and visualize a great result. Keep the idea of prosperity, of achievement, and of attainment firmly fixed in your mind. Never entertain a failure thought. Should a negative thought of defeat come into your mind, expel it by increasing the positive affirmation. Affirm aloud, "God is now giving me success. He is now giving me attainment." The mental vision which you create and firmly hold in consciousness will be actualized if you continually affirm it in your thoughts and if you work diligently and effectively. This creative process simply stated is: visualize, prayerize, and finally actualize.

People in all walks of life who accomplish notable achievements know the value of this law in their experience.

Henry J. Kaiser told me that at one time he was building a levee along a riverbank, and there came a great storm and flood which buried all his earth-moving machinery and destroyed the work that had been done. Upon going out to observe the damage after the water receded, he found his workers standing around glumly looking at the mud and the buried machinery.

He came among them and said with a smile, "Why are you so glum?"

"Don't you see what has happened?" they asked. "Our machinery is covered with mud."

"What mud?" he asked brightly.

"What mud!" they repeated in astonishment. "Look around you. It is a sea of mud."

"Oh," he laughed, "I don't see any mud."

"But how can you say that?" they asked him.

"Because," said Mr. Kaiser, "I am looking up at a clear blue sky, and there is no mud up there. There is only sunshine, and I never saw any mud that could stand against sunshine. Soon it will be dried up, and then you will be able to move your machinery and start all over again."

How right he is. If your eyes are looking down in the mud and you feel a sense of failure, you will create defeat for yourself. Optimistic visualization combined with prayer and faith will inevitably actualize achievement.

Another friend of mine who started from the lowliest beginnings has performed some outstanding achievements. I remember him in his schooldays as an awkward, unpreposssessing, very shy country boy. But he had character and one of the keenest brains I have ever encountered. Today he is an outstanding man in his line. I asked him, "What is the secret of your success?"

"The people who have worked with me across the years and the unlimited opportunity given any boy in the United States of America," he replied.

"Yes, I know that is true, but I am sure you must have some personal technique, and I would be interested in having it," I said.

"It all lies in how you think about problems," he replied. "I attack a problem and shake it to pieces with my mind. I put all the mental power I have upon it. Second, I pray about it most sincerely. Third, I paint a mental picture of success. Fourth, I always ask myself, 'What is the right thing to do?' for," he said, "nothing will be right if it is wrong. Nothing that is wrong will ever come out right. Fifth, I give it all I've got. But let me emphasize again," he concluded, "if you're thinking defeat, change your thoughts at once. Get new and positive thoughts. That is primary and basic in overcoming difficulties and in achieving."

At this very minute, as you read this book, potential ideas are in your mind. By releasing and developing these ideas you can solve your financial problem, your business situation, you can care for yourself and your family, and attain success in your ventures. A steady inflow and practical use of these creative thoughts can remake your life and you along with it.

There was a time when I acquiesced in the silly idea that there is no relationship between faith and prosperity; that when one talked about religion he should never relate it to achievement, that it dealt only with ethics and morals or social values. But now I realize that such a viewpoint limits the power of God and the development of the individual. Religion teaches that there is a tremendous power in the universe and that this power can dwell in personality. It is a power that can blast out all defeat and lift a person above all difficult situations.

We have seen the demonstration of atomic energy. We know that astonishing and enormous energy exists in the universe. This same force of energy is resident in the human mind. Nothing on earth is greater than the human mind in potential power. The average individual is capable of much greater achievement than he has ever realized.

This is true regardless of who is reading this statement. When you actually learn to release yourself you will discover that your mind contains ideas of such creative value that you need not lack anything. By the full and proper use of your power stimulated by God power, you can make your life successful.

You can make just about anything of your life—anything you will believe or will visualize, anything you will pray for and work for. Look deeply into your mind. Amazing wonders are there.

Whatever your situation may be, you can improve it. First, quiet your mind so that inspirations may rise from its depths. Believe that God is now helping you. Visualize achievement. Organize your life on a spiritual basis so that God's principles work within you. Hold firmly in your mind a picture not of failure but of success. Do these things and creative thoughts will flow freely from your mind. This is an amazing law, one that can change anybody's life including your own. An inflow of new thoughts can remake you regardless of every difficulty you may now face, and I repeat—*every difficulty.*

In the last analysis the basic reason a person fails to live a creative and successful life is because of error within himself. He thinks wrong. He needs to correct the error in his thoughts. He needs to practice right thinking. When the 23rd Psalm says,

"He leadeth me in the paths of righteousness," it not only means the paths of goodness, but the paths of right-mindedness as well. When Isaiah says, "Let the wicked forsake his way and the unrighteous man his thoughts," (Isaiah 55:7) it not only means that a person is to depart from evil and do good, but that he is to change his thinking from wrong to right, from error to truth. The great secret of successful living is to reduce the amount of error in oneself and increase the amount of truth. An inflow of new, right, health-laden thoughts through the mind creatively affects the circumstances of life, for truth always produces right procedures and therefore right results.

Years ago I knew a young man who for a while was one of the most complete personality failures in my entire experience. He had a delightful personality, but he failed at everything. A person would employ him and be enthusiastic about him, but soon his enthusiasm would cool and it was not long until he was out of that position. This failure pattern was repeated many times. He was a failure as a person as well as an employee. He missed connections with everything. He just couldn't do anything right, and he used to ask me, "What is wrong with me that everything goes wrong?"

Still he had a lot of conceit. He was cocky and smug, and had the irritating habit of blaming everybody but himself. Something was wrong with every office with which he was connected or every organization that employed him. He blamed everybody else for his failures—never himself. He would never look inside himself. It never occurred to him that anything could be wrong with him.

One night, however, he wanted to talk with me, and as I had to make a drive of about a hundred miles to deliver a speech he drove there and back with me. On our return we stopped along about midnight at a roadside stand for a hamburger and a cup of coffee. I don't know what was in that hamburger sandwich, but since this incident I have had a new respect for hamburgers, for of a sudden he shouted, "I've got it! I've got it!"

"You've got what?" I asked in astonishment.

"I've got the answer. Now I know what's the trouble with me. It's that everything goes wrong with me because I myself am wrong."

I clapped my hand on his back and said, "Boy, at last you are on your way."

"Why, it's as clear as a crystal," he said. "I have been thinking wrong, and as a result I have created wrong outcomes."

By this time we were out in the moonlight standing alongside my car, and I said to him, "Harry, you must go one step further and ask God to make you right inwardly." I quoted this passage from the Bible, " 'Ye shall know the truth, and the truth shall make you free.' " (John 8:32) Get the truth into your mind and you will be free of your failures.

He became an enthusiastic practicing follower of Jesus Christ. Through real faith and a complete change of thoughts and personal habits, wrong thinking and wrong acting were removed from his nature. He straightened out by developing a right (or righteousness) pattern instead of an error pattern. When he was made right, then everything began to go right for him.

Following are seven practical steps for changing your mental attitudes from negative to positive, for releasing creative new thoughts, and for shifting from error patterns to truth patterns. Try them—keep on trying them. They will work.

1. For the next twenty-four hours, deliberately speak hopefully about everything, about your job, about your health, about your future. Go out of your way to talk optimistically about everything. This will be difficult, for possibly it is your habit to talk pessimistically. From this negative habit you must restrain yourself even if it requires an act of will.

2. After speaking hopefully for twenty-four hours, continue the practice for one week, then you can be permitted to be "realistic" for a day or two. You will discover that what you meant by "realistic" a week ago was actually pessimistic, but what you now mean by "realistic" is something entirely different; it is the dawning of the positive outlook. When most people say they are being "realistic" they delude themselves: they are simply being negative.

3. You must feed your mind even as you feed your body, and to make your mind healthy you must feed it nourishing, wholesome thoughts. Therefore, today start to shift your mind from negative to positive thinking. Start at the beginning of the New Testament and underscore every sentence about *Faith*. Continue doing this

until you have marked every such passage in the four books, Matthew, Mark, Luke, and John. Particularly note Mark 11, verses 22, 23, 24. They will serve as samples of the verses you are to underscore and fix deeply in your consciousness.

4. Then commit the underscored passages to memory. Commit one each day until you can recite the entire list from memory. This will take time, but remember you have consumed much more time becoming a negative thinker than this will require. Effort and time will be needed to unlearn your negative pattern.

5. Make a list of your friends to determine who is the most positive thinker among them and deliberately cultivate his society. Do not abandon your negative friends, but get closer to those with a positive point of view for a while, until you have absorbed their spirit, then you can go back among your negative friends and give them your newly acquired thought pattern without taking on their negativism.

6. Avoid argument, but whenever a negative attitude is expressed, counter with a positive and optimistic opinion.

7. Pray a great deal and always let your prayer take the form of thanksgiving on the assumption that God is giving you great and wonderful things; for if you think He is, He surely is. God will not give you any greater blessing than you can believe in. He wants to give you great things, but even He cannot make you take anything greater than you are equipped by faith to receive. "According to your faith (that is, in proportion to) be it unto you." (Matthew 9:29)

The secret of a better and more successful life is to cast out those old, dead, unhealthy thoughts. Substitute for them new, vital, dynamic faith thoughts. You can depend upon it—an inflow of new thought will remake you and your life.

# 14

# Relax for Easy Power

"EVERY NIGHT IN these United States more than six million sleeping tablets are required to put the American people to sleep."

This startling statement was made to me several years ago by a drug manufacturer at a convention of that industry where I was giving a speech. Though his assertion seemed incredible, I have been told by others who are in a position to know that the above estimate is now an understatement.

In fact, I heard another good authority assert that the American people are using about twelve million doses of sleeping tablets per day. That is enough to put every twelfth American to sleep tonight. Statistics show that the use of sleeping tablets has risen 1000 per cent in recent years. But a more recent statement is even more startling. According to the vice-president of a large drug manufacturing concern approximately seven billion one-half-grain tablets are consumed yearly, which works out at about nineteen million tablets per night.

What a pathetic situation. Sleep is a natural restorative process. One would think that any person after a day's work would be able to sleep peacefully, but apparently Americans have even lost the art of sleeping. In fact, so keyed up are they that I, a minister with ample opportunity to test the matter, must report that the American people are so nervous and high-strung that now it is almost next to impossible to put them to sleep with a sermon. It has been years since I have seen anyone sleep in church. And that is a sad situation.

A Washington official who loves to juggle figures, especially astronomical figures, told me that last year in the United States there was a total of seven and a half billion headaches. This works itself out at approximately fifty headaches per head per annum. Have you had your quota yet this year? Just how this official arrived at these figures he did not say, but shortly after our conversation I noticed a report that in a recent year the drug industry sold eleven million pounds of aspirin. Perhaps this era might appropriately be termed "The Aspirin Age," as one author has called it.

An authoritative source declares that every other hospital bed in the United States is occupied by a patient who was put there not because he encountered a germ or had an accident or developed an organic malady, but because of his inability to organize and discipline his emotions.

In a clinic five hundred patients were examined hand running and 386, or 77 per cent, were found to be ill of psychosomatic difficulties—physical illness caused largely by unhealthy mental states. Another clinic made a study of a large number of ulcer cases and reported that nearly half were made ill, not as the result of physical troubles, but because the patients worried too much or hated too much, had too much guilt, or were tension victims.

A doctor from still another clinic made the observation that in his opinion medical men, despite all extraordinary scientific developments, are now able to heal by the means of science alone less than half the maladies brought them. He declares that in many cases patients are sending back into their bodies the diseased thoughts of their minds. Prominent among these diseased thoughts are anxiety and tension.

This unhappy situation has become so serious that in our own Marble Collegiate Church, Fifth Avenue at 29th Street, New York City, we now have twelve psychiatrists on the staff under the supervision of Dr. Smiley Blanton. Why psychiatrists on the staff of a church? The answer is that psychiatry is a science. Its function is the analysis, diagnosis, and treatment of human nature according to certain well-authenticated laws and procedures.

Christianity may also be thought of as a science. It is a philosophy, a system of theology, a system of metaphysics, and a system of worship. It also works itself out in moral and ethical codes. But Christianity also has the characteristics of a science in that it is based upon a book which contains a system of techniques and formulas designed for the understanding and treatment of human nature. The laws are so precise and have been so often demonstrated when proper conditions of understanding, belief, and practice are applied that religion may be said to form an exact science.

When a person comes to our clinic the first counselor is perhaps a psychiatrist who in a kindly and careful manner studies the problem and tells the patient "why he does what he does." This is a most important fact to learn. Why, for example, have you had an inferiority complex all your life long, or why have you been haunted by fear, or, again, why do you nurse resentment? Why have you always been shy and reticent, or why do you do stupid things or make inept statements? These phenomena of your human nature do not just happen. There is a reason why you do what you do and it is an important day in your life experience when at last you discover the reason. Self-knowledge is the beginning of self-correction.

Following the self-knowledge process the psychiatrist turns the patient over to the pastor who tells him how to do what he ought to do. The pastor applies to the case, in scientific and systematic form, the therapies of prayer, faith, and love. The psychiatrist and the minister pool their knowledge and combine their therapies with the result that many people have found new life and happiness. The minister does not attempt to be a psychiatrist nor the psychiatrist a pastor. Each performs his own function but always in co-operation.

The Christianity utilized in this procedure is the undiluted teachings of Jesus Christ, Lord and Saviour of man's life. We believe in the practical, absolute workability of the teachings of Jesus. We believe that we can indeed "do all things through Christ." (Philippians 4:13) The Gospel as we work with it proves to be a literal fulfillment of the astonishing promise, "Eye hath not seen, nor ear heard, neither have entered into the heart of man, the things which God hath prepared for them that love Him." (I Corinthians 2:9) Believe (in Christ); believe in His system of thought and practice; believe and you will overcome all fear, hate, inferiority, guilt, and every form and manner of defeat. In other words, no good thing is too good to be true. You have never seen, never heard, never even imagined the things God will give to those who love Him.

In the work of the clinic one frequent problem is that of tension. This, to a very large degree, may be called the prevailing malady of the American people. But not only the American people seem to suffer from tension. The Royal Bank of Canada some time ago devoted its monthly letter to this problem under the title, "Let's Slow Down," and says in part: "This monthly letter does not set itself up as a counselor of mental and physical health, but it is attempting to break down a problem that bedevils every adult person in Canada," and, I might add, in the United States as well.

The bank letter goes on to say: "We are victims of a mounting tension; we have difficulty in relaxing. Our high-strung nervous systems are on a perpetual binge. Caught up as we are in the rush all day, every day, and far into the night, we are not living fully. We must remember what Carlyle called 'the calm supremacy of the spirit over its circumstances.' "

When a prominent banking institution calls to the attention of its customers the fact that they are failing to derive from life what they really want from it because they have become victims of tension, it is certainly time something was done about the situation.

In St. Petersburg, Florida, I actually saw a machine on the street equipped with a sign, "What is your blood pressure?" You could put a coin in a slot and get the bad news. When you can buy a reading on blood pressure like you buy gum out of a slot machine, it indicates that many people have this problem.

One of the simplest methods for reducing tension is to practice the easy-does-it attitude. Do everything more slowly, less hectically, and without pressure. My friend Branch Rickey, famous baseball man, told me that he would not use a player no matter how well he hits, fields, or runs if he is guilty of "overpressing." To be a successful big-league baseball player there must be a flow of easy power through every action and of course through the mind. The most effective way to hit a ball is by the easy method, where all the muscles are flexible and operating in correlated power. Try to kill the ball and you will slice it or maybe miss it altogether. This is true in golf, in baseball, in every sport.

From 1907 through 1919, except for one year, 1916, Ty Cobb's batting average led the American League, a record so far as I know that has never been surpassed. Ty Cobb presented the bat with which he performed his extraordinary feats to a friend of mine. I was permitted to take this bat in my hand, which I did with considerable awe. In the spirit of the game I struck a pose, as if to bat. Doubtless my batting stance was not in any sense reminiscent of the immortal slugger. In fact, my friend, who was himself at one time a minor league baseball player, chuckled and said, "Ty Cobb would never do it that way. You are too rigid, too tense. You are obviously overtrying. You would probably strike out."

It was beautiful to watch Ty Cobb. The man and the bat were one. It was a study in rhythm, and one marveled at the ease with which he got into the swing. He was a master of easy power. It is the same in all success. Analyze people who are really efficient and they always seem to do things easily, with a minimum of effort. In so doing they release maximum power.

One of my friends, a famous businessman who handles important affairs and varied interests, always seems to be at ease. He does everything efficiently and quickly but is never in a dither. He never has that anxious, frazzled look on his face which marks people who cannot handle either their time or their work. I inquired the secret of his obviously easy power.

He smiled and replied, "Oh, it isn't much of a secret. I just try to keep myself in tune with God. That's all. Every morning after breakfast," he explained, "my wife and I go into the living room for a period of quietness. One of us reads aloud some inspirational piece to get us into the mood of meditation. It may be a poem or a few paragraphs of a book. Following that we sit quietly, each praying or meditating according to his own mood and manner, then together we affirm the thought that God is filling us with strength and quiet energy. This is a definite fifteen-minute ritual and we never miss it. We couldn't get along without it. We would crack up. As a result I always seem to feel that I have more energy than I need and more power than is required." So said this efficient man who demonstrates easy power.

I know a number of men and women who practice this or similar techniques for reducing tension. It is becoming a quite general and popular procedure nowadays.

One February morning I was rushing down the long veranda of a Florida hotel with a handful of mail just in from my office in New York. I had come to Florida for a midwinter vacation, but hadn't seemed to get out of the routine of dealing with my mail the first thing in the morning. As I hurried by, headed for a couple of hours' work with the mail, a friend from Georgia who was sitting in a rocking chair with his hat partially over his eyes stopped me in my headlong rush and said in his slow and pleasant Southern drawl, "Where are you rushing for, Doctor? That's no way to do down here in the Florida sunshine. Come over here and 'set' in one of these rocking chairs and help me practice one of the greatest of the arts."

Mystified, I said, "Help you practice one of the greatest of the arts!"

"Yes," he replied, "an art that is passing out. Not many people know how to do it any more."

"Well," I asked, "please tell me what it is. I don't see you practicing any art."

"Oh, yes, I am," he said. "I am practicing the art of just sittin' in the sun. Sit here and let the sun fall on your face. It is warm-like and it smells good. It makes you feel peaceful inside. Did you ever think about the sun?" he asked. "It never hurries, never gets excited, it just works slowly and makes no noise—doesn't push any buzzers, doesn't answer any telephones, doesn't ring any bells, just goes on a-shining, and the sun does more work in the fraction of an instant than you and I could ever do in a lifetime. Think of what it does. It causes the flowers to bloom, keeps the trees growing, warms the earth, causes the fruit and vegetables to grow and the crops to ripen, lifts water to send back on the earth, and it makes you feel 'peaceful like.'

"I find that when I sit in the sun and let the sun work on me it puts some rays into me that give me energy; that is, when I take time to sit in the sun.

"So throw that mail over in the corner," he said, "and sit down here with me."

I did so, and when finally I went to my room and got at my mail I finished it in no time at all. And there was a good part of the day left for vacation activities and for more "sittin' in the sun."

Of course I know a lot of lazy people who have been sittin' in the sun all their lives and never amounted to anything. There is a difference between sittin' and relaxing, and just sittin'. But if you sit and relax and think about God and get yourself in tune with Him and open yourself to the flow of His power, then sittin' is not laziness; in fact, it is about the best way to renew power. It produces driving energy, the kind of energy *you* drive, not the kind that drives you.

The secret is to keep the mind quiet, avoiding all hectic reactions of haste, and to practice peaceful thinking. The essence of the art is to keep the tempo down; to perform your responsibilities on the basis of the most efficient conservation of energy. It is advisable to adopt one or two workable plans through the use of which you can become expert in the practice of relaxed and easy power.

One of the best such plans was suggested to me by Captain Eddie Rickenbacker. A very busy man, he manages to handle his responsibilities in a manner indicating reserves of power. I found one element of his secret quite by accident.

I was filming a program for television with him. We had been assured that the work could be done quickly, leaving him free to go to the many other matters on his daily agenda.

However, the filming was long delayed beyond the time anticipated. I noted, however, that the Captain showed no signs of agitation. He did not become nervous or anxious. He did not pace up and down, putting in frantic calls to his office. Instead, he accepted the situation gracefully. There were a couple of old rocking chairs at the studio, apparently intended for use in a set other than ours. He sat in one rocker in a very relaxed manner.

I have always been a great admirer of Eddie Rickenbacker and I commented on his lack of tension. "I know how busy you are," I said, "and I marvel at the way you sit quiet, composed, and peaceful like."

For myself, I was a bit disturbed largely because I regretted to take so much of Captain Rickenbacker's time. "How can you be so imperturbable?" I asked.

He laughingly replied, "Oh, I just practice what you preach. Come on, easy does it. Sit down here beside me."

I pulled up the other rocking chair and did a little relaxing on my own. Then I said, "Eddie, I know you have some technique to attain this impressive serenity. Tell me about it, please."

He is a modest man, but because of my persistence he gave me a formula which he says he uses frequently. I now use it myself and it is very effective. It may be described as follows:

First, collapse physically. Practice this several times a day. Let go every muscle in the body. Conceive of yourself as a jellyfish, getting your body into complete looseness. Form a mental picture of a huge burlap bag of potatoes. Then mentally cut the bag, allowing the potatoes to roll out. Think of yourself as the bag.

What is more relaxed than an empty burlap bag?

The second element in the formula is to "drain the mind." Several times each day drain the mind of all irritation, all resentment, disappointment, frustration, and annoyance. Unless you drain the mind frequently and regularly, these unhappy thoughts will accumulate until a major blasting-out process will be necessary. Keep the mind drained of all factors which would impede the flow of relaxed power.

Third, think spiritually. To think spiritually means to turn the mind at regular intervals to God. At least three times a day "lift up your eyes unto the hills." This keeps you in tune with God's harmony. It refills you with peace.

This three-point program greatly impressed me, and I have been practicing it for some months. It is an excellent method for relaxing and living on the basis of easy does it.

From my friend Dr. Z. Taylor Bercovitz, of New York City, I have learned much of the art of working relaxed. Often when under pressure, with an office full of patients and telephone calls coming in, he will suddenly stop, lean against his desk, and talk to the Lord in a manner both natural and respectful. I like the style of his prayer. He tells me that it runs something like this: "Look, Lord, I am pushing myself too hard. I am getting jittery. Here I am counseling people to practice quietness, now I must practice it. Touch me with your healing peace. Give me composure, quietness, strength, and conserve my nervous energy so that I can help these people who come to me."

He stands quietly for a minute or two. Then he thanks the Lord and proceeds with full but easy power to do his work.

Often in making sick calls about the city he finds himself in a traffic jam. He has a most interesting method of using these potentially irritating delays as opportunities to relax. Shutting off his engine, he slumps in his seat, putting his head back, closing his eyes, and has even been known to go to sleep. He says there is no reason to be concerned about going to sleep because the strident honking of horns will awaken him when traffic begins to move.

These interludes of complete relaxation in the midst of traffic last for only a minute or two, but they have energy-renewal value. It is surprising how many minutes or fractions of minutes during the day you can use to rest where you are. If even in such fractional periods you deliberately draw on God's power, you can maintain adequate relaxation. It isn't length of relaxation time that produces power; it is the quality of the experience.

I am told that Roger Babson, the famous statistician, frequently goes into an empty church and sits quietly. Perhaps he reads one or two hymns and in so doing finds rest and renewal. Dale Carnegie, under tension, goes to a church near his New York City office to spend a quarter-hour in prayerful meditation. He says he leaves his office for this purpose when busiest. This demonstrates control of time rather than being controlled by it. It also indicates watchfulness lest tension develop beyond a controllable degree.

I encountered a friend on a train from Washington to New York one night. This man is a member of Congress and he explained that he was on his way to his district to speak at a meeting of his constituents. The particular group he was about to address was hostile to him, he said, and would probably try to make things very difficult for him. Although they represented a minority in his district, he was going to face them just the same.

"They are American citizens and I am their representative. They have a right to meet with me if they want to."

"You do not seem to be much worried about it," I commented.

"No," he answered, "if I get worried about it, then I will be upset and will not handle the situation well."

"Do you have any particular method for handling such a tense situation?" I asked.

"Oh, yes," he replied, "they will be a noisy crowd. But I have my own way of meeting such situations without tension. I will breathe deeply, talk quietly, speak sincerely, be friendly and respectful, hold my temper, and trust in God to see me through.

"I have learned one important fact," the Congressman continued, "and that is in any situation be relaxed, keep calm, take a friendly attitude, have faith, do your best. Do this, and usually you can make things come out all right."

I have no doubt about the ability of this Congressman to live and work without tension, and, what is more, successfully to attain his objectives.

When we were doing some construction work at my farm in Pawling, New York, I watched a workman swinging a shovel. He was shoveling a pile of sand. It was a beautiful sight. Stripped to the waist, his lean and muscular body worked with precision and correlation. The shovel rose and fell in perfect rhythm. He would push the shovel into the pile, lean his body against it, and drive it deep into the sand. Then, in a clear, free swing it came up and the sand was deposited without a break in the motion. Again the shovel went back into the sand, again his body leaned against it, again the shovel lifted easily in a perfect arc. One almost had a feeling that he could sing in rhythm to the motion of this workman. Indeed the man did sing as he worked.

I was not surprised when the foreman told me that he is considered one of his best workmen. The foreman also spoke of him as good-humored, happy, and a pleasant person with whom to work. Here was a relaxed man who lived with joyous power, master of the art of easy does it.

Relaxation results from re-creation, and the process of re-creation should be continuous. The human being is meant to be attached to a continual flow of force that proceeds from God through the individual and back to God for renewal. When one lives in tune with this constantly re-creative process he learns the indispensable quality to relax and work on the basis of easy does it.

Now, how to master this skill. Here are ten rules for taking the hard way out of your job. Try these proven methods for working hard easily. They will help you to relax and have easy power.

1. Don't get the idea that you are Atlas carrying the world on your shoulders. Don't strain so hard. Don't take yourself so seriously.

2. Determine to like your work. Then it will become a pleasure, not drudgery. Perhaps you do not need to change your job. Change yourself and your work will seem different.

3. Plan your work—work your plan. Lack of system produces that "I'm swamped" feeling.

4. Don't try to do everything at once. That is why time is spread out. Heed that wise advice from the Bible, "This one thing I do."

5. Get a correct mental attitude, remembering that ease or difficulty in your work depends upon how you think about it. Think it's hard and you make it hard. Think it's easy and it tends to become easy.

6. Become efficient in your work. "Knowledge is power" (over your job). It is always easier to do a thing right.

7. Practice being relaxed. Easy always does it. Don't press or tug. Take it in your stride.

8. Discipline yourself not to put off until tomorrow what you can do today. Accumulation of undone jobs makes your work harder. Keep your work up to schedule.

9. Pray about your work. You will get relaxed efficiency by so doing.

10. Take on the "unseen partner." It is surprising the load He will take off you. God is as much at home in offices, factories, stores, kitchens, as in churches. He knows more about your job than you do. His help will make your work easy.

# 15

# *How to Get People to Like You*

WE MIGHT AS well admit it, we want people to like us.

You may hear someone say, "I don't care whether people like me or not." But whenever you hear anyone say that, just put it down as a fact that he is not really telling the truth.

The psychologist, William James, said, "One of the deepest drives of human nature is the desire to be appreciated." The longing to be liked, to be held in esteem, to be a sought-after person, is fundamental in us.

A poll was taken among some high-school students on the question, "What do you most desire?" By overwhelming majority the students voted that they wanted to be popular. The same urge is in older people as well. Indeed it is doubtful if anybody ever outlives the desire to be well thought of, to be highly regarded, or to have the affection of his associates.

To be master of the art of popularity, be artless. Strive deliberately after popularity and the chances are you will never attain it. But become one of those rare personalities about whom people say, "He certainly has something," and you can be certain you are on the way to having people like you.

I must warn you, however, that despite your attainments in popularity you will never get everybody to like you. There is a curious quirk in human nature whereby some people just naturally won't like you. A quatrain inscribed on a wall at Oxford says:

"I do not love thee, Dr. Fell,  
The reason why I cannot tell;  
But this alone I know full well,  
I do not love thee, Dr. Fell."

That verse is very subtle. The author did not like Dr. Fell. He didn't know why but he just knew he didn't like him. It was most likely an unreasonable dislike, for undoubtedly Dr. Fell was a very nice person. Perhaps if the author had known him better he would have liked him, but poor Dr. Fell never did become popular with the author of those lines. It may have been due simply to a lack of *rapprochement*, that baffling mechanism by which we either do or do not "click" with certain people.

Even the Bible recognizes this unhappy fact about human nature, for it says, "If it be possible, as much as lieth in you, live peaceably with all men." (Romans 12:18) The Bible is a very realistic book and it knows people, their infinite possibilities as well as their imperfections. The Bible advised the disciples that if they went into a village and after trying their best to get along with people still couldn't do so, they were to shake off the very dust of the village from their feet—"And whosoever will not receive you, when ye go out of that city, shake off the very dust from your feet for a testimony against them." (Luke 9:5) This is all by way of saying that you will be wise if you do not let it too seriously affect you if you do not achieve perfect popularity with everyone.

However, there are certain formulas and procedures which, if followed faithfully, can make you a person whom other people like. You can enjoy satisfactory personal relationships even if you are a "difficult" person or by nature shy and retiring, even unsocial. You can make of yourself one who enjoys easy, normal, natural, and pleasing relationships with others.

I cannot urge you too strongly to consider the importance of this subject and to give time and attention to its mastery, for you will never be fully happy or successful until you do. Failure in this capacity will adversely affect you psychologically. To be liked is of profounder importance than mere ego satisfaction. As necessary as that is to your success in life, normal and satisfactory personal relations are even more important.

The feeling of not being wanted or needed is one of the most devastating of all human reactions. To the degree to which you are sought after or needed by other people will you become a fully-released person. The "lone wolf," the isolated personality, the retiring individual, these people suffer a misery which is difficult to describe. In self-defense they retire ever further within themselves. Their ingrowing, introverted nature is denied the normal development which the outgoing, self-giving person experiences. Unless the personality is drawn out of itself and can be of value to someone, it may sicken and die. The feeling of not being wanted or needed produces frustration, aging, illness. If you have a feeling of uselessness, if nobody needs or wants you, you really ought to do something about it. It is not only a pathetic way to live but is serious psychologically. Those who deal with the problems of human nature constantly encounter this problem and its unfortunate results.

For example, at a Rotary Club luncheon in a certain city two physicians were at my table: one an elderly man who had been retired for several years, the other the most popular young doctor in town. The young doctor, looking frazzled, dashed in late and slumped down with a weary sigh. "If only the telephone would stop ringing," he complained. "I can't get anywhere because people call me all the time. I wish I could put a silencer on that telephone."

The old doctor spoke up quietly, "I know how you feel, Jim," he said. "I used to feel that way myself, but be thankful the telephone does ring. Be glad people want and need you." Then he added pathetically, "Nobody ever calls me any more. I would like to hear the telephone ring again. Nobody wants me and nobody needs me. I'm a has-been."

All of us at the table who sometimes feel a bit worn by numerous activities did a lot of thinking as we listened to the old doctor.

A middle-aged woman complained to me that she didn't feel well. She was dissatisfied and unhappy. "My husband is dead, the children are grown, and there is no place for me any more. People treat me kindly, but they are indifferent. Everyone has his own interest and nobody needs me—nobody wants me. I wonder, could that be a reason I do not feel well?" she asked. Indeed that could very likely be an important reason.

In a business office the founder of the firm just past seventy was walking restlessly and aimlessly around. He talked with me while his son, present head of the business, whom I had come to see, was on the telephone. The older man said gloomily, "Why don't you write a book on how to retire? That is what I need to know. I thought it was going to be wonderful to give up the burdens of the job," he continued, "but now I find that nobody is interested in anything I say. I used to think I was a popular fellow, but now when I come down here and sit around the office everyone says hello, then they forget me. I might as well stay away altogether for all they care. My son is running the business and he is doing a good job of it, but," he concluded pathetically, "I'd like to think they needed me a little bit."

These people are suffering one of the most pathetic and unhappy experiences in this life. Their basic desire is to be sought after and this desire is not being satisfied. They want people to appreciate them. The personality longs for esteem. But it isn't only in retirement that this situation develops.

A girl of twenty-one told me that she had been unwanted ever since birth. Someone had given her the notion she was an unwanted child. This serious idea had sunk into her subconscious, giving her a profound sense of inferiority and self-depreciation. It made her shy and backward, causing her to retreat into herself. She became lonely and unhappy and was, in fact, an underdeveloped personality. The cure for her condition was to revamp her life spiritually, especially her thinking, which process in time made her a well-liked person by setting her personality free of herself.

Countless other people, not particularly victims of deep, unconscious psychological conflicts, have never mastered the knack of being popular. They try hard enough. They even go to extremes, often acting in a manner they do not really enjoy, but which they employ only because of their intense desire to have people like them. Everywhere today we see people putting on an act because of their inordinate desire for popularity in the superficial sense in which the word is often used in modern society.

The fact is that popularity can be attained by a few simple, natural, normal, and easily mastered techniques. Practice them diligently and you can become a well-liked person.

First, become a comfortable person, that is, one with whom people can associate without a sense of strain. Of some persons it is said, "You can never quite get next to him." There is always a barrier that you can't get over. A comfortable person is easy-going and natural. He has a pleasant, kindly, genial way about him. Being with him is not unlike wearing an old hat or an old pair of shoes, or an easy old coat. A stiff, reserved, unresponsive individual never meshes into the group. He is always just a bit out of it. You never quite know how to take him or how he will react. You just aren't easy-like with him.

Some young people were talking about a seventeen-year-old boy whom they liked very much. Of him they said, "He is good company. He is a good sport. He is easy to be with." It is very important to cultivate the quality of being natural. Usually that sort of individual is large-souled. Little people who are much concerned about how you treat them, who are jealous of their place or position, who meticulously stand on their prerogatives, are stiff and easily offended.

A man who is an outstanding example of these truths is James A. Farley, former Postmaster General of the United States.

I met Mr. Farley for the first time a number of years ago. Months later I met him in a large crowd of people and he called me by name. Being human, I never forgot that, and it is one reason I have always liked Mr. Farley.

An interesting incident illustrates the secret of this man who is an expert in how to get people to like him. I was to speak in Philadelphia at a book-and-author luncheon along with Mr. Farley and two other authors. I did not actually witness the scene I am about to describe, as I was late in arriving, but my publisher did. The speakers at this luncheon were walking along the hotel corridor together when they passed a colored maid standing by a cart loaded with sheets, towels, and other equipment with which she was servicing the rooms. She was paying no attention to this group of people as they turned aside to avoid her cart. Mr. Farley walked up to her, put out his hand, and said, "Hello, there. How are you? I'm Jim Farley. What's your name? Glad to see you."

My publisher looked back at her as the group passed down the hall. The girl's mouth was wide with astonishment and her face broke into a beautiful smile. It was an excellent example of how an unegotistical, comfortable, outgoing person is successful in personal relationships.

A university psychology department conducted an analysis of the personality traits by which people are liked or disliked. One hundred traits were scientifically analyzed and it was reported that one must have forty-six favorable traits in order to be liked. It is rather discouraging to realize that you must have so large a number of characteristics to be popular.

Christianity, however, teaches that one basic trait will go far toward getting people to like you. That trait is a sincere and forthright interest in and love for people. Perhaps if you cultivate this basic trait, other traits will naturally develop.

If you are not the comfortable type of person, I suggest that you make study of your personality with a view toward eliminating conscious and unconscious elements of strain which may exist. Do not assume that the reason other people do not like you is because of something wrong with them. Assume, instead, that the trouble is within yourself and determine to find and eliminate it. This will require scrupulous honesty and it may also involve the assistance of personality experts. The so-called "scratchy" elements in your personality may be qualities which you have taken on through the years. Perhaps they have been assumed defensively, or they may be the result of attitudes developed in your younger days. Regardless of origin they can be eliminated by a scientific study of yourself and by your recognition of the necessity for change followed by a process of personality rehabilitation.

A man came to our clinic at the church seeking help in the problem of personal relationships. About thirty-five years of age, he was the type of person whom you would certainly look at twice if not three times. He was splendidly proportioned and impressive. Superficially regarding him it was surprising that people should not like him. But he proceeded to outline an unhappy and continuous set of circumstances and instances to illustrate his dismal failure in human relations.

"I do my best," he explained. "I have tried to put into practice the rules I have been taught about getting along with people, but get nowhere with the effort. People just don't like me and what is more I am aware of it."

After talking with him it was not difficult to understand the trouble. There was in his manner of speech a persistently critical attitude thinly veiled but nonetheless apparent. He had an unattractive manner of pursing his lips which indicated a kind of primness or reproof for everybody, as if he felt just a bit superior and disdainful toward other people. In fact there was about him a noticeable attitude of superiority. He was very rigid, with no flexibility of personality.

"Isn't there some way to change myself so that people will like me?" he demanded. "Isn't there some way I can stop unconsciously rubbing people the wrong way?"

The young man was decidedly self-centered and egotistical. The person he really liked was himself. Every statement, every attitude was unconsciously measured in terms of how it reacted on himself. We had to teach him to love other people and to forget himself, which was of course a complete reversal of his development. It was vital, however, to the solution of his problem. I found that this young man was irritable with people and he picked on them in his own mind, though no outward conflicts with other persons developed. Inwardly he was trying to make everybody over to suit himself. Unconsciously people realized this, though perhaps they did not define the trouble. Barriers were erected in their minds toward him.

Since he was being unpleasant to people in his thoughts, it followed that he was less than warm in his personal attitudes. He was polite enough and managed not to be boorish and unpleasant, but people unconsciously felt coolness in him, so gave him the "brush-off" of which he complained. The reason they did so was because in his mind he had "brushed them off." He liked himself too well, and to build up his self-esteem he disliked others. He was suffering from self-love, a chief cure for which is the practice of love for others.

He was bewildered and baffled when we outlined his difficulty. But he was sincere and meant business. He practiced the suggested techniques for developing love of others in place of self-love. It required some fundamental changes to accomplish this, but he succeeded in doing so.

One method suggested was that at night before retiring he make a list of persons he had met during the day, as, for example, the bus driver or the newsboy. He was to picture mentally each person whose name appeared on the list, and as he brought each face up before him he was to think a kindly thought about that person. Then he was to pray for each one. He was to pray around his little world. Each of us has his own world, people with whom we do business or are associated in one way or another.

For example, the first person outside the family whom this

young man saw in the morning was the elevator man in his apartment house. He had not been in the habit of saying anything to him beyond a perfunctory and growled good morning. Now he took the time to have a little chat with the elevator man. He asked him about his family and about his interests. He found that the elevator operator had an interesting point of view and some experiences which were quite fascinating. He began to see new values in a person who to him previously had been a mechanical robot, who ran the elevator up and down to his floor. He actually began to like the elevator operator and in turn the elevator man, who had formed a pretty accurate opinion of the young man, began to revise his views. They established a friendly relationship. So the process went from person to person.

One day the young man said to me, "I have found that the world is filled with interesting people and I never realized it before."

When he made that observation he proved that he was losing himself, and when he did that, as the Bible so wisely tells us, he found himself. In losing himself he found himself and lots of new friends besides. People learned to like him.

Learning to pray for people was important in his rehabilitation, for when you pray for anyone you tend to modify your personal attitude toward him. You lift the relationship thereby to a higher level. The best in the other person begins to flow out toward you as your best flows toward him. In the meeting of the best in each a higher unity of understanding is established.

Essentially, getting people to like you is merely the other side of liking them. One of the most popular men who lived in the United States within the lifetime of most of us was the late Will Rogers. One of the most characteristic statements he ever made was, "I never met a man I didn't like." That may have been a slight exaggeration, but I am sure Will Rogers did not regard it as such. That is the way he felt about people, and as a result people opened up to him like flowers to the sun.

Sometimes the weak objection is offered that it is difficult to like some people. Granted, some people are by nature more likable than others, nevertheless a serious attempt to know any individual will reveal qualities within him that are admirable, even lovable.

A man had the problem of conquering feelings of irritation

toward persons with whom he was associated. For some people he had a very profound dislike. They irritated him intensely, but he conquered these feelings simply by making an exhaustive list of everything he could possibly admire about each person who annoyed him. Daily he attempted to add to this list. He was surprised to discover that people whom he thought he did not like at all proved to have many pleasing qualities. In fact, he was at a loss to understand how he ever disliked them after becoming conscious of their attractive qualities. Of course, while he was making these discoveries about them, they, in turn, were finding new and likable qualities in him.

If you have gone through life up to this point without having established satisfactory human relationships, do not assume that you cannot change, but it will be necessary to take very definite steps toward solving the problem. You can change and become a popular person, well liked and esteemed, if you are willing to make the effort. May I remind you as I remind myself that one of the greatest tragedies of the average person is the tendency to spend our whole lives perfecting our faults? We develop a fault and we nurse it and cultivate it, and never change it. Like a needle caught in the groove of a defective record on a victrola, it plays the same old tune over and over again. You must lift the needle out of the groove, then you will have disharmony no longer, but harmony. Don't spend more of your life perfecting faults in human relations. Spend the rest of your life perfecting your great capacities for friendliness, for personal relations are vitally important to successful living.

Still another important factor in getting people to like you is to practice building up the ego of other persons. The ego, being the essence of our personalities, is sacred to us. There is in every person a normal desire for a feeling of self-importance. If I deflate your ego and therefore your self-importance, though you may laugh it off, I have deeply wounded you. In fact, I have shown disrespect for you, and while you may exercise charity toward me, even so, unless you are finely developed spiritually, you are not going to like me very well.

On the other hand, if I elevate your self-respect and contribute to your feeling of personal worth, I am showing high esteem for your ego. I have helped you to be your best self and therefore you appreciate what I have done. You are grateful to me. You like me for it.

The deflation of another person's ego may be mildly done perhaps, but one can never evaluate how deep the depreciation goes from even a remark or an attitude that is not meant to be unkind. Here is the way in which ego is often deflated.

The next time you are in a group and someone tells a joke and everybody laughs with appreciation and pleasure except yourself, when the laughter has died down say patronizingly, "Well, that is a pretty good joke all right. I saw it in a magazine last month."

Of course it will make you feel quite important to let others know of your superior knowledge, but how does it make the man feel who told the joke? You have robbed him of the satisfaction of having told a good story. You have crowded him out of his brief moment in the limelight and usurped attention to yourself. In fact you have taken the wind out of his sails and left him flat and deflated. He enjoyed his momentary little prominence, but you took it away from him. Nobody in that group is going to like you for what you did, and certainly not the man whose story you spoiled. Whether you like the joke or not, let the storyteller and the others enjoy it. Remember he may be a little bit embarrassed and shy. It would have done him good to have received a response. Don't deflate people. Build them up and they will love you for it.

While writing this chapter I enjoyed a visit with an old and dear friend, Dr. John W. Hoffman, one-time president of Ohio Wesleyan University. As I sat with him in Pasadena, I realized once again how much this great personality has always meant to me. Many years ago, on the night before my graduation from college, we had a banquet at our fraternity house at which he was present and made a talk. After dinner he asked me to walk with him to the president's house.

It was a beautiful moonlit night in June. All the way up the hill he talked to me about life and its opportunities and told me what a thrill awaited me as I entered the outside world. As we stood in front of his house he put his hand on my shoulder and said, "Norman, I have always liked you. I believe in you. You have great possibilities. I shall always be proud of you. You have got it in you." Of course he overestimated me, but that is infinitely better than to depreciate a person.

It being June and the night before graduation and excitement being in my heart, my sentiments were pretty close to the surface, and I said good night to him through a mist of tears which I tried to conceal. It has been many years since then, but I never forgot what he said nor how he said it on that June night long ago. I have loved him all across the years.

I discovered that he made similar statements to many other boys and girls long since become men and women and they, too, love him because he respected their personalities and was constantly building them up. Through the years he would write to me and to others congratulating us on some little thing that we had done, and a word of approval from him meant much. Little wonder this honored guide of youth has the affection and devotion of thousands of people whose lives he touched.

Whomever you help to build up and become a better, stronger, finer person will give you his undying devotion. Build up as many people as you can. Do it unselfishly. Do it because you like them and because you see possibilities in them. Do this and you will never lack for friends. You will always be well thought of. Build people up and love them genuinely. Do them good and their esteem and affection will flow back toward you.

The basic principles of getting people to like you need no prolonged and labored emphasis, for they are very simple and easily illustrate their own truth. However, I list ten practical rules for getting the esteem of others. The soundness of these principles has been demonstrated innumerable times. Practice them until you become expert at them and people will like you.

1. Learn to remember names. Inefficiency at this point may indicate that your interest is not sufficiently outgoing. A man's name is very important to him.

2. Be a comfortable person so there is no strain in being with you—be an old-shoe, old-hat kind of individual. Be homey.

3. Acquire the quality of relaxed easy-goingness so that things do not ruffle you.

4. Don't be egotistical. Guard against giving the impression that you know it all. Be natural and normally humble.

5. Cultivate the quality of being interesting so that people will

want to be with you and get something of stimulating value from their association with you.

6. Study to get the "scratchy" elements out of your personality, even those of which you may be unconscious.

7. Sincerely attempt to heal, on an honest Christian basis, every misunderstanding you have had or now have. Drain off your grievances.

8. Practice liking people until you learn to do so genuinely. Remember what Will Rogers said, "I never met a man I didn't like." Try to be that way.

9. Never miss an opportunity to say a word of congratulation upon anyone's achievement, or express sympathy in sorrow or disappointment.

10. Get a deep spiritual experience so that you have something to give people that will help them to be stronger and meet life more effectively. Give strength to people and they will give affection to you.

# 16

# *Prescription for Heartache*

"PLEASE GIVE ME a prescription for heartache."

This curious and rather pathetic request was made by a man who had been informed by his doctor that the feelings of disability of which he complained were not of a physical nature. His trouble lay in an inability to rise above sorrow. He was suffering from "an ache in his personality" as a result of grief.

His doctor advised him to secure spiritual consultation and treatment. So continuing to use the terminology of medicine, he repeated his question, "Is there a spiritual prescription which will reduce my constant inner suffering? I realize that sorrow comes to everyone and I should be able to meet it the same as others. I have tried my best but find no peace." Again he asked with a sad, slow smile, "Give me a prescription for heartache."

There is indeed a "prescription" for heartache. One element in the prescription is physical activity. The sufferer must avoid the temptation to sit and brood. A sensible program which substitutes physical activity for such fruitless brooding reduces the strain on the area of the mind where we reflect, philosophize, and suffer mental pain. Muscular activity utilizes another part of the brain and therefore shifts the strain and gives relief.

An old country lawyer who had a sound philosophy and much wisdom told a sorrowing woman that the best medicine for a broken heart is "to take a scrubbing brush and get down on your knees and go to work. The best medicine for a man," he declared, "is to get an ax and chop wood until physically tired." While this is not guaranteed to be a complete cure for heartache, yet it does tend to mitigate such suffering.

Whatever the character of your heartache, one of the first steps is to resolve to escape from any defeatist situation which may have been created around yourself, even though it is difficult to do so, and return once again to the normal course of your life. Get back into the main stream of life's activities. Take up your old associations. Form new ones. Get busy walking, riding, swimming, playing—get the blood to coursing through your system. Lose yourself in some worth-while project. Fill your days with creative activity and emphasize the physical aspect of activity. Employ healthy mind-relieving busyness, but be sure that it is of a worth-while and constructive nature. Superficial escapism through feverish activity merely deadens pain temporarily and does not heal, as, for example, parties and drinking.

An excellent and normal release from heartache is to give way to grief. There is a foolish point of view current today that one should not show grief, that it is not proper to cry or express oneself through the natural mechanism of tears and sobbing. This is a denial of the law of nature. It is natural to cry when pain or sorrow comes. It is a relief mechanism provided in the body by Almighty God and should be used.

To restrain grief, to inhibit it, to bottle it up, is to fail to use one of God's means for eliminating the pressure of sorrow. Like every other function of the human body and nervous system, this must be controlled, but it should not be denied altogether. A good cry by either man or woman is a release from heartache. I should warn, however, that this mechanism should not be used unduly nor allowed to become a habitual process. Should that happen, it partakes of the nature of abnormal grief and could become a psychosis. Unrestraint of any kind should not be allowed.

I receive many letters from people whose loved ones have died. They tell me that it is very difficult for them to go to the same places they were in the habit of frequenting together or to be with the same people with whom they associated as a couple or as a family. Therefore they avoid the old-time places and friends.

I regard this as a serious mistake. A secret of curing heartache is to be as normal and natural as possible. This does not imply disloyalty or indifference. This policy is important in avoiding a state of abnormal grief. Normal sorrow is a natural process and its normality is evidenced by the ability of the individual to return to his usual pursuits and responsibilities and continue therein as formerly.

The deeper remedy for heartache, of course, is the curative comfort supplied by trust in God. Inevitably the basic prescription for heartache is to turn to God in an attitude of faith and empty the mind and heart to Him. Perseverance in the act of spiritual self-emptying will finally bring healing to the broken heart. This generation, which has suffered fully as much if not more heartache than people in preceding eras, needs to relearn that which the wisest men of all time have known, namely, that there is no healing of the pain suffered by humanity except through the benign ministrations of faith.

One of the greatest souls of the ages was Brother Lawrence, who said, "If in this life we would know the serene peace of Paradise, we must school ourselves in familiar, humble, and loving converse with God." It is not advisable to attempt to carry the burden of sorrow and mental pain without Divine help, for its weight is more than the personality can bear. The simplest and most effective of all prescriptions for heartache then is to practice the presence of God. This will soothe the ache in your heart and ultimately heal the wound. Men and women who have experienced great tragedy tell us that this prescription is effective.

Another profoundly curative element in the prescription for heartache is to gain a sound and satisfying philosophy of life and death and deathlessness. For my part, when I gained the unshakable belief that there is no death, that all life is indivisible, that the here and hereafter are one, that time and eternity are inseparable, that this is one unobstructed universe, then I found the most satisfying and convincing philosophy of my entire life.

These convictions are based upon sound foundations, the Bible for one. I believe that the Bible gives us a very subtle, and as will be proved ultimately, a scientific series of insights into the great question, "What happens when a man leaves this world?" Also the Bible very wisely tells us that we know these truths by faith. Henri Bergson, the philosopher, says that the surest way into truth is by perception, by intuition, by reasoning to a certain point, then by taking a "mortal leap," and by intuition attaining the truth. You come to some glorious moment where you simply "know." That is the way it happened to me.

I am absolutely, wholeheartedly, and thoroughly convinced of the truth of which I write and have no doubt of it, even to an infinitesimal degree. I arrived at this positive faith gradually, yet there came one moment when I knew.

This philosophy will not ward off the sorrow which comes when a loved one dies and physical, earthly separation ensues. But it will lift and dissipate grief. It will fill your mind with a deep understanding of the meaning of this inevitable circumstance. And it will give you a deep assurance that you have not lost your loved one. Live on this faith and you will be at peace and the ache will leave your heart.

Take into your mind and heart one of the most marvelous texts in the Holy Bible—"Eye hath not seen, nor ear heard, neither have entered into the heart of man, the things which God hath prepared for them that love Him." (I Corinthians 2:9)

This means that you have never seen, no matter what you have seen, however wonderful it is, you have never seen anything to compare with the marvelous things that God has prepared for those who love Him and who put their trust in Him. Moreover, it says that you have never heard anything to compare with the astonishing marvels that God has laid up for those who follow His teachings and live according to His spirit. Not only have you never seen nor ever heard but you have never even dimly imagined what He is going to do for you. This sentence goes all out in promising comfort and immortality and reunion and every good thing to those who center their lives in God.

After many years of reading the Bible and being intimately connected with all the phases of the lives of hundreds of people, I wish to state unequivocally that I have found this Biblical promise to be absolutely true. It applies even to this world. People who really practice living on a Christlike basis have the most incredible things happen to them.

This passage also relates to the state of existence of those now living on the other side and our relationship, while we live, to those who have preceded us across that barrier which we call death. I use the word "barrier" somewhat apologetically. We have always thought of death as a barrier with a concept of a separatist nature.

Scientists working today in the field of parapsychology and extra-sensory perception and experimenting in precognition, telepathy, clairvoyance (all of which were formerly considered paraphernalia of the cranks, but which are now of sound, scientific usage in the laboratories), are expressing themselves as believing that the soul survives the barrier of time and space. In effect, we are on the edge of one of the greatest scientific discoveries in history which will substantiate, on a laboratory-exploratory basis, the existence of the soul and its deathlessness.

For many years I have been accumulating a series of incidents, the validity of which I accept and which bear out the conviction that we live in a dynamic universe where life, not death, is the basic principle. I have confidence in the people who have described the following experiences and am convinced that they indicate a world impinged upon or intertwined with our own through the meshes of which human spirits, on both sides of death, live in unbroken fellowship. The conditions of life on the other side, as we know them in mortality, are modified. Undoubtedly those who have crossed to the other side dwell in a higher medium than we do and their understanding is amplified beyond ours, yet all the facts point to the continued existence of our loved ones and the further fact that they are not far away, and still another fact implied, but no less real, that we shall be reunited with them. Meanwhile, we continue in fellowship with those who dwell in the spirit world.

William James, one of America's greatest scholars, after a lifetime of study said he was satisfied that the human brain is only a medium for the soul's existence and that the mind as now constituted will be exchanged at last for a brain that will allow the owner to reach out into untapped areas of understanding. As our spiritual being is amplified here on earth and as we grow in age and experience we become more conscious of this vaster world all around us, and when we die it is only to enter into an enlarged capacity.

Euripides, one of the greatest thinkers of antiquity, was convinced that the next life would be of infinitely greater magnitude. Socrates shared the same concept. One of the most comforting statements ever made was his remark, "No evil can befall a good man in this life or in the next."

Natalie Kalmus, scientific expert in technicolor, tells about the death of her sister. The following account given by this scientifically trained woman appeared in the inspirational magazine *Guideposts*.

Natalie Kalmus quotes her dying sister as saying, " 'Natalie, promise me that you won't let them give me any drugs. I realize that they are trying to help relieve my pain, but I want to be fully aware of every sensation. I am convinced that death will be a beautiful experience.'

"I promised. Alone, later, I wept, thinking of her courage. Then as I tossed in bed on through the night, I realized that what I thought to be a calamity my sister intended to be a triumph.

"Ten days later the final hour drew near. I had been at her bedside for hours. We had talked about many things, and always I marveled at her quiet, sincere confidence in eternal life. Not once did the physical torture overcome her spiritual strength. This was something that the doctors simply hadn't taken into account.

" 'Dear kind God, keep my mind clear and give me peace,' she had murmured over and over again during those last days.

"We had talked so long that I noticed she was drifting off to sleep. I left her quietly with the nurse and retired to get some rest. A few minutes later I heard my sister's voice calling for me. Quickly I returned to her room. She was dying.

"I sat on her bed and took her hand. It was on fire. Then she seemed to rise up in bed almost to a sitting position.

" 'Natalie,' she said, 'there are so many of them. There's Fred . . . and Ruth . . . what's she doing here? Oh, I know!'

"An electric shock went through me. She had said Ruth. Ruth was her cousin who had died suddenly the week before. But Eleanor had not been told of Ruth's sudden death.

"Chill after chill shot up and down my spine. I felt on the verge of some powerful, almost frightening knowledge. She had murmured Ruth's name.

"Her voice was surprisingly clear. 'It's so confusing. So many of them!' Suddenly her arms stretched out as happily as when she had welcomed me! 'I'm going up,' she said.

"Then she dropped her arms around my neck—and relaxed in my arms. The will of her spirit had turned final agony into rapture.

"As I laid her head back on the pillow, there was a warm, peaceful smile on her face. Her golden-brown hair lay carelessly on the pillow. I took a white flower from the vase and placed it in her hair. With her petite, trim figure, her wavy hair, the white flower, and the soft smile, she looked once more—and permanently—just like a schoolgirl."

The mention of her cousin Ruth by the dying girl and the evident fact that she saw her clearly is a phenomenon that recurs again and again in the incidents which have come to my attention. So repetitive is this phenomenon and so similar are the characteristics of this experience as described by many that it amounts to a substantial evidence that the people whose names are called, whose faces are seen, are actually present.

Where are they? What is their condition? What sort of body have they? These are questions that are difficult. The idea of a different dimension is probably the most tenable, or it may be more accurate to believe that they live in a different frequency cycle.

It is impossible to see through the blades of an electric fan when it is in a stationary position. At high speed, however, the blades appear to be transparent. In the higher frequency or the state in which our loved ones dwell, the impenetrable qualities of the universe may open to the gaze of one passing into the mysteries. In deep moments of our own lives it is entirely possible that we enter to a degree at least into that higher frequency. In one of the most beautiful lines in English literature, Robert Ingersoll suggests this great truth, "In the night of death, hope sees a star and listening love can hear the rustle of a wing."

A famous neurologist tells of a man who was at death's door. The dying man looked up at the physician sitting beside his bed and began to call off names which the physician wrote down. The doctor was personally unfamiliar with any name mentioned. Later the physician asked the man's daughter, "Who are these people? Your father spoke of them as if he saw them."

"They are all relatives," she said, "who have been dead a long time."

The physician said he believes his patient did see them.

Friends of mine, Mr. and Mrs. William Sage, lived in New Jersey and I was often in their home. Mr. Sage, whom his wife called Will, died first. A few years later, when Mrs. Sage was on her deathbed, the most surprised look passed across her face, and it lighted up in a wonderful smile as she said, "Why, it is Will." That she saw him those about her bed had no doubt whatsoever.

Arthur Godfrey, famous radio personality, tells of being asleep in his bunk on a destroyer in World War I. Suddenly his father stood beside him. He put out his hand, smiled, and said, "So long, son," and Godfrey answered, "So long, Dad."

Later he was awakened and given a cablegram telling him of the death of his father. The time of his passing was given, and it was the precise period during which Godfrey in his sleep "saw" his father.

Mary Margaret McBride, also a famous radio personality, was overwhelmed with grief upon the death of her mother. They had been very close to each other. She awakened one night and sat on the edge of her bed. Suddenly she had the feeling, to use her own words, that "Mama was with me." She did not see her mother nor hear her speak, but from that time on, "I knew that my mother isn't dead—that she is near by."

The late Rufus Jones, one of the most famous spiritual leaders of our time, tells about his son Lowell who died at twelve years of age. He was the apple of his father's eye. The boy took sick when Dr. Jones was on the ocean bound for Europe. The night before entering Liverpool, while lying in his bunk, he experienced an indefinable, inexplicable feeling of sadness. Then he said that he seemed to be enveloped in the arms of God. A great feeling of peace and a sense of a profound possession of his son came to him.

Upon landing in Liverpool he was advised that his son had died, his death occurring at the precise hour when Dr. Jones had felt a sense of God's presence and the everlasting nearness of his son.

A member of my church, Mrs. Bryson Kalt, tells of an aunt whose husband and three children were burned to death when their house was destroyed by fire. The aunt was badly burned but lived for three years. When finally she lay dying a radiance suddenly came over her face. "It is all so beautiful," she said. "They are coming to meet me. Fluff up my pillows and let me go to sleep."

Mr. H. B. Clarke, an old friend of mine, was for many years a construction engineer, his work taking him into all parts of the world. He was of a scientific turn of mind, a quite restrained, factual, unemotional type of man. I was called one night by his physician, who said that he did not expect him to live but a few hours. His heart action was slow and the blood pressure was extraordinarily low. There was no reflex action at all. The doctor gave no hope.

I began to pray for him, as did others. The next day his eyes opened and after a few days he recovered his speech. His heart action and blood pressure returned to normal. After he recovered strength he said, "At some time during my illness something very peculiar happened to me. I cannot explain it. It seemed that I was a long distance away. I was in the most beautiful and attractive place I have ever seen. There were lights all about me, beautiful lights. I saw faces dimly revealed, kind faces they were, and I felt very peaceful and happy. In fact, I have never felt happier in my life.

"Then the thought came to me, 'I must be dying.' Then it occurred to me, 'Perhaps I have died.' Then I almost laughed out loud, and asked myself, 'Why have I been afraid of death all my life? There is nothing to be afraid of in this.' "

"How did you feel about it?" I asked. "Did you want to come back to life? Did you want to live, for you were not dead, although the doctor felt that you were very close to death. Did you want to live?"

He smiled and said, "It did not make the slightest difference. If anything, I think I would have preferred to stay in that beautiful place."

Hallucination, a dream, a vision—I do not believe so. I have spent too many years talking to people who have come to the edge of "something" and had a look across, who unanimously have reported beauty, light, and peace, to have any doubt in my own mind.

The New Testament teaches the indestructibility of life in a most interesting and simple manner. It describes Jesus after His crucifixion in a series of appearances, disappearances, and reappearances. Some saw Him and then He vanished out of their sight. Then others saw Him and again He vanished. It is as if to say, "You see me and then you do not see me." This indicates that He is trying to tell us that when we do not see Him, it does not mean He is not there. Out of sight does not mean out of life. Occasional mystical appearances which some experience indicate the same truth, that He is near by. Did He not say, ". . . because I live, ye shall live also." (John 14:19) In other words, our loved ones who have died in this faith are also near by and occasionally draw near to comfort us.

A boy serving in Korea wrote to his mother, saying, "The strangest things happen to me. Once in a while at night, when I am afraid, Daddy seems to be with me." Daddy had been dead for ten years. Then the boy wistfully asks his mother, "Do you think that Daddy can actually be with me here on these Korean battlefields?" The answer is, "Why not?" How can we be citizens of a scientific generation and not believe that this could be true? Again and again proofs are offered that this is a dynamic universe, surcharged with mystic, electric, electronic, atomic forces, and all are so wonderful that we have never yet comprehended them. This universe is a great spiritual sounding house, alive and vital.

Albert E. Cliff, well-known Canadian writer, tells of the death of his father. The dying man had sunk into a coma and it was thought he was gone. Then a momentary resurgence of life occurred. His eyes flickered open. On the wall was one of those old-time mottoes which said, "I Know That My Redeemer Liveth." The dying man opened his eyes, looked at that motto, and said, "I *do know* that my Redeemer liveth, for they are all here around me—mother, father, brothers, and sisters." Long gone from this earth were they all, but evidently he saw them. Who is to gainsay?

The late Mrs. Thomas A. Edison told me that when her famous husband was dying he whispered to his physician, "It is beautiful over there." Edison was the world's greatest scientist. All his life he had worked with phenomena. He was of a factual cast of mind. He never reported anything as a fact until he saw it work. He would never have reported, "It is very beautiful over there" unless, having seen, he knew it to be true.

Many years ago a missionary went to the South Sea Islands to work among a cannibal tribe. After many months he converted the chief to Christianity. One day this old chief said to the missionary, "Remember the time you first came among us?"

"Indeed I do," replied the missionary. "As I went through the forest I became aware of hostile forces all around me."

"They did indeed surround you," said the chief, "for we were following you to kill you, but something prevented us from doing it."

"And what was that?" asked the missionary.

"Now that we are friends, tell me," coaxed the chief, "who were those two shining ones walking on either side of you?"

My friend, Geoffrey O'Hara, famous song writer, author of the popular World War I song, "Katy," also "There Is No Death," "Give a Man a Horse He Can Ride," and other songs, tells of a colonel in World War I whose regiment was wiped out in a bloody engagement. As he paced up and down the trench he says he could feel their hands and sense their presence. He said to Geoffrey O'Hara, "I tell you, there is no death." Mr. O'Hara wrote one of his greatest songs using that title, "there is no death."

Of these deep and tender matters I personally have no doubt whatsoever. I firmly believe in the continuation of life after that which we call death takes place. I believe there are two sides to the phenomenon known as death—this side where we now live and the other side where we shall continue to live. Eternity does not start with death. We are in eternity now. We are citizens of eternity. We merely change the form of the experience called life, and that change, I am persuaded, is for the better.

My mother was a great soul, and her influence on me will ever stand out in my life as an experience that cannot be surpassed. She was a wonderful conversationalist. Her mind was keen and alert. She traveled the world over and enjoyed wide contacts as a Christian leader in missionary causes. Her life was full and rich. She had a marvelous sense of humor. She was good company, and I always loved to be with her. She was considered by all who knew her an unusually fascinating and stimulating personality.

During my adult years whenever I had the opportunity I would go home to see her. I always anticipated the arrival at the family home, for it was an exciting experience in which everyone talked at once as we sat around the breakfast table. What happy reunions—what glorious meetings. Then came her death, and we tenderly laid her body in the beautiful little cemetery at Lynchburg in southern Ohio, a town where she had lived as a girl. I was very sad the day we left her there, and went away heavy-hearted. It was in the fullness of summertime when we took her home to her last resting place.

It came autumn, and I felt that I wanted to be with my mother again. I was lonely without her, therefore I decided to go to Lynchburg. All night long on the train I thought sadly of the happy days now gone and how things were utterly changed and would never be the same again.

So I came to the little town. The weather was cold and the sky overcast as I walked to the cemetery. I pushed through the old iron gates and my feet rustled in the leaves as I walked to her grave where I sat sad and lonely. Of a sudden the clouds parted and the sun came through. It lighted up the Ohio hills in gorgeous autumn colors, the hills where I grew up as a boy, which I have always loved so well, where she herself had played as a girl in the long ago.

Then all of a sudden I seemed to hear her voice. Now I didn't actually hear her voice, but I seemed to. I am sure I heard it by the inward ear. The message was clear and distinct. It was stated in her beloved old-time tone, and this is what she said, "Why seek ye the living among the dead? I am not here. Do you think that I would stay in this dark and dismal place? I am with you and my loved ones always." In a burst of inner light I became wondrously happy. I knew that what I had heard was the truth. The message came to me with all the force of actuality. I could have shouted, and I stood up and put my hand on the tombstone and saw it for what it is, only a place where mortal remains lay. The body was there, to be sure, but it was only a coat that had been laid off because the wearer needed it no longer. But she, that gloriously lovely spirit, she was not there.

I walked out of that place and only rarely since have I returned. I like to go back there and think of her and the old days of my youth, but no longer is it a place of gloom. It is merely a symbol, for she is not there. She is with us her loved ones. "Why seek ye the living among the dead?" (Luke 24:5)

Read and believe the Bible as it tells about the goodness of God and the immortality of the soul. Pray sincerely and with faith. Make prayer and faith the habit of your life. Learn to have real fellowship with God and with Jesus Christ. As you do this you will find a deep conviction welling up in your mind that these wonderful things are true indeed.

". . . if it were not so, I would have told you." (John 14:2) You can depend upon the reliability of Christ. He would not let you believe and hold convictions so sacred in nature unless they are absolutely true.

So in this faith, which is a sound, substantial, and rational view of life and eternity, you have the prescription for heartache.

# 17

# *How to Draw upon That Higher Power*

FOUR MEN WERE sitting in the locker room of a country club after a game. Talk about golf scores drifted into a discussion of personal difficulties and problems. One man was especially despondent. The others, his friends, realizing his unhappy state of mind, had arranged this game to get his mind off his difficult situation. They hoped a few hours on the golf course might afford him some relief.

Now, as they sat around after the game, various suggestions were offered him. Finally one of the men arose to go. He knew about difficulties, for he'd had plenty himself, but he had found some vital answers to *his* problems. He stood hesitantly, then laid his hand on his friend's shoulder. "George," he said, "I hope you won't think I am preaching at you. Really, I'm not, but I would like to suggest something. It's the way I got through my difficulties. It really works if you work at it, and it's this. 'Why not draw upon that Higher Power?' "

He slapped his friend affectionately on the back and left the group. The other men sat mulling this over. Finally the discouraged man said slowly, "I know what he means and I know where the Higher Power is. I only wish I knew how to draw upon it. It's what I need all right."

Well, in due course he discovered how to draw upon that Higher Power, and it changed everything for him. Now he is a healthy, happy man.

The advice given at the golf club is really very wise. There are many people today who are unhappy and depressed and just not getting anywhere with themselves or with conditions. And they do not need to be that way. Really they don't. The secret is to draw upon that Higher Power. And how is that done?

Let me tell you about a personal experience. When quite young

I was called to a large church in a university community and many of my congregation were professors in the university as well as leading citizens of the city. I wanted to justify the confidence of those who gave me such an outstanding opportunity and accordingly worked very hard. As a result I began to experience overstrain. Everyone should work hard, but there is no virtue in overtrying or overpressing to such an extent that you do not work efficiently. It is somewhat like making a golf shot. Try to "kill" the ball and you execute the shot poorly. You can do likewise in your job. I began to get rather tired and nervous and had no feeling of normal power.

One day I decided to call on one of the professors, the late Hugh M. Tilroe, a great friend of mine. He was a wonderful teacher, and he was also a great fisherman and hunter. He was a man's man, an outdoor personality. I knew that if I did not find him at the university he would be out on the lake fishing, and sure enough there he was. He came ashore at my hail. "The fish are biting—come on," he said. I climbed in his boat and we fished awhile.

"What's the matter, son?" he asked with understanding. I told him how hard I was trying and that it was getting me down nervously. "I have no feeling of lift or power," I said.

He chuckled. "Maybe you're trying too hard."

As the boat scraped the shore he said, "Come in the house with me." As we entered his cabin he ordered, "Lie down there on that couch. I want to read you something. Shut your eyes and relax while I find the quotation."

I did as directed, and thought he was going to read me some philosophical or perhaps diverting piece, but instead he said, "Here it is. Listen quietly while I read it to you. And let these words sink in. 'Hast thou not known? Hast thou not heard, that the everlasting God, the Lord, the Creator of the ends of the earth, fainteth not, neither is weary? There is no searching of his understanding. He giveth power to the faint; and to them that have no might he increaseth strength. Even the youths shall faint and be weary, and the young men shall utterly fall. But they that wait upon the Lord shall renew their strength; they shall mount up with wings as eagles; they shall run, and not be weary; and they shall walk, and not faint.' " (Isaiah 40:28-31) Then he asked, "Do you know from what I am reading?"

"Yes, the fortieth chapter of Isaiah," I answered.

"I'm glad you know your Bible," he commented. "Why don't you practice it? Now relax. Take three deep breaths—in and out slowly. Practice resting yourself in God. Practice depending upon Him for His support and power. Believe He is giving it to you now and don't get out of touch with that power. Yield yourself to it—let it flow through you.

"Give your job all you've got. Of course you must do that. But do it in a relaxed and easy manner like a batter in a big-league ball game. He swings the bat easy-like, and doesn't try to knock the ball out of the park. He just does the best he can and believes in himself because he knows that he has lots of reserve power." Then he repeated the passage again. " 'They that wait upon the Lord shall renew their strength.' "

That was a long time ago, but I never forgot that lesson. He taught me how to draw upon that Higher Power, and believe me, his suggestions worked. I continue to follow my friend's advice, and it has never failed me in the more than twenty years that have passed since then. My life is crowded with activity but that power formula gives me all the strength I need.

A second method for drawing upon that Higher Power is to learn to take a positive, optimistic attitude toward every problem. In direct proportion to the intensity of the faith which you muster will you receive power to meet your situations. "According to your faith be it unto you," (Matthew 9:29) is a basic law of successful living.

There is a Higher Power, and that Power can do everything for you. Draw upon it and experience its great helpfulness. Why be defeated when you are free to draw upon that Higher Power? State your problem. Ask for a specific answer. Believe that you are getting that answer. Believe that now, through God's help, you are gaining power over your difficulty.

A man and his wife who were in real trouble came to see me. This gentleman, a former magazine editor, was a distinguished figure in music and artistic circles. Everyone liked him for his geniality and friendliness. His wife was held in similar high regard. She was in poor health and as a result they had retired to the country where they were living in semi-seclusion.

This man told me he had experienced two heart attacks, one quite severe. His wife was in a steady decline and he was deeply concerned about her. The question he put was this: "Can I get hold of some power that can help us recover ourselves physically and give us new hope and courage and strength?" The situation as he described it was a series of discouragements and defeats.

Frankly I felt that he was a bit too sophisticated to permit himself to adopt and utilize the simple trust that would be necessary if faith were to rehabilitate him. I told him I rather doubted he had the capacity to practice simple faith enough to open the sources of power according to the techniques of Christianity.

But he assured me he was in earnest and was open-minded and would follow any directions given. I saw his honesty and the real quality of his soul and have had a great affection for him ever since. I gave him a simple prescription. He was to read the New Testament and the Psalms until his mind was saturated with them. I gave him the usual suggestion of committing passages to memory. Principally I urged him to utilize the formula of putting his life in the hands of God, at the same time believing that God was filling him with power, and his wife also, and that the two of them were to believe unfalteringly that they were being guided in even the most commonplace details of their lives.

They were also to believe that in co-operation with their physician, whom I happened to know and admire, that the healing grace of Jesus Christ was being given them. I suggested that they picture the healing power of the Great Physician as already working within them.

Seldom have I seen two people who became more gloriously childlike in their faith and whose trust was more complete. They became enthusiastic about the Bible and would often telephone me about "some wonderful passage" they had just found. They gave me fresh insights into the truths of the Bible. It was a truly creative process working with this man and his wife.

The next spring Helen (that is the wife's name) said, "I have never experienced a more wonderful springtime. The flowers this year are the loveliest I have ever seen, and have you noticed the sky with its extraordinary cloud formations and the delicate colors at dawn and sunset? The leaves seem greener this year, and I have never heard the birds sing with such ecstasy and melody." When she said this there was an ecstatic light on her face and I knew she had been reborn in the spirit. And she began to improve physically, regaining a large share of her old-time strength. Her native creative power began to flow forth once again and life took on new meaning.

As for Horace, there has been no more heart trouble, and physical, mental, and spiritual vigor mark him as extraordinarily vital. They have moved into a new community and have become a center of its life. Wherever they go they touch people with a strange uplifting force.

What is the secret which they discovered? Simply that they learned to draw upon that Higher Power.

This Higher Power is one of the most amazing facts in human existence. I am awestruck, no matter how many times I have seen the phenomenon, by the thorough-going, tremendous, overwhelming changes for good that it accomplishes in the lives of people. Personally, I am so enthusiastic about all that the Higher Power can do for people that I am loath to bring this book to a close. I could recite story after story, incident after incident of those who by laying hold of this power have had a new birth of life.

This power is constantly available. If you open to it, it will rush in like a mighty tide. It is there for anybody under any circumstances or in any condition. This tremendous inflow of power is of such force that in its inrush it drives everything before it, casting out fear, hate, sickness, weakness, moral defeat, scattering them as though they had never touched you, refreshing and restrengthening your life with health, happiness, and goodness.

For many years I have been interested in the problem of the alcoholic and in the organization known as Alcoholics Anonymous. One of their basic principles is that before a person can be helped he must recognize that he is an alcoholic and that of himself he can do nothing; that he has no power within himself; that he is defeated. When he accepts this point of view he is in a position to receive help from other alcoholics and from the Higher Power—God.

Another principle is the willingness to depend upon the Higher Power from whom he derives a strength which he does not himself possess. The working of this power in men's lives is the most moving and thrilling fact in this world. No other manifestation of power of any kind is equal to it. Materialistic power achievement is a romantic story. Men discover laws and formulas and harness power to do remarkable things. Spiritual power also follows laws.

Mastery of these laws works wonders in an area more complicated than any form of mechanics, namely, human nature. It is one thing to make a machine work right. To make human nature work right is something else. It requires greater skill, but it can be done.

I sat one day under swaying palm trees in Florida listening to the story of a demonstration of Higher Power activity in the life of a man who narrowly escaped tragedy. He told me that he started drinking at the age of sixteen, "as it was the so-called smart thing to do." After twenty-three years, beginning as a social drinker, he "came to the end of the road on April 24, 1947." A growing hatred and bitterness toward his wife who had deserted him and toward his mother-in-law and sister-in-law culminated in his decision to kill these three women. I relate the story as he told it to me, in his own language.

"To strengthen myself for this gory task I went into a bar. A few more drinks would give me the courage to commit this triple murder. As I entered the bar I saw a young man by the name of Carl drinking coffee. Although I had hated Carl from boyhood I was utterly astounded to note his immaculate appearance, and I was also astonished to see him drinking coffee in a bar where he had spent on an average of $400 a month for drinks alone. Also I was mystified by what seemed a strange light on his face. Being fascinated by his appearance, I approached Carl and asked, 'What happened to you that you are drinking coffee?'

" 'I have not had a drink for a year,' Carl replied.

"I was utterly amazed, because Carl and I had been on many drinking bouts together. A strange incident in this affair is that even though I hated Carl I was strangely moved. I could not help but listen when he asked, 'Ed, did you ever want to quit drinking?'

" 'Yes, I have quit a thousand times,' I replied.

"Carl smiled and said, 'If you really want to do something about your problem, get sober and attend a meeting at the Presbyterian Church at nine on Saturday. It is a meeting of Alcoholics Anonymous.'

"I told him I had no interest in religion, but that maybe I would come. I was unimpressed, but still I could not get that light in his eyes out of my mind.

"Carl did not insist that I attend the meeting, but repeated that if I wanted to do something for myself he and his associates had an answer to my problem. After making that statement Carl left and I stood up to the bar to order a drink, but somehow it had lost its appeal. So, instead, I went home, the only home I had remaining, my mother's home.

"May I explain that I had been married for seventeen years to a very fine girl, but being an impatient person and having no faith in me due to my drinking, she finally decided upon getting a divorce, so not only my job and all my material assets but my home also were completely lost.

"Upon getting to my mother's home I wrestled with a bottle until 6 A.M., but still could not take the drink. I kept thinking of Carl's appearance. So on Saturday morning I went to Carl and asked him what I could do to keep from taking a drink until nine o'clock that night when the meeting would be held.

"Carl said, 'Every time you come to a bar or whisky sign or beer garden, just say one little prayer—"Please, God, get me past this place," ' and then he added, 'Run like hell. That will be co-operating with God. He will hear your prayer and the running will be your part.'

"I did exactly as Carl told me to do. For many hours, anxious and shaky, accompanied by my sister, I walked around the streets of the town. Finally at eight o'clock my sister said, 'Ed, there are seven drinking joints between here and the place where you are to attend the meeting. You go by yourself, and if you don't make it and come home drunk we will still love you and hope for the best, but somehow I feel that this meeting will be different than any you ever attended.' With God's help I got by those seven places.

"At the church entrance I happened to look around and the sign over one of my favorite drinking places glared me straight in the eyes. The battle to decide whether to go into that bar or into the Alcoholics Anonymous meeting is one I shall never forget, but a Power greater than myself pulled me to the meeting.

"Upon entering the meeting room I was utterly astounded to receive the firm handshake of my ex-hated friend, Carl. My resentment toward him was disappearing. A round of introductions began to many men in all walks of life—doctors, lawyers, bricklayers, millwrights, coal miners, construction workers, plasterers, laborers—all types were there. I had been drinking with some of these men for the last ten to twenty-five years and here they were all sober on a Saturday night, and, above all, they were happy.

"What happened at that meeting is rather vague. All I know is that a rebirth had taken place. I felt different deep within.

"Happily leaving the meeting room at midnight, I went home with a glorious air-lifting feeling and slept peaceably for the first time in more than five years. Upon awakening the next morning, I recall something clearly saying to me, 'There is a Power greater than yourself. If you will turn your will and your life over to the care of God as you understand Him, He will give you strength.'

"It was Sunday morning, and I decided to go to church. I attended a service where the preacher was a man whom I had hated from childhood. (The author wishes to comment at this point how inevitably hate is associated with emotional and spiritual sickness. When the mind is emptied of hate, a long step has been taken toward recovery. Love is a tremendous curative force.) This preacher was one of those sedate, swallowtailed-coat-wearing Presbyterian ministers. I had no use for him, but that was my fault. He was all right really. I sat nervously through the singing and the collection taking. Then the preacher read his Scripture, and his sermon was based upon the theme, 'Never belittle anyone's experience—he had it.' I shall never forget that sermon as long as I live. It taught me a valuable lesson—never to belittle an experience because someone had it, for he and God know the depth and sincerity of that experience.

"Later I came to love this minister as one of the greatest, most sincere men I have ever known.

"Just where my new life began is a matter that is difficult to determine. Whether it was when I met Carl in the bar, or wrestling past the drinking places, or at the Alcoholics Anonymous meeting, or at the church, I do not know. But I, who had been a hopeless alcoholic for twenty-five years, suddenly became a sober man. I could never have done this alone, for I had tried it a thousand times and failed. But I drew upon a Higher Power and the Higher Power, which is God, did it."

I have known the narrator of the foregoing story for several years. Since becoming "dry" he has had to face some difficult financial and other problems. But never once has he weakened. In talking with him I find myself strangely moved. It isn't what he says or even the way he says it, but one is conscious of a power emanating from this man. He is not a famous person. He is an everyday, hard-working salesman, but the Higher Power is in him, flowing through him, operating within his experience, and it transmits itself to others. It transmitted itself to me.

This chapter is not intended as a dissertation on alcoholism, although I will use still another reference in connection with this problem. I cite these experiences to show conclusively that if there is a Power able to deliver a person from alcoholism, this same Power can help any other person to overcome any other form of defeat he may face. There is nothing more difficult to overcome than the problem of alcoholism. The Power that can accomplish that difficult feat can, I assure you, help you to overcome your difficulties whatever they may be.

Let me give still another experience. I narrate this incident for the same purpose, namely, to emphasize that there is a Power which can be applied, drawn upon, and used that mysteriously but surely gives to people who demonstrate faith the most remarkable victories.

In the Hotel Roanoke at Roanoke, Virginia, one night a man who has since become a good friend told me the following story. Two years before he had read my book, *A Guide to Confident Living*. At that time he was considered by himself and by others to be an utterly hopeless alcoholic. He is a businessman in a Virginia town and is of such ability that despite his drinking problem he was able to keep going with fair success. He had absolutely no control over his drinking, however, and evident deterioration was taking place.

Upon reading the book above mentioned, the idea was lodged in his mind that if he could only get to New York he could be cured of his difficulty. He came to New York but was dead drunk when he arrived. A friend took him to a hotel and left him. He recovered sufficient consciousness to call a bellboy and told him that he wanted to go to the Townes Hospital, a famous institution for alcoholics, presided over by the late Dr. Silkworth, one of the greatest men in the field of alcoholism—now deceased but never to be forgotten.

After robbing him of one hundred or more dollars which he had in his pocket, the bellboy delivered him to the hospital. After several days of treatment, Dr. Silkworth came in to see him and said, "Charles, I think we have done for you all that we can do. I have a feeling that you are well."

This was not Dr. Silkworth's usual practice, and the fact that he handled this case in this manner causes one to sense the guiding hand of a Higher Power.

Still somewhat shaky, Charles made his way downtown until he found himself outside the office door of the Marble Collegiate Church, 1 West 29th Street, New York City. It happened to be a legal holiday and the church was closed. (Other than such holidays the church is always open.) He stood there hesitantly. He had hoped that he might go into the church and pray. Not being able to gain entrance, he did a strange thing. He took from his wallet one of his business cards and dropped it through the mail slot in the door.

The instant he did that a tremendous wave of peace came over him. He had an amazing sense of release. He put his head against the door and sobbed like a baby, but he knew that he was free, that some tremendous change had happened to him the validity of which is attested by the fact that from that minute on there has been no turning back. He has lived in complete sobriety from that moment.

There are several features about this incident which mark it as impressive. For one, Dr. Silkworth seemed to have released him from the hospital at the proper psychological, spiritual, and shall we say supernatural moment, indicating that the doctor himself was the subject of Divine guidance.

When Charles told me this story in the Hotel Roanoke two years after it happened, I had a feeling as he related it that I had heard it before in precise detail. But he had never told me this story. In fact, I had never previously talked to him. It occurred to me that perhaps he had written the story to me and I had read it, but he said he had never written me. I then asked him if he had told the story to one of my secretaries, associates, or any other person who could have related it to me, but he said he had never told the story to any other individual save his wife and I had not met her until that night. Apparently this incident had been transmitted to my subconscious at the time it happened for now I "remembered" it.

Why did he drop the card in the mail slot? Perhaps he was symbolically reporting to his spiritual home, reporting to God. It was a dramatic and symbolic separation of himself from his defeat and the turning to a Higher Power which immediately took him out of himself and healed him.

The incident indicates that if there is deep desire, intensity of longing, and a sincere reaching out after the Power that it will be given.

In this chapter I have related victory stories out of human experience each in its own way indicating the continual presence and availability of a life-renewing Power, beyond but resident within ourselves. Your problem may not be alcoholism, but the fact that the Higher Power can heal a person of this most difficult malady emphasizes the tremendous truth related in this chapter and throughout the entire book that there is no problem, difficulty, or defeat that you cannot solve or overcome by faith, positive thinking, and prayer to God. The techniques are simple and workable. And God will help you always, just as the writer of the following letter was helped.

"Dear Dr. Peale: When we think of all the wonderful things that have happened to us since we first met you and started coming to the Marble Church, it seems nothing short of a miracle. When you realize that just six years ago this month I was totally broke—in fact thousands of dollars in debt—a complete physical washout—and had hardly a friend in the world because of my excess drinking—you can see why we have to pinch ourselves every now and then to realize that our good fortune isn't all a dream.

"As you well know, alcohol wasn't the only problem I had six years ago. It has been said that I was one of the most negative people you ever saw. That's only a half truth. For I was filled with gripes, all sorts of irritation, and was one of the most supercritical, impatient, cocky individuals that you could have possibly met even in all your travels.

"Now, please don't think I feel I have overcome all these obsessions. I haven't. I am one of those people that have to do a day-to-day job on myself. But gradually, by trying to follow your teachings, I am learning to control myself and be less critical of my fellow man. And it is like being released from a prison. I just never dreamed that life could be so full and wonderful. Sincerely, (Signed) Dick."

Why not draw upon that Higher Power?

# EPILOGUE

YOU HAVE FINISHED this book. What have you read?

Simply a series of practical and workable techniques for living a successful life. You have read a formula of belief and practice which should help you win victory over every defeat.

Examples have been given of people who have believed and who have applied the suggested techniques. These stories have been told to demonstrate that through the same methods you can obtain the same results as they did. But reading is not enough. Now please go back and persistently practice each technique given in this book. Keep at it until you obtain the desired results.

I wrote this book out of a sincere desire to help you. It will give me great happiness to know that the book has helped you. I have absolute confidence and belief in the principles and methods outlined in this volume. They have been tested in the laboratory of spiritual experience and practical demonstration. They work when worked.

We may never meet in person, but in this book we have met. We are spiritual friends. I pray for you. God will help you—so believe and live successfully.

NORMAN VINCENT PEALE

# *The Amazing Results of* **Positive Thinking**

TO CHERISHED ASSOCIATES

Smiley Blanton

Daniel A. Poling

Herman L. Barbery

Eugene McKinley Pierce

Donald Wayne Hoffman

Mary F. Brinig

# Contents

# A Word to the Reader

**Hundreds of people** wrote this book. I have simply put together the combined experiences of many men and women.

This is a result book. It is the story of thrilling things which took place in the lives of thousands of people when they applied the principles of dynamic change.

Since publication of *The Power of Positive Thinking,* a book which teaches effective living through right thinking and practical religious faith, thousands of readers have communicated with me. They told how, by the application of positive thinking principles to their own life situations, they have mastered fear, healed personal relationships, found better health, overcome inner conflicts and gained strong new confidence.

Writers of these letters invariably expressed themselves in terms of joy and faith in God. Readers repeatedly said that they started reading the Bible, and they told how it took on new meaning. Indeed, they declared that they drew from it faith and happiness they had not previously known. They discovered new values in the church, and the use of practical spiritual techniques became an exciting adventure. These letters came from Catholics, Protestants and Jews alike, and told how God had become a living reality. Many referred to experiencing Jesus Christ in their lives, and this spiritual phenomenon is described with deep feeling as being very warm, rich and personal. New potentials were found in spiritual living, especially in the power of prayer. Some who had gone regularly to church for years, but with no joy or sense of lift, spoke wonderingly of fresh discoveries in faith.

What excitement, what sense of wonder, what new life,

what love of their fellow men, and of life itself, these people told about.

While readers have graciously expressed appreciation of the teachings outlined in *The Power of Positive Thinking*, many have found either new uses for the suggested methods or, in some cases, exciting new formulas for effective living, which in their enthusiasm they sent to me. These discoveries of fresh techniques should, I felt, be passed on to others for the helpfulness they are certain to bring.

So wonderful were the letters and word-of-mouth statements concerning the workability of the positive way of life that, when I gathered many of them together in book form, a natural title was *The Amazing Results of Positive Thinking*. This book is a laboratory demonstration of the real experiences of many people with formulas that actually changed lives.

Through these formulas thousands of people have discovered a way of thinking and living that changed sorrow to joy, weakness to strength, failure to success, despair to hope, and defeat to victory. This new book explains how the same principles can help you. And, after reading these results, perhaps you will want to put these powerful techniques to work in your life. Then won't you write me about your own results, that I may pass them on to encourage and help others.

To you, my reader and friend, God bless and guide you always. And He will, too.

NORMAN VINCENT PEALE

# I

# Does Positive Thinking Always Work?

DOES POSITIVE THINKING ALWAYS WORK?

Yes.

Now, I realize this is a rather bold statement. And someone may object: "Is that so. I had lots of problems. I read positive thinking and I still have problems." Someone else may say, "Well, I had a business that was in the doldrums, and I tried positive thinking, and my business is still in the doldrums. Positive thinking didn't change the facts. Failure exists. If you deny that, you're just being an ostrich, burying your head in the sand."

So often, people don't really understand the nature of positive thinking. A positive thinker does not refuse to *recognize* the negative, he refuses to *dwell* on it. Positive thinking is a form of thought which habitually looks for the best results from the worse conditions. It is possible to look for something to build on; it is possible to expect the best for yourself even though things look bad. And the remarkable fact is that when you seek good, you are very likely to find it.

This seeking-the-positive is a deliberate process, and a matter of choice. Not long ago I received word that a friend of mine had been fired. In talking with Bill, I learned the circumstances. He had been summarily dismissed. No explanation was given except there had been a policy change, and he was no longer needed. To make matters worse, nine months earlier Bill had received a handsome offer from a competing firm, he had talked the matter over with his boss, and his boss had persuaded him to stay on, saying: "We need you here, Bill. And frankly, things look pretty good for you."

Well, of course, Bill reacted rather bitterly to all of this. He went around feeling unwanted, insecure, rejected. His ego had been hurt. He became morose and resentful, and in a state of mind like that, he wasn't in a very good condition to look for another job.

This is exactly the kind of situation where positive thinking can do its best. One day, Bill dug out an old copy of *The Power of Positive Thinking*, and read it through. What possible good was there in his condition, he wondered? He didn't know. But he could see plenty of negative factors, and he clearly realized that these negative emotions were dragging him down. If he was going to put positive thinking to work, the first thing he had to do was get rid of the negative feelings.

Here, at least, was a place he could begin. So he practiced the principle of thought replacement. That is, he deliberately filled his mind with positive affirmations and crowded out the negative thoughts. He began a systematic program of prayer and told the Lord: "I believe You have a plan for my life, so there must be some purpose in my getting fired. Instead of railing against my fate, I humbly ask You to show me the purpose in what has happened." Once he began to believe there had been a reason and some meaning behind what had happened to him, it was easier to rid himself of resentment against his former employers. And once that happened he was "employable" again.

One day, shortly after he had reached this point in his thinking, Bill met an old friend. They got to talking, and the friend asked how things were.

"Oh, I've just been fired," Bill said, casually.

The friend was surprised. "Well you're certainly honest enough about it," he said. "What happened?"

Bill told him, and he finished by saying: ". . . and I know the Lord has a job for me somewhere else."

"The *Lord!* Aren't you worried?"

"Not at all. Something better will turn up. In my philosophy, when one door shuts another will open if you just have faith and put it in God's hands."

A few days later Bill received a telephone call from his friend, saying that there was a long-unfilled opening in his company, and asking him if he wanted the job—salarywise it wasn't as good as his last position, but it had potential. Bill took it. There was no doubt about the fact that in his new job he was in a better position to be of service to people. He realized this very shortly and soon discovered that his new activity was one he had always wanted. He became stimulated and excited about his work in a way that he had almost forgotten at his previous place of employment. He would grow. This, he felt sure, was part of the plan that God had in mind.

Now the important thing to analyze here is *why* positive thinking worked. It's not that some magic entered the picture and created a job out of the ether. There was a definite scientific principle at work. When Bill had his mind filled with resentments and angers and hatreds, he was destroying his own value as an employee. He was making it impossible for himself to do his best at the business of job-seeking. On the day Bill met his friend, if he had been bitter and full of sly defenses, do you think his friend would have considered him a good person to recommend for the new job? There is no mysticism at work here. This way of thinking and of acting is, above all, down-to-earth common sense.

Positive thinking is looking at events with the knowledge

that there will be both good and bad in life, but that it is better to emphasize the good. And as you do that, good seems to increase.

The other day I went out the door of my office and hailed a cab. As soon as I got in the taxi, I could tell that my driver was a happy man. He was whistling. First he whistled a tune from, "My Fair Lady," and then he launched himself into a version of "Stars and Stripes Forever." After a while I said to him, "You seem to be in a happy mood."

"Why shouldn't I be?" he said. "I've just learned something. I've learned that there's no percentage in getting excited, or in the dumps, because things average out."

And he went on to explain what he meant. Early that morning he had taken his cab out, hoping to take advantage of the morning rush hour. It was a bitterly cold day. The driver said it was ". . . the kind of temperature where, if you touch metal, your hand will stick to it." And as luck would have it, no sooner had he started his day than he had a flat tire. He was angry. Muttering, he got out his jack and lug wrench and tried to take off the tire. It was so cold he could only work for a few minutes at a time. And while he was struggling, a truck stopped. The driver jumped out and, much to the taxi-driver's surprise, began to help him. When the tire was back in place, the trucker gruffly waved off the cabby's thanks, got in his truck and drove off.

"Well, this put me in a high mood," the cabby said to me. "Already things were averaging out. First, I was angry with the flat, then I felt good because of that trucker's help and right away things started going good. Even the money has averaged out. I've never had a busier morning, one fare after another in and out of the cab. Things average out, Mister. Don't get excited when a situation gets rocky; things average out."

Here was a positive thinker, all right. He said he was never again going to let life's mishaps annoy him. He was just going to live by the theory that things average out OK. That is real positive thinking, and it will work, too, because things always come around to a brighter view when you wait them out and work them out optimistically. The law of averages is always on the positive thinker's side. A positive thinker chooses to keep his mind fixed on the bright future that is always just around the corner, and in this way he helps make the dark moments more cheerful, productive and creative. That attitude gets you around the "corner" quicker, too.

It is a fact of life that all of us will come face to face with plenty of frustration, difficulty and trouble. But there isn't one of us who needs to be defeated by these obstacles. If you face life with the sincere faith that through the aid of the Almighty you can overcome your troubles, then you will keep defeat at arm's length. And this applies in all the circumstances life can bring.

One evening in San Francisco, I had the pleasure of dining in the home of a charming lady named Elena Zelayeta. I have never attended a dinner party presided over by an individual of happier personality or more irresistible gaiety. Elena is Mexican, and the dinner she served that evening was a 17-course Mexican dinner (small courses)—the most delicious repast I could hope to experience. She cooked it herself—and she is totally blind.

Elena Zelayeta once ran a restaurant in San Francisco. It was a beautiful place, full of color and life. Then her eyesight began to fail. Soon she was blind, living in darkness. One day the telephone rang and she groped her way to answer it and received the shocking news that her husband had just been killed in an accident.

Blindness—and now her husband suddenly dead. She sat by the telephone, utterly crushed, wondering what she was going to do. She was dejected for weeks, living in helplessness. But in this most complete darkness, emotionally and physically, she perceived finally, by the help of her strong faith, that there was something positive to which she could attach herself. She did not choose to dwell on the negative, she sought the positive, and she found it in a most remarkable way. As she struggled in shock and sorrow, suddenly she felt "as if a great, strong hand gripped her and lifted her up."

Putting sincere faith and strong positive thinking against her sad conditions, she determined that she would conquer her grief, loneliness and handicap. So complete was her ultimate victory that presently she picked up her life again as a career woman. How well Elena Zelayeta succeeded is shown by the fact that in recent years she has lectured on cooking up and down the West Coast, sometimes to as many as a thousand women at a time. She has written three successful cook books and a book of inspiration. She operates a frozen food business with her two sons and goes to the office every day.

She has to cook by sense of feel and taste and smell. But these, she says with a smile, are what cooking is all about anyway. This inspiring woman is one of the most marvelous examples of positive thinking I have ever ran across. Naturally I sought for her secret of conquering adversity. While we were having dinner at her home, Mrs. Zelayeta made this powerful statement, which is the guiding principle of her life. It is the formula through which she found victory. "Always act," she said, "as if it were impossible to fail, and God will see you through."

Always act as if it were *impossible* to fail!

Elena Zelayeta is the type of person William James the philosopher-psychologist would call "tough minded." The world, according to this great thinker, is made up of two kinds of people—the "tough-minded" and "tender-minded."

The tender-minded are the ones who wilt under obstacles and difficulties. They are cut to the quick by criticism and lose heart. They are the ones who whine and fail. But the tough-minded individuals are not like that. They are people from all walks of life, the manual workers and the merchants, the mothers and the fathers, the teachers, the old people, and the young people too, who have a strong element of toughness built into them by Almighty God. By toughness is meant the inner power to stand up to a difficulty; to have what it takes to take it.

Up in the little town of Carmel, New York, where we publish *Guideposts* magazine, lived a boy named Jim Mackey. Jim was fourteen years old; a lovable boy and real man, one of the truly tough-minded people of this world. He was a natural born athlete, one of the very best. But early in his high school career, he began to limp. It soon developed that he had a cancer. An operation was required, and Jim's leg was amputated. As soon as he was out of the hospital, he went around to the high school on his crutches, talking cheerfully about how he was going to have a wooden leg soon. "Then I'll be able to hold up my socks with a thumb tack," he said. "None of you guys can do that!"

As soon as the football season started, Jim went to the coach and asked if he could be one of the team managers. For weeks he appeared regularly for practice, carrying the coach's set of plays and infusing the team with his contagious, fiery courage. Then one afternoon he missed a practice. The coach was worried. He checked, and learned that Jim was in the hospital having another examination. Later, he learned that the examination had revealed lung cancer. "Jim will be dead," said the doctor, "within six weeks."

Jim's parents decided not to tell the boy about his death sentence; they wanted him to live as normal a life as he could for the last few weeks. So, Jim was soon back at practice again with his big smile and his offering of enthusiasm and courage. With his inspiration the team raced through the season undefeated, and to celebrate they decided to throw a banquet. Jim was to receive a victory football autographed by each member of the team. The banquet, however, was not the success it should have been. Jim was not there. He was too weak to attend.

A few weeks later, however, Jim was back again, this time at a basketball game. He was pale, very pale, but aside from that he was the same old Jim, smiling, laughing, making jokes. When, after the game, he went to the coach's office the entire football team was there. The coach scolded him gently for missing the banquet. "I'm on a diet, Coach," said Jim with a grin that covered his pain. Then one of the team members presented him with the victor's football. "We won it because of you, Jim," he said. Jim said a quiet thanks with tears in his eyes. The coach and Jim and the other boys talked about plans for the next season, and then it was time to go. Jim turned, and at the door he said, looking at the coach with a steady, level gaze:

"Good-bye, Coach."

"Don't you mean, 'so long,' Jim?" the coach asked.

Jim's eyes lighted up and his steady gaze turned into a smile. "Don't worry, Coach," he said. "I'm all set." And with that he was gone.

Two days later, he was dead.

Jim had known all along about his death sentence. But he could take it, for you see he was a tough-minded positive thinker. He made of this sad and tragic fact a creative experience. But, someone might say, he died; his positive thinking didn't get him very much. This is not true. Jim knew how to reach out for faith and how to create something warm and uplifting from the worse possible situation. He wasn't burying his head in the sand; he knew full well what was in store for him, and yet he chose not to be defeated! Jim was never defeated. He took his life, short as it was, and used it to instill courage, faith and laughter, permanently, into the lives and minds of the people who knew him. Could you, in any possible way, say that a person who succeeded in doing that with his life had been a failure?

That's what positive thinking is; it is tough-mindedness. It is refusing to be defeated. It is making the most of what you have to deal with in life. I have always been a reader of the works of the apostle of tough-mindedness: Thomas Carlyle. Recently I went up to Ecclefechan, the little Scotch village where he was born, to see if I might find there something of the strength of mind and character he possessed. Carlyle was the son of a stone mason. He started off to Edinburgh for his education with a shilling in his pocket and he walked into immortality.

Carlyle grew up in the little town of Ecclefechan, halfway between the Scottish border and the town of Dumfries. He loved Ecclefechan and Dumfrieshire. He might have been buried in Westminster Abbey but he preferred Ecclefechan. Queen Victoria once asked Carlyle what he considered the most beautiful road in Britain, and he answered, "The road from Ecclefechan to Dumfries." And then she asked him what he considered the second most beautiful road, and he answered, "Why, it's the road back to Ecclefechan."

I visited Carlyle's grave in the cemetery of his beloved Ecclefechan and sat at his graveside reading some of his words. Carlyle's message came to me anew—the essence of which is never give up; never give in; stand up to it—fight it through. God will aid you. According to Carlyle's understanding, life asks of each of us, "Will you be a hero, or will you be a coward?" It is just that direct and forthright. Where did Carlyle get such ideas? Of course, from the most rugged Book ever put together. "Be strong and of good courage; be not afraid, neither be thou dismayed; for the Lord thy God is with thee whithersoever thou goest." (Joshua 1:9)

Will you be a hero, or will you be a coward? Will you be tough-minded or tender-minded. The positive thinker will not be a coward. He believes in himself, in life, in humanity and in God. He knows his own capacity and his own ability. He is undaunted and invincible. He will draw the best from whatever comes.

The formula he uses is one by which he is changed from weakness to strength. Some time ago the Chase Manhattan Bank started excavation for a new skyscraper. Most of Manhattan Island is composed of solid bed-rock. This is the reason we can have structures that pierce the sky. But early excavations revealed that this site was not solid rock, as had been supposed, but contained a large pocket of quicksand! And of course it would be very difficult indeed to build a skyscraper on such a base.

So the bank people called in experts to suggest ways for meeting this situation constructively. One expert suggested pilings; another said to seal it off with caissons; but the cost would be prohibitive. Geologists were consulted: How long would it take to turn quicksand into sandstone? About a million years, the geologists answered. Well, the bank didn't feel they could wait that long. They then called in some soil solidification people, and this is where their search ended. These experts knew how to handle the quicksand problem. They sank pipes down into the quicksand and pumped into it a solution of sodium silicate and calcium chloride. In a few days the quicksand solidified into sandstone hard enough to permit the erection of a sixty-floor skyscraper building.

Does this seem miraculous? No, because it was done according to a sound, scientific principle; a proven, scientific formula. But I have seen "miracles" that make this achievement fade into insignificance. I have seen weak, defeated personalities who have had infused into them a special mental-spiritual formula called positive thinking, and I have seen them become as solid as rock. They have become strong people, well able to bear the weight of life most successfully.

This kind of transformation is available to all of us. It is in this sense that positive thinking always works. Positive thinking is able to transform us from cowards to heroes, from tender-minded to tough-minded individuals, from weak, negative, vacillating people to men of positive strength.

Although the life-changing power of positive thinking is available to all, some people experience difficulty in making it work. This is because of some strange psychological barrier that stands between them and the full use of positive thinking? One that keeps cropping up, is simply that they do not *want* it to work. They do not want to succeed. Actually, they are afraid to succeed. It's easier to wallow in self-pity. So, we create our own failure, and when a suggestion (such as positive thinking) comes along that will help overcome that failure, we subconsciously see to it that the suggestion doesn't work, and so we believe the principle, rather than ourselves is at fault. But when we understand such unhealthy mental reactions, then positive thinking begins to work. Recently I received this letter from a reader who lives in Petaluna, California:

> For the first time in my life I can see where I have created my own bad luck by my thought pattern. Since reading your book about positive thinking and trying to clear my mind, I find little resentments cropping up I thought I'd forgotten years ago. Such silly little things to carry along with me all these years.
>
> Certainly if you have helped me rub out these little termites, I owe you a great deal for showing me the way. I, too,

have a pattern of failure and defeat. I never expected the best and I never got it, either. From here on out I'm going to go after the things I want, with confidence.

I feel God gave me a good chance and I just didn't have sense enough to use it. My faith will certainly deepen as I remove these mental blocks that I have so industriously set up. Believe me I built them strong!

This woman states that, for the first time, she sees that she has been creating her own bad luck by her thoughts. We have to stop creating our own failure. We have to stop being afraid that success will come our way.

I have a very good friend who is outstanding in the field of industrial medicine. He is the medical director of one of the nation's giant companies. He has come up from the worst kind of failure to the finest kind of success. Like the quicksand, he was made into rock, but by a spiritual formula of great strength. The other day I received a letter from him which had this paragraph in it:

I struggle constantly with success. For me, it has an insidious sweetness far more difficult to handle than the bitterness of failure, and much more uncertain as a stepping stone to spiritual progress.

I will call this man simply Dr. Tom, because he has such a spectacular story hidden in his past that I cannot name him fully. His was a dramatic struggle with success. He did not want it. It frightened him so thoroughly that he came close to killing himself rather than face it. In 1938 Dr. Tom was on the staff of a state mental hospital. Exactly ten years later he was paroled from this same hospital *as a patient!*

Dr. Tom started out in life with all the advantages. In fact, he had so many advantages that they got him in trouble. He had social position, a fine education, wealth, health and good looks. A nurse sat beside him in private school until he was nine years old; his father gave him an open checkbook when he was in high school. If Tom wanted anything, he just wrote a check; it was as simple as that. But along with this ease went trouble. People were always watching him, expecting great things from him because he came of such an outstanding family and "wonderful" environment. Nothing that Tom did seemed to live up to people's expectations. He never got any satisfaction out of success; in fact, success always seemed to get people annoyed with him: "Of course he's successful," they'd snap. "He ought to be!"

So Tom's subconscious mind did the thing that so many of our minds do. It said, "All right. If I can't get satisfaction from success, I'll get it from failure." And he proceeded to fail magnificently. When he was in college he started drinking. At medical school, his drinking became excessive. Drug addiction compounded his troubles. He married, set up a practice and had a child; the degeneration continued. In about ten years he reached the place where "just one" drink would start him off on a wild, blind drinking orgy that would last for days, even weeks. After one of his long disappearances, Dr. Tom came home to find that commitment papers had been made out against him. He was put in the violent ward of the state hospital, the same hospital where he had served as a doctor only a few years earlier.

"For forty-five days," Tom says, "I was out of my mind with D.T.'s. I was in solitary confinement, eating out of a tin plate like an animal. Then I began to come out of it and for another eighty-six days I lay in a comatose state, halfway between life and death. Surely this was as low as a man could sink. And then, suddenly—my heart still pounds when I think of it—I heard words spoken very slowly, and very distinctly.

'As far as the east is from the west, so far have I removed your transgressions from you.' (Psalm 103:12) Nothing has been the same for me since."

What had happened? Tom didn't know. He only knew that he had changed. He became calm. He was released from solitary confinement and allowed the comparative freedom of the ward. There he met two men who befriended him, and introduced him to Alcoholics Anonymous. In time, under the sponsorship of his AA friends, he was paroled from the hospital.

It was at this point that I met Tom at a religious conference where I was speaking. Scarcely have I ever known a man so thirsty for the water of life, so hungry for the bread of life. He wanted God, and God wanted him, and they found each other.

Dr. Tom did not go back to his practice right away. He felt he wasn't ready for that. He wanted to get a job on his own, one that had no relation to his childhood education. The only work he could find was a manual laboring job in the city dump. Think of that! A highly skilled, wealthy young man working as a laborer on the city dump and in the very southern community of his birth. But it was what Tom wanted. He wanted to see if he could be accepted for himself, and not for his family or his money.

One day while he was working, several of the "city fathers" came down to the dump for an inspection. Dr. Tom recognized some of his former schoolmates. He was suddenly filled with shame that they might recognize him, and he turned his back, bent down, and pretended to be working with something on the ground. A Negro fellow-worker saw him do this, and at the same time saw the neatly dressed city fathers. He must have sized up the situation quickly because, without saying a word, he turned and did Dr. Tom's work for him until the visitors left. To my mind that is one of the greatest, kindliest acts of understanding and brotherhood that I have ever heard about. Dr. Tom and his Negro friend never spoke about it, but it created a bond between them that was to have a wonderful effect on the young doctor. He took from it the strength that he needed.

"That man's name was Frank," Dr. Tom told me. "Frank will never know what he did for me. He accepted me. He taught me that I could be accepted for myself. First I had the acceptance of God, there in the hospital's solitary ward. Then I had the acceptance of man. It was what I needed in order to start again."

Today, Dr. Tom is again practicing medicine very successfully. He has a kind of enthusiasm about him, and a basic solidarity that comes from the new tough-mindedness that he has found. He was transformed from a "coward" to a "hero," to use Carlyle's terms. Of course, not many of us have such dramatic experiences with our fear of success, but it is nonetheless true that we often *don't want* positive thinking to work. We subconsciously see to it that our failure patterns remain intact.

But this is not the only block that can keep positive thinking from being effective. Sometimes there are strong negative elements in our lives that we refuse to clean out. We make feeble efforts to put positive forces to work, but they get stymied behind negative forces.

One night after I finished speaking at a dinner meeting in a hotel ballroom a man came up to me with the challenge: "I've been reading your stuff," he said, "I've tried it and it won't work."

"Why won't it work?" I asked him.

"That's what I'd like to know," he blustered.

Having a little time before taking a late plane I invited him to my hotel room for a talk. "I didn't mean to be impolite," he said as we sat down to chat. "But I'm trying to find out what's wrong. I seem to have lost my grip. I'm nervous and tense. I have a wonderful wife and family, a good business, a nice home, and I go to church. You'd think I'd be happy. But . . ." The recital went on and on. One trouble after another. And positive thinking, he said, did him no good at all.

After some discussion it occurred to me to throw out this question: "Are you doing anything wrong?"

"Nothing much," he muttered.

"What?" I asked.

"There's no point in going into that. I'm not doing anything that is in any way connected with my troubles. I'm only doing what everybody does."

"What does everybody else do?" I asked.

"Well," he said, "there is a little affair with a woman in Milwaukee."

"How little?" I asked.

He hesitated, "Well, maybe not so little."

"Maybe we had better face it. The plain truth is that you know you are doing something wrong, something you are ashamed of, something that could very well be the reason positive thinking isn't working for you."

"But how?" he demanded, on the defensive.

"Because guilt has a way of closing off your personality," I continued. "It sprouts fear and self-doubt; it restricts the power that gives vitality to the thought-flow. Constructive thinking becomes more difficult. Also, there is the self-punishment mechanism to deal with. When you are doing something wrong, you want to punish yourself to get relief from conscience distress. So actually, you try to make yourself fail, strange as it may sound. Of course all this blocks the positive feelings and thoughts that you do have. It's possible that all your misery and conflict stems from this sour area in your life."

"Well, what do I do about it?" he asked. Then he continued, "I guess I know the answer—stop doing it, get forgiveness—is that it?"

"That's it," I agreed. "And then you must forgive yourself. Do you want to start now?" He nodded. I could see that he was in earnest so I prayed, and he prayed. I made him pray out loud because he really had a lot to unload. And because he was sincere in his desire for change, God came into the picture and poured spiritual strength into him. Then his positive thinking really started working. Gone now is the woman in Milwaukee. Gone are the guilt and conflict feelings. As he became spiritually organized he found that it was quite possible for him to apply the principles of positive thinking with effective results. Naturally, this change did not happen all at once, but it *did* happen, and of course that's the important thing. One of the greatest facts in this world is that when a man changes, really changes in the God-centered way, everything changes.

Again, there is nothing mysterious about this. It is just common sense. We do something wrong, we feel guilty about it, and we expect punishment. If this remains uncorrected, the tendency is to punish ourselves, often through failures. That is the way the human mind is made. To correct the situation we must first clean out the wrong-doings; then the guilt feelings disappear and the need to punish ourselves with failures is thus eliminated. When this process has been completed, the principles of positive thinking can be tremendously effective.

One of the most important reasons why positive thinking seems not to work sometimes is that it has not really been put to a test. Positive thinking requires training and study and long perseverance. You have to be willing to work at it, sometimes for a long while, as was the case of a woman who spent four months of good solid, even painful effort before she got the results she sought. She wrote the following:

Dear Dr. Peale:

On the morning of January 21, 1956, I awoke with a headache. I am a registered nurse and I didn't think much of it at the time. A headache for a mother of three children is not an unheard of thing. Little did I know, as I downed a couple of aspirins, that this one was to be my constant companion for the next eight months.

Why should I have a headache? Seven doctors later, a badly depleted bank account, and a skin full of the newest drugs found me fifteen pounds lighter, an almost raving maniac, the sight badly impaired in one eye, blood pressure sky high and the headache.

My husband and I are devout Catholics. I was beyond the ability to pray so my husband prayed for both of us. He prayed God would direct him to help for me. It was in a chiropractor's office that I learned the power of positive thinking. I did not believe all this doctor told me, but when your book, *The Power of Positive Thinking,* fell into my hands I began to believe it might be so. Fortified with the spoken word of this sage doctor, plus the written material in your book, I began to apply to myself the principles.

To the degree I was able to understand and change my concepts from negative to positive—my headaches lessened. It took four months. I took no medication during this time and by September of that same year I had the last of the headaches.

I must add, our medical expenses have dropped about 80 per cent since I've changed my pattern of thinking. Do you know how a nurse thinks? Well, I'll tell you. One of the children has a running nose. Now, to the average person it is a running nose, but not to a nurse. It's pneumonia! She shoots that concept out into the air, and into the child's head. The child accepts it and puts the picture into reality.

How do I know this—because I did it. Hospital insurance records will bear me out. I was so good at it I was able to put not one of our children in the hospital, but all three of them at once, plus myself.

Now when they get a cold I look at it for what it is, a cold. And you know something—that's just as far as it goes. They throw it off in a couple of days.

Notice that it took four months of hard work to get results. This registered nurse understood the principle of positive thinking all right, but it wasn't until she was willing to put it to a test, go all out with it, make an effort really to change herself that she got rid of her headaches and experienced radical change within herself.

Ben Hogan, one of the greatest golfers of all time, practices what he calls muscle memory. He gets out on the links and swings the very same golf shot over, and over, and yet over again until his muscles "memorize" the exact pattern they have to follow. It is the same with our thinking habits. They have to be trained by a deliberate learning process to react the way we want them to react when we are faced with life's problems. Our mind has to be *trained* to think positively.

A final thing that I would like to mention has to do with belife. Positive thinking will not work unless you believe it will work. You have to bring your faith to bear on your thinking processes. The reason a lot of people do not get anywhere with positive thinking is that their faith is diluted. They water it down with timid little doubts. They do not dare to believe! But when you *do* believe, what amazing results you have.

There is D. H. Metzger, for example. But first let me refer to one of the most effective positive thinkers I have ever been privileged to know, my friend, Roger Burman, New York Sales Manager for the National Cash Register Company. Roger has a passion for helping others. He is always bringing out latent possibilities and guiding men in overcoming difficulties.

Roger Burman's teaching of positive thinking was a godsend to one of his top salesman, D. H. Metzger, who suddenly was afflicted with a growth in the throat. During the days of crisis Dave Metzger was able to say, "My mind was alerted to think right and have faith. I knew my life was at stake, but the feeling of doing right at the right time added confidence as to my future."

Then Dave Metzger encountered an even greater crisis, learning to speak again. How could he ever sell unless he could speak? Roger Burman told him that, with God's help, he could and would; and he did, too. In fact he became a top salesman, one of the most successful in his line. In his desire to help others Dave said:

> In order that I may be helpful to others who may find themselves in a similar predicament, more or less, I would like to emphasize that I put into practice Dr. Norman Vincent Peale's philosophy as outlined in his *Power of Positive Thinking,* of getting to the point of emptying one's mind of all negative thoughts, all unhappy thoughts and all pessimistic thinking and filling that vacuum with happy thoughts, filling the mind with a determination to get well at all costs. I pictured in my mind a return of my former faculties and good health. By following the specialist's prescribed exercises, I visualized my return as a leading salesman for my company once again.
>
> "Faith power works wonders" and I quote it from Dr. Peale's book. I cannot stress the value of this philosophy, the magic power of positive thinking for anyone who has any kind of a problem.
>
> This whole new experience has renewed the statement: "Salesmen talk too much." Finding it necessary to say the "mostest" in the "leastest" number of words I have framed my word story in such a manner and in such a tone that the results have been most gratifying. I speak slower and lower, and find the customer leaning forward if he misses a word. I am not dominating the situation and giving the customer

a chance to say "yes" much sooner than before. In this way I do not tax my strength. I "word plan" my sentence and now give the buyer a chance to be part of the sales. I confess I used to be part of that Etc., Etc., and Etc.

Conrad Hilton, an inspiring friend of mine for many years, magnificently demonstrated positive thinking in his victory over adversity in the building of his vast hotel empire. In his dynamic book, *Be My Guest*, he tells us that his parents gave him a two-part formula to which he owes much of his success. His mother said "pray" and his father said "work." Pray and work; how wise!

My own parents helped me similarly. My father said "think" and my mother said "believe." What power is in those four words when taken together; pray, work, think, believe!

Belief that is bold and daring—there is the formula. It carries all before it. Nothing can permanently stand against it. It magnificently focuses power. "If ye have faith . . . nothing shall be impossible unto you." (Matthew 17:20) Faith in God, faith in God's power in you, faith in life itself—that is the essence of positive thinking; not timid doubt, not weak speculation, but big, bold, daring faith—this is the victory.

Does positive thinking always work?

Of course it does; positive thinking will work if you are willing to work at it. It is not an easy discipline. It takes hard work and hard belief. It takes honest living, and a strong desire to succeed. And you will need to keep working at it constantly to achieve success in applying positive thinking. Just when you believe you have mastered it, you will have to develop it again.

My friend Justin Dart, head of Rexall Drugs, one of our greatest salesmen and business leaders said, "Positive thinking is just like golf. You get a good stroke or two, and you think you've mastered the game. But the next thing you know, you flub your shots again. So, with positive thinking you have to work at it again and then again, ever relearning it."

How right Mr. Dart is. You must do a day-to-day job on yourself, conditioning and reconditioning your thinking. But the results are really amazing. They are worth all the effort and change-in-habit that is required, as I will demonstrate in the chapters that follow.

II

# Precondition Your Mind to Success

YOU CAN precondition your mind to success. This is a basic principle of positive thinking. You can actually forecast what your future failure or success will be by your present type of thinking.

And right here I think it is important to define what we mean by success. Naturally we do not mean mere achievement, but rather the more difficult feat of handling your life efficiently. It means to be a success as a person; controlled, organized, not part of the world's problem but part of its cure. That is the goal we should have for ourselves: the goal of successful living, of being a creative individual.

I learned a valuable lesson in successful living from a Pullman porter. I had a speaking date in Olean, New York, and my travel schedule called for an overnight trip on the Erie Railroad. My journey got off to a wonderful start the moment I stepped into the sleeping car. I was greeted by the porter, a big, genial, friendly man.

"Good evening, sir," he said. "Are you ready for a good night's sleep?"

"I sure am," I replied. "I can't wait to get into bed."

As he showed me into my compartment I saw that the bed was already made up. It was really an inviting sight. The sheets and covers were tight and neatly turned back, the bedroom was immaculate with a generous supply of towels, the temperature was exactly right. "You certainly know how to prepare an attractive room," I commented. I got into bed, read a few verses from my Bible, and then fell into a deep sleep. The next thing I knew it was nine o'clock and I usually wake up automatically at seven.

"Good morning, sir," said the porter as I was going in to breakfast. "How did you sleep?"

"Fine," I said, "just fine."

"Well, I'm not surprised; I knew you would. But you should have seen the man who got on just after you. First thing he said was, 'I know I'm not going to sleep, porter.' And then nothing was right. He wanted to be moved to the center of the car. He didn't like the way his bed was facing. The room was too cold and then it was too hot. Do you know the difference between you two gentlemen and why you slept well and he didn't?"

"No. I'm interested."

"You slept well because you had made up your mind to it. That other man had made up his mind not to sleep. A long time ago I discovered that those who ride with me sleep if they think they are going to sleep. They precondition their minds to sleep."

It was worth making the trip just to get that remark which contained such amazing insight. You can precondition your mind. You can precondition it to sleep, or to insomnia. You can precondition it to success, or to failure. In other words, that which you constantly think is going to happen, tends to happen. At this very minute, as you are reading this book, you are what your thoughts have made you over a long period of time. And it is possible to figure out, almost scientifically, what kind of person you will be ten years from now by analyzing the kind of thoughts you are now holding in your mind. Are they negative, destructive thoughts? Are you preconditioning yourself to failure? Or are they positive, healthy thoughts, so that you are forecasting your own success?

Let me tell you about a friend of mine, Norman A. McGee. Better still, here's a story from the *Savannah Morning News* about him:

> Ten years ago, the Southland Oil Corporation was just an idea in the fertile brain of Norman A. McGee. Today it is a flourishing Savannah corporation occupying 24 acres at the Georgia State Port with fixed assets topping the $2,000,000 mark.
>
> "I've been lucky many times," the 43-year-old McGee says. "On the other hand, I've resorted to prayer often, too. I believe anybody could have done it with persistence and faith—and a wife like mine."
>
> McGee had this idea about forming a corporation for the distribution of oil products and he had worked hard to interest others in it. The prospects looked good, but McGee had no income and he was down to his last $1,000 in the bank.
>
> "I asked my wife," McGee recalls, "what should I do? Keep on trying, or give up and take a job?"
>
> Her answer made Southland Oil possible. "Keep on trying," she said. "Don't ever give up!"

What is McGee's secret? He thinks, he prays, he believes, he works and he has a wife who would never let him quit. What marvelous assets! He preconditioned himself to success. And he isn't working only for himself either. He is active in the Presbyterian Church and was elected to the legislature.

Now listen, my friend. You can also gain success. Stop thinking failure. Start thinking success. Think and pray and work. Get a goal, clearly define it, and never give up. But first start working on your thoughts. Precondition them with sound positive thinking. When you precondition your mind, you are in the process of transforming your life. We transform our lives by how we think. The Bible says ". . . be ye transformed by the renewing of your mind." (Romans 12:2) Thoughts are things. Thoughts are dynamic, thoughts are vital and creative, thoughts actually change conditions. If you hold defeatist thoughts, hate thoughts, dishonest thoughts, failure thoughts—these are destructive. If you have honest thoughts, love thoughts, if you have service thoughts, success thoughts—these are creative. By the renewing of your mind you can be transformed as a person. Your condition may be transformed by the substitution of positive thinking for negative thinking. This is being done every day as my contacts reveal. The following letter is an example:

> Five years ago, right after my husband returned from the service, I had a complete physical and nervous breakdown. I was not able to face life. I became weak and nauseated after having given a simple devotional for our Sunday school class.
>
> I became panicky and made excuses when asked to do things socially. When more than one or two unusual things faced me at a time, I would go to bed with nervous chills and a real and intense sickness. Then depression would set in, and I would feel so guilty and bad about leaving my family in the lurch and at upsetting them, that I would have a long hard battle before I could again face a full day's routine. I was miserable.
>
> All this time my husband was taking his place in the community. Civic clubs, church and business were demanding more and more of his time and talent. I knew that as far as our marriage was concerned, I was being outgrown and the years would see us with nothing in common . . . he an active and happy person away from home and I more of a recluse each day.

Then came help! I found out about positive thinking. My husband ordered some literature about positive thinking, and here it was! I started reading with the feeling of, "I might as well try this, too." But this was new. Real. Something definite to work with.

Now time has passed. Six months ago when they asked me to be president of our Sunday school class I said no. I had no more than hung up the phone than I realized that this was God giving me a chance to overcome my sense of defeat. After a prayer, I phoned the committee and accepted the nomination. Then, until I took office, I prayed daily that God would let it be His work.

I have never faced that class with anything except a perfect calm and peace of heart. I am now secretary of our School Parents; work two days a week for my husband; bowl every week and do all my own housework. I seldom have even an hour of depression. My husband loves his home and we do civic work together. Thank you, Dr. Peale, and God bless you.

Here is a woman whose life was completely changed by a change in her thought pattern. She changed the conditions of her life by changing the conditions of her mental life. Disraeli, the great English statesman, made this wise remark: "Nurture your mind with great thoughts for you will never go any higher than you think." Therefore, think big. I believe the trouble with all of us is that we have a tendency to think only little thoughts about everything: about ourselves, our family, our children, our business. So we get little results.

I really believe it is a law—you will get no bigger results than your thoughts are big. Big thoughts get big results; little thoughts get little results. One of the most successful men I have ever known was William Danforth, who headed the Purina Company. When Mr. Danforth was a boy he was puny. He would have qualified well for one of the "before" pictures in a body building advertisement. He has told me that he was small in thought, too. He did not think well of himself, and this insecurity was compounded by the slenderness of his physique.

But all this changed. William had a teacher in school who must have been one of the world's great builders of men. Privately, one day his teacher took him aside and said, "William, your thinking is all wrong. You think of yourself as a weakling and you are becoming one. But this need not be. I *dare* you to be a strong boy."

"What do you mean?" the boy asked. "You can't just dare yourself strong."

"Oh, yes, you can. Stand up here in front of me." Young Danforth stood up before the teacher. "Now take your posture, for instance. It shows that you are thinking weakness. What I want you to do is to think strength. Pull in your stomach, draw it up under your rib cage. Now. Do this. Think tall. Believe tall. Act tall. Dare tall. Stand on your own two feet and live tall like a man."

And that is what William Danforth did. The last time I saw him he was eighty-five years old. He was vigorous, healthy, active. And the last thing he said to me as we were parting was: "Remember, stand tall."

Justin Dart, head of the Rexall Drug Company, once played guard for Northwestern University. Before an important game the coach called him aside and said, "Go out there today and play as a great guard should. You can do it!"

Justin told me, "I know the coach overestimated me, but he gave me a new mental concept of myself. I shall never forget how I ran out on the field, running tall."

Big thinking, tall thinking. It is this that makes men big and conditions them to success.

One of my readers describes himself as a business doctor. John, as I shall designate him, takes ailing businesses and makes them well again. And he tells me that in nine out of ten cases there is nothing much wrong with the business except the personnel. "A sick business is usually run by sick men," he says. "The trick is to get the men to thinking of themselves as successful; and then the business will be successful."

John told me about a boy he met at one of the companies he was doctoring. This boy was about as low on the totem pole of that business as he could possibly be. He was the fifth assistant to the shipping clerk; he spent his days sticking on labels. But there was something appealing about him, and one day my friend said to the boy, "I see no reason why you couldn't be a great success if you *thought* you could be. You are a bright boy. You have the brains and the personality. I hope you're not content with sticking on labels. Have you ever thought of becoming a salesman?"

"Oh no, no. I couldn't do that," the boy said quickly.

"Don't answer so fast," said John. "I think you'd make a good salesman. I'm going to speak to the front office about switching you to another job."

The boy was upset. It made him feel insecure. He was used to sticking on labels. But John had his way and in a few days the boy was out of his blue denims and into a smart suit, reporting for instructions.

"What do you want me to do?" said the boy. "I couldn't possibly sell anything."

"Well now, the first thing I want you to do is to take a good look at that door over there." The boy looked. On the glass panel were the words "Sales Manager," and under it was the name of the present sales manager, an older man who was scheduled to retire in a few years.

"Now," said our business doctor, "I want you to photograph mentally a picture of that door. Only I want you to substitute your own name for the name you see there now. Close your eyes. Can you mentally see that door? Can you see your own name on it?" The boy nodded yes. "All right, then.

Here's what you do. Hold that picture firmly in your mind; then work hard, study hard all the time, believe that your name will eventually be on that door, and I know that it will."

"And was it?" I asked.

"What do *you* think? I never saw anyone work so hard and so long and so persistently. When I thought he was ready to go out and sell I went with him on his first trip. I left him at Wheeling, West Virginia. The boy looked at me and said, 'When you leave me I'm all alone, but I'll do my best.' "

"But I reminded him, 'You're not alone. Just remember that; and remember also, you know how to sell. And that Partner who is with you will help you.' "

A look of satisfaction came over John's face. "He turned out great, that boy, and finally became the best sales manager that company has ever had."

The manner in which you precondition your mind is extremely important because, whether good or bad, strong or weak, that preconditioning tends to become a reality. Whatever you picture about yourself either as a success or a failure will likely come to pass. "There is a deep tendency in human nature," said a psychologist, "to become precisely like that which we habitually imagine ourselves to be." Now imagination isn't fantasy. Imagination is the art or science of the projected image. You might call it image-ing. And the sort of image of yourself that you hold is very important—for that image may become fact.

The thought is ancestor of the deed. If you precondition your mind with thoughts of success, the deeds of success naturally tend to follow. But, notice that an important ingredient of this pattern is to ask for God's help. Let me just say that again: A very important part of the secret of using positive thinking in any form is to include the active participation of God. This is borne out time and again in our mail.

I ordered *The Power of Positive Thinking* from Montgomery Ward at Fort Worth. At that time I was out of work. I called all over the country to find work. Everything looked very black for me and my family, then one day I just happened to see this book. Well, I didn't tell anyone about it but just ordered it and when it came I got busy reading it.

In a few days I began to get some confidence in myself, which I didn't have before, and God gave me courage. So one night I read where you could take God as a partner in your business so I asked him to be my partner. I got me a welding machine for I am a welder; and then I got a contract to build some cattle guards for the county. I kept asking God to be my partner so I finally got me a truck and put my stuff on, welding machine and equipment. Everything on credit. Didn't know how I was going to come out, just kept on fighting, having faith in God and praying.

All of a sudden my prayers began to be answered. I got some oil field welding pipe and got a pipeline contract that really gave me a push. He liked my work and gave me another line.

I could write about many things, but it is getting late. I can say one thing, through this book I got to know God more and the way you can have joy out of life that I didn't know before. Now I know what you can do with faith in God. Thank God, and you, for sending me on my way to success.

And then in a completely different vein, there is this letter from a woman who faced a terrible ordeal, but who preconditioned her mind to a successful adjustment. Here, too, note the important role God played in her success.

During the last year I have had three operations for cancer, the last one involving the amputation of my right arm and shoulder. I have been so thankful for God's presence during this time.

I had quite a struggle deciding whether to let the doctors do the extensive surgery they felt was necessary. I read the chapter "How To Use Faith in Healing" in *The Power of Positive Thinking* several times and prayed for guidance. I came to the conclusion that the best thing to do was to let the doctors do all they could and trust God for the rest. Once I was able to put myself completely in His hands I found peace and was able to go to the operating room without fear.

I made a very rapid recovery and now, eight weeks after surgery, am making preparations to be fitted with an artificial arm. I have been amazed at the way I have been able to accept this handicap without bitterness and depression.

Taking the power of God into your life is one of the most essential steps in preconditioning your mind to success. Forecast that you are going to achieve a certain goal, and then move steadily toward that goal. But if you have given yourself a really difficult assignment, you cannot achieve it by yourself. You need the help of God. The pathetic fact is that many of us do not live as people who have the Kingdom of God within us. We do not really use the great forces that Almighty God has put into us. Draw fully and confidently upon the power of God that He placed within you when He created you.

These are the powers that are available to all of us on our road to success. They are available, but they are of no use unless we take advantage of them. Far too often people spend their whole lives close to these riches without ever tapping them. They are like an old man I once heard about down in Texas. He had a small ranch which never amounted to much. All his life he had scrimped for a living and eventually he grew old and died.

The property was sold. The new owner drilled a well and struck a rich deposit of oil. Of course, the oil was there all the time waiting to gush forth. Many of us are living like that: we are sitting right on top of the richest sources of power that can be imagined, and we do nothing about it at all. It is there, waiting to be tapped. But the exploitation of these resources is up to you. Precondition your thinking to this truth and successful living can be yours.

It doesn't matter who you are or how often you've failed. Neither does it matter how old you are. Successful living can always be yours. I received a letter from a woman in Georgia describing the amazing transformation in the success-pattern of her father after he discovered what God could really do with his life. Before he tapped the powers of the Almighty, this lady told me, her father was a very unsuccessful person. He lost all his money in the market and after that he became bitter and resentful. He changed his work and tried to make the climb back, by himself, but failed again. But read the daughter's letter:

> . . . he was terribly unhappy. He had no belief. He didn't believe in God, he didn't even believe in himself. He shut out all friendships, and did nothing but criticize people. You can imagine the effect this had on his children. I don't remember ever having a peaceful meal at home. None of us could gain any weight because we were so tense all the time.
>
> About eighteen months ago my mother and father moved to Florida. He wanted to start all over again. Well, as you can probably guess things didn't work out well, and he became more unbearable than he was back in the dark days. He finally became so despondent that last September he had a serious heart attack. Later it was decided that he would have to have an operation.
>
> It was while he was waiting for the operation that God came in. First of all, God told my sister and me at exactly the same time to send Dad some material about positive thinking. Dad read it and took God into his life.

> Well now, here is your miracle, Dr. Peale. I was in Florida in February and my father looks twenty years younger. He is full of health and vitality. He keeps a Bible by his chair all the time. He loves everybody now, and he made three big sales in one day just while I was there. He constantly talks unashamedly of God and after witnessing this metamorphosis I am convinced that nothing, absolutely nothing, is impossible in this world as long as God is given half a chance.

Success is available to all of us if we will follow the basic principles of positive thinking.

You must never conclude, even though everything goes wrong, that you cannot succeed. Even at the worst there is a way out, a hidden secret that can turn failure into success and despair into happiness. No situation is so dark that there is not a ray of light. So if you face circumstances that you think are extremely difficult, if not utterly hopeless, I urge you to read and ponder the experience of Mr. and Mrs. J. P. Lingle of Missouri.

A couple of years ago Mrs. Lingle wrote me after reading *The Power of Positive Thinking* as follows:

> Three years ago, after fourteen years with a national chain variety store, my husband and I had an opportunity to open a store of our own. We were quite undecided, and turned the decision over to God, asking that, if it were His will to please provide the money we would need to get started; and if it were not His will, to keep us from getting it.
>
> Well, friends and relatives actually came and offered money to help us, and we felt that was our answer.
>
> But it seemed to have been wrong from the beginning—we could never make ends meet and were constantly, for two and one-half years threatened with lawsuits, telegrams demanding payment, etc.
>
> We are $10,000 in debt, and have no material assets other than a seven-year-old car and our furniture. My husband is

making $310.00 a month after taxes, so that doesn't leave much to pay off debts. We refused to go into bankruptcy as too many people would have been cheated out of what we rightfully owe them, and we felt God wouldn't want us to do it that way, even though we could have, legally. It's especially hard to keep faith when we get a nasty letter from a creditor or I look at the staggering debts compared with the miniature salary.

If you would just send me a word that will help me through this, I would be deeply grateful. I'm not experienced enough to know how to handle my spiritual thinking at a time like this.

Well, I wrote the Lingles describing some steps which I thought might be helpful. But I thought that the *most* helpful thing I could do was to put them in touch with a successful positive thinker who lived near them. I asked him to talk with them. I am going to call this man simply "Mr. S." because Mr. S. believes in keeping his good works secret. He follows the spiritual principle of not letting the right hand know what the left hand is doing.

Mr. S., I knew, believed strongly in the spiritual principle of sharing, not only as a means of maintaining a successful way of life, but also as a means of obtaining it in the first place. He promptly went to see the Lingles and found that they were so deeply engrossed with their problem that they could talk of nothing but their $10,000 debt. He told them that the first step in solving their problem was to start sharing, to begin at once to give away at least 100 per cent of the little that was coming in.

"But," they protested, "we are $10,000 in debt!"

"So what," Mr. S. replied. "My wife and I went broke back in 1933. We were in your very same situation—only we were $63,000 in debt. And we tithed our way out." He explained the principle of sharing, how it stimulates and maintains success. He pointed out one of the most subtle rules of successful living; namely, that unselfish giving makes real receiving possible.

Mr. S. prayed with this couple and together they surrendered the problem into the Lord's hands, promising to follow His guidance as it would be revealed to them. They broke with their self-pity, worry and tension. They let the problem go into God's hands; they let God take over. Then they were ready to start doing business on a creative and positive spiritual level. And incidentally, as they found, this is where being practical begins. They began to tithe their time, money and effort—in other words, they began to share themselves.

The first result to be recorded was in a letter from Mrs. Lingle in August, about four months after she wrote me the first time.

> I wanted to let you know that I haven't had a single worry day. I even received a letter from a creditor and it didn't upset me in the least, which is a remarkable change in itself.

And a little later there was another report from the Lingles on the effects of tithing:

> Have you time for an "inspiration story?" I have one. Two weeks ago, we received a notice from the State Tax Department informing us we were being assessed for $90. In addition the points were worn out in our car, and our liability insurance on the car had expired.
>
> We had no more than received the assessment notice, (and had no idea where the money was to come from) when the Monroe Calculator office man here called and said he could sell our calculator (we've been trying to sell it for five months) at a price which would cover the tax, the auto re-

pairs and buy the necessary insurance! Isn't that wonderful? But there's more to come!

I hadn't had any luck finding work that would allow me to be home with Skippy (our little boy). But, following the principles of tithing one's self, on an impulse, I stopped by the church here and went to the office, introduced myself and told them I had a typewriter at home; and if they ever had extra work to do, I would like to take it home and do it in an effort to give some of my time to the church.

Well, they were almost stricken dumb! They explained they had lost a secretary, and were so snowed under, my offer was truly an answer to prayer! So I brought several stencils home and cut them; and then the next day ran them, and lots more, off on the mimeo for them.

That night I received a phone call from an office I had called two months ago about work and had almost forgotten about. They wondered if I would be interested in doing extra work—*cutting stencils*—at $1.25 per hour to start. There wouldn't be any regular hours for me, I could come in each day whenever I wanted and go home whenever I wanted! Don't you find that inspiring?

And so it went, blessing after blessing, guidance after guidance to these happy people. They prayed, they trusted, they gave, and they got right up on top of their difficulties. Mr. Lingle made a new business connection as a store manager and he did all right, too, as the following happy letter from Mrs. Lingle, written two years later, indicates:

I just can't wait any longer!

Here is another story for you of how God is looking after us. It happened after your last visit.

You remember we had been looking for a car since last October, when our seven-year-old Studebaker started giving us fits. We found the one we wanted then, in October, a secondhand Buick, but we felt that we didn't need such a fine one. So Jim kept looking and looking, but none came up to the Buick in price, mileage, cleanness and all things considered.

So one day he said, "Well, we know we don't need that nice a car; we know we don't have the down payment, but if that's the car we're supposed to have, the down payment will come to us, and the car will still be on the lot waiting when it does."

You know, in Jim's business, he gets a percentage on any profit made during the year, but we were only open two months in 1958 and, of course, the profit the store made was eaten up by the opening expenses.

So imagine our surprise when Jim got a note from the office saying they were going to pay him a bonus on his profit, just as if there had been no opening expenses, but they felt he had worked hard and deserved it. They just don't do things like that! And instead of the usual 10 per cent, it was 15 per cent! So there was our down payment! And after four months of waiting, the car was still there!

Remember you asked how much we had been able to repay on our $10,000 debt when we talked on the phone? Well, next month, it will have been two years and we have repaid $4,000 since then! Well, four down and six to go. What a challenge!

And here is the last report to date from the Lingles. Note in it how the Lingles have now completely absorbed the principle of sharing:

This will tell how we are doing at the present time. We are far from being out of debt, but far from out of faith, too.

As for some of the spiritual principles which have helped us, there is no doubt that *helping others who are in need* stands at the top of the list. I'm enclosing a copy of the type of note we send when we discover someone who could use a little boost. In so doing, I'm letting out our secret, but perhaps, Dr. Peale, if you desire to use the idea, other people will pick it up and it's the sort of thing that can snowball into something wonderful. Here is the note which we send:

> Dear Friends:
>
> Every week Jim and I put back an offering in a little envelope we have for "others." Then when we learn of someone who could use a little boost—as we often have—we send something to them with a note like this.
>
> We know Stan has a job now, but Saturday you said you only had a dollar, so maybe this will help out with his lunches and carfare until his first pay check comes in.
>
> We don't want it back for ourselves, but there are two things we would like you to do—don't tell anyone about it, and when you begin to get on your feet again, find someone who could use it, and repay us by giving it to them under the same conditions.
>
> No one knows we do this, and it must be kept just between God and you and us. And if you want to know our reasons, I'll give you a clue. Read Matthew 6:1-4.

Well, let's run down the list of principles of successful living that we have been talking about in this chapter.

*First,* it is important to define what success means to you. Define your goal clearly, pinpoint it. Be sure that your goal is in harmony with God's desires for you. For example, don't make the mistake of having only material success as your goal: God wants a lot more for you than superficial material wealth. He wants real wealth for you, the wealth of life that is successful in all its aspects: economic, social, spiritual, intellectual, physical. It is His desire to give you real riches. Don't underestimate the good things that God wants for you and will give you if you will only learn to receive.

*Second,* study until you really grasp the life-changing power of the truth that you can precondition your own success. Paint a picture of yourself as succeeding, hold that picture ever before you, and it will materialize. With positive thinking you can actually change the conditions of your life.

*Third,* bring God into a central place in your thought pattern. Pray, seek His guidance, strive to bring your effort into harmony with His teachings.

*Fourth,* to maintain your success with poise and without tension, learn to share. Share your success liberally with others. Teach others how to think positively, how to achieve the same results with their lives that you do with yours. In this way you will be guaranteeing the continued flow of creative ideas in and around you: you will be paying the premiums on an insurance policy protecting the success you have achieved.

Use these four principles steadily and regularly in your life, and success—the true success of bountiful living—will be yours. Start now to precondition your mind to success.

III

# No More Failure for You

HIS NAME was Bob. He was a big man, but shy. He was a salesman. But Bob's record was perilously near the bottom.

Yet, only a year after his superiors had decided to give Bob one last chance, he passed every other salesman to become the company's top producer. At the annual sales meeting, the manager called Bob to the platform to receive the prize as top man for the year. As the manager handed him a check he said: "Bob, you're a mystery. You've never been anywhere near the top in sales before, but now you've reached it. Besides, you came up from near the bottom. How did you do it? Tell the boys here."

Bob was embarrassed. He shifted from one foot to the other and his face turned red. "There's nothing I can tell them," he said. "I just got hold of something that changed me into a new man."

"What was that?" the manager asked curiously.

"Well, I simply found thirteen words—and those words changed everything. You see, when I was told you'd have to let me go if I didn't improve, I got to thinking. I went home that night and sat in my chair thinking some pretty honest thoughts with myself.

"Well, after a while, I happened to see an old Bible my mother had given me but which I hadn't looked at very often. She told me if I ever got into trouble I'd find an answer in that Book. Well, I was in real trouble. Maybe this was the time. Anyway, I took it from the shelf, blew the dust off it, and began to leaf through. But it wasn't until I was almost going to close it that I found exactly what I needed."

He hesitated in some embarrassment. Talking religion wasn't his line, but he continued doggedly. "I found these thirteen words: 'Behold, I make all things new . . . He that overcometh shall inherit all things.'

"Well, those words hit me like a ton of bricks. If anyone needed to be made new it was I.

"Right there I prayed to God to make me a new man, to help me stop being such a flop. I meant this too, and I felt much better. I had the best sleep in weeks. I felt a little confidence for the first time.

"Next morning, I said those thirteen words to myself several times. And because I made up my mind to change everything about me and make it all new like the words I said, I went downtown and shot some of my last few bucks for a new suit and tie and took them home. I undressed, got into the tub and scrubbed myself hard. It seemed like I wanted to wash all the failure off of me. Then I dressed, and before going out, knelt down and prayed to God to help me. I looked in the mirror and, believe it or not, I actually looked like a new man. I know that sounds crazy, but it's the way I felt, too.

"I said, 'God, I'm going out now to make calls and I'm a new man. I'll do better with Your help. I found myself taking a lot more interest in the prospects I called on. I was more enthusiastic. I began to sell. I was enjoying myself, too. Everything went better. I guess that's all there is to it."

The man who told me this story said, "You could hear a pin drop. Then the boys tore off the lid with cheering like you'd never heard at a sales meeting." And why not, for they had seen actual proof that a man, with God's help, can make himself over, despite all failures.

So you do not need to put up with continued failure. I know this to be a fact and not theory. My reason for being so certain is because of the many people who have convincingly demonstrated the power to change from failure to success. Such change may no come easily, but it can and does come and that is the main thing. When you decide, really decide, that there shall be no more failure for you, and carry out the principles outlined in this chapter and book, there is no doubt there need be no more failure for you.

I base this assertion upon the many amazing results which have been reported to me by those who have practiced positive thinking.

For example, in a western state I stayed in a large and beautiful hotel. When I checked out, the manager came over to say good-bye.

"A fine hotel you have here," I said in thanking him for a pleasant stay.

He smiled and said quietly, "I owe it all to God and the help I received from positive thinking." Later he wrote me a sincere and moving statement of his dynamic change.

> I used to be the biggest worry and fear man alive. When I had nothing to worry over, I would dream one up to stay in step with all the confusion and upheaval I lived in. This was a condition dating back from early childhood.
>
> Five years ago this coming September, I came across some of your writing about positive thinking. This article aroused a tremendous amount of interest, and I knew immediately that here I had found something which could help me. I began to collect all the material you had written and listened to your Sunday radio broadcasts.
>
> Dr. Peale, it is not easy to shake off long established habits,

but the one thing which helped me most was that I began to read the Bible, and in very short order I realized that I wanted God to help me, and I received Jesus Christ.

I came across in your writing where you suggested draining out all your bad thoughts, like water out of a faucet, and replacing them with clean, healthy thoughts. I did this and had a real brain washing. Gone are the worries, fears and emotions. I might also like to mention that I gave up drinking.

Today I am happy. I love everything I come in contact with and have acquired your habit of staying on top of every situation.

The principles of positive thinking work when applied with the honesty and sincerity this man used. Let me suggest an experiment. Take a pencil and paper and list your three chief failure areas; three points at which you are currently failing, or at least not doing as well as you desire.

It may be you do not get along too well with other people. Perhaps you are having trouble controlling desire. Is it for alcohol, sex, tobacco, or perhaps simply too much fattening food? Could be you simply cannot seem to master efficiency. Maybe you are easily discouraged, or negative. Whatever they are, big or little, list your failure areas in the order of their importance. Then let's see what to do about turning these failures into successes.

The first thing is to get an answer to that basic question, "Why do you have these failure points?"

That may be difficult to determine, and you may even require professional help to ferret out the real reasons for your failures. Many of us tend to blame external factors for our failure. But actually, more often the place to look is within ourselves. And here we come upon some strange and complex facts. For one thing, psychologists tell us that there is even such a quirk as a failure wish. Success, for some psychological reason, seems too dangerous for many people. They cleverly find ways to avoid it, unconsciously, of course. They do not really want to succeed. So, when you give the reason for your failure, be sure it's the true reason.

But let us suppose that you really want to do something about failure. What corrective formula can you use? There is one simple formula that I have known to produce amazing results. It is a definite one, two, three positive-thinking procedure. If applied with maximum effort, it will almost certainly result in no more failure for you. Here's the formula:

Try, really try.
Think, really think.
Believe, really believe.

Let's take that first point; *Try, really try*. Probably this doesn't have too much appeal, because trying can be very hard, so hard, in fact, that few people will actually attempt it. Or they may attempt it, but do not have what it takes to keep on trying. Let's face it, when was the last time you tackled one of the failures on your list with the determined attitude that you were going to get in there and try, *really* try? Most failure is simply due to the fact that we take the line of least "persistence." We do not make a prodigious effort to succeed.

Eddie Arcaro, the famous jockey, says that only a few horses really try. "Seventy per cent of them don't want to win," he declares, and he ought to know. In this respect it would seem that we are like race horses; we too seldom try, really try, to win.

William James, the famous psychologist, recognized the difficulty of making a great effort. He speaks of "the first layer of fatigue." This is the tiredness that comes after a little unusual effort. You try for a short while, become fatigued, then simply quit. But God built an enormous reservoir of reserve energy into your system, which is available if you will just push down to it—just give a little more effort. It is like the accelerator on some automobiles which produce a sudden burst of added energy and power whenever needed by simply pressing down harder. Personality is constructed in much the same way. Push down hard on your personality accelerator and this extra power will come surging forth. We seldom give ourselves the extra push that penetrates below the first layer of fatigue to where vast untapped power lies. But when you do, you get amazing results.

The secret is in putting your *whole* mind to it. Actually we seldom use our full mental power—certainly not our full spiritual potential. We might as well admit we do not give a problem all we've got; only in the rarest instances or in the greatest crises. If you put your whole mind to a difficulty you will be astonished at your own power over it.

Do you really want power over your failures? Do you want it enough to try, really try? You can have it if you do. This applies in any failure area. A remarkable example of the victory-producing power over sheer, dogged effort, plus faith, is described in the following letter from a reader in New York. The writer herself says she hasn't much education. Indeed, the lack of punctuation adds to the letter's charm, so I am going to copy it just as it is written.

> I'm a little old lady in my late 60's, and I would like to tell you all the ones that have no faith that with the power of faith one can achieve miracles. I'm sorry I have no education and can't even spell right, but I'm going to try and relate to you my first great problem of my life and how I did draw on the power of faith.
>
> I was born a cripple with dislocation of both my hips and doctors said I would never walk but as I grew up and looked at others walk I said to myself please God help me. I know

you love me, I was six years old and my heart was broke and so one day I tryed to stand up between two chairs and down I would go but I didn't give up. Every day I'd speak to God and tryed again and again until I held myself up for a few seconds and I can't describe to you the joy in my heart being able to stand on my feet. I gave one scream to mamma. I'm up. I can walk!

Then I went down again. I can't never forget the joy of my parents and when I tryed again my mother handed me the end of a broom stick while she held the other end and said, Give one step forward with one foot and then another and that is how my faith helped me to walk the duck walk thats what the doctors calls it but I have been so grateful ever since then.

Three years ago I had an accident and I broke my left ankle and was in the hospital and they took exrays of my legs. Then the doctors came to me and said lady how did you walk? And I said God was my doctor and they said its a miracle you have no socketts and no joints on your hips how did you stand up? And memories came back to me and I have waited 60 years to find out that I have no socketts and no joints for I never knew why.

Then the doctors were afraid that with the accident and broken ankle and my age I would not walk again but God came to my rescue again and to the surprise of all I'm walking again, and still holding my job of taking care of four children of a widow mother while she works. I'm a widow too and had to work very hard to grow my children. My husband died with the spanish flu in 1919. I had two little girls and a son was born two month later. I scrubbed floors on my knees for 17 years and never was sick in life. I don't know what an headache is.

Now here is a person who knows what it is to try, really try. "Every day I'd speak to God and tryed again and again until I held myself up," she said. And I like that advice of her mother, too: "Give one step forward with one foot and then another." That's what trying means. It means being willing to keep at your problems until they are solved. Keep at it, try, keep at it; that constant attack attitude will ultimately overcome any failure.

So with regard to your own problem area, or your own failure area, are you tackling it well, only half-well, or just well enough to get by? Are you putting an honest, all-out effort into the solution? The fact cannot be repeated too often, namely: You can eliminate your failure pattern by learning to try, really try.

Difficulties should act as a spur. Charles de Gaulle once said, "Difficulty attracts the man of character because it is in embracing it that he realizes himself." That's real stuff. Try and try and keep on trying and God will come to your aid. God is always with the man who is willing to make a gallant and repetitive effort.

I witnessed the Millrose Games in Madison Square Garden. These are great games in which the finest athletes in the country compete in various track events: running races, pole vaulting, high jumping. And I saw something that was truly wonderful, the breaking of the world's indoor high jump record by John Thomas, a seventeen-year-old freshman from Boston University.

I saw John Thomas become the champion high jumper of the world. One month before the Millrose Games, he jumped 6′9″; two weeks before the games, he jumped 6′11¾″. On the night of the games themselves, before a hushed fifteen thousand people, he broke the world's record. To quote one sports writer: "In one of the greatest moments of sports, he took off toward the ceiling and topped the bar at seven feet."

Only seventeen years old and world's champion indoor high jumper! The crowd went wild. John was immediately besieged by photographers, reporters, people hugging him and shaking his hand. But he paid scant attention to them.

In fact, he waved them aside. He wasn't through trying yet. He had made one world's record. He could have rested on his laurels, but he was a boy who knows what it is to keep trying, and there was another record he wanted that night. He wanted to go after the outdoor record too. That was 7′1.2″. It was a record held by a Russian. John told the officials to put the bar at 7′1.25″. And once again fifteen thousand people dropped into a deep silence. One time John failed. Twice, he failed. A third time . . . he failed.

Now, I had a curious reaction to all this. At first I said to myself that John Thomas had made a mistake. He had taken the edge off his victory. But then I was ashamed of myself. When I got to thinking about what that boy had done, I saw that he was not out for the glory; he was driven by some godlike impulse to try for something always just a little bit out of his reach. Something greater.

They wouldn't let him try further that night. But I came away with the feeling that I had been watching one of the greatest athletes of all time in the making, because he knew what it was to reach up and try, and even when he had won, to try again for a higher goal. And this feeling proved itself three weeks later when, in the same Madison Square Garden, John "took off toward the ceiling" again, and this time topped the bar at 7′1.25″, thus becoming the world's champion for both the indoor and the outdoor jump. He tried, really tried. And it paid off in victory.

How about your own efforts? Are you willing to stretch yourself? Have you honestly given your problem that big extra try and done it more than once? Once isn't enough. It takes many tries. And you will be surprised at what real trying will release in you. For so many people failure is simply a matter of not making the expenditure of physical and mental effort that is needed for victory. Look over your failure list. Can you say that each of these failures has been probed with an honest, all-out effort, the kind of trying that makes champions? If not, test the theory of trying, and trying some more, and see what happens.

The second part of the formula for overcoming the failure pattern is to think, really think . . . positively. I believe that the power of positive thought is so great that you can think yourself through any failure. You can think yourself out of any problem.

An illustration is the fourteen-year-old boy who read a want ad in the newspaper in which a job for a boy of his age was offered. When he arrived next morning at the appointed place, on time, he found twenty boys already in line.

This would have stumped a less forceful and resourceful boy, but this lad had what it takes to handle a situation. He thought. He made use of his head, which is a thinking machine designed by the Creator to help a person solve problems. His mind was not negative. He could think, really think, and so an idea was born. What a wonderful thing a thought-out idea is. It's powerful.

Taking a piece of paper he wrote a few lines; then, stepping out of line and asking the boy behind him to hold his place, he went over to the secretary of the man doing the hiring and said politely, "Please, Miss, will you kindly hand this note to your boss? It's important. Thank you very much."

The secretary was impressed by the boy; he was courteous, pleasant and forceful. A lesser boy she would no doubt have brushed aside, but this youngster was different. He had that attractive, indefinable quality called force. So she complied with his request and took the note in to her employer.

He read it, grinned, and handed it back to her. She read it and laughed. This is what it said:

"Dear Sir, I am the twenty-first kid in line. Please don't do anything until you see me."

Did he get the job? What do you think? A boy like that

will inevitably go places and do things. He knew, though young in years, how to think, really think. He had already developed the ability to size up a problem quickly, attack it forcefully, and do the very best about it.

If the problem happens to be yourself, as actually a great many of life's problems are, solutions come more surely and even more easily when you think, really think. The *Saturday Evening Post* carried an interesting article about Tommy Bolt, who won the National Open Golf Championship in 1958. The subtitle of this article read, "It was clean, positive thinking that changed my life." It is a story of how a champion was made by positive thinking.

It seems that Mr. Bolt used to be called the "terrible tempered Mr. Bolt." He missed the championship a couple of times, due to his terrible temper. On one occasion, in a rage because he had missed a putt, he deliberately broke all of his clubs. Frequently he broke his five iron. To use his own colloquial phrase, he would just "wrap the five iron around a tree." Gradually the fans got onto this. Spectators followed Tommy Bolt around the course, and they would congregate at the greens and chant, "Miss it, miss it!" And he would accommodate them by missing. Then he would go into one of his rages, and the spectators were delighted. Mr. Bolt, not knowing how to think properly, was emotionally unstable, Wrong thinking, expressed in temper, resulted in failure to reach his goals.

Finally Tommy Bolt read a couple of books which straightened out his thinking. One of these was by Bishop Fulton J. Sheen. Another, as I was pleasantly surprised to learn, was one of my own books. And here is some of Tommy Bolt's testimony about his experience.

"I reformed my thinking," he says. "I reconditioned my attitudes, I strengthened my faith and put my trust in Someone bigger than I was, and it worked. My new positive attitude never wavered, once I started. Clean positive thinking changed my life. I wanted to keep my thinking clear and straight. The things I read put a safety valve on my temper and formed a sort of protective coating against outside influences and distractions." The last sentence is a classic, but now comes one that is even more so: "I promised the Lord I would help Him help me." That's a tremendous idea, for God needs your help with you. Tommy Bolt used his failures to spur him on to success. Failure, for him, became a challenge, and that of course is what failure should always be.

It is absolutely vital to learn to think positively if failure patterns are to be overcome. You must recondition your attitudes until you have turned negativism into positivism. In this I am always reminded of a dynamic and unforgettable schoolteacher I had when I was a boy. All of a sudden, for no apparent reason, he would stop the class, walk up to the blackboard and write in big, bold letters the word, CAN'T. And then he would turn to the class and smile and chant to them:

"What do I do?"

And the kids would laugh and chant back to him, "Knock the T off the CAN'T!!!

He whisked an eraser over the "t" and the word became CAN. That's the kind of teaching we need to give ourselves. Knock the T off the Can't, and make it Can. This is the way to think, really think yourself away from your failures. If the word Can't ever gets firmly embedded in your mind it will cause all sorts of trouble.

It is astonishing how even successful enterprises can go badly when you take on the can't attitude. Years ago I knew an old gentleman who ran a lunch counter along the highway. It was a time of depression in business. The old man was fortunate enough to be a little blind and deaf. I say fortunate, because he didn't have to read about the depression or hear the negative conversation of his friends. So, not knowing there was a depression, he had a remarkably successful business. He painted his stand, he delivered a good article; he put up bright signs along the road which almost conveyed the aroma of his sandwiches. He made his merchandise so delicious that people who "had no money," would stop and buy his food.

The old man worked hard and sent his boy to college. There the boy took courses in economics and learned how bad things were. When he came home for Christmas and noticed the thriving business, he went to his father and said, "Pop, something's wrong around here. You shouldn't be as successful as you are. Why, you act as if you didn't know there was a depression on!"

And he told his father all about the depression, and how people were retrenching everywhere. As the father began to think it over and look around him, and listen to the negative thoughts, he said to himself: "Maybe I'd better not repaint my stand this year. I'd better save my money because there's a depression. And I'd better cut down on the amount of hamburger I put in these sandwiches. And what's the use of putting out signs if nobody has any money." And so he stopped all positive efforts. The result: business soon fell off. When the boy came back for the Easter vacation the father told him, "Son, I want to thank you for the information you gave me about the depression. It's absolutely true. I feel it in my business. A college education, son, is a wonderful thing."

That is what happens when negative thinking gets lodged in our minds. Such thoughts should be drained out constantly. Dr. Sara Jordan, co-founder of Boston's Lahey Clinic, has a wonderful way of putting it. "Every day give your brain a shampoo." What a thought! Get rid of all the dust and dirt and grime of negative thinking. Start off every day with clean, sparkling thoughts that will have nothing in them to impede the flow of success to you.

Give your brain a shampoo every morning. Get your day started right mentally and it will continue right. One winter morning I had occasion to get up very early. I went into the living room and looked out at the glorious morning sky. It suddenly occurred to me that Emerson was right when he said that ". . . The sky is the daily bread of the soul." Our apartment faces west, overlooking Central Park, an area in the heart of the city, four miles long and one-half mile wide. The sky that morning was like a gigantic fireplace, with flames shooting up over the city. There was a soft blanket of broken clouds overhead and, across the park, windows were golden as they reflected the rising sun. The whole city was as still as an etching. The air was clear as crystal. The snow was clean and fresh. Suddenly I felt a strong instinct to pray and the prayer became one of joy and exhilaration. It was an unforgettable experience.

That day was a wonderful day. There were no failures in it, and I am sure it was because I had washed my mind clean before the day ever began. I felt stimulated and on a higher level of energy all day long. There is an anonymous poem that describes this type of experience graphically:

*Every morning, lean thine arms awhile*
*Upon the window-sill of Heaven,*
*And gaze upon the Lord . . .*
*Then, with that vision in thy heart,*
*Turn strong to meet the day.*

I have made this a kind of morning habit and can assure you of the amazing value of this technique for starting off a day—"lean upon the window-sill of heaven," leave off looking so hard at your difficulties, and instead, "gaze upon the Lord." In so doing you will have strength and peace and power. This practice has powerful revitalizing potential.

What are the things that you may wash out of your mind by a daily mental and spiritual shampoo? Resentments, of course, and fears and hatreds; also, the negative and selfish thoughts that impede the flow of power through your personality are flushed out. Such daily mental shampoo or thought cleansing re-establishes the perspective that leads to successful action.

Some years ago I was in Hollywood as technical advisor for a motion picture called "One Foot in Heaven." One of the character actors working in this picture was a man named Harry Davenport. Harry told me a story about an experience he had with right-thinking a few years earlier. It seems that, at one time, he had been in a profession slump.

"I was actually a failure," said Harry. "And when I began to analyze what had happened to me, I saw that my motives had been all wrong. Performing before an audience I would think about how great I was, and had no special interest in the people of the audience. Well, it didn't take long for that kind of self-centered thinking to transmit itself to the audience, and ultimately it threatened my whole career. For if you think only of yourself, people pick it up and don't like you. I wasn't getting good jobs. After a while I became really disturbed and began to pray about it, and the answer I got was this: Project an attitude of love to your audience and see what happens.

"I thought that was a strange idea, but I was in such desperate straits that I would have tried anything. A few days later I received a call to play a part; it was not an important role, but I took it. Before the play started, I stood off stage in the wings and looked out over the audience. I saw a business man out front who seemed very unhappy. He looked like he had been dragged there by his wife, and wanted to be elsewhere. 'Well, I will try making you happy tonight,' I said silently. 'I will project love to you, and try to give you a pleasant evening.' And do you know I have never had a better performance or felt greater happiness in my work. It was the turning point in my career. Today I wouldn't dare give a performance without first seeing to it that my thinking is in proper order."

This conversation was one of the most determinative of my own life. I decided then and there never to go on the platform to make a speech or into the pulpit to deliver a sermon without sending out genuine love thoughts to my audience or congregation. I look out at the people present and pray that through me, as a medium, God may help each one. I wouldn't think of attempting a speech without carrying through this formula.

The same principle and procedure applies to anyone in any kind of work. Jim Johnson, my friend who operates a big hotel in Harrisburg, Pennsylvania, spends a definite period each day sending out such thoughts to his employees, and has created a wonderful spirit in his organization. At night when he leaves for his home, he stops his car across the river and looks back at the towering hotel. From there he sends out thoughts of good will and prayer to all the guests behind those windows and to all the workers who staff the hotel throughout the night. As you might suspect, this kind of thinking gives one a positive and wise attitude toward life. Jim once said something I never forgot. "I never knew a storm that didn't blow itself out."

And, last of all, believe, really believe. Believe in whom? In God, in Jesus Christ, and, with real humility, believe in yourself. Believe that you are going to be victorious and that very belief will go far toward bringing you the victory you believe in. Why does the Bible talk about faith so much?

Because if you really believe, you can do tremendous things. You can if you believe you can. Believing opens the channels of creative, dynamic good. It sets power to flowing in even the most difficult circumstances.

One of the world's most accomplished positive thinkers is Casey Stengel, pilot of the New York Yankees. During one World Series, when the Yankees were fighting it out with the Milwaukee Braves, positive thought power brought really spectacular results. The Yankees had had an easy year of it in the American League. They had no real competition at all, and they won the pennant so early that it worked to their disadvantage, for they played rather colorless ball toward the end of the season. The Yankee players were not really on their toes by the time the World Series started. The Yankees lost three out of the first four games. It looked like an ignominious defeat for Casey Stengel and his team. He had to win the next three games in a row if he was going to take the Series.

And that is exactly what Casey did. He got his players fired up to the point where they played super-human baseball. It was one of the most thrilling exploits I have ever witnessed, and at the time I found myself wondering what magic Casey used to turn such defeat into victory. Later I found the answer. I read an article in *Sports Illustrated* about Mr. Stengel, and in this article were two sentences that describe him perfectly. I copied them and memorized them, because to me they are really powerful sentences. "Defeat does not awe Casey, and he is on good terms with hope." And the other was, "In the worst moment of defeat, he was looking for victory."

There you have it. Casey Stengel never once believed in defeat. He believed in victory. He "knew" he was going to win that Series, and he managed by some peculiar alchemy to transmit this belief to the Yankee ball team. And, of course, with that kind of certainty behind them, they were invincible.

I am going to close this chapter with a deeply moving letter that I received from a young mother. If you have any doubts as to the amazing results of positive thinking, you will surely lose them after reading this letter. We get thousands of letters in my office, from people in all kinds of circumstances. Some are enough to break your heart. They are filled with stories of pain, suffering, heartache, disappointment—it is most pathetic, all the troubles people have to deal with in life. But it is also inspiring to read about how tremendous people become when they develop that magic ingredient of belief. You can believe yourself to victory over the greatest obstacles in the world, as did Mrs. Harry Fike of Bexley, Ohio, who writes:

Dear Dr. Peale:

On October 30 of last year when I was pregnant five and one-half months I had an unfortunate accident—a rupture of the membrane enclosing the baby. This had happened to me in two previous pregnancies with the resulting loss of the baby. On the first two occasions the doctors told me such an accident was absolutely hopeless and I accepted their decision. I remember going to the hospital and saying on the delivery table, "It is hopeless. My baby is too small and will die," and that is what happened, exactly.

This time another doctor told me, "It's up to you and God." At first I panicked, but soon got hold of myself, My instructions were not to move. So I propped myself in an upright position in bed and vowed I would not move for at least a month—which I did not. With a four-year-old and a two-year-old this was easier to say than to do. But with the help of my husband I stayed there one month to the day, never lying down or turning to the side. Whenever the situation seemed threatening I would thank God that the baby was going to be all right. I prayed constantly for myself, but most of the time I thanked God for His blessings.

Every time someone talked discouragingly to me I simply told them that everything would be all right. One month later I went into labor, but I was not afraid. Even the resident doctor in the labor room told me that my baby would be too small. I heard him on the hall telephone telling my doctor that I thought the baby would be large enough but it was wishful thinking. I watched the baby's birth and when I saw him I almost panicked again seeing how tiny he was. But his eyes were open and he was struggling for breath. He was also deep purple. He weighed 2 lbs. 9 ozs.

My pediatrician arrived at the hospital and met me coming out of the delivery room. While all others shook their heads he smiled and said, "It is possible for him to survive." He didn't spout the discouraging statistics to me as most of the others did. On the fourth day my obstetrician came in and told me the baby was barely breathing, but I can remember saying, "But he *is* breathing." I called my pediatrician and he said the next time the obstetrician comes in and talks that way, tell him to jump out the window. So I hung on and thanked God over and over again.

After seven weeks my baby was discharged weighing 5 lbs. 3¾ ozs. He has been home a week, has a wonderful appetite and weighs 6 lbs. In four days he will be two months old and he wasn't even due until February 8th. No one will ever discourage me in believing the power of faith.

How about that for a human experience of faith over defeat? She simply determined that, with God's help she would not fail. I sent the letter back to that mother to save for her baby when he grows up. What a priceless and inspiring possession it will be to him.

So, take another look at your failures in the light of these three principles: ***Try, really try. Think, really think. Believe, really believe.*** Put these powerful principles to work on your failures, and they can be overcome. As you work with positive and creative ideas you can so develop yourself that there will be no more failure for you.

IV

# The Kind of People People Like

You want to be liked. So do I. To be liked and appreciated is a deep-seated human desire. That is why Dale Carnegie sold several million copies of his book *How to Win Friends and Influence People.* That is why tooth paste and gargles and deodorants are sold by the millions from ads which promise popularity for fifty-nine cents. In poll after poll the personal wish that comes up strongest is the desire to be well liked.

And so the problem of getting alone well with others is no trifling matter; it is an important skill which must be mastered if we are to be effective and happy. And how is it done?

A first answer is a simple one, but one that is extremely vital, as experts will testify. I was having lunch with two good friends of mine, C. K. Woodbridge and Carol Lyttle, Chairman of the Board and Vice President of the Dictaphone Corporation, respectively. Our conversation was concerned mainly with the techniques of effective living. Since these two men are outstanding in sales work, I asked what, in their opinion, was the basic requirement of a successful salesman. Mr. Woodbridge answered me quickly. "It's to like people. Of course a man must believe in and know his product. He must be a hard worker and a positive thinker. But first of all he must like people."

I think that is the basic ingredient of popularity, too. Essentially, popularity is a form of salesmanship in that you "sell" yourself, if I may use that concept. When a man genuinely likes other people, he himself is quite certain to be liked in return. So, a primary step in being well liked is simply to like other people and like them sincerely, not for a purpose.

Of course, this is not always easy. Some people are more difficult to like than others. But the more you practice liking people, the easier it becomes. This is not done by blithely saying, I am now going to like everybody. While, as I said, it is simple, it is not that simple. Liking other people is the *result* of a way of life. It is the result of certain disciplined thought patterns. And one of the principal thought patterns for liking other people is positive thinking. It is taking a positive and not a negative attitude toward everyone.

It amazes me how often I hear the phrase, "I began to love everybody," when people are telling about the results of positive thinking in their lives. Here are a few examples culled from letters that come from Oshkosh, Fort Worth, San Diego and Louisville.

> . . . and then I just began to love everybody.
>
> . . . so that is the way things stand now. I like everybody and get along fine with them.
>
> . . . Then a strange thing began to happen to me. I began loving everybody.
>
> . . . Before I read *Positive Thinking,* frankly, I loved only myself; but then I went beyond myself. Now I actually like everyone. I can in all honesty say that.

It's not hard to understand why this is true. When people get rid of fear, anxiety and self-centeredness they develop a kind of ecstatic joy and delight in living. The world seems so different and newly wonderful that they tend to love everybody and everything. And they become so warm-hearted and delightful that people take a real liking to them. They change from withdrawn, worrying persons to ones with vitality and charm. They become "out-flowing" personalities; that is, personalities which now flow outward toward others in kindness and helpfulness.

If you are primarily concerned with yourself, you really haven't much chance of being one of the people people like. To become of that enviable type you'll just have to shift your primary attention away from yourself to other people. William James said, "The deepest drive in human nature is the desire to be appreciated." That also goes for the other person; he, too, wants to be appreciated by you. If you are abnormally concerned with yourself, craving attention, but absorbed in yourself, you will have no time to appreciate others and no inclination to do so, for that matter. And the other fellow wanting attention and regard, failing to get it from you, isn't going to be too enthusiastic about you.

I have a friend who is a natural-born positive thinker, and that's a blessing, for most people have to cultivate it. His name is Charles Heydt. Charlie is one of the great "appreciators" of this world. And as a result he is very well liked by everyone. When my secretary buzzes and tells me that Charlie Heydt is on the line, my face always brightens. I am delighted to talk to him, because Charlie is a builder-upper. If he sees an article that I have written for some magazine, he will take time out to call, or even to write a letter. "Dear Norman: By golly that was a good article. Something that needed to be said, too. You sure came up with a ringer."

It is not surprising, of course, that Charlie Heydt is one of the people people like. Being a builder-upper is essentially a question of paying attention to the other person's needs and the inevitable result of this is that the builder-upper himself becomes a beloved person.

If you want to be liked and respected, get to loving other people. Really put yourself out in interest and love for them, and stimulate them to bring out their best. Then, like bread on the waters, interest and love will come back to you a hundredfold.

One of my readers told me a story about Henry Ford which I like very much. He and this friend were lunching together when suddenly Henry Ford asked this question. "Who is your best friend?"

His companion named several persons, but Ford took a pencil and wrote these words on the tablecloth: "Your best friend is he who brings out the best that is within you."

Look behind actions and see the real person. If you try to help him be his best self, you will win esteem and confidence. If, in trying situations, you show a deep understanding and patience for a person, not only he, but others also will like you very much indeed.

I received a letter from a woman in Philadelphia who works on this principle. She had a difficult office manager to deal with:

> . . . the day the office manager opened up a tirade against me, I wanted to quit. Actually I started to look for another job. Then, what I had been reading about positive thinking caught up with me. Now was the time for me to put it to work.
>
> So I took a chance. I wrote the boss a letter and told him I was very appreciative of his giving me a job and an opportunity of working in his business, but I felt that he could double his business if the atmosphere around the place was more amiable.
>
> Did he realize that every time he called his office manager, the man became paralyzed? His brain went numb, he dropped whatever was in his hand on the nearest desk; that when he lit into the office manager he, in retaliation, lit into

the people in the office? I told him I wanted to be a Christian. Why can't we all start loving one another around this place?

That was some weeks ago and to date I haven't been fired. The conditions are 90 per cent improved and everybody is happier. I know the boss came up the hard way and I feel sorry for him, so I am going to redouble my efforts to help him all I can.

This woman, thinking positively, reacted to a difficult situation, not emotionally, but intelligently. She looked behind the "crippled condition" of the frightened office manager and had the keen insight to see that he acted as he did because he was insecure. She lifted the situation to a higher level of understanding because she was looking behind actions to the people themselves. Naturally she was a well liked and respected person in that office. She had learned to listen with understanding to a person's troubles even when he communicated through odd behavior rather than words. She knew that behavior often speaks as plainly as words, sometimes even more plainly. Many of us listen to words, but not to the harsher language of behavior, and therefore are blundering in our human relations.

And many of us, unfortunately, do not even know how to listen to words. The art of listening is certainly one of the great secrets of being well liked. Most of us tend to talk too much when people come to us with a problem. We try to give advice, whereas more often the thing that is needed is silence and the ability to transmit to the other person the sense of patient, understanding love.

My friend Arthur Gordon, the writer, tells a poignant story about a newspaper editor in a small town. He was often at his desk until late at night writing editorials and doing other work. One night about midnight there was a rap on his door. "Come in," he called. The door opened and there before him was the haggard face of a neighbor, a man whose little boy had recently been drowned. The editor knew the story. This man had taken his wife and son out canoeing. The canoe had overturned; the wife was saved, but the child had drowned. Ever since the tragedy the father had been beside himself. Apparently he had been walking the streets in a daze and had been drawn by the editor's light—perhaps by the editor's understanding and kindness.

"Here, Bill," said the newspaperman. "Sit down and rest yourself a while."

The broken-hearted father sat down, then slumped forward in utter dejection and silence. And here the editor did an interesting thing. Instead of filling the void with a lot of talk, he simply went back to work. He was not upset by the other man's silence. After awhile he asked, "Would you like to have a cup of coffee, Bill?" He poured Bill a steaming cupful. "Drink that, old boy. The heat inside you will do you good." They sipped their coffee. Still there was no conversation.

After quite awhile the neighbor said, "I'm not ready to talk yet, Jack."

"That's OK. Just sit there as long as you want. I'll keep on with my work."

Much later Bill said, "I'm ready to talk." Then for a solid hour he poured it all out, while Jack listened. Bill went over the tragedy in meticulous, minute detail—what actually happened, what would have happened had he done this, what would not have happened had he done that, blaming himself for everything. He talked on and on until about three o'clock in the morning. Finally he stopped talking and said, "That's all I want to say tonight."

The editor came over, put his arm around his shoulder and said, "Go home, Bill, and get some sleep."

"May I come and talk to you again?"

"Any time," the editor told him. "Whenever you want to, day or night. God bless you."

That was all the editor did; he listened quietly, sympathetically and with love in his heart. And he was beloved by everybody in his community because he had this ability to listen creatively. He stimulated people to talk out their problems and find their own solutions. They all liked him for that.

Out in Ottumwa, Iowa, there is a man by the name of Al Stevens, a good friend of mine, who also knows how to listen creatively. Al Stevens is in a business that often stirs up a good deal of ill will; he is a bill collector. He owns the Wapello Adjustment Bureau. Businessmen pay him to collect bad debts. For years Al's was like any other collection agency. He made his calls, cajoled, pleaded, and sometimes he had to be rather firm. But then one day he came across the principles of positive thinking and he decided to run his business along those lines.

"Suppose," he said to himself, "that I take a more positive approach. Suppose I try to see each of these debtors as people who are faced with serious problems that are getting them into debt. Suppose I try to help them solve their problems . . ."

So Al Stevens turned his collection agency into a human service bureau aimed at helping other people. On his first intervew after he had made his decision, he met a twenty-seven-year-old housewife who owed a seven months old bill to a local merchant. Al didn't ask for money right away. Instead he said, "I know you have a problem or you wouldn't be in debt. I'm confident that we can work it out. Let's see if there isn't some solution." The kindly yet positive tone in which he spoke inspired a spirit of confidence.

He learned that a series of medical bills had consumed all the family's savings. Heavy debts had followed. Depression set in. The husband couldn't seem to hold a job and soon he and the wife were fighting all the time. Al figured out that the basic problem these people faced was the lack of a sense of organization. They couldn't seem to conquer their debts, no matter what they did. Al saw his job—he had to restore these people's confidence by showing them how to organize their way out of their difficulties. Then and there he had the young housewife write down all her family's debts in one column, and in another column, all their assets. Then, together, they worked a system of rotating payments.

"For eighty-five cents a day you can have all of your debts paid within a year. Can you manage that?" Al asked. The young woman was now sure that she could . . . and she did. Nine months later she was completely debt free, the husband had a good job, and their marital relations were on a much better footing.

Is it any wonder that Al Stevens is known as the Debt Doctor around Ottumwa? He is so beloved in his town that many of his customers send him Christmas cards. People go out of their way to cross the street and wish him a Happy New Year. Imagine that—sending cards and good wishes to your bill collector! When you start to think positively about your relations with other people, when you start to see their behavior as the result of problems which they are not handling successfully, you quickly become one of the people people like.

There is another quality that is possessed by an astounding percentage of sought-after people and it is this: they seem to know how to help their friends to accept themselves. Anyone who can do that will always gain affection. It is amazing how self-conscious people are, and it makes them most unhappy.

Self-conscious people are often those who have never learned to accept themselves. It's a very misery-producing state of mind, and self-defeating, too. Because the individual is suffering inwardly, other people unconsciously pick up tension and rigidity from his attitude and he never quite makes the grade with them. At least he thinks he doesn't and, in thinking it, he helps to create unsatisfactory relationships.

One of my readers is a writer of note and a popular public speaker. He is about 5'8" in height, which is only a shade below average. But he was very self-conscious about his height. He would never allow himself to be pictured with a group of men lest he appear dwarfed by them. He became shrinking and retiring and avoided social contacts as much as possible. He happened to read in one of my books about an old friend of mine, a rugged character who had a formula which he often gave to those who were having trouble, either with themselves or with circumstances, and it was this: Think big, pray big, believe big, act big and you'll be big.

That formula really took hold with this man and he began practicing it. It started him on the study and practice of positive thinking which led ultimately to a normalizing of his attitudes toward himself. He accepted himself. Now he has no self-consciousness at all about his height. I have heard him say that height isn't measured by the length of a man's legs or the size of his frame, but it's how tall he is above his ears that counts. Now, big men look up to him even though they have to glance down to do it. He learned to accept himself and his height and, in so doing, found his real size—which is plenty big. He often tells me that he loves me because he feels that I helped him accept himself. And I feel the same toward those who helped me accept myself.

I used to be very self-conscious of my speech because I felt that I never could get just the right words. Oftentimes I would grow hot and almost blush because of my awkwardness of expression, especially in small groups in personal conversation. Strangely enough, I was not bothered by this before an audience. If a person from a university background was present, for example, one whose use of words was exceptionally cultivated, it gave me an enormous inferiority complex and tended to cause me to close up and retreat. The inhibitions and inferiority feelings caused by this self-consciousness was one of my most painful struggles.

The man who together with the never failing support of my mother helped me conquer this sensitivity was Professor Hugh M. Tilroe, Dean of the College of Public Speaking of Syracuse University. He taught me the importance of being myself, of not trying to be like any other person or following any style or mode of speech. "Use plain, simple, every day English," he said, "words everyone understands. And just talk like yourself; you sound all right to me."

Professor Tilroe was a member of my church and I was very young. I asked him if he would criticize my sermons from the standpoint of technique. "Not on your life," he responded. "If you want instruction in public speaking, register at the University and pay your bills and I'll teach you in class. But when I come to church, you are the teacher and I am the pupil in the great school of Christ. You just be yourself and speak out of your heart."

To this day and until the end of my days, I shall love this man, for he helped me to accept myself and be myself.

If you always have a genuine interest in people and always think of them as important, if you are concerned about them, it will vastly add to your success and happiness and they will like you in return. This requires having something constructive to give to others and a skill in communicating it. Knowing how to help people is an art and the person who knows how to do it can always know that he will have the lasting affection of many.

One of my readers runs a clothing store in upstate New

York. This man's business was in a run-down condition a few years ago. The store was drab and dark and unattractive. Merchandise lay on the tables in sloppy piles. The owner himself was in a state of gloom and negativism which paralleled the physical condition of his store

One day an old friend, who was concerned about the storekeeper, came in to see him. "How's business?" the friend asked.

"Awful," was the answer. "Simply terrible."

The friend walked around studying the situation and he said, "Really, I'm not surprised. Just take a look at the condition of this place. What's eating you, Fred? You used to have the snappiest store in town."

The storekeeper said, "The trouble is I haven't enough money to freshen things up. I know how everything looks. If I could just collect my outstanding accounts I'd have enough to start fixing things the way they once were."

"You can't collect any of your debts?" asked the friend. "That's strange. Maybe I can help you. Let's just take a look. Would you mind showing me the names of those who are behind in payments?"

The storekeeper brought out his accounts and pointed to a list of some ninety-six customers who owed him money. The friend took out a pencil and pointed at random to a name. "Tell me something about this person," he said.

The storekeeper looked at him in surprise. "What do you mean?"

"You don't know this customer—anything about him, his family, his problems, his needs?"

The storekeeper was astonished. "Of course not. I haven't time for that kind of stuff. He's just an account to me and one who doesn't pay, at that."

The friend chose another name. "What about this one?" The story was the same. The storekeeper had to admit that he did not know, personally, more than ten of the ninety-six people he carried on his books as bad debts.

"All right now," the friend said, "will you try an experiment? Send out all of these bills as usual, but this time say a prayer for the person who will be receiving it. In your prayer express the desire that each person have a happy and prosperous use of the clothing which you have sold him. Pray that things will go well with him. Then at the bottom of the bill add a word of personal interest. I do not care what it is. Simply, 'I hope you are enjoying the sweater,' or 'If there is any problem with this pair of shoes, be sure to bring them in and we will see what we can do about it.' Then add a cheery word like 'Lots of luck,' or 'Hope the family is all well.'

"Then, at the first opportunity, learn something personal about each one of these people. When this customer comes to you again think of him not as a sale, but as a person you are going to help. These are not accounts—they are people. Your job is to serve human beings through your store, helping them to the best of your ability."

Well, the storekeeper was not sure this was a very businesslike approach, but he was at the point where he was willing to try anything. So, to please his friend and with a new feeling of faith, he decided to try the experiment of praying for each of the persons he was billing and adding the personal note.

And then was he surprised. Right away an amazing thing happened. Of the ninety-six people, over half promptly remitted in whole or in part. Others wrote back that they were sorry to be slow in their payments and asked if it would be all right if they paid next month. Some few even came by personally to pay their bill. The storekeeper was so impressed with the first success of the experiment that he decided to double his efforts. From that day his philosophy of business changed and today he is a very greatly liked and sought after member of his community. People think of him first as a friend and then as the man from whom they buy their clothes. Being liked is so simple; just be concerned in a helpful way about people.

I would like to mention another characteristic that almost all popular people have. It is a kind of urbane imperturbability. They are not easily irritated or annoyed. Some people seem to be able to rise above their irritations and they are fun to be with because they are poised and even-tempered. They seem to live on an upper level emotionally and are not easily riled up. They keep in a good humor and spirit.

In California I met Mrs. Sadie Bunker, a remarkable lady now over sixty-five who has come to be known as the "flying grandmother." Three years before, she had decided she would be a licensed pilot. She studied, practiced, got her license and now flies her own plane all the time. Recently she passed all the tests necessary to go on a sound-breaking flight. She told me she thought everybody ought to have a plane. When things get on her nerves she just goes to the airport, takes her plane seven thousand feet up in the air and right away everything seems different. "You look down on the earth and it looks like an awfully nice place; and the people, too, seem different from up above," she explained.

While you and I may not be able to get into a plane whenever we get irritated and go up to a higher altitude in the physical sense, anyone can, by positive thinking, take altitude in his mind and spirit. The higher your spiritual altitude the less irritated you will be and the more fun you will be as a companion. Just be sure you always stay on top of things.

Suppose, for instance, that you are being criticized. Does criticism get under your skin, hurt your feelings, make you irritable and therefore unpleasant to be around? Or are you able to handle criticism in such a way that you gain friends? Anyone can handle criticism if he tries. And the secret is to keep your thinking positive. Note the following letter:

> I am a member of our City Council. At a recent meeting one Councilman became incensed when the rest of us disagreed with him over a bill. He stalked out of the chambers in wrath and into the arms of reporters.
>
> The next day the newspapers quoted him as berating each of us for attempts to block progress. In his anger he attempted to cause sectional bitterness.
>
> Fortunately, before the news reporters interviewed me I had been doing some reading in positive thinking. I shall always be grateful for the thoughts on this subject because it gave me the power to make the right kind of reply. I answered softly and constructively. That was several weeks ago and I am still hearing approval of my kindly feelings toward the angry councilman.

People who are able to turn criticism into a positive situation are going to attract friends. One of the most beloved public figures in this country today is former President Herbert Hoover. Some time ago I had a good visit with Mr. Hoover and asked him this question. "At one time," I said, "you were probably the most criticized man in the United States. Nearly everybody seemed to be against you. It was customary to sneer at you. Nowadays, of course, you are America's grand old man and everybody on both sides of the political fence admires you. But when you were being so criticized, didn't it ever get inside you and bother you?"

Mr. Hoover looked at me with genuine surprise in his penetrating eyes and said, "Of course not."

Rather amazed, I asked, "But how come?"

"All you have to do in life," he said, "is to use your head. That is what you have it for—to use. When I decided to go into politics I sat down and figured out what it would mean. I weighed the cost. One thing was sure, I would get some very hard criticism. But in spite of that I went ahead. So when I got the criticism, I wasn't surprised. I had expected it and there it was. I was, therefore, better able to handle it. You see," he smiled, "I'm a positive thinker."

He looked at me for a moment. "But that is not the whole answer. I am a Quaker." He did not amplify that remark, for he knew that I would understand. Quakers cultivate peace at the center. Irritation is simply absorbed in a deep spiritual peace in the mind and heart.

And so, being able to handle criticism, Mr. Hoover was destined to outlive the slurs of political life and become one of our best liked Americans. His philosophy is one that all of us could well follow, whether in public or private life. We are going to be criticized; you can count on that all right. This is one of the facts of living. By urbanely recognizing that fact we can develop the right spiritual attitude for handling criticism creatively. And it won't get you down when it comes if you are mentally and spiritually prepared for it.

Senator Paul Douglas of Illinois tells of a Quaker meeting where he learned a great lesson in handling criticism. As you know, the Quakers practice silence in their worship. Sometimes they sit for a long time without anybody saying anything. At this particular meeting the only person who spoke was an old man who rose and made this statement:

"Whenever a man differs with you or criticizes you, try to show him by every look, by your demeanor, and by your actions that you love him."

That was all the old man said, but Senator Douglas instantly knew that, as the Quakers phrase it, this man had "spoken to his condition."

One of the most practical anti-criticism formulas ever outlined is this: "Love your enemies, bless them that curse you, do good to them that hate you, and pray for them which despitefully use you, and persecute you." (Matthew 5:44) This is wonderful teaching when put into action, for it enables you to remain poised and confident in the face of the hostile words and actions of others. And those who watch you handling criticism in this way will instinctively be drawn to you. You will be the kind of person other persons like. As a matter of fact, people tend to like a criticized person (providing he is criticized a great deal by a great many) on the basis of the kicked dog psychology. And if the criticized person takes it quietly without rancor, not striking back but constantly loving, he will gather in friends faster than his critics can manufacture enemies.

That Scripture verse about loving enemies and treating people kindly is actually the subtlest technique ever devised for getting the love of everyone. It proves once again, if proof is needed, that Jesus Christ is the wisest of all teachers of the skill of living.

It is so easy to hate, so easy to be negative, so easy to accept defeat and live on a low level. It is easy, but it is also frustration and misery, because we never can be happy, deep in our souls, until we live according to what we are; namely, sons of God with the Kingdom of God within us.

In my correspondence with those who are working with the principles of positive thinking, I have noticed something else about the kind of people people like. And it is this; those who have what you might call up-beat personalities, who inspire others, who supply courage, strength and hope are deeply appreciated. All of us need courage, we need strength and hope, sometimes we need these qualities desperately. So, when people are able to draw this strong spirit from you, the natural result is that you become important to them. You gain a place in their hearts.

I know full well the effect of such people on me, and many others also testify to the effect upon them of the inspirational personality. The man who believes in something, who has some real convictions, who lives by a strong and sturdy faith and shares it freely becomes an influence in men's lives.

For example, one of my esteemed friends, George E. Sokolsky, the famous newspaper columnist, is a strong positive thinker and the word defeat is not in his vocabulary. He experienced several illnesses and I saw little of him for quite a while as he restricted his activity. But a few days ago he telephoned me about helping some people and I noted the old time vigor and verve in his voice.

"You seem on top of things, George," I commented.

"Sure thing," he replied. "We're supposed to be on top of things."

"But you've been through so much, what is your secret?"

"Secret! It's no secret. We have Someone with us, haven't we?"

He went on to tell about going into the hospital for examination. Then the doctors came in and put the X-ray pictures up against the window. "Know how to read an X-ray?" they asked.

George took a long look and said, "Sure, I've got cancer . . . let's cut it out."

"They told me," he explained, "because they knew I could take it."

His heart doctor called to check his heart, to determine whether it could take an operation since he had experienced a coronary. He was amazed at Sokolsky's calmness. "You astonish me by your composure," the doctor said. "If I had your attitude I would live ten years longer."

"But," said George, "I have faith so I'm completely at ease. I'm in God's hands."

Following nearly five hours on the operating table, upon

Sokolsky's return to consciousness, the surgeon said, "Well, you're alive."

"How do you know I'm alive?" returned his vigorous patient. "There's only one way I can know I'm alive—can I do my work. If I can't work, I am dead. Bring me a pad and pencil and I'll try writing a column. Then I'll know whether I'm alive."

The column was one of the best of his entire career.

Another up-beat personality is Colonel Frank Moore, head usher in my church in New York. Frank is a positive thinker who takes his Christian faith into business activity as well as into personal life.

In his office is a large conference table around which his executive staff of seven persons gathers regularly for important conferences. The table accommodates eight chairs. Colonel Moore at the beginning of his service in this organization commented to his staff upon the importance of the decisions they would reach in conferences and referred to the necessity for Divine guidance. In view of the fact that there was normally a vacant chair at the table, he wondered if it might not be a good idea always to leave the chair at the head of the table vacant to remind each person of a Presence who would always guide in decisions.

Slowly at first, but with growing appreciation for what it did to the meetings, the suggestion was accepted. The information regarding the vacant chair got around through the other offices and when joint meetings were held that chair was never occupied. The news spread outside the organization and a quiet but definite influence seemed to be derived.

Back of the table on the wall a prayer was reproduced on a framed mat 18 x 24 inches. It so impressed buyers and others that in one year alone over two thousand copies were requested and given away. This is the prayer:

**O Lord, grant that each one who has to do with me today may be happier for it. Let it be given me each hour today what I shall say, and grant me the wisdom of a loving heart that I may say the right thing rightly. Help me to enter into the mind of everyone who talks with me, and keep me alive to the feelings of each one present. Give me a quick eye for little kindnesses that I may be ready in doing them and gracious in receiving them. Give me a quick perception of the feelings and needs of others, and make me eager hearted in helping them. Amen.**

Want to be liked? Lift people's spirit. Give them a little extra inspiration. Help build up their strength. They will like you for it. You'll have a warm place in their hearts for always.

So let's review some of the things we have been talking about in this chapter. What are the secrets of popularity? How do we go about becoming the kind of people people like?

1. In the first place, start now to like other people. How do you do this? One of the most successful ways is through positive thinking. Positive thinkers become out-flowing personalities, they cease to be obsessively concerned about themselves, and they begin to be concerned for others. They "love everybody" as is evidenced by the many times this phrase has cropped up in the letters people write me about the results of positive thinking. Once they begin to "love everybody," they themselves become lovable. They are sought out, needed personalities.

2. Always try to bring out the best in other people and you will be welcomed wherever you go. Learn to "listen" to behavior as well as to words that are spoken. People are often trying to communicate with you, for good or bad, through the way they act as well as by what they say. When you learn to listen to the problems people have, you are in a

position to help them bring out the best that is within themselves.

3. Make your friends feel comfortable with themselves. People have a hard time accepting themselves. Help them do that and everyone will enjoy having you around.

4. Be calm, poised and cheerful. Learn how to rise above the irritations that life holds for us all. Develop an ability to fly to higher "spiritual altitudes," so that criticisms and petty unpleasantnesses will no longer ruffle you. Take for its full meaning the Biblical injunction, "Love your enemies, bless them that curse you, do good to them that hate you, and pray for them which despitefully use you, and persecute you."

5. Be an up-beat personality so that people may receive inspirational support from you. You'll become very important to their lives.

Practice these principles in your daily life, and it will follow automatically that you will become one of the people people like.

# V

# There Can Be Lots of Fun in Life

How good it is to be alive! What a glorious morning! I've really never felt better. This promises to be a wonderful day.

This may sound a bit exuberant but it's the way I feel this morning. I'm happy, I feel good. I'm getting ready to have a lot of fun today. When I walk down the street wouldn't be surprised if I whistled, just like when I was a youngster.

Come to think of it, it's been a long time since I heard anyone whistling on the street in New York City. And this isn't just an observation of my own. I was talking to Bill Arthur, the other day. Bill is managing editor of *Look* magazine. "Have you noticed that no one ever walks down Madison Avenue whistling?" he asked. Bill was raised in Louisville, Kentucky and he remembers his childhood days as a time when people seemingly knew how to get more fun from life than they do today.

Why is this? If it is true of you, what can you do to bring the want-to-whistle back into your attitude-of-living? What can you do to gain the natural, unaffected kind of joy that comes from deep down inside? I heard recently about a well-known psychiatrist who is working on a program called Positive Mental Health. Whenever he describes the results he hopes to obtain, he talks about his dog. "I come home from work and my dog greets me with a bound and a yelp and a kind of frenzy of joy. What a contrast this is to the gloom and depression I see on human faces during the day. This animal has the secret of deep fun. *This* is the way we should be able to react to life."

Now I'm not suggesting that we start bouncing all over the place. We've all known people who make themselves a little ridiculous by overdoing this kind of enthusiastic happiness. I've often suspected that such people are only feigning happiness. But all of us have also known the rare and wonderful individual who is full of *deep* fun. There's the key. It's a fun that is not on the surface, not light or superficial but one that derives from a deep sense of happiness at being what you are and where you are and doing what you are doing. Catch such a completely well adjusted person unawares, and you are apt to find him singing or whistling.

Let me repeat. I really feel happy today. And I think I can spot the origin of this good feeling, too. Yesterday afternoon it was a bright Sunday, and my wife Ruth and I took a walk with our young daughter, Lizzie. (I can't break myself of the habit of calling her Lizzie, although her mother would much prefer Elizabeth.) We had a lot of fun together. We walked up Fifth Avenue along the park, stepping out briskly, with our heads held high and our spirits held high, too. "It's fun to walk tall," Lizzie and Ruth and I agreed.

We walked a mile or more, all of us feeling dynamic, gay and enjoying life. We passed the Frank Lloyd Wright building, the Guggenheim Museum, on upper Fifth Avenue. "Isn't that beautiful!" said Lizzie. Well, I had never thought of that building as being particularly beautiful, but through her eyes I took a second look. (I was thinking a little taller, perhaps.) And when I looked that second time, I sensed the joy that the great architect had built into this structure. It spirals upward. It really transmits an emotion of enthusiasm and happiness and vigor. For the first time I began liking that building. Perhaps it was just the way I was feeling.

But that's the point. When you feel right, you tend to be joyful, you tend to have a sense of deep fun and your appreciation of everything expands. Dr. Henry C. Link, the psychologist, would never see a patient who was in a state of depression without first sending him for a vigorous turn around the block. "Walk rapidly around the block ten times," Dr. Link would say. "This will exercise the motor centers of the brain, and the blood will flow away from the emotional-activity centers. When you come back, you will be much more rational and receptive to positive thoughts."

Your physical condition has a lot to do with your ability to enjoy life. When you are refreshed and rejuvenated, life takes on new meaning. Proper exercise and proper rest are essential ingredients of joyful emotions. Some scientists, according to an account I read, recently made some experiments with what they call "massive doses of sleep." Using drugs, they induced sleep in people who were tired and aging, and they reported a regeneration of tissues, a prolonging of life, the disappearance of disease and of course with this, the appearance of a new vitality and joy in living.

So, the first step in attaining this wonderful sense of the deep fun of life is to feel right. And treat your body right if you want your feelings to be right.

And the second step is to think right. Treat your mind right. Think positively. The positive thinker trains himself in the attitude of joy. He expects it, and then he finds it. What you look for, you will find—that is a basic law of life. Start looking for joy and you'll find it. For when you look for it, you will be able to see and recognize it. Some good friends of mine, Elsie and Otto Palmer, who live in Brooklyn, N.Y. looked for it and found it. They wrote:

> It is extremely difficult to give expression to one's innermost feelings; but since we have been learning about positive

thinking, we feel you should know that we, too, are experiencing that wonderful something within that makes us want to sing for joy and tell the world about it.

The application of your techniques has revolutionized our lives. While we have been brought up in a religious home, we never before understood how helpful and practical religion could and should be. It has given us a completely new and happy outlook on life to the extent that each day is begun with great expectancy and joy.

I have made it a habit to expect a pleasant surprise each day and it has never failed to come to pass with one exception; and that is, the degree of the surprise depends on the degree of faith I put into my expectancy. If I am very sure, luke warm, or cool—to that degree will the surprise come to pass.

I like the paragraph in this letter that speaks about expecting a pleasant surprise each day. This is first-rate positive thinking. The people who look forward into the future expecting to see great things are people who are going to be happy.

The other night I was driving up Park Avenue with a wonderful man, Dr. Arthur Judson Brown. Dr. Brown is 101 years old, and he has the spirit and verve of a teenager. "Just look at that skyline," he said. "New buildings everywhere. I think it's just great the way this town is always changing, always improving itself."

That's the way a *young* person thinks. I asked Dr. Brown what he thinks of modern young people. "I thank God for them," he said. "They are really great, these youngsters. They're so much wiser and better than I was at their age. They're going to create a new world for us. There is a new day on the way, and I'm looking forward to it."

At 101 years of age, he's looking forward to a great new day! I apologized to Dr. Brown for keeping him out so late at night. It was nearly eleven, and I thought he would normally be in bed at that hour. "Oh, not at all," he said. "I'm often up until midnight. But I'll get my rest tomorrow. I've learned, long ago, not to push myself too much. You ought to learn that too, you youngsters. Tomorrow I'll get up and have a leisurely breakfast and read the paper; and if I don't see my name in the obituary column, I'll go back to bed for some extra sleep."

The thing that determines whether or not a person is happy is an *inward* state or condition. It is what goes on in the mind that tells the story of whether you are happy and positive or sad and negative. Marcus Aurelius Antonius said, "No man is happy who does not think himself so." William Lyon Phelps remarked, "The happiest person is he who thinks the most interesting thoughts."

So, if you're not happy, you can experience this deep fun in life by doing a constructive job on your thoughts. If your mind is filled with grudges, hate, selfishness or off-color thoughts, why naturally the clear light of joy cannot filter through. You'll need to shift to a different mental life, an up-beat attitude, if you want a lot of fun out of life.

A reader I have known for some years was originally one of my "miserable" friends. A miserable friend is a person who makes everybody around him unhappy because he is unhappy himself. You might come into the presence of this man in a more or less jaunty frame of mind but he was a jauntiness-extractor. In no time at all he would take the jauntiness out of you.

In the course of time this man moved away, though he remained on my mailing list for positive thinking material. Then, three or four years later, I saw him again. He was so changed it was as though he had been reborn, which is exactly what had happened to him. He had been mentally reborn and spiritually, too. He was definitely a different person. I was so impressed by his change that I asked how he had managed it.

"I went on a seven day mental diet," he replied. He explained that he had become interested in a pamphlet by Emmet Fox called, "The Seven Day Mental Diet," which I had recommended to my readers. Observing that Americans are physically diet conscious, Dr. Fox urged people to undertake a mental diet as well. He made the point that a man becomes what he thinks.

And what is the seven day mental diet? It is this: you resolve that from a given minute you will, for seven days thereafter, watch your every word. You will not say a single negative thing, or a mean thing, or a dishonest thing. You will not make a depressing remark for seven days.

Now that is, of course, a big undertaking. "I tried it one day and failed," my friend said. "I tried it again, and went two days this time before I slipped. I tried again, unsuccessfully, and then again." But this is the kind of man who, when he goes out for anything, goes all out. "I asked God to help me, for I knew I just had to change myself or else! Then finally, for a whole week I succeeded. Not once, for seven days, did I fail. Then I thought I would ease off and just slump back a little into the old ways. But do you know, I found that there was a difference within myself. Actually, I could not slip back. I was changed, not completely of course; but I was not the same person. Since then life has become different. Now my mind is free of negative thoughts and I get real fun out of living." This is one of those sound new angles on positive thinking that readers pass along.

The two most important moments in the day are when you first open your eyes, and the moment when you drop off to sleep. These are the brackets of your conscious day. If those moments are packed full of positive, joyful thoughts, your day will be full of positive, joyful living. Elbert Hubbard said, "Be pleasant until ten o'clock in the morning and the rest of the day will take care of itself." Henry David Thoreau used to give himself good news first thing in the morning. He would tell himself how lucky he was to have been born. If he had never been born, he'd never have known the crunch of snow underfoot, or the glint of starlight; he'd never have smelled the fragrance of a wood fire nor would he have seen the love light in human eyes. He started off each day with thanksgiving.

My old friend from college days, Judson S. Sayre, President of the Norge Corporation, gets up every morning, looks in the mirror and says, "I am going to make good things happen today." And sometimes when he tends to become discouraged, he stops everything and thinks of some of the happiest experiences of his life. His spirit rises again. During the forty years I've known him, I've never seen him when he didn't radiate optimism and joy.

An excellent go-to-sleep technique is suggested by J. Harvey Howells in *This Week* magazine. "When the last good night has been said and the head is on the pillow, the soul is utterly alone with its thoughts. It is then that I ask myself, 'What was the happiest thing that happened today?' "

This has a great effect not only in setting the tone for a deep and peaceful night's sleep, but also in conditioning the mind to anticipate the new day soon to dawn.

This happiest thing may be only a little experience like the aroma of a flower, golden sunlight through a soft glass curtain, a chance word of friendship, a little kindness done, a fragment of melody. But to go mentally searching through the activities and fleeting impressions of the day for that one happiest thing; this is a most rewarding adventure on the borderline of sleep.

And Emerson used to end his day in a wonderful way. He

would see to it that he finished it, completely. "Finish each day and be done with it," he advised. "You have done what you could. Some blunders and absurdities no doubt crept in; forget them as soon as you can. Tomorrow is a new day; begin it well and serenely and with too high a spirit to be cumbered with your old nonsense."

He knew better than to let his day end with regrets. Emerson was a door shutter. He shut the door on the day, and forgot it. He was like Lloyd George who, one day, was taking a walk with a friend and was carefully closing every gate after him. "You don't need to close those gates," said the friend.

"Oh yes," said Lloyd George. "I've spent my life shutting gates behind me. It's necessary, you know. You shut the gate behind you and the past is held there. Then you can start again."

In becoming a joyful person, it is extremely important to clean up mistakes, sins, errors; then forget them and go forward. "Forgetting those things which are behind, and reaching forth unto those things which are before." (Philippians 3:13) This is to be smart and wise.

The kind of people to whom life with Christ has become a personal friendship are as natural as they can be in their enjoyment of religion. My friend Floyd McElroy, for example, is one. He and his wife Edith invited us to dinner with some other friends in their apartment on Fifth Avenue overlooking Central Park.

When we sat down to dinner Floyd did not call on me, his pastor, to offer thanks. I loved what he did. He offered the blessing himself and I thought it was one of the best I ever heard. Floyd said in his humble and unaffected manner, "Lord we thank You for our friends and we are happy that they are with us tonight. You have been so good to all of us and we are grateful. And now give us a gay and jovial evening in Jesus name. Amen."

This kind of religion, in my judgment, is the real thing and it is a big natural part of life. Why do people insist upon making religion stilted and unnatural, and above all, getting pained looks on their faces when it is mentioned. When you've got the real article, you can hardly contain yourself, you're so happy. You are walking toward the sun.

The McElroys are people that I like to call "shadow leaders" rather than "shadow pushers." And what might that be? One sunny day I was standing with a friend at a window in one of New York's tall office buildings looking down on Fifth Avenue at 42nd Street near the Public Library. The friend I was with, Amos Parrish, is one of the nation's great merchandising experts and a man with a picturesque, imaginative mind. I knew that an idea was agitating him because he was scratching his chin and had a reflective look. Suddenly, pointing down at the sidewalk in front of the library he said, "A lot of those people down there are shadow pushers."

"What do you mean, shadow pushers?" I asked.

"Why don't you see," he replied. "They are walking away from the sun and their shadows go ahead of them. They are shadow pushers. Those others," he continued, pointing again, "are shadow leaders. They are walking toward the sun, so their shadows fall behind them."

The difference is very significant, for if you are leading the shadow, you are master of life; but if you are trying to push shadows, life can be hard indeed. You can't have any real fun in life if you always have your back to the sun pushing shadows.

Another important principle in leading a happy fun-loving life is to learn to love and esteem the best in people. My father taught me the great truth that how you think about people, how you treat them and react to them, is extremely important to your own happiness. "Treat each man as a child of God is the secret," he said. "Hold him in esteem and it will make both him and you happy."

On Christmas Eve, when I was very young, I was out with my father doing some late Christmas shopping in our home town of Cincinnati. My father had as big a heart of love as any man I ever knew. It made no difference who a person was, he loved and talked with them all. And he was an extremely happy man. He had respect and esteem for every person. He saw beneath their exteriors, not as they appeared to be, but rather as they really were. And he had sharp insight, too. He knew people.

On this occasion I was loaded down with packages and felt tired and irritable. I was thinking how good it would be to get home when a beggar, a bleary-eyed, unshaved, dirty old man came up to me, touched my hand with his and asked for money. I recoiled from his soiled hand and rather impatiently brushed him aside.

"You shouldn't treat a man that way, Norman," said my father as soon as we were out of earshot.

"But, Dad, he's nothing but a bum."

"Bum?" he said. "There is no such thing as a bum. He is a child of God, my boy. Maybe he hasn't made the most of himself but he is a child of God, nonetheless. We must always look upon a man with esteem. Now, I want you to go and give him this." My father pulled out his pocketbook and handed me a dollar. That was a lot for his means. "And do exactly the way I tell you. Go up to him, hand him this dollar and speak to him with respect. Tell him you are giving him this dollar in the name of Christ."

"Oh," I objected, "I don't want to say that."

My father insisted. "Go and do as I tell you."

So I ran after the old man, caught up with him and said, "Excuse me, sir. I give you this dollar in the name of Christ."

The old man looked at me in absolute surprise. Then a

wonderful smile spread over his face. A smile that made me forget he was dirty and unshaven. I could see his real face through the streaks of grime. His essential nobility came out. Graciously, with a sort of bow, he said, "I thank you, young sir, in the name of Christ."

My irritation and annoyance faded like magic. And suddenly I was happy, deeply happy. The very street seemed beautiful. In fact, I believe that in the moment I held that man in full and complete esteem, I came very close to Christ Himself. And that, of course, is one of the most joyful experiences any person can ever have. Since then I have made every effort to see people as my father saw them. And that has brought me untold satisfaction. I have often returned to the exact spot where this incident took place, on Fourth Street, Cincinnati.

Giving is another joy producer. This may mean giving money or time or interest or advice; anything that takes something out of you and transfers it to other people, helpfully. Anything that gets you out of yourself, actually helps you find yourself. It's a strange principle but it's true, nevertheless, that those who give the most have the most of whatever they give.

I recall a young businessman who was ambitious. To get money and get ahead was his idea. And there is nothing wrong with that idea if you keep yourself in the center of a sharing process at the same time. He gave to his job all he had and then some. He was not naturally selfish, but he wanted to go places and so he concentrated upon himself rather exclusively.

He read everything that had to do with self-improvement. So it was that he bought *The Power of Positive Thinking*. It was "right down his alley" he said. He put positive thinking principles into action though he had a materialistic slant on it! But he went all out with it; and as a result, he "took off like a jet for the top echelon" to quote his picturesque, though not too modest, words.

But soon he began developing tension and anxiety symptoms, the former from overdrive, the latter because he feared he couldn't sustain the fast, competitive pace he had set for himself. Then developed a pathetic reaction often experienced by those who "get ahead." Such men have a lot of fun arriving, but when they arrive there isn't as much fun in it as they expected. The top can turn out to be a rat race and ulcers, if being at the top is all you're interested in.

"Why don't I get fun out of life any more?" this man asked me. "I've hit the top through positive thinking and look—I'm still not forty. What's the matter with me? Am I stale or something?"

We checked him over for the usual causes of unhappiness. We started by looking into his participation, or lack of it, in things which wouldn't "get him something."

"Why, I can't believe it," I said. "You're not giving a thing to anyone except your family, to whom you give everything."

The church which he attended with fair regularity got exactly one big dollar a week from him—about a twentieth of what he should have been giving on his income. He gave the community chest just as little as he could get away with. It wasn't that he was tight. This dollar-pinching was rather a holdover from his old insecurity feelings when he was a poor boy starting out. As for giving of his time and thought to help others, this didn't check out at all on his personal evaluation test.

"No wonder there's no fun in life for you," I said. "You've got to get outside of yourself. You've stopped the creative process. You're run down because everything has been coming in and nothing going out. You're like the dead sea, inlets but no outlets, and that means mental and spiritual stagnation."

Now, he wasn't as bad as this sounds. The fact that he was worried about the way he felt and frankly was willing to discuss it, humbly asking for guidance, showed him to be a pretty real person. And a real person can always get answers to problems like this.

We therefore gave him a positive thinking program which he had missed by stressing the materialistic values in positive thinking. Sure you can use it to make money but if you use it only that way it will fold back on you as it did with this man. So, we stepped it up into a higher level, into a positive thinking he hadn't seen before. This was designed to release him and remake him and it did.

1. He was to increase his giving to the Lord's work to 10 per cent of his income. Some of this was to go to the church, some to individuals (for whom there would be no tax exemption claim) and some to other charitable institutions.

2. He was to look for someone who needed help outside his family and friends, someone who might never be able to help him in return. The help might be monetary or in the form of advice, or justly friendly interest. Perhaps he might select a deserving boy and help him get an education or get started in business.

3. He was to stop rushing long enough to give himself to people—a few leisurely words with those who were part of his daily life: the waiter, the policeman on the corner, the news vendor, the elevator operator, or even his wife and children.

4. He was to go to his pastor and offer to help in some of the church's business problems. More than that he was to offer to call on a few people to carry the helpful ministry of the church to them, people in the hospital for example.

"Gosh that sounds like a time-consuming layout to me," he complained.

"Sure," I said, "that's exactly right. You must learn to give, not only money and good will, but time for the benefit of other people. But the pay-off will be more than worth it. You'll get back your old sense of fun if you follow this plan. It's either-or, take it or leave it." I knew my man, I knew he wouldn't leave it. He went for the businesslike approach when he knew it was sound. And this was.

To sum up this case history, which strung out over many months, he did follow the program and he did recover the ability to get a lot of fun out of life. He became an active factor in his community life. Moreover, the tension and anxiety subsided. Maybe he staved off a heart attack, who knows?

Still another element in the total joy-in-life formula is to know for a fact that you are able to meet and overcome the hardships, sorrows and tough circumstances of this world. This kind of happiness is priceless. This is that deep fun we were talking about earlier.

One thing after another happening to you can literally "knock the life out of you." The expression is realistic, life is knocked out of you, for a fact. Blow after blow can leave you pretty limp and discouraged. Ultimately you may feel so beaten that you crawl through life instead of standing up courageously and masterfully, taking things as they come and handling them with sure skill and force. There is no fun in life for the crawler-through-life. The licked are always unhappy. But those who know in their hearts that they are equal to every challenge, minor or major, are the ones who get a huge amount of fun out of life.

A man on a plane said "I'm a positive thinking Exhibit A! I don't say that boastfully, but because it's done so much for me. I was the world's worst self-defeating person. I blamed everyone for my failures—even the government. But I knew who was my worst enemy. As someone put it, 'If I could kick the pants of the man causing all my troubles I couldn't sit down for a week!'"

"And believe me it wasn't funny." Then he described a series of defeats and disappointments sufficient to take the heart out of any man. "At first I shied off positive thinking because you tied God into it and I didn't go for that religious approach. I took the psychology in the book and let the religion alone. But while I mentally agreed with the psychology, it didn't take with me. Perhaps I was too negative. But I noticed that you were always urging your readers to read and apply the Bible to problems. Frankly, I hadn't opened a Bible in years. But finally I started reading. At first I couldn't get a thing out of it and wondered why you were so keen for it. So I limited myself to looking up your references. I really tried to follow the things you suggested.

"I was reading the 84th Psalm and the eleventh verse struck me . . . 'No good thing will he withhold from them that walk uprightly.' (Psalm 84:11) 'Walk uprightly'—what did that mean? But it wasn't hard to figure out that I was crawling like a worm. I should stand up like a man and quit griping and being sorry for myself. I was full of self-pity. *Uprightly*—that was the word! Stand up to things—that was what I should be doing! And I got the idea that if I did that, God wouldn't hold back any good thing. So I started walking as sprightly as I could, not cringing like I had been doing. I also saw that *uprightly* meant no double dealing. I decided I'd straighten some things out, with God's help.

"I now see why you tie religion and practical psychology together. Religion makes it work, puts the oomph into it."

That's really an idea to get hold of. Or better still let it get hold of you. "No good thing will he withhold from them that walk uprightly." It gave this man new fun in living. He really had it.

But what about sorrow and grief? An effective demonstrator of positive thinking who achieved out of sorrow a quiet joy in life is Mrs. Anne Scherer of Switzerland. I met Mr. and Mrs. Scherer several years ago at the Beau Rivage Palace Hotel in Lausanne where he was the manager. Some months later Mr. Scherer died suddenly. Mrs. Scherer worked on, under the new manager, as hostess of the hotel. Recently when I returned to Lausanne it was evident that in her modest way Mrs. Scherer had adjusted quite well to her sorrow problem. She had achieved a quietly serene spirit that obviously derived from a deep source of strength.

"I admire the way you have managed to pull through this sad time with such fine spirit," I said. "You did the right thing by going back to work and keeping yourself busy."

Then Mrs. Scherer answered with an extraordinary philosophy of sorrow. "Actually it wasn't going back to work that did it for, you see, work is not a medicine, it is a drug. It desensitizes, but does not heal. It is only faith that heals."

That insight is a classic. Work desensitizes, but it does not heal. It is faith that heals. When we are suffering from deep emotional wounds, of course, we cannot have real happiness; not until the wounds are healed. Some of us make the mistake of thinking we can cure them with work, or perhaps with play; with drink or attempted forgetfulness. As Mrs. Scherer pointed out, these efforts only desensitize the wound for a while. But they do not cure. It is when one learns to apply faith in depth that a true curative process is begun.

A man from out West used to come to New York every now and then on business, and he would call me on the telephone. He had a deep emotional wound and his mood was invariably dejected, his thinking gloomy and somewhat cynical. This negative reaction to sorrow, negative to the point of being abnormal, went on for several years and then, all of a sudden, he wrote me a ten-page letter. I left it lying on my desk for a while before undertaking to read it. But I got into it and I was amazed; it was full of joy and hope. Here was the buoyant testimony of a man who at last had found himself and was telling me how happy he was.

What had happened? Well, this man finally decided he was on the wrong track with his gloomy attitudes and resolved to study and "try to apply" positive thinking techniques to his sorrow problem. He said, "I evolved some techniques you didn't give in your book and they worked beautifully. Perhaps you would like to pass them along to others." And I am glad to do just that for these ideas are sound. I give them to you just as I received them.

This man's "five-fold program of faith" follows:

> First, I pray twenty-five times a day. Yes, I mean that; but these are fragmentary prayers as I walk or drive or work at my desk. I guarantee that if anybody will pray twenty-five times a day he will change the character of his thoughts and change his life. Perhaps this is what the Bible means when it tells us to "pray without ceasing."
>
> Second, I soak my mind with Bible passages. I must have committed a couple of hundred texts by now. I say them over and think of them as going down and down into my subconscious.
>
> Third, I take a piece of paper and see how many good thoughts I can write down about people I know and about situations, too. This was the toughest thing in the whole process as I had a lot of gripes about lots of people. And as to situations, I was always negative and pessimistic. However, I've found that if you think mean thoughts about people it makes you unhappy. But pleasant thoughts about people make you happy all over. And if you make yourself

think that things are going to be O.K. that makes you happier too; and thinking that way often makes them turn out that way.

Fourth, I see how many times every day I can tell the Lord how much I love Him. This love-for-God feeling really does something to you. There was a time I would have ridiculed such a thing, but no more. The more I express my love for God the happier I become.

Fifth, I try to keep all sin out of my life. This is a big order, but even making the effort gives me a clean and happy feeling.

As I said I tried this man's program on quite a few people and where they really worked at it, it proved effective. It is my belief that this spiritual formula will, as he indicates, go far toward curing anybody of unhappiness.

Who wants to live with joy? Who wants to feel like whistling on Madison Avenue or any other street? Pray twenty-five times a day. Soak the mind with Bible passages. See how many good thoughts you can think about people. Tell the Lord you love Him. Get sin out of your life. It is not easy. It takes self-discipline. It requires your doing something about yourself. But really there is no need for you to be unhappy. Simply do a rehabilitation job on your thoughts. Try spiritual living, really try it. You will discover for yourself that there's lots of fun in life.

VI

# The Wonderful Law of Abundance

THERE IS a law of abundance operating in life. And this abundance is for you.

Abundance is a wonderful word. I like the sound of it; it's full and rich. The root of this word, I'm told, is the Latin *undare* which means "to rise up in waves." So actually, when you think and practice abundance you stimulate all manner of good things to rise up toward you in waves.

I received a letter from a young man in Washington, D. C. A year ago this man, Lloyd, was in all sorts of trouble. His marriage was on the rocks, he was drinking, he couldn't hold a job; he had been fired seven times from positions with the Hot Shoppes restaurant chain. Certainly Lloyd couldn't say that all manner of good things were rising up toward him in waves, or even in dribbles.

Then Lloyd began to hear about the amazing effect that positive thinking had on people's lives. He read and studied *The Power of Positive Thinking* and all the books and articles he could find on the subject, and he made up his mind to try these techniques for himself. First, he had to deal with the past. Who would hire him with his record? But that was negative thinking. Sure he had failed before, but that did not have to determine the future.

In *The Power of Positive Thinking* he had read those dynamic words from the Bible, "Forgetting those things which are behind, and reaching forth unto those things which are before, I press toward the mark . . ." (Philippians 3:13)

Lloyd went out once more and applied for a job . . . at the Hot Shoppes; right back where had been fired seven times. With his chin held high, but scared and frightened, and saying over those words from Philippians, Lloyd walked into the office of the personnel director. His new faith enabled him to tell this man that he wanted to work again. And an amazing thing happened. The personnel director said that if he could find one manager who would take Lloyd on, he could work there again. This firm, as I have since learned, began and operates on positive spiritual principles.

"I'm thankful to say," writes Lloyd, "that I found a manager who remembered my good qualities as well as the bad, and gave me another chance." He was hired as a waiter at this drive-in restaurant. Then and there Lloyd set a new pattern for himself. His letter continues:

> I made two very simple promises to God and to myself, something which I've never dared do before, for to me a promise to anyone is serious but to God it is more so.
>
> First, I promised to read my Bible and pray—really pray—every day. Second, I promised to tithe, to give a tenth of my income to God regardless of whether I had a good night as a waiter or a bad one. I decided to go for that promise in the Bible: "Bring ye all the tithes into the storehouse—and prove me now herewith, saith the Lord of hosts, if I will not open you the windows of heaven, and pour you out a blessing, that there shall not be room enough to receive it." (Malachi 3:10)
>
> Now, I'm no saint and have plenty of faults but for once in my life I've found a happy, peaceful, workable relationship with my God. Often on the curb (drive-in service) when someone has failed to tip and my blood pressure starts to rise, somewhere from the Bible, or some phrase from one

of your books will come to mind and I try to give that much *better* service to the next car.

This morning, after I came home from work, I was reflecting on the past year, and I suddenly realized that the problems I had a year ago no longer exist.

And then Lloyd made an amazing statement. I think of it as a most constructive result of positive thinking. Remember, this statement comes from a young man whose life has been remade.

I never thought I could afford to tithe before. But now I can't afford not to!

What dynamic thinking! The exclamation point at the end of the sentence is Lloyd's own. He felt like exclaiming to the world the power of the new idea he had uncovered. When he began to tithe, to give in earnest of himself and his money, he unleashed one of the most potent spiritual principles in the universe. He discovered a basic fact of successful living: that to receive the good things of this life you must give.

This is the secret of the law of abundance.

Let me repeat it for you, because the idea contained in that sentence is literally life changing. It will make your life full and abundant and satisfying beyond anything you have ever imagined.

To receive the good things of this life, you must first give.

Firmly imbed that idea in your consciousness. Say it over and over. Let your mind dwell on it until it becomes a fundamental part of your thought pattern. To receive the good things of this life, you must first give. I cannot over-emphasize its importance. It can change anyone's situation.

This creative law of vital living is expressed in familiar words: "He that findeth his life shall lose it: and he that loseth his life for my sake shall find it." (Matthew 10:39)

And the law is again stated in a sentence which I, personally, regard as one of the most important in the entire Bible: "I am come that they might have life, and that they might have it more abundantly." (John 10:10)

Poverty-stricken and defeated living has no place in the planning of a Creator who crammed this world to overflowing with riches and blessings beyond description. It is man who has messed up the supply of good to all. By his crude interference with the laws of Divine abundance, both socially and personally, he merely exits when all around him are values, not simply in sufficient supply, but in prolific abundance. Such a simple thing as the giving of self, of thought, of money, of time, of helpfulness starts it flowing.

Sometimes the results of putting this technique into practice seem almost miraculous. I choose the following illustration from among many because it is so down-to-earth and about plain everyday people like most of us. And it's one of those situations we call "desperate." But no situation need be thought of as desperate, really; not with the law of abundance to call upon.

A few years ago a woman living in Florida was really up against it. She had moved there from Illinois with enough, she thought, for a humble but secure future; she had a small private income from investments in popular common stocks.

Well, as happens to so many people, something came along to upset all her plans. "The best laid schemes of mice and men gang aft a-gley, and leave us nought but grief and pain for promised joy," wrote Robert Burns. And it's so true.

Certainly that was true for this lady because, when the 1929 crash came, she was completely wiped out. She lost all her money. Fortunately, her home was paid for, so she had a roof over her head but no income, and naturally she was worried.

"What can I do?" she wrote to an old and invalid aunt who lived in Pennsylvania. "Actually, things are so bad that I don't know where I'm going to find enough money to buy food. Right now, believe it or not, I have only a loaf of bread and some cheese in the kitchen, but by the time I get an answer back from you even that will be gone. I'm really up against it."

Well, when the invalid aunt got that letter she sat down and wrote a reply by return mail. She didn't have any money herself but she gave her niece something better, a dynamic motivation, the idea of abundance, the concept of supply. She gave her a formula for getting out of her predicament.

"The trouble with you," wrote the aunt, "is that you are thinking of starving when God will supply abundantly. You are thinking of getting instead of giving, so the secret of your situation is to give, give, give!"

You might say that's the kind of advice you can expect from an old aunt, living in a rocking chair; but as a matter of fact, the apparently unrealistic advice showed a sharp, keen insight into the deeper nature of things.

On the day the aunt's letter arrived in Florida, her niece was almost destitute. She had exactly two slices of bread left in the house. You may not remember, but I recall very well the unbelievable condition that developed during the depression back in the thirties. This type of situation was common then.

When the postman arrived, she tore open the letter hoping, perhaps, there would be something green inside. She didn't see anything green. She turned the letter over and opened the envelope wider and searched inside, but the aunt had sent no money at all. And then she read the note.

She was annoyed. Impatiently she tossed the letter aside. And just as she did there was a knock at the door. Still somewhat annoyed, she opened it and there stood a neighbor, an old man, a dignified elderly gentleman who lived down the road a way. He was embarrassed, terribly embarrassed to come to her door this way, he said, but would she by any chance happen to have something to eat. He was on his way home from a fruitless search for work. His wife wasn't well, and he just had to have something for her to eat. He couldn't believe, he said sadly, that he would ever be in such a condition.

The words from the aunt's letter came rushing back. "The secret of your situation is give, give, give." On impulse, this lady walked back to her kitchen and picked up a piece of bread. Half of all she had. She started back with it, and then she stopped. "The secret of your situation is to give, give, give!" She thought a moment and then returned to the kitchen and got the other piece of bread too, and she wrapped them both in a piece of paper and when she handed them to the old man she did so with an apology for not having more to offer. The grateful old man never knew that she had given him every bit of food there was in the house.

Now, the things that happened next are going to sound a bit on the extravagant side. They are going to appear exaggerated. All I can do is to assure you, further, that even more exciting things are happening to people every day. The door to this lady's house had hardly closed when there came another knocking. There stood a neighbor with a whole *loaf* of bread in her hand, fresh out of the oven. And the next day an unexpected dividend check arrived for $10, which this lady quickly shared. And then, a few days thereafter, a check for $50 arrived "as a belated birthday gift" from a brother. "It just occurred to me that you might be a bit low," he wrote. This, of course, was quickly shared too, because by this time our lady had come to the same conclusion that Lloyd was going to reach years later at the Hot Shoppes. She just couldn't afford not to share.

So this is the way the law of abundance works. It is there, ready to shower you with all manner of good things. All you need to do is stimulate the flow of abundance. And that is accomplished by developing certain stimulators; that is, certain attitudes and habits which will start and maintain the flow of abundance.

One is definitely and deliberately to work with abundance thoughts. Set yourself to eliminate all lack thoughts from your mind. Practice the abundance concept until it becomes habitual. See or picture your life as full of rich values. Conceive of yourself as being a stimulating part of the flow of good, not bad, of prosperity, not poverty. Help other people to think and act similarly, for there can be no permanent abundance for one unless it spreads to many. Prosperity, widely enjoyed, always lifts the level of abundance for everyone.

And there is another significant fact: those who apply the law of abundance, right thinking, right acting, outgoing service keep the flow of values in motion. Even when men, by wrong thinking, interrupt the smooth operation of another of God's great laws, the law of economics, those who keep in harmony are still able to draw upon the vast basic prosperity of God's abundant world.

Catherine Thrower tells of a study class composed of business people who were working with the principles in Charles Fillmore's book *Prosperity*. It was in a period of business recession. Each student was asked to "pour living words of truth into their situation," believing they would be prospered in their work regardless of recession. This was a city where the psychology of lack was very strong. Each class session began with such an affirmation as the following:

> I am the rich child of a loving Father. All that the Father has is mine. Divine intelligence is now showing me how to

claim my God-given blessings of wealth, health and happiness. All that is mine by Divine heritance now comes to me in abundance.

Each student was expected to pour positive thinking into the atmosphere of office, business establishment or home. He was to turn the energy of his thinking upon "plenty" ideas rather than upon "lack" ideas and thus to counter with thought-vitality the negativism expressed all around him.

These business people studied, learned and applied the simple principles of the law of abundance. They thought creatively, they helped each other, they shared with God and man, they worked creatively and thus they set the immense force of positive ideas against the dismal defeatism everyone was talking.

Results began to show. Two secretaries became so valuable to their firms that they received pay increases at a time when many salaries were being cut. A lawyer became so helpful to his clients that his receipts for professional services took a swift upturn. A steel man, whose business was supposed to be particularly affected by recession, unexpectedly received several good orders. One abundance student, a saleslady in a downtown department store, as a result of her application of abundance principles, did so much business in an organization riddled by negative thoughts that she was the only clerk to receive a commission for having sold more than her quota.

In such experiences as those mentioned, positive thinking stimulated fresh and creative ideas. Abundance begins in your thoughts, in the form of new slants, fresh insights concerning problems. These produce better results. Buried deeply in your mind are all the potential values you need for a complete life. The Bible tells us "the Kingdom of God is within you." What a promise! Think of it; all the riches of

God's great Kingdom are potentially resident in your mind. It remains only to learn the method of releasing them into abundance. And by abundance, of course, is meant every good: health, well-being, sufficiency, usefulness—every creative value in life.

I have a friend in St. Joseph, Missouri, who showed me recently how right thinking can act as a stimulator of abundance. This friend's name is Jack Spratt. His first name isn't really "Jack," it's Elliott; but with a last name like Spratt it seems that no one can resist the temptation to call him Jack. And he is a living demonstration of the amazing results of positive thinking.

One day when I was visiting Mr. Spratt we got to talking about the law of abundant supply. "It's an amazing thing," Mr. Spratt said, "how a simple change in thinking can affect a man's whole career." And then he told me how, whenever he has a salesman who has begun to slow down on sales, maybe get a bit stale, he calls him into his office.

"Joe," he says, "I want you to give me your order book. I'm taking it away from you."

Well, that scares the salesman pretty badly; he thinks Mr. Spratt is discharging him. But Mr. Spratt is not; actually he is re-charging the salesman. He takes away the order book, but he gives the man an opportunity to find himself, to start abundance flowing again.

"Now Joe," says Mr. Spratt, "I want you to go out and make the rounds of your customers."

"But you've got my order book," Joe answers.

"That's because I don't want you to take a single order," says Mr. Spratt. "Don't even try to get an order. You're going out on a new angle of salesmanship. You are going to sell yourself on the law of abundance."

"What's the idea, I haven't been getting enough orders as it is, and now you want me to stop taking them entirely?"

And then Mr. Spratt says, "The trouble with you, Joe, is that you've been hoarding yourself. You've got to give yourself away. Now here's what I want you to do. Make your rounds as usual; but this time, for one week, I want you to go to each of your customers and give yourself to him. I mean, do something good for at least one of them each day this week. Help them to have something they really need, something like courage, faith, hope. Give them just plain old friendship. Think about them as people, not as customers. Then, after you've given yourself away for a week, come back and see me."

Mr. Spratt told me that usually at the end of such a week, the salesman is quite a different person. A revitalized enthusiasm shows in his voice and a kind of excitement has come into his relations with his customers. And then, in most cases, amazing things begin to happen to his sales record. Orders start to flow in. And they don't come out of gratitude, either. A man substituting a go-out-to-give system for a go-out-to-get attitude breaks down barriers with people and releases creative qualities within himself.

"The key idea, of course," said Mr. Spratt, "is the tithing of yourself and your time as well as your money. When this is done miraculous things begin to occur in you, in your job, in your family life, in everything. I've seen it work a hundred times right here in St. Jo. The more you try to keep of yourself, the less you have to keep; and the more you give yourself away, the more you have to give away."

Tithe yourself, give yourself, share yourself. What a lot of power there is in that idea, and how it stimulates the flow of abundance whether your need is for abundant material things, or ideas, or happiness. Tithing yourself means giving yourself to people and to God; doing something for your fellow man and for God's work in the world. As you do this humbly and sincerely, good things will flow back toward you. Try it for yourself. See for yourself.

At one time I received a letter from a young mother who complained that she was getting a raw deal.

> Who is it that has to do all the cooking and all the ironing and scrubbing around here? Me.
>
> Who is it who is scullery maid while the others play? Me!
>
> My lot is an unhappy one and I don't mind saying so. This house is not a place of love, Dr. Peale; it is a house where there is one overworked maid-of-all-work and that maid is me. And what do I get out of it? Nothing! Absolutely nothing, but work and more work.

Well, I wrote back that I certainly was sorry she felt that way about her home. It is sad indeed when a woman does not like her job as wife-mother-homemaker. Obviously she had developed a self-centered thought pattern that was keeping her from receiving and enjoying the flow of love that her family would want to send out to her. She was blocking it off and in so doing was making herself tired and irritable.

I suggested to this young woman that she put into effect a new philosophy; just to see what would happen. Suppose, I suggested, that instead of waiting for love and appreciation to come from others, she stimulate the flow of these healthy emotions by giving them away first.

"When you cook," I said, "you use seasonings. You use salt and pepper and spices. Why not 'season' your home life? Try, for one month, adding a generous tablespoon of love to your recipe. As you stir in the other seasonings think these words, maybe even say them aloud: 'I am now adding love. This will make the meal more enjoyable for everyone.' Try the same thing with your cleaning. Sweep out your old, injured thoughts and bring in thoughts of love. Sprinkle thoughts of appreciation over your family's clothes as you prepare them for ironing. But the important thing is this: don't wait for someone else to begin. You start the love-flow yourself, and then write me again and let me know how things are."

Well, I didn't have to wait long to find out how the experiment worked. Three weeks later I got a letter from this woman. It went, in part, like this:

> I must admit, Dr. Peale, that at first I thought your ideas were a little extreme. Imagine adding a tablespoon of love to a recipe, sweeping out negative thoughts, sprinkling clothes with affection! But frankly things were so bad around here and I was feeling so miserable that I decided to try your ideas anyway, as queer as they seemed. All I can say is, it's amazing how they did work!
>
> The very first night, for instance, my husband paid me a compliment on my cooking; it was the first he had given me in a long time, and do you know what he said? "What's your secret ingredient, Baby? This is really good!"
>
> Well, I was surprised to hear myself reply that it *was* a secret, but that I had lots more where it came from. And it's been the same way with other things around the house. Not always compliments; sometimes it's simply a look of appreciation, and sometimes it's even a helping hand. Anyway, I can see now that a whole new world lies before me.

These are but a few of the stimulators of the law of abundance. They all have one denominator in common; in each case the flow of abundance was started when a person dared to open himself up, ceased to be afraid, and believed that good things were going to flow toward him; and then underlined his belief by first giving away much of himself to others. It is a fact that negative thought will attract negative thought, and positive thought will attract positive thought.

If you live on a basis of pinched, patched, poor, little thoughts, you will attract others of similar outlook. But if you make the first, bold move to get rid of your shabby thoughts, and replace them with fresh, healthy, abundance thoughts you will attract more such thoughts to yourself.

Abundance does not come by praying for things, money, possessions. Instead pray for insights and ideas. These you can turn into useful implements to enrich your life.

Actually, all values are in the mind. Creative achievement is in the mind. You have abundance within you. You can think your way to all manner of good if you will only *think: think* new thoughts.

Abundance is never likely to come to the "grooved-in thinker." That phrase was often used by the late great scientific genius Charles F. "Boss" Kettering, inventor of the automatic self-starter.

Some people, he pointed out, simply get into mental ruts and stay there. They have capacities, just as the people have who do things, but they won't ask questions and won't think, or if they do it's negative thinking. They even defend their failures and sometimes actually call it the will of God, if they are piously disposed. In this abundant universe anyone, except the infirm and very aged perhaps, can think his way into abundance. And actually I could cite cases of people flat on their backs in bed who carry on worthwhile activities, even paying businesses.

Kettering shows how the negative or grooved-in thinker shuts off abundance and how the positive thinker stimulates it in full measure. He told the following story about his early experiences in the automobile industry.

> In the early days of cars, we finished them off, like pianos, with varnish. For the cheaper cars, the job took seventeen days; more expensive ones took thirty-five. One day I called

in all the paint experts and asked if we could shorten that part of automobile production. They thought maybe two days could be lopped off.

"Why can't you paint a car in one hour?" I asked.

"The paint won't dry," they said.

That was the best advice of the experts; so, with my question still in my mind I went looking. One day I saw lacquered pin trays in a jewelry store on Fifth Avenue in New York. I bought one for $11.50. The jeweler told me he bought the trays from a little laboratory over in New Jersey. So I went out there.

When I asked for a quart of his lacquer, the man was startled. He had never made a quart of it before. When I told him I wanted to use it on an automobile, he shook his head. "It won't work. Put it in your spray guns and it will dry before it hits the door."

"Can't you slow it down?"

"Nope, that's impossible!"

Of course it wasn't impossible. One question led to another, then another. Finally, by working closely with one of the paint manufacturers, we obtained a lacquer which could be sprayed on and a car completely finished in a few hours. Grooved-in thinking could have stopped us cold, back at the horse-and-carriage level.

And when we first put the self-starter in the automobile, the Detroit Edison people had a special meeting of the American Institute of Electrical Engineers. They wanted me to explain the self-starter, which I did; but about halfway through, a dignified gentleman interrupted.

"I move this meeting come to an end," he said. "This man doesn't know what he is talking about. He has profaned every fundamental law of electrical engineering!"

He was a victim of grooved-in thinking.

So, to stimulate abundance, *think*. Really think there is a way to better conditions. And, if you can think it in your mind, you can think it into actuality. Believe, pray, think, give—these are the four horsemen of abundance. Don't be a grooved-in thinker!

In Hong Kong I met a most remarkable man named Mr. Chou, a refugee from the Chinese communists. Mr. Chou, formerly a wealthy merchant in the old China, loved freedom so much that he and his family walked out of Red China with nothing; nothing, that is, except courage and faith and love; nothing, but positive thinking. He had known what it was to live abundantly in the material sense; but in Hong Kong he also knew what it was to live on a very, very meager scale. In fact, he was in plain, miserable poverty.

When he and his family first arrived without money or any source of money, they built a shack made of a couple of packing boxes insulated with burlap bags. They did their cooking on an open fire in front of their shanty home. After Mr. Chou had been in Hong Kong for several weeks, living on this subsistence level, he managed to get a humble job. It paid ten Hong Kong dollars a month ($1.60 U.S.)!

And yet the remarkable thing is that Mr. Chou was neither bitter nor resentful. He made every effort to improve his condition; but when his efforts failed he knew how to shift gears mentally and think abundantly regardless of setbacks. He tried to arrange for living quarters for his family in a Methodist housing project nearby called Wesley Village. Mr. Chou was a Methodist and Wesley Village was a nice cottage community especially built to house refugees. The two-room cottages were situated on a sunny hillside and were neat, warm and attractive; but they cost 50¢ a day (8¢ U.S.). This was much more than Mr. Chou could afford so his dream was not realized.

But even so, on the day when his friends and neighbors who could afford to live there packed up their possessions and struggled up the hill to Wesley Village, Mr. Chou was on the spot to help them. He carried the heaviest boxes. He laughed and sang as he carried in the belongings of the fortunate ones. He was happy for them. He helped the aged grandmothers and the very young children. How much he wanted to move his own family there too; but since he couldn't, he rejoiced with those who could. Mr. Chou knew how to think abundantly. Wasn't he a true follower of Christ who promises: "I am come that they might have life, and that they might have it more abundantly." (John 10:10)

To me the wonderful point in this story is that Mr. Chou possessed abundant happiness, outgoing unselfishness, good will and cheerfulness even while his fortunes were at an extremely low ebb. But there is something about a personality such as his that attracts good will from others. You should see this man's radiant face—it warms your heart just to look at him.

Before long someone found a job for Mr. Chou that paid 35 Hong Kong dollars, more than tripling his previous wage. The law of abundant supply was working. And shortly after that a vacancy occurred in the Wesley cottage community. Is it any wonder that Mr. Chou and family were asked to take it? This Chinese man will always remain in my memory as one of the truly great souls I have met in my lifetime.

His experience clearly demonstrates that the law of abundance operates even in most desolate and desperate circumstances. It stimulates forces which result in astonishing readjustment of conditions and, what is perhaps more important, constructive attitude toward conditions. Mr. Chou gave freely (at a time when many might have said he had nothing to give) and so he received abundantly. By this law of thinking and living one can do a creative job with the toughest possible conditions.

When you are in tune with the law of abundance the good things of life shall rise up toward you in waves. You will know emotional, physical (perhaps even material) wealth far beyond your present dreams. If today you are experiencing something less than abundant living, review this chapter and select one of the abundance stimulators that applies to your situation. Give it full cooperation. Live with it, believe in it, make it part of your unconscious thought pattern. You'll know this has happened when the new technique no longer requires effort. At the end of six months I am sure your life will be enriched beyond measure.

VII

# What to Do About What You're Afraid Of

YOU CAN do something about your fear. You can overcome it. And to do that, simply develop faith as did this young naval officer.

He wrote me about his victory in the same factual manner he would report an engagement with an enemy.

> I am the commanding officer of this ship, a job which carries both pleasure and responsibility in large measure. It is as fine a task as could be assigned a young officer and I am grateful for the opportunity.
>
> My problems arise from the fear of failure, from the habit of worry, and from the lack of self-confidence. An imposing array of shortcomings, I know. Of all the methods tried to overcome or alleviate these weaknesses the only one proven successful has been Faith.
>
> From this realization stems my gratitude to you, for the simple, down-to-earth, and above all, believable manner in which you picture the power of reliance on God. I have been a skeptic in the past but you make further doubt so illogical as to be impossible. The strength I gather from you has enriched my life and made possible a hitherto unknown happiness.

How much time and energy do you spend on fear?

None? When did you last knock on wood or walk around a ladder or throw a pinch of salt over your shoulder? When did you suddenly feel your heart pounding for no apparent reason? Was it when you awakened in the night, tense, mouth dry? Maybe you felt it as you went in to call on a prospective customer?

We are a curious generation when you come to think about it. We have developed the resources of the earth and advanced our scientific knowledge to a remarkable degree; we are masters in so many areas. Yet we are not really masters of our own anxieties. We still live in fear.

Actually, ours is a frightened generation. Albert Camus, the French author, calls this "the century of fear." There is even a modern symphony called, "Age of Anxiety." That's something when we make music based on fear.

Not only do we have all the normal, old-fashioned fears but we now have a big new fear in the nuclear bombs which can strike across oceans. And even if they never strike, we can still worry about a sinister invisible killer called "fallout" which may wreak its damage on us and future generations. A scientist recently said, "We have a free-floating anxiety induced by the atom bomb, by space missiles and every destructive device."

"Free-floating anxiety!" What an apt way to describe the fear of our time. This is not the fear which the caveman felt when he heard the growl of the saber-toothed tiger. That fear triggered the caveman to run, or (if he was inventive) to tie a piece of rock to a stick and get himself that tiger's skin for a coat. Of course, this is the basic and original purpose of fear; to impel us to action in order to save our lives. And this use of fear is as valid today as it ever was. When we check our tires because we are afraid they are wearing thin, that's healthy use of fear.

But this is not the type of fear on which most of us expend our time and strength. Today we are afflicted more often with a vague uneasy anxiety that's hard to name. We can't fight back at this fear because we don't really know what we're scared of. Or perhaps we are fearful of so many things that attacking any of them seems futile. Fear, for us, isn't always a specific pinpointed menace that we can act on and do something concrete about, but a cloud that hovers over us, just out of reach, and casts its black shadow on everything we do.

It's a hazy, pervasive apprehension. Some time ago I was lecturing in Wichita, Kansas and had to fly to Cincinnati. Mrs. Olive Ann Beech, of the Beech Aircraft Corporation kindly loaned me a plane and pilot for that seven-hundred mile flight. When we were flying over the Mississippi the weather, which was sunny, became hazy.

"We'll have to go up above the haze level," said the pilot. "Ground heat, dust and smoke often make a low-lying haze. We'll go up another thousand feet and get above it."

We emerged into an altogether different world, one that was clear and with far visibility. This is what we have to do in our thinking; lift our thoughts above the haze level of our own conflicted, fear-ridden thoughts. We need to rise above the cloud of fear, anxiety and worry into an upper level where we can think clearly and rationally.

It is most important to do something about fear. Fear is an enemy of your happiness. It affects your ability to think, thus hampering your efficiency, and poses danger to your health.

My own heart specialist and good friend Dr. Louis F. Bishop says: "It is not generally realized how many cardiovascular symptoms can be produced by tension and anxiety. Anxiety states are very common, and whereas it can be stated that a certain amount of anxiety is good for everybody, because it spurs you to get things done, at the same time it can be very crippling. It may produce symptoms affecting almost any organ of the body.

"The heart itself reacts in various ways to anxiety. The rate may be remarkably increased; the rhythm may be affected; a stressful or anxious situation may produce a serious irregularity of the heart. Anxiety may also produce, as is well known, particularly in the middle-aged, attacks of precordial pain, known as angina pectoris. Tension may play a role as a precipitating factor in the closure of one of the vessels supplying the heart with blood—the condition known as coronary thrombosis."

Dr. Leo Rangell, Clinical Professor of Psychiatry at U.C.L.A., says, according to the *Los Angeles Times*: "Bacteria and other micro-organisms find it easier to infect people who worry and fret."

But do not be alarmed. You have the power to overpower fear. It need not be allowed to harm you at all. The great fact is that you can, if you will, do something constructive about what you're afraid of. The ability to do this is one of the greatest results of positive thinking. Positive thinking presupposes a firm mind control. When you control your thoughts you will be able to control your emotions, including fear and worry.

I received a letter from a lady in Philadelphia whose little boy, named Carl, was troubled with fears. He was having nightmares; he was afraid of his playmates; he had grown thin and was constantly tired. She wanted to know if she could come to see me. Well, there is nothing sadder than a little boy full of fear and I wanted to help if possible, so we fixed an appointment.

When the time for the appointment arrived, it was a beautiful, springlike day, which was a bit unusual as it was the fifteenth of January. When this mother walked in (she came without Carl), I made some passing remark about what a fine day it was.

"Sickness weather," said this woman. "It's not healthy to have it warm this time of year. Watch out for influenza when you get a warm stretch in January."

That was just the start. This woman was afraid of everything. Within the first five minutes of our conversation, she mentioned that she had not brought her son with her from the hotel because she was afraid of the "dirty" air in the subways. She was afraid of all the "foreigners" she saw on the streets. She was afraid to go up on the Empire State Building for fear of the pressure on her ears. This was the tone of her talk. After we had visited in this way for a while, I brought the conversation around to Carl. I mentioned to her that his problem was by no means unique.

"So many children have fears," I said. "Where do you think they come from?"

This woman didn't know. She thought perhaps children were born with their fears.

"Not at all," I said. "Most fears are acquired from the people around them, especially, of course, from their parents."

"What you're trying to say is that Carl gets his fears from me?"

"I assure you this is nothing to be ashamed of," I said. "It is the way of human nature. You probably picked up your own fear thoughts from your parents and they from their parents and so on. The important thing is to break the chain."

"And how can I do that?"

"With positive thinking. Fear is a negative thought, and one helpful way to get rid of it is to think of your mind as a scale, a balance. On one side of the scale are all of your negative thoughts. On the other side are all of your positive thoughts. Right now, your scale is pretty badly out of balance; your negative thoughts far outweigh your positive thoughts . . . and, of course, these are being reflected in your son. The solution is to outweigh your fears.

"Try this method. The next time you have a negative thought, put a positive thought in the other scale. Take, for instance, the weather. It's a beautiful day outside. When you leave here, say to yourself, 'What a health-giving day! In fact it's so unusually clear that this would be a good day to take Carl up the Empire State Building to see the view.'"

The woman laughed—but doubtfully, "Do you think it would really work?" I replied, "It will work. Stick with it until that emotional scale is completely balanced; and then stick with it some more, until your positive thoughts outweigh your negative thoughts. When you have done this for, let us say, three months, let me know how Carl's fears are coming."

It was more than three months before I heard from this woman, nearer six, actually. But she really did make the experiment. When she finally wrote me, her letter reflected a state of healthy, happy excitement. She said:

> You've no idea what an amazing effect on our lives this simple plan of outweighing your fears has had. We have had to do a lot of struggling with them, but I do believe they are under much better control. Carl is much more relaxed and has fun with his playmates. He no longer seems so afraid or tense. I like to feel that I have, at last, broken that chain of inherited fears. One of these days I hope I can report that they are conquered altogether.

The basic idea employed here is an indirect approach to the problem of handling fears. Instead of tackling the anxiety and fear directly, by which process they often refuse to budge, we tried the indirect method of floating the fears out.

This is one of the best strategies for ridding yourself of fears; much better than trying to force them out by mustering your will power, which may be weak anyway. Rather let the rising tide of faith do the job for you. Fill your mind with such a large quantity of faith that your fears will actually be floated away. By this method God's power will do for you what you cannot do for yourself. Your part is simply to believe, trust and surrender yourself to His power. Let His tremendous strength lift you above fear.

Those who have used this principle of positive thinking in dealing with fear have had amazing results. But how do you fill your mind with faith to this degree? One of the methods is what we call the practice of the presence of God.

For example, I received a letter from Mrs. Grace Lichtenstein of Oakland, California, telling how one lady used this same positive technique to handle a situation that usually arouses panic and fear.

> A woman was caught in an elevator which had stopped between floors. The manager of the building called to her and asked if she were alone. She replied, "No, not alone." He assured her the elevator would soon be repaired and urged her not to worry.
>
> When finally the elevator was repaired, and the door opened, the lady was quite alone. The man looked at her in surprise. "Lady, you said you were not alone."
>
> "No," she replied calmly, "I wasn't alone. God was with me."

How many people, who constantly live with fear thoughts, could have answered as calmly as she did? There is a profound comfort and security in believing, for a fact, that God is with you. Perhaps the greatest comfort in this world is, "I am not alone." When you know this for yourself, your fears will lose their hold upon you.

Next time you are afraid, next time your heart pounds or anxiety clutches at your mind, repeat the following eight confidence-building words from Isaiah 41:10: "Fear thou not; for I am with thee." Say them over and over to yourself, listen intently to them as if God were actually with you speaking to you. He is, of course, so try to sense His presence. When you are able to do this with a sense of conviction, then you will experience release from your fears.

In the great crises of life, when men really need to have a sense of the Lord's presence in order to endure, they can get it. In Belgium I visited what was once a notorious Nazi prison, located midway between Antwerp and Brussels and known as the Breendonk. It is now maintained by the Belgium government as a sacred place of memory, and the flag flies over it proudly.

To the Breendonk during the Occupation, the Nazis took loyal, patriotic Belgium citizens who had the audacity to oppose their tyranny, kept them like animals in miserable cells and strove by indescribable maltreatment and torture to crush their spirits; but the prisoners stood up against all this. Passing through the dark, dank, dismal passageways that have been left just as they were in those days, one gets an awful sense of the degradation of man and at the same time an uplifting sense of the greatness of man.

I said to our guide, "How could people stand up against anything so terrible?"

"I'll show you the answer," he said, and he took us back into one of the darkest of the cells. There in the corner, carved crudely in the stone, was an outline of the face of the Saviour, Jesus Christ. The guide said, "When the going got hard these men, one by one, would come in here and put their hands on His face. It was their way of remembering that they were not alone.

"One night the Nazis came to our house and took my father. We never saw him again. We heard, after the war, that he probably died here; but we cannot be sure. We were told that he was one of those who came to this very cell to feel the face of Christ. I know he would do that for he was a devout Christian. I am comforted by the thought that our Lord was with my father to make him unafraid of whatever he had to suffer."

What an answer to fear. *We are not alone!* Practice this tremendous truth until it becomes a positive conviction. I AM NOT ALONE. Make it personal. No fear on earth is greater than this thought.

This truth suggests that one big factor in doing something about fear is to keep your head and not panic. As long as you can think calmly, you can think rationally. When you can do this you will get along all right. The only way God can guide you is through your thoughts and even He cannot get through panicky thoughts to direct you. But God will help you maintain calmness as you practice positive thinking. In a radio talk describing certain aspects of positive thinking, I said: "There is a passage in the Bible, in Luke, ninth chapter, first verse, where we are told that Jesus called unto His disciples and 'gave them power and authority over all devils.' "

Now, did you ever have any idea you might have a devil in you? By devils I mean the devil of hate, the devil of sensuality, the devil of dishonesty or the devil of fear? When the Bible says men may be possessed by devils, it is of course a truth. And modern psychological medicine confirms it. I have known people who have had devils in them. In fact I have felt devils within myself: meanness, hate, fear, resentment, jealousy. These things are well named, for devils they are, considering all the misery they cause. But an enormous fact to depend upon is that Jesus gave his disciples power and authority over devils so that they may rise up in a vast strength and cast them out in His name.

A businessman in Tennessee wrote me of his experience with this truth.

Dear Dr. Peale:

About three years ago I found myself engulfed with doubts and fears. They crept in and peace crept out. For months I was swamped with a tormenting depression. I felt as if I were almost lost and there was no God. I prayed and I did everything I could think of.

One day I found myself impatient, if not angry, that He would let me go on this way. I told Him I was angry and asked Him to forgive me.

I found information in the writing of Reverend J. A. MacMillan of the Christian and Missionary Alliance faith about the authority of the believer. I saw I was a victim of doubts and fears which are really evil demons. I acknowledged it. I cried out to God and I asked Him for this authority.

Then, as if I were in the presence of a person, I spoke to these doubts and fears and commanded them to leave me in the name of Jesus. A miracle happened. As if a light were turned on, the doubts and fears fled and my soul leaped for joy in a peace that is hard to describe.

For five months now I have been getting up around five o'clock to read the Bible and to meditate and pray. Peace has so flooded my soul that it is like liquid joy.

This man learned that Christianity is not some little, nice thing, a mere intellectual system of thought. It is rather a very strong power given to those who truly accept it. It is the power of God unto salvation to all who will believe. And if you really want freedom, Jesus Christ will give you power and authority to say to these devils of fear, or hate or sensuality or whatever: I command you to leave me.

That is man-sized christianity and its blessings are yours if you want them badly enough. But you will have to develop some very real and strong faith. Say to the Lord, "I am tired of fooling with this fear; I want peace and relief." Don't go cringing and crawling in front of life. We are supposed to be men, strong men of faith, filled with power. Take the Gospel of Jesus Christ, really take it in depth; and transplant it into your mind, and you can have power and authority over your fear. Stand up to your fear and in the name of God and His son Jesus Christ command it to leave you. Then believe it is gone. Repeat this process until you feel a deep sense of victory.

One thing we must watch is that a fear thought has a way of popping into your mind when you least expect it and when it can do the most damage. At such times it is particularly important, as we have said before, not to try a frontal attack against the fear, but to use the displacement and substitutionary method of eliminating it. If you constantly fill your mind with faith thoughts, the fear thoughts will be firmly and surely displaced in due course of time. Of course, no change of personality of this character may be accomplished without effort. But that it can be accomplished there is no doubt at all.

A woman wrote me in French from Switzerland to report on the remarkable effects of such thought changing and displacement.

Dear Friend:

Allow me to start my letter so. You do not know me. I know you well after reading your book.

I am the daughter of a French Presbyterian minister. I have been brought up by real Christian parents, but having lived through two wars, I lived in terrible fear of the future. What would I ever do if I lost my husband? How would I ever bring up my three boys with very little money? And so on.

Then I became dreadfully ill with eczema, which was real torture. It lasted, on and off, for seven years. The doctors could not find the origin of this eczema. But I found it in reading your book. Fear had actually poisoned my blood. As I was itching on the inside, so also I itched on the outside, and I assure you it was agony.

So after reading your book I followed your advice. I started reading the Psalms. I copied all the verses which were helpful. I followed the way you said, of letting these verses soak into my mind. At last I fell upon the last verse of the Fourth Psalm: "I will both lay me down in peace, and sleep: for thou, Lord, only makest me dwell in safety." (Psalm 4:8) Security, that is what I needed. I can find it in God. I have found it in God.

And as for money, I found these verses in Job which set me free from money worries: "Then shalt thou lay up gold as dust . . . Yea, the Almighty shall be thy defense. . ." (Job 22:24-25)

So now at last I have understood, now that I am over fifty, that the spiritual reserves within me are unlimited, and I can call upon Him and be well and joyful.

This woman literally crowded out fear by crowding faith in, faith in the form of great spiritual truths which were received deeply into her mind.

Harold Medina, you recall, was the famous judge who presided over the long trial of eleven top U. S. communists who had been charged with conspiracy to overthrow the United States government by violence. This trial was an extremely difficult experience. Emotions were high; tempers were short. And a great deal of the emotion and temper was directed at the judge in person.

He soon became aware of the fact that this was not entirely an accident. Something unusual was happening. It seemed that the defendants were more interested in breaking up the trial than they were in obtaining an acquittal. They were after a mistrial. They could achieve this goal in one of two ways: either by creating a tremendous confusion, or else by putting Judge Medina himself under such a strain that he would break.

The defense worked both plans at once. Throughout the trial, there was great difficulty in keeping order. Witnesses were insolent; attorneys were devious. But the attack that came closest to breaking up the entire trial was directed against Judge Medina himself. Somehow or other the master planners for the defense found out that the judge was afraid of high places. He had what is known as acrophobia, a fear of heights.

When Harold Medina was a small boy his father took him to Niagara Falls. Harold saw the crowd of people pressing up against the railing, looking down at the falls, but he could not go near that rail. He was afraid he would jump over. Time and again throughout his childhood and young manhood, Medina faced this fear and handled it simply by avoiding it.

But now, suddenly, he could no longer avoid it. Judge Medina's chambers were on the twenty-second floor of the skyscraper federal courthouse in New York City overlooking Foley Square. One day the judge became aware of crowds down below shouting about him. "Medina will *fall*, like Forrestal." It was just a few days after Defense Secretary James Forrestal had fallen to his death from a hospital window. Was it just his imagination, Judge Medina wondered, or were these people stressing the word "fall." Quickly he stepped back from the window.

Bit by bit, Medina became aware of the deliberateness of the campaign. The word "fall" began to be stressed all around him. He found it underlined in letters, circled in newspaper clippings; he heard it stressed in conversations. He managed to carry on, but the strain was beginning to tell. One evening as he was preparing to go to bed, his wife opened the window of their apartment to let in some air. It was a stifling night, but Judge Medina said:

"Close that window, please, Ethel."

His wife looked at him, puzzled. He had never mentioned to her the fear of falling that he had had as a child. "I'm not fooling," he said, and then he told her about the signs, the chants, the whispers and the underlinings. Mrs. Medina was convinced. After that, they slept with the window open only a crack, from the bottom.

"Now the problem was," said Judge Medina talking about the experience later, "what do you do when you cannot avoid your fears? When I was a child the solution was simple; I just shunned the things that would make me afraid. Now I couldn't do that. What could I do? How does a man face a fear he cannot avoid? I'll tell you the answer . . . prayer.

"I don't mean a prayer directed only toward my fear of falling. I didn't suddenly say, 'Now, Lord, You have got to take away my acrophobia.' I mean a whole prayer pattern that asked for strength and guidance in *all* that I was doing. It was prayer that I had been building since I was a boy, when my mother knelt with me at bedtime to read from her Episcopal Book of Common Prayer. I inherited not just a Sunday kind of prayer, but a daily, often hourly kind of prayer. I prayed constantly, on and off throughout the day, any time when I was thankful, or under stress, or when I was in any kind of trouble.

"It was prayer alone that kept me going during the sixth and seventh months of the trial. There was no visitation, no sudden apparition, but there was the slow renewal of strength. With it came the firm realization that I would be able to meet whatever lay ahead of me . . . free of my old fear."

Do you see what Judge Medina was doing? He did not try to fight this one fear; he did not struggle and strain trying to rid himself of his acrophobia. He floated his fear away with a total prayer program that acted in the same way the tide did in raising that old tanker out of the Jersey mud flat. He so completely filled his mind with faith thoughts, that there simply was no room for fear thoughts, and they were firmly and finally floated away.

Judge Medina told this story in our monthly, inspirational magazine, *Guideposts*. It illustrates how a man can use prayer to eliminate his fears, even old deep ones. But this is not the only way that prayer can be used to conquer anxiety. There is also intercessory prayer when many people pray for a given objective.

One of the editors of *Guideposts* is a man named John Sherrill. In September, 1957, John had an experience which convinced him of the power of other people's prayers to dispel fear. Right up until the morning September 20, of that year, John was leading a fairly normal life. He was married, he and his wife (and the bank) owned a house in the suburbs of New York; they had three children and a four-year-old Ford automobile. Theirs was a happy, creative life.

Then, on this morning, John got a telephone call from his doctor. The doctor wanted to see him right away. A few days earlier, John had had a small mole removed from his left ear. Now he was told the shocking fact that it was highly malignant. Without an operation, the doctor said, his chances of being alive at the end of a year were one in nine.

With an operation, he had one chance in three. Further examination by specialists at Memorial Center and Presbyterian Hospital confirmed the diagnosis. Immediate surgery was recommended by every doctor.

A few days after that operation, I received a letter from John which I would like to share, in part, with you. This is what he had to say about the fear that took hold of him when he learned about the cancer:

> . . . Fear is such a devastating emotion, Dr. Peale . . . it harried us day and night. I woke up in the night and knew that I was afraid. I answered the children's questions automatically; my mind was elsewhere. I spent hours with Tibby [his wife] going over insurance, wills, finances. When I tried to force my mind to more healthy matters, I could not: I was afraid.
>
> And then, Dr. Peale, something remarkable happened. As our friends began to hear the news of the cancer, they needed to feel they were helping and their immediate response was to pray. The first prayer that we learned about, I think, was the one that you said for us from your pulpit that Sunday. After that, prayer rose about us like a flood.
>
> There was prayer at *Guideposts,* both in the New York and Carmel office. Did you know, Dr. Peale, that your friend, Tessie Durlac, asked her synagogue to pray for us, and that she called long distance to the Prayer Tower at Unity? Our assistant art director, Sal Lazzarotti, told me he almost drove off the road saying the rosary on his way home Friday after he heard the news. "I haven't been saying the rosary too regularly, God," he said, "but starting tonight it's going to be different."
>
> Prayer was in the air we breathed. We were surrounded by it, submerged in it. Early the following week I was admitted to the hospital. To my amazement the atmosphere there was one of prayer, too. No sooner had I settled down in my bed in Room 609 when I heard a weird and haunting note, almost

a cry, permeate the corridor. In the room next to mine an Orthodox Jewish patient was celebrating Rosh Hashana, the Jewish New Year. The nurse told me I had heard the cry of the ram's horn, which for centuries has been used to summon men to prayer.

During these days in the hospital, I was praying too. But there was something strange about my own prayers; they were not for myself, they were for others. I must emphasize, Dr. Peale, that I am trying simply to report facts. I prayed for others, not from any deliberate sense of selflessness, but because I genuinely did not feel the need to pray for myself. This struck me as odd until I realized the reason. *Suddenly, on the night before the operation, I was aware that I was free of fear!*

Was this the tangible result of all the prayers? I think it was. On the night before the operation I felt such a surge of health that is was hard to realize I was in a hospital. At six o'clock the next morning a nurse roused me and gave me a needle.

"This will make you sleepy," she said.

I laughed. "You wake me up to give me something to make me sleepy?"

They came and wheeled me into the operating room. It was as if I, and the white-masked nurses, and the doctors were in the center of a force that dispelled fear. The closest I can come to describing it is to say that I felt as if I were deeply and personally loved.

And that, of course, must be a perfect condition for healing.

The operation was over. There was a week of tortuous waiting. Then the doctor brought me his report. He did not tell me the results of the operation right away. He shined a light into my eyes, probed and thumped, and then, in a matter-of-fact voice, he said: "Your report is the best one I could possibly have for you. There is no evidence of residual melanoma."

Does this mean that there has been a cure? I am not a doctor, and I do not pretend to understand the vagaries of cancer. Has it all been removed? Will it come back? No one really knows. But I do know about another kind of cure, one that may be more important.

With as much honesty as I can possibly muster, I must say that I personally have experienced the power of prayer to heal the most devastating disease of all—the power of prayer to heal fear.

So John Sherrill's fear was healed. And of course this experience means that yours can be healed also—no matter what it is—if you will let prayer open for you the tremendous world of faith. We have God's own promise that our fears can be overcome: "For I the Lord thy God will hold thy right hand, saying unto thee, Fear not; I will help thee." (Isaiah 41:13)

And He will, too. Place your fears in God's hands and leave them there.

And now let's sum up what to do about what you're afraid of:

1. Know what it is you are afraid of. Pinpoint it. Isolate it. Set it off and see it for what it is. Know exactly what you have to deal with.

2. Study the origins and reasons for being afraid of this or that. If you are not absolutely sure that you know the reason or reasons, then you had better get some expert counseling.

3. Get the fear out into the open. Divest it of all the mystery. Get it out where you can really attack it. Often you will be surprised what a puny thing has been frightening you all this time.

4. Cram your mind full of faith thoughts, for fear cannot occupy the mind when it is full of faith. Remember always that faith is stronger than fear. So, the more faith you have the less fear you'll have. It's that simple, though this process requires some hard discipline.

5. Just do your very level best. You can do no more. Then practice until you strongly develop it, the ability to leave results calmly to the good Lord.

6. Stand up to your fear and challenge it to do its worst. Usually there will be no worse, for actually most fear is an unreal bluffing of the imagination.

7. For the real fears that have substance in fact, you have what it takes to meet them. God will help you release the necessary mental and spiritual strength. Pray.

8. Affirm always that by the grace of God you are more than equal to any fearsome situation.

9. Keep uppermost the most powerful thought and fact of all—"*I am not alone*. God is my friend, my *support*. He is always with me."

10. Finally, if you would like further help, I shall be glad to send you free upon request, my pocket-sized twenty-four page booklet entitled, *Quit Worrying*. Write to: Foundation for Christian Living, Pawling, New York, if you would like a copy.

VIII

# How to Feel Real Security

A SENSE of security is one of the most priceless assets you can have. With it, you can be efficient and contented. Without it, you may not be able to function effectively at all.

I received a letter recently, a really remarkable letter, from a woman who had lost all the security props that one usually depends upon. She was fifty-four years old and had been married thirty-one years when her husband suddenly asked for a divorce. So, she lost her husband. She simultaneously lost her "home" since, for her, home meant the place where she and her family lived. She lost her son when he was killed in an automobile accident. And then her daughter married, and in a very real sense this was a loss too—as any mother knows who has ever cried at a wedding.

So where did she turn? Here is an excerpt from her letter:

> It wasn't easy to lose my son or give up my daughter in marriage, or my husband, or my home, or my friends; but I found that security is within one's self, and not in persons, places or things and we really don't possess anything except in our consciousness.

That is a philosophical classic, that sentence. She tried finding security in the three traditional ways: persons, places and things; and she came to the conclusion that she couldn't possess anything except in her own consciousness.

What she meant by this is that security is a spiritual matter and not a physical one. The fact is, *only* in spirit will we ever be able to find security. In order to feel confident and secure we must have a secure spiritual life; that is, we must get close to God.

This precept has very good foundation in psychology. Victor Frankl, world-famous psychiatrist and professor at the University of Vienna, practices what he calls *Logo Therapy*, or God Therapy. It has been his observation that much of the mental trouble we experience today stems from the fact that "we have broken with the sense of the reality of God." Along with this goes a loss in the sense of life's meaning. We feel a decline in well-being; we feel hopelessness and insecurity. But when a person does establish a closeness to God, a great sense of security follows, says Dr. Frankl.

How practical a sense of God's presence can be is shown in this letter from the vice-president of an important company in the midwest:

> You have gotten me to going around talking to the Lord just like I talk to the president of this company. I do not call that praying, or what the average prayer sounds like. But in reading and following your advice these past years I have come to actually feel that the Lord is with me in my office, or when I am traveling, or walking, or in a conference. In fact, I know He is near me and I have frequent conversations with Him just as naturally as with any friend. You have taught me that the Lord is a constant companion.
>
> I can tell you that in the last six years since I have been practicing this, it does not make any difference what the problem is in this business, the Lord is with me and helping me. I do not talk to Him, perhaps, in the same way in which you do. You are working on the sacred front and I am working on the secular front, but it all comes out at the same place. You and I know that God is with us.

> Why did I have to be sixty years of age before I discovered the wonderful, practical value of religion in my daily life! Everything has been different since I discovered the amazing truth that God can be my constant companion.

So runs this letter from a businessman. This man's life has been revitalized and renewed, his whole outlook changed, his grip on himself strengthened, his record of achievement enhanced. He has found security in God.

So we are on very realistic grounds when we talk about getting close to God and finding security. But the big question is, how does one get close to God? Since many people ask me this question, I have worked out a formula that I have tested often and found very helpful.

1. Feel a deep need of God.
2. Have a deep desire for God.
3. Pray in depth to God.
4. Live in partnership with God.

The most difficult part of this formula, I think, is to learn how to pray in depth. When this happens, lives are really altered. It is as if you are able to focus all the strength-giving, life-changing powers of God on your soul at once. God's power is around us all the time. Occasionally we are able to focus it on our problems with definite effect. And sometimes we are able to focus it with a mighty power that shakes us to the depths of our very beings.

It is as though God's power were sunlight. The sunlight is around us daily, affecting our lives. As children we learned how to bring the rays of the sun together with a piece of glass and generate enough energy to set fire to paper. Recently, the Army engineers developed a series of lenses and mirrors which concentrate and re-concentrate the simple rays of the sun to such a degree that they could develop the thermal power of an atomic bomb! This force is so great that it can cut through a four-inch beam of steel as easily as if the beam were composed of ice. And this astonishing force is simply the concentrated rays of the sun. Similarly, the power of God through concentrated positive faith can cut through our problems with tremendous results.

This is what it is like to pray in depth.

Have you ever had that experience? You can have it, when you reach for it and pray with all your heart and soul and mind. When you really pray with powerful intensity of belief and earnestness, you can burn out your insecurity and gain new confidence in yourself and in life.

I had such an experience twenty-five years ago, which is as vivid to me now as when it occurred. Mrs. Peale and I were in England staying in the little town of Keswick, in the English Lake District. And it was there I had one of my most profound experiences of prayer. This was the situation.

I was filled with insecurity and lack of confidence. I had just become pastor of the Marble Collegiate Church, a famous and distinguished church on Fifth Avenue in New York City. I was young, had come to the big city from upstate New York; and some people said I couldn't handle the job. I became convinced they were right. I floundered and was frightened and just knew I was going to fail. That was the mental condition I was in when my wife and I took this trip to England and found ourselves in Keswick.

We were sitting on a bench in the lovely, formal garden of the Keswick Hotel. We had been married for only two years and my wife was young, but she was a forceful young girl, and a spiritual one. She said to me very plainly, "Norman, I don't know what to make of you. I listen to you preach sermons and know you are sincere; but I also know that you are thinking of yourself too much. You have ability but it will never be realized until you surrender your self-consciousness and all your insecurities to God."

She put her hand upon mine. A soft hand, but a determined one. She said, "Let us sit right here and pray this thing through. We are not going to leave this garden or this bench until you really let God take over your life." I looked into her eyes, and I know that what she was saying to me was the truth.

So we sat there together for a long, long time. Then I started praying. And by some self-releasing I really prayed; and it was an agonizing prayer, trying to get free from myself. Finally, in the depths of that prayer, I felt a Presence giving me release. It was an amazing sense of release and from that moment my feelings of insecurity and lack of confidence had less strength. Ultimately, with God's help, I was able to break their power over me. Years later when Ralph Edwards on his "This Is Your Life" program suddenly asked me what my greatest spiritual experience had been, I unhesitatingly told him, and the millions watching, that it was this one at Keswick.

Anyone can find an answer to insecurity if he will pray with everything he has, and pray until he actually senses God's presence. This isn't easy or superficial: it is like drilling for deep water. The shaft has to sink far below the usual water levels, but once these deep-down sources of supply are tapped they will not dry up with every passing drought.

*The Power of Positive Thinking* has brought me many good friends. One is Elmer Cary and he has developed a very workable technique for living close to God and overcoming insecurity.

Now, Elmer has an unusual job. He sells cemetery lots. As a matter of fact, he is the world's greatest salesman of cemetery lots, having set a record during an international contest. You might think he would be a long-faced, lugubrious character, but this is not so. He has brought a warmth, a genuine naturalness and a spirit of dedicated service to his work. Elmer is really a great persuader; so much so that, although he sells lots in Houston and I live in New York City, I find it all I can do to keep from buying one of his properties whenever he unleashes his salesmanship on me.

One time we were traveling across the ocean on the *S.S. Constitution*. It was the first time Elmer had ever been overseas, but even so, he was a better sailor than I. The weather, actually, was rough and after a couple of days of being tossed about, I became slightly green around the gills. In fact, I went to bed.

Well, I'd not been in bed for long when Elmer knocked on the door and came bouncing in looking unpleasantly healthy. There's nothing worse, when you're seasick, than seeing one of your shipmates feeling good.

"Well, what's the matter with you!" he asked. He seemed genuinely surprised to see me flat on my back.

"I just thought I'd lie down a while," I said wanly, trying not to show how I really felt.

"You're not sick?"

"Well, you might say I've felt better in my life. As a matter of fact, I do feel kind of woozy."

"Now look," he said, "where's your positive thinking? Let me give you a lesson in right thinking. The trouble with you is you're not in harmony with God and His wondrous works. The sea is His—He made it. God made this ship through men's hands. And here it is in its natural element, moving like a thing alive on the waves. It rides the sea with graceful and beautiful symmetry. You ought to come up on deck and feel the spume flying off the waves, and watch the great billowing clouds in the sky, and hear the whistling of the wind. It's really great! And up there you will know one of the best fellowships with God, in the wonder and glory of the elements."

"My, that's wonderful talking," I said admiringly. "Where did you get it?"

"From one of your talks," grinned Elmer.

So I got dressed and went up on deck with Elmer and we stood there facing the flying spray and spume that he had spoken of so rhetorically. After the first few wobbly moments I began to get the feel of it. We stood swaying to the ship's motion and identifying ourselves with God's ocean and His waves. And I, too, began to sense the rhythm and wonder of a ship mastering a sea. Never again on that trip did I feel the slightest edge of seasickness.

Elmer says that the secret of his confidence and security is living with God. He used to feel quite insecure. One thing, he is short of stature; and this shortness bothered him a lot, especially since he was quite slender as well. And for another thing, Elmer once told me that he never liked his name. "I didn't like 'Elmer,' " he said. "Why my mother and father ever named me 'Elmer' is something I will never know! But I discovered a long time ago that confidence doesn't come from the way you look, or from what people call you. Confidence comes from living close to God. You can't live close to God and feel insecure."

"No," I answered, "and the size of a man is not determined by the length of his legs but by what's in his head."

I think that one phrase Elmer used is worth memorizing. "You can't live close to God and feel insecure." Elmer Cary spends a lot of time at the task of living close to God. He told me once that every morning he spends more than thirty minutes, figuratively putting on the whole armor of God.

"I protect myself with 'the helmet of salvation' . . ." he says with a twinkle in his eyes. "That keeps my mind and my thoughts safe. Then I put on 'the shield of faith' to protect my heart and keep it strong. But I still have fears to live with, so I put on 'the sword of the Spirit' and with it I go out to do battle with the things that otherwise would frighten me." (Ephesians 6:13-17)

Is it any wonder that Elmer Cary is full of self-confidence? "You can't live close to God and feel insecure," he says. That, my friends, is it! The Bible puts it another way: "In the fear of the Lord is strong confidence." (Proverbs 14:26) What does "fear of the Lord" mean? I never did like that phrase too well because I feel certain the word "fear" conveys the wrong concept. Either "awe" or "respect," I think, would be closer to the intended meaning. In respect of the Lord there is strong confidence. When an individual is close to God, in harmony with God, then his weaknesses, his self-doubts, his shyness, his bashfulness disintegrate.

I know another man who spends a particular time every day getting close to God, and in this way achieves a strong confidence. He is the well-known writer, Roy L. Smith. Not long ago he suggested that instead of having the usual "coffee break" we should have a "Bible break." "Why wouldn't that be a good idea?" he suggested. "Well, as a matter of fact, we could have a Bible break right along with the coffee break."

This idea impressed me as unique and sound and I advocated it in my own writings and speeches. One reader became particularly interested in the idea and decided to try it. So, five days a week he read the Bible while having coffee in his office. He began with the New Testament. He read it through and then went back and read it through again, for it had gripped him. Then things began to occur that had life-changing potentialities. "I found things were beginning to happen to me. For one thing, surprisingly, I wasn't as nervous. I didn't feel so negative about things. Then I discovered that people were more friendly. There were some curious situations which could only be ascribed to God's guidance. All in all, the Bible breaks gave me a new insight into the nature of security and confidence."

This is a wonderful confidence-producing technique. I am absolutely convinced that if a man were to carry out such a program faithfully, five days a week, for one year, he would be an altogether different person. Nothing would floor him. The reason I am so sure of this is that I have seen it work; not only with a Bible break explicitly, but with a little booklet called *Thought Conditioners* that we wrote and published back in 1951. In a small footnote at the bottom of page 109 in *The Power of Positive Thinking,* I offered a free copy of *Thought Conditioners* to anyone who would like to have one. As a result we have given away well over one million copies of this forty-page booklet.

The ideas we worked out in *Thought Conditioners* seem to have caught on. Time after time people have told me that these powerful nuggets of scriptural thought have altered their lives. Since this volume you are reading is a book about the amazing results of positive thinking, I would like to mention two ideas from this booklet.

*Thought Conditioners* is a pocket-sized booklet containing forty creative and dynamic Scripture passages. The idea is this: As you can air-condition a room, so you can thought-condition your mind. First of all, you must be willing to go into the program with the idea that you are about to perform a major operation on your thoughts. You are definitely going to get rid of all those old insecure thoughts. In their place you are going to substitute real faith and security thoughts. It will be an operation by displacement. One way in which this is done is by a simple memorization of each and every one of the texts suggested in *Thought Conditioners.* Take one example:

> What things soever ye desire, when ye pray, believe that ye receive them, and ye shall have them. (Mark 11:24)

Next you meditate briefly on the technique for using this Thought Conditioner. For this one the explanation reads:

> To pray successfully you must employ affirmation and visualization. From a picture in your mind, not of lack or denial or frustration or illness, but of prosperity, abundance, attainment, health. Always remember you will receive, as a result of prayer, exactly what you think, not what you say. If you pray for achievement but think defeat, your words are idle because your heart has already accepted defeat.
>
> Therefore practice believing that even as you pray you are receiving God's boundless blessings and they will come to you.

Throughout the day refer to the Scripture passage and repeat it until it is thoroughly memorized. Then, on the second day, select another Thought Conditioner, and *add it to the first.* This is the way thought-conditioning works. As you repeat one right after the other, the second will "hammer and drive" the first deeply into your mind. The next day a third is added, then another and another on succesive days. This will strongly displace any negative thoughts that are now resident there. Keep this process up steadily for forty days, each day saying all the verses you have learned before until finally you have committed to memory all forty and know them so well you can repeat them in your sleep. The effect upon you will astonish you. Thousands of people bear testimony to the powerful results of this method.

I will defy anybody to remain insecure, or to lack confidence, if he will deeply saturate his mind, and keep it saturated, with these creative thoughts. How well thought-conditioning works was illustrated by a man I met at a luncheon meeting of a state association of businessmen. A diamond-in-the-rough type of man walked up to the head table where I was sitting and said, "Doctor, I just wanted you to know that I am in the state legislature today because I read *The Power of Positive Thinking* and sent for that *Thought Conditioners* booklet of yours. They mean so much to me that I couldn't carry on without them. They turned me from a person full of insecurity into a man of real confidence. Through following the plan of using those Scripture texts, I was able to overcome my fears and inferiority so much that I went into politics which, as you know, means liking and working with people. By thought-conditioning my mind I emptied out my insecurity. No, I didn't do it," he corrected himself, "God did it for me. Now I am trying to do something for God and my country." The man seated beside me at the table overhearing this conversation said, "I've seldom seem such a change in anyone as in Jack. So it was thought-conditioning that did it!" He asked for the booklet to work the plan on himself.

A few months later I stopped at a motel out West. The manager came up and handed me an old, dirty, battered copy of *Thought Conditioners*. "I just wanted you to know, Dr. Peale, that this little book is the reason I'm successful in this business today. I used it to pull myself out of a very bad debt situation, and now I'm doing right well."

I suggested to him that he get a fresh copy. His copy looked pretty dog-eared. "Let me send you one when I get back to New York," I said.

"No, sir," he said. "This is the one that did it. I've got

sentiment for this particular copy and I wouldn't exchange it for anything." Then he went on to say, "At first I thought the idea of merely committing Bible verses to memory was too simple, and that your idea of reconditioning your thoughts was sort of on the queer side. I'd never heard anything like that before. But then, from somewhere I found the will actually to do the memorizing. It was so helpful that I kept on doing it and all I can say is that this simple practice has changed my life. It burned out all the old negative, defeatist thoughts and substituted more confidence than I've had in years."

A man from Connecticut who experienced some pretty bad times tells in the following letter how he found security and a new business career. His is another demonstration of the amazing power of positive thinking:

While going through a very trying period of losing my business about five years ago, a friend suggested *The Power of Positive Thinking* and I became a disciple of your teachings from the first chapter. I also sent for a copy of *Thought Conditioners* and followed instructions to the letter, working, studying and praying for a way out of my difficulty. I know that you won't be surprised to hear that the way out appeared before I had committed all the verses in *Thought Conditioners* to memory. I was led to close the business and talked to each of my creditors in person and was surprised at the way my fear of them was suddenly taken away. I found them all very agreeable to give me a chance to see what I could work out without having to resort to bankruptcy. I was led to talk with my banker and was able to arrange a mortgage loan of $3500 on my home and was able to pay all my debts in full. I just can't put into words the relief I experienced in clearing this mountain of despair up in such a short time, truly proving "The things which are impossible with men are possible with God," and your words in *Thought Conditioners*: "Keep relaxed. Don't worry. Avoid getting panicky . . ."

The very next day after this demonstration of the power of prayer I landed a job with an aircraft company as an aircraft mechanic, after having been away from that field for over ten years, and have rapidly risen to my present position where I am trusted with the most difficult repair jobs on the aircraft in the factory. Another proof of God's POWER.

A few months later I formed my own band with a group of dedicated musicians. This was the first time I had fronted a band in fifteen years and we were a success from the first date we played, and new fields are opening for us all the time.

So to develop more confidence within yourself, try using *Thought Conditioners*. Saturate your mind with them. Let these dynamic principles work for you, and I am sure you will have a deeper feeling of security than you have ever enjoyed. Actually, you do not need the booklet, though I will be glad to send you a copy. You can go through the Bible taking out your own texts which speak of faith, and peace and strength. But insert at least one every day deeply into your mind until it really takes hold of you.

There is one last thing which is quite important in living confidently. And that is the values which the church affords you. A church is a wonderful source of security because this is where people, for generations, have congregated in an effort to bring the health-producing, life-changing laws of God together in a single concentrated experience. Church worship is much more than a formal duty to perform. It is your exposure to the greatest of all power. In fact, a vital church is the greatest power relay station in existence.

Through it flows the vibrant life-changing energy of Almighty God Himself.

The church has probably produced more real, sensible and effective positive thinkers than any institution in the world. And that is because it reaches the power of faith. It provides peace of mind and heart, and these qualities are very essential to efficient mental processes. The church puts hope and love and confidence into men's minds. True, you will find some gloomy, depressive, negative, even mean people in churches. There are two things that may be said about this phenomenon: First, the exposure just hasn't taken; and second, it's good that such people are in the church, for it means there is still hope of doing something with them. Of course the basic reason the church produces positive thinkers is due to the life-changing force in Christianity, the basic genius of which is that, when taken into one's life, it can dramatically eliminate weaknesses and add strength. Christianity can literally make a new man of anyone who wills it so.

In *The Power of Positive Thinking* the reader was constantly urged to practice the teachings of Jesus Christ, or if not of the Chrisitan faith to practice the laws of God as he has been taught. Church worship was advocated as an invaluable aid in solving personal problems, of contributing to human welfare and helping one to know God.

One of my readers, a man who had no church contact whatsoever, resisted that particular emphasis in the book. He said, "I took the common sense of the book but skipped the religion. As a matter of fact, I thought you just brought that in because you happen to be a minister." However, he became convinced by my insistence, and one Sunday he attended a neighborhood church. Unfortunately, the minister devoted his sermon to a denunciation of businessmen, strangely seeming to regard them all as evil influences. The church was only partially filled and the spirit was without lift or enthusiasm. This man did not sense or note the spiritual power I had promised he would find.

My reader was so incensed that he sat down and wrote me a rather sharp letter and ended by saying that this finished him with the church. However, he did admit that he felt a real sense of need and would continue to work with the book—but no church, that was "out, period!" for him.

I wrote back suggesting that it was hardly fair to judge a minister by one sermon or to dismiss such a great and vast institution as the church because of one unfortunate contact. I gave him the name of a church not too far from his home where I knew the minister to be a pastor of radiant spirit and infectious faith.

My friend, a bit mollified, went to this church. He found it filled with a great congregation of eager people.

> They all struck me as happy and everyone was so friendly. The minister was obviously a man of conviction. He was so sincere and kindly and down-to-earth that he got to me. I kept on going.
>
> The minister called on me and invited me to join a group of fellows who met for lunch once a week. To my astonishment they actually had a good time together talking about religion and how they were applying it to personal and business problems. I was amazed by all this and continued attending these luncheons. I soon realized that you were right in your book; Christianity is actually a way of life. At least it was for these guys. One day one fellow told how insecure he had been, how he had suffered all his life from feelings of inadequacy and inferiority.
>
> Well, that was me all over, and I listened carefully as he told how, through this fellowship of spiritually-minded men,

he had found peace and a new strength to solve his own problems. So I decided that this was for me if I could only get it.

On Sunday in church we have a quiet period and the big congregation silently prays. Some real power is developed—there's no doubt about that. Suddenly, one Sunday, I felt a wonderful sense of peace. It wasn't like me, or at least like I thought I was, but tears came to my eyes. I actually felt God's presence. It had to be that, for all that old insecurity seemed gone. It was simply wonderful, the greatest thing that ever happened to me.

So ends the letter of a man who found security through spiritual fellowship.

Finally, to sum up, I recommend the use of the following formula for gaining a sense of security and confidence:

1. Study yourself to discover where *your* real security lies. Check over the things upon which you are now depending for security. Persons? Places? Things? Are they really satisfactory? Or do you need to look for a more basic security in the spiritual realm by getting close to God?

2. For getting close to God, practice the following:

First, feel a deep need of God.
Second, have a deep desire for God.
Third, pray in depth to God.
And fourth, live in partnership with God.

3. Take God as your actual working partner. Let God guide your thoughts and actions.

4. Practice systematic thought displacement to dislodge your insecure thoughts and replace them by confidence thoughts.

5. Associate with people of a confident and secure frame of mind. These feelings are contagious.

6. Read and implement positive ideas about everything in your life.

7. Find a positive, dynamic church where victorious living is taught and practiced. Become a vital part of such a creative spiritual community. Give to it. Draw from it. Believe, share and practice a power-packed faith.

Do the above and a strong confidence will displace your insecurity.

IX

# How to Handle Your Difficulty

A DIFFICULTY can break you, or it can make you. It all depends on how you take hold of it, and what you do with it. "Mishaps are like knives, that either serve us or cut us, as we grasp them by the blade or the handle," said James Russell Lowell.

Grasp a difficulty by the "blade" and it cuts; grasp it by the "handle" and you can use it constructively. It may be hard to get hold of that handle but it can be done—that's for sure. And there are some practical techniques for so doing that have been tried and tested.

But before we get to them let me say that actually you ought to be glad you have some difficulties; life would not be worth living without them. While this element in life may have its unpleasant aspects, difficulty is still essential to growth and direction.

Recently on a flight from New York to Los Angeles on a Boeing Jet 707 airplane, I noticed a line of small blades midway down the wing surface and also on the tail. These blades I was told are called vortex generators. Their function is to cause the air flow to swirl as it passes over the rear wing area. Engineers tell me that the rear assembly of these big planes does not steer truly if the air situation is too smooth, so vortexes must be generated. The element of roughness must be inserted to attain precise directional accuracy.

God's wisdom is demonstrated by the fact that He installed vortex generators in our human experience.

Many people write to me complaining about the problems they have. "Why must there be so many problems?" they ask.

Actually, problems are a sign of life! In fact the more problems, the more you are a part of life. The only place I've ever been where people have no problems is a cemetery and there they are all dead. Be glad that God trusts you with some problems. Thank Him for the compliment. He believes you have what it takes to handle them.

In this chapter we shall outline a technique for handling difficulty and this can be very important to you for, as Confucius says, "Settle one difficulty and you keep a hundred away."

In handling difficulty, first of all, get yourself as quiet, calm and composed as you can. You can never competently handle a difficulty unless you are quiet mentally. It is so very important to think calmly. When a difficulty arises, the first tendency is to become upset, even panicky. Nervously we assume that the problem has to be solved right away, quick; that something must be done immediately.

When you are mentally hectic, rational answers to difficulties tend to elude you; but when you become quiet your mind gets down to its real business, which is rational thinking.

So I must stress the importance of learning the use of silence in meeting life's difficult problems. "Silence is the element in which great things fashion themselves," said Carlyle. Silence conditions the mind to those sharper illuminations which surely come from God working in your thoughts. Divine guidance is always spoken in a still, small voice. You can scarcely hear it in confusion—certainly not in excited panic, nor when your mind is filled with anxiety. You cannot perceive God's will or receive His guidance in the midst of noise, especially noise within. So, the technique is to let yourself down into the relaxed and deep quietness of faith and confidence in which clear thinking is possible. Then a sense of direction will be opened to you for dealing with your difficulties.

The Japanese seem to practice quietness to a high degree of efficiency. It is one of their characteristics that I admire most—their ability to be quiet, composed and unruffled in the face of difficulty. Recently when I was in Japan, I spent some time studying quietness techniques. The practice of quietness is actually an important ritual in Japan; sometimes it is called *Ryōmi*. In English perhaps the nearest meaning of the word is "the taste of coolness" or "a refreshing." What a wonderful idea! When you have a problem, get "the taste of coolness." We put it another way, "keep cool." But to keep cool you must first get cool. In Japan this is done in an unusual but effective manner.

Let us say it is a pleasant summer evening. The first thing is to sit in a hot Japanese bath and reflectively soak yourself. A bath is frequently more like a pool—a hot thermal pool. Everybody goes into the same bath together. Most Westerners balk at this beyond the family group. You relax, become quiet, and after awhile you feel like philosophizing.

Then you come out of the bath and put on a *yukata,* the name for a cotton kimono. You proceed into a cool room which is without furniture and sit on the floor on a soft straw matting called *tatami.* You sit quietly, listening to the wind bells tinkling in the gentle breeze and watching the *gifu* latterns swaying overhead.

Then you are brought a little bowl of amber tea. You don't gulp the tea down hurriedly in American style; rather you savor it thoughtfully, even commune with it. The Japanese linger long over a cup of tea, making of it an act of serenity. The idea is to induce quiet reflection; to relax and grow still, thus entering into the essence of peacefulness. You talk very little but rather meditate in an effort to cultivate the creative values of silence. In this way your mind brings the scattered ends of life together, the heat goes out of your thinking, and you get the taste of coolness. The effect of this practice on problem solving is amazing. Problems seem the more readily to dissolve. And they are resolved. This is a most effective method for perceiving difficulties clearly in their deeper implications. It is extraordinarily helpful in arriving at sound solutions.

Since you and I don't live in Japan, we have to develop our own kind of *Ryōmi*. Actually, one already exists in our own religious tradition. Christianity and Judaism are basically Oriental faiths and the value of quietness and meditation is emphasized in the Bible. "Come ye yourselves apart into a desert place and rest a while." (Mark 6:31)

Indeed, one of the best places to find creative quietness in our country is in a church. If you have a problem that you have difficulty in solving and wish to find a quiet place for meditation, I suggest that you go into an empty church when no service is in progress. Sit quietly in a pew and think of your mind, and then of your muscles, as letting go their tension. Let down and down, until you are relaxed.

Then practice consciously sensing God's presence. Say the following affirmative prayer, repeating it several times slowly: "You are here, Lord . . . You are now touching me with Your healing peace . . . My mind is becoming quiet. You are now giving me the answer . . . Your answer . . . The right answer to my problem." Then empty out any wrong thinking which you may be holding. Forgive everyone. Quietly say, "I forgive ———— (mention name)." Enumerate a few things for which you are thankful and others for which you ought to be thankful. Don't hurry, but rest quietly in the Lord. Try this experiment in creative quietness. It's really a wonderful method for handling difficulty.

Another method is to associate yourself with spiritually-minded people who have developed some skill in the use of creative quietness. I once had a very perplexing personal difficulty and had not been able to get an answer. While I was struggling with it I attended a Quaker Meeting. In a Quaker Meeting the practice of silence is a well-developed spiritual skill. It is a practical demonstration of the principle suggested in two Scripture passages: "Be still, and know that I am God." (Psalm 46:10) And "In quietness and in confidence shall be your strength." (Isaiah 30:15) Even to the unpracticed, the deep and vital silence-power of a Quaker Meeting has a way of getting through to you.

Before the silence period began, a man said something which was most enlightening: "If anyone here has a problem, drop it now into the deep pool of spiritual quietness."

It was an apt description, for the silence that followed was indeed like a deep pool. I took that problem, which had been baffling me, and said, "All right. We'll see what happens." And I let it drop into that pool of spiritual quietness. We continued to sit and wait and pray and listen to the silence and to the Reality within the silence. I don't know how long we sat there, for the passing of time was not important; but suddenly as clear as crystal, came the answer to my problem. And it proved to be so right an answer. I saw that I had been thinking and searching in wrong directions. But intuitively I now recognized this solution for what it was: God's answer.

It is always very important to find God's answer, and then to follow it. Mencius (second only to Confucius among the sages of China) says: "To follow the will of God is to prosper; to rebel against the will of God is to be destroyed."

One of the greatest people I ever knew for handling problems through mind-power plus Divine guidance was a wonderful old man, Harlow B. Andrews, who lived in Syracuse, New York. "Brother" Andrews we all called him. Brother Andrews is said to have operated the first supermarket in the United States. Years ago he brought in perishable goods from California by fast express trains and sold them in his big Andrews Brothers store. He is credited with developing the first dishwasher. He was a highly effective businessman.

Brother Andrews had only three years of schooling, but his was a great mind and he used it to the maximum. His method of thinking through a problem was an amazing combination of common sense, scientific analysis, intuition and prayer. I had a chance, once, to see his mind at work on a tough problem of my own about which I had asked Brother Andrews' help. As I outlined my problem I paced nervously up and down in front of his desk.

"Wait a minute, hold your horses, don't pace around so much," said Brother Andrews. "Sit down and get relaxed. Let's get that mind of yours untensed. How do you expect to think when your mind is so tied up."

After he had me sitting relaxed and laughing a bit with him, he said, "Now let's examine this difficulty." He began talking the problem through, step by step, detail by detail, with consummate exactitude. He really took it apart and studied every aspect. He gave me the impression of walking around the difficulty, poking at it here and there with his gnarled old finger saying: "Let's see if we can find a soft spot." Or, "Let's chip a little off here, a little there and get it down to size where you can handle it, son."

He walked around it mentally, and I walked around with him. "Every problem has a soft spot," he declared. "But we don't know enough. What are our little minds compared to the great mind of God. Let's take it up with God." So saying, he prayed, outlining the problem in detail. The prayer itself was a process of thinking it through, of analyzing it. He knew God so well that he talked to God as though He was right there with us. (I believe He was, too.) And as Brother Andrews talked to the Lord about my problem it began to clarify in my thinking. It was remarkable how my nervousness passed off and suddenly I just knew the solution would come.

Brother Andrews' advice came to mind recently when I had a phone call from a well-known figure in baseball. He told me about a difficult decision he had to face. "I'd like you to pray with me about this matter. Will you?"

I told him I would, and advised him, "Don't worry. You'll get the right answer. Don't push it."

He answered, "I'm not worrying, nor am I tense. It's only that I have to have the answer by tomorrow, that's all. But I know I'll get the answer that God wants me to have." Then he used a phrase which I liked very much. He said, "I'm walking around this problem with prayerful thought." That really is an interesting idea: "I'm walking around the problem with prayerful thought."

Later I learned that my friend had made the choice that had seemed to him the more difficult of two alternatives which he described at the time he talked with me. In explaining his decision he said, "I took the job I thought the Lord wanted me to take." That had been the outcome of walking around the problem with prayerful thought. Incidentally, it turned out very well indeed.

Use the power of your human mind fortified with Divine guidance to organize the attack against a difficulty. No matter what your situation or however difficult the nature of your problem, or how hopeless it seems, this organized, analytical-spiritual attack will get results, and right results, too.

Another very good technique for handling a problem is just to stay with it; in other words, don't give up. It's amazing what simple *persistence* will do where you use it intelligently on your difficulties.

When everything goes wrong and you seem particularly inadequate, what shall you do? Just keep on pitching. And tenaciously hold a positive picture of the outcome. Put your faith in God . . . all your faith. You will get through if you persevere.

That's the way the great men of history handled their problems. It is a good idea to read about those men and get acquainted with the inspiring persons of all time who didn't know how to quit.

There is another element in winning victory, and that is the element of belief. "Believe you can, and you can." Belief is one of the most powerful of all problem dissolvers. When you believe that a difficulty can be overcome, you are more than halfway to victory over it already. One of the greatest of all principles is that men can do what they think they can do.

For example, it was generally accepted for a great many years that it was impossible to run a mile in four minutes. But then along came a lanky, frail-looking English physician named Roger Bannister who didn't look like he had the strength to run a mile at all. But one fine day, back in 1954, Roger Bannister ran the mile in four minutes flat.

Why had no one ever run the mile so fast before? Bannister feels it was because people didn't think it could be done, and that seems to be a very reasonable conclusion. Back in 1886, a man named Walker ran the mile in 4:12 3/4, a world record. And thirty-seven years later Paavo Nurmi ran it in 4:10¾ shaving two seconds off the earlier record. That was a wonderful achievement. I remember reading about it in the papers at Boston where I was living at the time. The fastest man on earth—Nurmi! Nobody, they said, will be able to beat his record!

But thirty-one years later Roger Bannister broke it. For the first time in history a man ran a mile in four minutes flat.

And now what has happened? Since Bannister's feat no less than twenty-three other runners have run the mile in *less* than four minutes. When asked whether this is due to scientific improvements in the style of running, Bannister says that it cannot be explained that way. He believes it is due to a change in psychology. Once the mile had been run in four minutes, the mental conception was accepted that it could be run in less, and this belief in the runner's mind was responsible for its being done.

This, of course, is positive thinking in its purest form. And the use of positive thinking in overcoming difficulties is becoming more and more widespread. I can tell this from my mail. Letters come in by the hundreds, even by the thousands, telling how faith thoughts and positive thinking attitudes have helped in surmounting difficulties.

For instance, one man says that he keeps a card index of every passage in the Bible dealing with faith. He commits these to memory. One text among hundreds which he has collected is this one: "I can do all things through Christ which strengtheneth me." (Philippians 4:13) Another text is: "If God be for us, who can be against us?" (Romans 8:31) He substitutes the pronoun "me" for "us" in the latter text.

Read the Bible regularly and when you come to a passage that states positive thinking in a fresh new way that appeals to you, put it in your collection of faith ideas. As you fill your mind with these great thoughts your own attitudes will become more positive and more vitally strong.

So keep positive thoughts from the Bible at your fingertips or more properly your "mindtips" throughout the day—thoughts that will be ready to help you meet any new difficulty that may arise. This method is a practical one and we recommend it.

In this connection I am reminded of my friend Arthur D. Rodenbeck of Dayton, Ohio. When I spoke to the National Home Builders great convention in Chicago, I had a very unique and dramatic introduction. The stage was set, special lighting arranged and dialogue prepared and rehearsed. The "star" of the cast was Art Rodenbeck, a successful home builder who told how positive thinking had pulled him through some difficult experiences.

To that big hushed audience Art Rodenbeck gave the following testimony to the power of Bible passages and the healing potency of God's Word in practical human problems. He said:

> I had plenty of problems, not financial, but with people. You know, people in the office, salesmen, foremen, mechanics—a big turnover—and nothing seemed to go right. Well, I was getting nervous and irritable and it began to affect my health. I was in pretty bad shape and actually on the verge of a crack-up. I read *The Power of Positive Thinking* by Dr. Peale and it helped. But then I went further. I got one of his pamphlets called *Spirit Lifters,* and I memorized thirty-two verses from the Bible. Everytime things were going bad, I'd mentally recite one of those verses. It did the trick; saved my mind and maybe my life.
>
> Later I went to New York and I found out about his Foundation, The American Foundation of Religion and Psychiatry, where people are helped by a permanent staff of

specially trained pastors, psychologists and some top psychiatrists.

Well, just a year ago I was having the same trouble and the *Spirit Lifters* saved me again. I was in deep trouble, financially this time, and I couldn't see my way out. But I drew all the strength I needed from those Bible verses just as you'd draw money from the bank, and it worked again. Right now, I'm sold out in Dayton and in Florida and my lumber company is doing fine. And I know that nothing can ever get me down again.

And here is a letter from a family in Massachusetts who describe another type of satisfying experience with positive thinking:

None of the letters that you receive can be more inspired by a deeper gratitude than that which is in our hearts. My husband (an engineer) and I sincerely feel that our seventeen-year-old boy would have lost the opportunity of a lifetime if it had not been for our daily letters based on your book, *The Power of Positive Thinking for Young People.*

After high school graduation this spring, our son received a full scholarship to a famous school in New York. This is a specialized, completely endowed college, necessarily very small. Candidates are carefully screened and admitted by their standing on the Board Exams. Only twenty are taken each year from all over the United States. The course is extremely tough, and a test of character as well as brains.

The first six weeks were a severe strain on our son who concluded from the evidence available that he was flunking. It would have been the first failure of his life; he was so upset we feared for a complete nervous breakdown.

I wrote him every day, and his father wrote as often as possible—the gist of our letters being to think positively. He began to do this, and also to pray seriously, from his heart, for the first time in his life.

As a result, he kept plugging instead of just giving up! And he has passed his mid-terms this month with an average of 84 per cent, standing seventh in his class. Only seventeen of the boys are left now, as three freshmen did flunk out! After questioning our son, we have concluded that their failure was due more to attitude than to lack of ability or intelligence. I just felt that I should let you know this story.

A chief reason that people are beaten down by difficulties is simply that they allow themselves to think they can be beaten. And one of the greatest techniques for overcoming difficulty, as we have said, is to learn to believe that they can be overcome; and that you can do the overcoming with God's help. In order to accomplish this you may have to do considerable growing, both mentally and spiritually; but that can be done also. It is possible to grow tall in the mind, taller than any problem. This is another way of saying that you are bigger than any difficulty.

I had lunch recently with a friend, John Powers, president of Prentice-Hall, Inc., my publishers. He makes interesting use of diagrams to illustrate his ideas. He draws them all over the paper at hand, and then perhaps over the tablecloth as well. On this particular day he drew a picture of a hugh mountain, and next to it a small man. "This mountain symbolizes a difficulty," said John. "Now how is this little man going to get on the other side?"

"That's easy," I said. "He will go around the end."

"Too wide, he can't do that."

"Well then, he will skirt the other end," I said.

But John shook his head, "That's just as wide."

"He will crawl over the top."

But John replied, "That won't work either for it's too high."

I thought and then said, "He will burrow under it."

"Too deep," he replied.

"O.K. then," I declared, "he will just haul off and plow right through it."

"That's out too," said John. "It's much too thick and he would only break himself."

"Well," I said, "it looks like an impasse; though I'm sure there is a way."

"There is indeed," said John Powers. "The answer is in your power of positive thinking. Rise over the difficulty by the enlargement of your thoughts. The man will grow tall in his thoughts until he is taller than the difficulty."

Of course that is the secret. There is apparently an unlimited extension facility in the human mind. Physically a man's height is limited. I once saw a man 7′6″ tall; but I presume the average height for a man is from 5′8″ to 5′10″. But man has the unique mental ability to extend far beyond those limits. In his mind he developed the ladder which made him, let us say, about twenty feet high. His brain produced the elevator which made him, perhaps, two hundred to three hundred feet high; and the jet airplane which raised his height to thirty thousand feet. You have a tremendous extension power within yourself.

"You teach that fact in positive thinking," John declared.

So here is our little man apparently blocked and baffled by the big mountainous difficulty confronting him. This is how he meets this seeming impasse. He starts thinking pure, unadulterated, positive thoughts. He explores the matter from every angle. He affirms that with God's help and his own creative powers he will get the answer. Then he prays and this prayer takes the form of affirmation, the expression of the belief that he can rise above even this huge difficulty. In his prayer he receives guidance about how to do it. Through prayer, also, comes the inspiration and motivating force which supplies lifting power. As a result he begins to grow in mind and spirit until he is taller than the problem and looks down upon it.

You are indeed greater than any difficulty—always remember that. Grow until you're bigger than your difficulty. That's really a power-packed idea, and the way to achieve this growth is through understanding of yourself, and through prayer and spiritual development. You can grow bigger than any difficulty you may face.

One of the great things that positive thinking does for people is that it teaches them to stop working against themselves. So many people actually practice self-defeat. By their thoughts they actually convince themselves that they can not handle their difficultes. They are defeated in their minds. And since you are intended to be master of your thoughts, if you have used your thinking negatively you are responsible for your own inability to deal successfully with your difficult problems.

One of the greatest blessings of my life is the association I have had through the years with laymen in the church. As a pastor I was supposed to be their guide and teacher but it's a two-way street; and I can never pay the debt I owe to them for their guidance and inspiration to me.

In my first church in Berkeley, Rhode Island, I formed a lifetime friendship with Rob Rowbottom. When I recently went back to Berkeley to speak at the dedication of the remodeled church, I had an interview with reporters from Pawtucket, Providence and Woonsocket newspapers. I was asked if I had learned the idea of positive thinking from Mr. Rowbottom.

I replied that many had contributed to my thinking but to Rob I owe the conviction that sound thinking and prayer to God will take you successfully through any difficulty. In my young and acutely impressionable years I watched him meet up with some very difficult problems. Nothing ever floored him. He would say, "Well, now let's see, let's pray and think and we'll come through this all right." Then he would chuckle and keep on hacking away at the difficulty, always with good spirit and always believing. It was marvelous the way things worked out. This quiet but determined man was actually an indomitable personality.

We discussed the principle of positive thinking after the reporter had raised the question. "Tell me your secret, Rob," I said.

His reply was priceless, one of the wisest statements I have ever heard. "When a problem arises, I think it through patiently and carefully. I analyze it and analyze it some more. Sometimes, in doing so, I go off alone where I can talk to myself. I can understand better by talking out loud." Then he added, and this I hope you will never forget, "*I never build a case against myself.*"

That is so very important. Stop working against yourself down in that mind of yours. God, your creator, is not a poor workman. He made you and He never intended that life should defeat you. He made life hard, to be sure, but He wants you to know that He will help you. "Hope thou in God: for I shall yet praise Him . . ." (Psalm 42:11) is one of the great words from His book. And another is, "God is our refuge and strength, a very present help in trouble." (Pslam 46:1)

So, with faith in that help, print those words of my friend Rob Rowbottom indelibly upon your mind: *I never build a case against myself.*

What thrilling victories people have who practice these principles of positive thinking. I have before me a letter from a man who was faced by one of the toughest kinds of problems. This is what he has to say about his difficulty:

For twenty-five years I had been progressing from a heavy drinker to a hopeless alcoholic. I had lost position after position; had been locked up for common drunkenness; had been confined to alcoholic wards; spent many weeks in mental wards where alcoholics were confined while being given treatment. I spent a year and a half a hopeless drunk on skid row in Philadelphia.

For years I was completely out of touch with my family. My marriage, never a happy on, dissolved. I am a photographer. At one time I had two portrait studios. These I lost. About 1950 I heard about Alcoholics Anonymous and attended some meetings. I tried to work the program but had too many reservations. Then, in a Jacksonville, Florida AA I met a fine woman and a year later we were married. However, not long afterward we both began drinking again and things went from bad to worse. Hospital after hospital.

One day I took to my bed with a bottle—my usual routine when a difficult problem arose—and passed out. My wife, to pass the time, went downtown to the library. Somehow she stumbled across a book of yours, *The Power of Positive Thinking*. She glanced through it and as she later told me, rushed home and put it on my night table. When I came to in my drinking bouts I usually liked to read something, as it seemed to calm me down.

So I reached out and picked up this book and began reading it. At first, of course, none of it made much sense. I remember closing it and placing it on the table. But a phrase I read made its way through my muddled thoughts. "If God be for us, who can be against us?" I tried visualizing Him there beside me and immediately felt assured and stronger. I then picked up the book again and commenced reading it from the beginning, feeling better as I went along. During the next days, reading a little each day, I could feel a resolve within me becoming stronger and stronger to regain and keep my sobriety.

My wife and I celebrated our fourth anniversay the other day. Four years without a drink. We don't have too much in the way of worldly goods, but we are very happy. I manage a portrait studio in a small town in Massachusetts. We have nice clothes, our own car, attend the Episcopal church, and hope to build our own home next year.

Here is a man who grew. He grew over his difficulties through the power of that one phrase, "If God be for us, who can be against us?" Completely defeated, he got hold of this tremendous force, the power of the Almighty, and with this he began to grow. And he built a case not against, but for himself!

There is a corollary to this idea. If it is true that by growing you can overcome your difficulties, it is also true that your difficulties can help you grow. Difficulties are growth stimulators. The Russians have a proverb which I find interesting in this connection: "The hammer shatters glass but forges steel." If you are like steel, if you have good, malleable stuff in you, the difficulties of life will forge you in strength and power.

It is interesting how many of our outstanding leaders have had this philosophy. President Eisenhower told me one day about an early memory he had of his mother as one of the wisest persons he had ever known. And her wisdom came from her religion. She created a wonderful spirit in the home, and she herself was the center of it.

He recalled one evening playing some kind of game with cards and complaining about the bad hands he was getting. Suddenly, his mother stopped the game and told him that when you play a game you have to take the cards as they come, and play them! She reminded him that life is like that. God deals the cards in life, and you've just got to play your best with what you have.

The President said he had never forgotten that advice and follows it to this day.

Thomas A. Edison took life in this same man-sized manner. He too was a tough, positive thinker. Former Governor of New Jersey, Charles Edison, his son, told me this fascinating story about his father. On the night of December 9, 1914, the great Edison industries of West Orange were practically destroyed by fire. Mr. Edison lost two million dollars that night and much of his life's work went up in flames. He was insured for only ten cents on the dollar because the buildings had been made of concrete, at that time supposed to be fireproof.

Young Edison was twenty-four, his father was sixty-seven. The young man ran about frantically, trying to find his father. Finally he came upon him, standing near the fire, his face ruddy in the glow, his white hair blown by the winter winds. "My heart ached for him," Charles Edison told me. "He was no longer young and everything was going up in flames. He spotted me. 'Charles,' he shouted, 'where's your mother?' "

" 'I don't know, Dad,' I answered."

" 'Find her!' he bade me. 'Bring her here. She will never see anything like this again as long as she lives.' "

The next morning, walking about the charred embers of all his hopes and dreams, Thomas A. Edison said, "There is great value in disaster. All our mistakes are burned up! Thank God we can start anew." And three weeks later, just twenty-one days after that disastrous fire, his firm delivered the first phonograph.

To sum up, I recommend the following:

1. Thank God you have difficulties. It's a sign you are alive.
2. Learn to stand back from your troubles and take a calm survey of them. The best way to do this is through the practice of quietness. In quietness and peace, take a level look at your problem.

3. Use your full mind power to analyze your difficulty. Then systematically chip away at it, bit by bit.
4. Think positively about your difficulty. Believe that you can overcome it. Do this and you are already well on the way to victory.
5. Learn the spiritual-practical method for handling a difficulty.
6. Let persistence work for you. Keep everlastingly at it, and you eventually will be victorious.
7. Grow to the high point where you can look down on your problem, and then use your problem to help you grow.
8. Calmly take life as it comes. Deal with your difficulties with controlled emotion and steadily keep on working for victory.
9. Never build a case against yourself.
10. Make use of the available power of the Almighty. Troubles will defeat you without God, but with His help you can handle any difficulty.

# X

# Don't Let Pressure Pressure You

It is a generally recognized fact that we live in a world that is full of tension. Tension surrounds us. It is in the rhythm of our cities and of our machines. It is in our talk and on our faces and in our bearing. It is built into our society. Certainly it shows in our work. Believe it or not, in New York City you can get the correct time by dialing N-E-R-V-O-U-S!

Fortunate indeed are those who do not let tension push them around; who do not let pressure pressure them. One evening, not long ago, when I was out on the West Coast, I had a very interesting talk on the subject of tension with Desi Arnaz. Desi and Lucy had just finished a hectic week at the studio, where they were filming scenes for a new show. But when I saw them in the living room of their country home, they were both as calm and cool as if they had just finished a refreshing week on vacation rather than on location.

"I've read that book of yours about positive thinking," Desi said suddenly. He has a way of fixing you with those wide-open, deep brown eyes of his when he talks. "You know," he said, "there're some pretty good parts in it."

Lucy laughed. "Just pretty good?" she asked.

"Especially that part, there, where you talk about tensions," he went on. "I really liked that part because we're in the business of tension, Lucy and me."

"You know what I did after I finished your book?" Desi said. And then he came up with a unique result of positive thinking. He leaned forward and pulled back his sleeve to show a bare wrist. "I threw away my watch."

I was a little startled. This wasn't exactly the kind of effect I had expected when I wrote *The Power of Positive Thinking.* But I felt better when I got the whole picture, because it turned out that although Desi does throw his watch away, he does it for just a few hours.

During the week, Desi's time is very tightly scheduled. At 8:05 in the morning he must do this; at 11:40 he must do that. Commercials must fit smoothly into the program, timed down to the exact second. And, of course, there are always delays and last minute changes to gum up plans and create tensions that mount higher and higher.

But always, after a while there comes a breather. Maybe it's a break in the production schedule. Or just a weekend, or a holiday. On these occasions, if it's winter, Desi and Lucy drive out to their house at Palm Springs, or if summer to one they own on the ocean. Both are beautiful places. The desert home is rimmed around by glorious mountains. The seashore home sits right on the edge of the Pacific. Out there in the desert and mountains, or next to the surf, they are far away from deadlines and appointment pads. But this is not enough. Just to make sure they won't be hounded by time, Desi throws away his watch.

He literally takes his watch off as soon as he walks into the house, tosses it into the dresser drawer and closes the drawer with a bang.

"After that," he said—and then he came up with a wonderful phrase—"I take a vacation from tension."

Isn't that a great idea! Take a vacation from tension. Desi does it by ignoring time. "I go down to the beach," he said. "And I lie down and let my mind and body relax. Then if someone calls me and says that it's time to eat, I tell them it isn't time to eat because I'm not hungry. If they come and say it's time for bed, I tell them the stars are out and the moon has just come up. It'll be time for bed when I get sleepy."

Later, of course, after the little vacation-from-tension is over, Desi has to go back to the dresser drawer and put the watch back on again. But he does it with a new sense of vitality; he is refreshed and ready to get back to work.

It isn't just the Desi Arnazes of this world who need to learn how to handle tensions. Almost everyone these days faces the same problem. Thousands of children no longer stroll out the door and walk leisurely off to school, thumping picket fences and breaking the ice that has formed on puddles along the way; they must hurry to catch the bus at the corner—it leaves precisely at 8:12 A.M.

Even the routine business of getting to work has become a tightly scheduled affair. I know one pathetic fellow who has to meet three deadlines before he can sit down at this desk in the morning. He must get up in time to catch the 7:28 bus that takes him to the railroad station. He must be at the station in time to catch the 7:43 train to New York. He must arrive in the city in time to catch a car pool that takes him fifty blocks uptown. The schedule is so tight that at every stoplight he wonders if he's going to be at his desk by the time the 9 o'clock "starting bell" rings.

I once asked this man what time he had to set the alarm in order to make that series of deadlines. His answer was a classic. I think about it whenever I think about twentieth century man and the way he is pushed around by time.

"Oh," he said casually, "I usually set it for approximately 6:32."

Approximately 6:32!

This is symbolic of a problem that thousands upon thousands of men and women face daily. How to handle unwanted tension.

Notice that word "unwanted." A certain amount of tension is a good thing. Normal tension keys you up, it stimulates you and keeps your creative processes operating at top efficiency. But perhaps it would be a good thing if we learned how to turn tension off and on as we turn off the energy that flows through an electric wire. We would then be able to use tension when it served our purposes, and stop it when it begins to overpressure us. When it came time to relax, all the pressures could be drained off with little vacations from tensions.

Actually, that turning off of pressurized tension can be done. Here's one way to do it. First, consciously tense up your whole body. Start with your eyebrows. Draw them together into a frown. Now move on down to your jaw muscles and your lip muscles and your throat muscles. Tense them without relaxing. Hold the tension in all these muscles and move on down to your shoulders; tighten the muscles there and clench your fists. Contract the muscles in your stomach and press your knees together. Finally, push your feet down against the floor.

If you have done this as outlined, just about every muscle in your body is now tight. Hold that for a minute. Note the amount of energy that it takes to keep yourself tense!

I suggest this experiment to demonstrate what we are doing to ourselves, for many of us go through life pretty much tightened up like this twenty-four hours a day. Not every muscle at once, perhaps. Maybe it's just the throat muscles, or the shoulder muscles. For a great many people it's the stomach muscles. But the point is that because of such tension much energy is being wasted. It is being dissipated through effort that shows no results except fatigue and irritability.

Now, go on with the experiment; let the tension relax. Reverse the process described above. This time consciously relax every mucle. Carry this relaxing through your eyebrows, your jaw muscles, lip muscles, throat muscles. Now your shoulders and your fists. Your stomach. Your legs. Think of yourself as letting go. Relax all muscles and sink back in your chair until you feel limp all over. Imagine that the chair is carrying every ounce of your weight. There is nothing for your muscles to do—you are relaxed, completely relaxed.

I have a friend who works in a health club in a large city. George gets his clients to try this experiment of tensing all the body muscles and then relaxing them. He may sometimes use an additional relaxing method. With the muscle tensions eased, George tells them to bring the thought of God to mind.

"You are now perfectly relaxed," George says. "The tensions are leaving your body. In place of the tension, healing thoughts are coming into your mind and into your body. Now, let's go deeper. Say to yourself, 'God is in me. God is in my whole being. Just a moment ago I was rushed and anxious. I was tense, but now I am released from tension. My energies are now operating in a normal and creative way.' "

And then George asks, "Do you notice anything different about yourself?"

And one does indeed. I have tried the exercise myself many times, and know that something very different is present. I feel refreshed, invigorated, a new sense of control, as if I had the power to tackle the most difficult problem.

"That's relaxed power," says George. "You can now take that power back with you to the office, or back into your home. You can take relaxed power into the most tensed-up situation and the pressures won't bother you at all."

This is an excellent technique for handling the physical tensions that have a way of seizing us and not letting go. But I am of the opinion that most physical tension is really mental tension that has been translated into a new dimension. Our minds get to racing with a problem; pretty soon our bodies get to racing too. Even when seated in a chair our bodies can race. The muscles tense up as if they were in motion, and before we know it, we find ourselves knotted up. You must find ways and means to keep pressure under control, to keep the great quality of relaxed quietness.

Some years ago my wife and I bought a farm about seventy-five miles north of New York City. While the chief purpose in getting the place was to give our children the benefit of country life, I also wanted that farm to try an experiment on myself. I had a theory that everyone should have a private retreat where he can retire from the hurrying, scurrying, tension-filled world, and renew his spirit. My theory was based on the words: "In quietness and in confidence shall be your strength." (Isaiah 30:15)

I was born a country boy and they say you may take the boy out of the country, but you can never take the country out of the boy. At any rate, I wanted an actual place away from the city where I could retire at times and give God a chance to re-create in me a quiet mind. I wanted to see if this return to the country had a noticeable effect on the mental and muscular tensions that I was feeling.

Out back of the old farmhouse, on the place we finally bought, there is an orchard. To reach it you walk past the barn and follow a little path over a small stream, then through a corn patch and along an old stone wall. Finally you come to a little hill hard by a woods. You are completely alone up there. If you strain your ears, you can hear the wind in the trees, or the far-off whistle of a New York Central train working its way up the valley. Occasionally, you might hear the lonesome barking of a dog.

Nothing happens to you right away, up there on that windswept hilltop. You have to give God a chance to reach into your soul with His healing power. It requires a sort of settling down. But after a while you become aware that there is a certain rhythm in nature, a rhythm you had not been conscious of before. You look around you. It is autumn, say. The world is slowly going to sleep. A squirrel chatters to himself as he gathers nuts for the winter. A leaf falls; its very fall is lazy and relaxed. Down in the valley the corn is standing in shocks; the harvest is in, the fields are asleep, not to awaken for months. The entire world, as you see it from up there on the hilltop, has a rhythm of its own.

And it is a slow, relaxed rhythm. It is not the hurried pace that you brought with you from the city. You came racing up the hill with your mind running to keep pace with your body. But up there on that elevation, if you sit back and let the rhythm of the universe seep into your bones, or more importantly, into your thought processes, you find that your mind has slowed down; you simply are not in the same rush you were before. You find yourself repeating, with a new sense of meaning, the words: "In quietness and in confidence shall be your strength." God has heard your prayer. You feel less tension, more peace, and greater strength.

Once recently, when I was telling this story to a tired and harassed business executive who had come to me for help, I had it pointed out that not everyone has a convenient, lonely hill to which he can retire. "No," I said, "but anyone can find a quiet place if he really wants one."

On a recent trip to the Orient I noticed that the Japanese have beautiful, small gardens scattered throughout their cities. Maybe it's a garden of stones or of sand or of moss; it doesn't matter. They can retire to their gardens for a few minutes of contemplation. And it is a most effective practice, as I myself discovered.

During the weeks I was in Japan I made good use of the quieting and relaxing qualities of those unique Japanese gardens. Two in particular were so unforgettable that I often find myself returning to them in memory to experience anew their healing touch.

A moss garden in Kyoto was the scene of frequent relaxing meditations. There, where the sun falls gently through lacy-leafed trees onto a soft floor of moss and gleams on little lily pads in miniature ponds, the confusing world retreats and peace abounds. One is supposed to sit as immobile as possible, letting the eyes rest upon this beauty and permitting the mind to open wider and even wider to receive peaceful impressions. The effect, when you have learned to yield to it, is amazing in its ability to heal tension.

The stone garden of Kyoto will ever remain a significant spot in my long study of the techniques for reducing tension. Located within the confines of a Buddhist temple, the garden is an area perhaps 75 x 40 feet. It consists only of sand in which are set fifteen stones of varying size and shape. Sand and stones, that is all. The stones, according to one theory, are supposed to represent the fifteen basic problems of human existence. They are so placed that only part of them are in your line of vision, on the theory that it is too much for the mind to consider all human problems at one time.

One is supposed to become physically and mentally still and, without being conscious of time, to contemplate life's deepest meaning.

On my last visit, the Japanese taxi-driver volunteered, "Do not hurry from Stone Garden. I will wait. No charge. If you worry about time you will miss what Garden has to say." I was the only Westerner in the Stone Garden at the time. Two venerable men in kimonos, a woman of uncertain age in Japanese dress, and a young couple in western clothes, holding hands but not speaking: these were my companions in meditation.

We all sat quietly, each thinking his own thoughts. Deep stillness prevailed, but I recall thinking that it was an alert stillness, full of dynamic force but no tension. Suddenly a phrase came to my mind: "Motion in stillness." I realized again that out of quietness comes vitality and force. Tension swirls one apart, but motion in stillness puts one together again. Quietness does not curtail, but stimulates drive; however, it is a drive that is organized and controlled.

The experience gave me an extraordinarily acute awareness of God. "In him we live, and move, and have our being," (Acts 17:28) was a Scripture passage I found myself repeating.

Later I addressed the Kyoto Rotary Club on "How to Live and Work Without Worry and Tension." In replying to my talk the club president said it was, "very appropriate since Japanese businessmen are Far Eastern Yankees, full of stress." I suggested that they visit their own shrines of healing quietness, just as I advise Americans to seek "the peace of God, which passeth all understanding." (Philippians 4:7) So, find your place of quietness for the practice of meditation, contemplation and prayer. It is one effective answer to tension.

A good friend of mine, Jesse L. Lasky, one of the founders of Hollywood as a motion-picture center, did this most impressively. In his house Mr. Lasky had a special room set aside which he called his Silence Room. It was simply furnished with a table, one stiff-backed chair, and a picture of the Matterhorn on the wall. On the table was a Bible.

Whenever Jesse became tense or found that pressure was mounting in him he would go into his Silence Room, shut the door and just sit for a while gazing at the picture of the majestic Matterhorn. "I will lift up mine eyes unto the hills," (Psalm 121:1) he would say to himself. Then he would open his Bible at random and read.

Jesse Lasky told me that he never failed to come out of his Silence Room refreshed and renewed in spirit. Anyone can find a quiet place of his own, if he really wants to. It is significant that a good many people nowadays are arranging, if not a room, at least a little spiritual meditation nook in the home. Islands of spiritual quietness, you might call them, in a time of tension.

Actually, a quiet place doesn't have to be a physical place; it can be in the thoughts. Years ago I developed a technique of my own for storing up peaceful experiences in my mind. I have used this technique literally hundreds of times, and can personally guarantee its effectiveness. It has done much in helping me master tension.

Here is what you do. Let's imagine that you are standing alone on a beach. The rest of the world has gone to sleep, but you were restless, so you got up, dressed, and took this walk on the beach. All of a sudden you find your eyes rising to the heavens. For the briefest moment you throw your soul out into the universe. You consciously expand yourself into an identification with the great God and His vast creation. You stand there and become at one with the pounding surf and the infinity of the skies.

Then you memorize the experience. It is like memorizing a poem. First you start with the things you can hear: the ocean and the wind and the sound of the beach grass rustling. Then you memorize the things you can feel; the spray in your face, the bite of the cool night air. And taste? There is salt in the air; if you run your tongue over your lips you can actually taste the ocean. Down your five senses you go, memorizing each one so that as you stand there you can bring it back at will.

And then the next time you find yourself tense, close your eyes and bring the scene back by conscious memory re-creation. Run down each of the senses and re-create the peaceful experience. In just a few moments you will bring back into your mind the feeling of harmony and of relaxation that you knew that night on that vast and empty beach.

One night at Pensacola a high-ranking naval officer told a group of us a wonderful story illustrating the importance of calm, emotional control in doing a vital job.

> The aircraft carrier *Essex* was entering Pearl Harbor, the first of her class, loaded with planes and gear from San Francisco, including five thousand Marines. All officers and men in Pearl were eager to see the first of the replacement ships, and her arrival was a significant event in the war.
>
> As she entered the channel a fire broke out on the hangar deck. Simultaneously a merchant ship was sighted coming out. The channel at Pearl was not wide enough for two ships under normal conditions and the situation was critical. Word of the fire was passed to the bridge and the officer of the deck called to the captain, "Fire on the hangar deck!"
>
> Every captain is seriously concerned about a fire on the hangar deck because of the many gasoline filled aircraft always present there, and because of the proximity of fuel and ammunition stowage.
>
> The captain was closely watching the approaching ship and did not appear to have heard, so the officer of the deck repeated his report more loudly. Without turning his head the Captain, who was noted for his imperturbability, said quietly, "Put it out."
>
> The two ships passed safely, and the fire was put out with little damage.

But some people are always telling me that the times are so filled with tension! Tension, they complain, is all around, so how can you keep from being tense. I repeat—tension exists in the mind, in your attitude toward confusion, noise and problems.

How do successful positive thinkers keep their lives poised and relaxed? There seems to be a definite pattern that they follow. For one thing, they do what Bernard Haldane suggests. They "study their successes." Some people keep poking around among their failures for know-how. There's not much wisdom in a failure, otherwise it wouldn't have been a failure. It's really only good as a reminder how not to do something.

But when you have succeeded, study how you did it, and see if you can apply the technique to the next job. You will then know that you know, and that you can, and your tension and nervousness will give way to the calmness of the man who knows that he can, and does it.

The successful person has had to learn how to organize, so that he is free from those swamped feelings that cause pressure to rise.

A great many of the successful positive thinkers with whom I have talked, or who have written me, are men who were thoughtful enough to realize they couldn't handle everything on their own. They were part of a team in which many others were important. They learned to train and encourage others, and trust them to do their part.

And, finally, men of this caliber know the real source of strength and peace. Having big minds, they are able to comprehend the importance of spiritual values in life. The bigger they are, the humbler they are.

And now, what about the times when it is *necessary* to live with tension. I guess one of the most confusion-ridden, ten-square-feet of real estate in the whole world must be the area under the information sign on the upper level of Grand Central Station, New York. I went there one day to ask a question. Out of the surging crowds there was constantly a little knot of people clustered up against the booth, each with a burning question that had to be answered right *now!*

I watched the man behind the desk handle people. And he showed no signs of tension. It was fascinating. Here was a small, bespectacled man, subjected to heavy pressures, trying to answer the questions of impatient and confused travelers. And yet he was one of the calmest people I have ever seen.

The next passenger to get his attention was a short, plump woman, a shawl tied over her head. I remember that she had little whiskers growing from her chin.

The information man leaned forward so he could single out her voice from all the noise around him. "Yes, madam?"

The information man looked up slowly and focused his eyes on this woman through the bottom lenses of his bifocals. "Let's see . . . where was it you were going?"

A smartly dressed man with a briefcase in one hand and an expensive hat in the other tried to break in with a question. The information man just kept on talking to the woman in front of him. "Where was it you were going?"

"Springfield."

"And that was Springfield, Ohio?"

"Massachusetts."

Without looking at his timetable he gave her the answer. "That train leaves on Track 25 in just ten minutes. You don't need to run; you have plenty of time."

"Did you say Track 25?"

"Yes, ma'am."

"Twenty-five?"

"Twenty-five."

The woman turned to leave and the information man focused his attention on the man with the expensive hat. But once again the woman asked him the track number. "Did you say it was Track 25?" she asked. This time, however, the man behind the desk was giving his attention to his new passenger, and he would no longer listen to the little woman with the shawl tied over her head.

Finally, there was a momentary lull, and I took the opportunity to ask the information man a question. "I've been admiring the way you handle the public," I said. "Tell me, how can you do it and keep so calm?"

And then this man raised his head and looked at me through his bifocals. "I don't deal with the public," he said. "I deal with one passenger. And then with another passenger. It's just one person at a time right on through the day. Now where was it you were going?"

I've never forgotten that phrase: one person at a time right on through the day. And I don't intend that I ever shall, for it is too important in the proper regulation of factors that make for tension. It's been a great help to me when many multiplying problems compete for my attention at once. When things start coming at me from every direction I remind myself: "One thing at a time." That's it. That policy can undercut tension and keep your emotions under good control.

"This one thing I do," said St. Paul. (Philippians 3:13) There is magic in that phrase. If life is crowding you, if pressures are mounting inside you and tensions are leaving you high-strung and irritable, memorize that phrase. "This one thing I do." Refer to it before you start to work, and then determine to live by it. Develop the habit of saying, "Just a minute please" to interruptions, whether they come in the form of people, ideas or noise. As you perfect the technique of doing only one thing at a time you will find that much of the tension has been eased away, and in its place has come a smooth power-flow.

If you learn to think in terms of peacefulness then, no matter how hectic your circumstances, you can live with calmness and peace of mind.

I saw this demonstrated in the case of a man I met one winter morning. To begin with, I make it a practice in my morning prayers to ask the Lord to guide me to anyone He wishes me to help during the day. I recommend this practice. It will lead you to many exciting adventures.

Well, on this particular day the telephone rang and a tense voice reminded me of a meeting I was supposed to attend in midtown Manhattan. I got the impression from the tense person who was calling that if I failed to show up or was late, civilization would fall. I dashed out of my apartment building urging Mike, our genial doorman, to get me a taxicab. But it was the morning rush hour and none was readily available. I live on upper Fifth Avenue and, failing to note a cab in sight, started walking rather rapidly toward Madison Avenue, a block away, where I felt the chances for getting a cab might be better.

Then I decided to practice the tension-free control which I advocate for others. I slowed down to a relaxed pace and humbly suggested to the Lord that if He wanted me at that meeting He would just have to make a cab available. And that is exactly what happened, for there at the corner was an empty taxi. And, as I soon discovered, my earlier prayer was answered, for this driver was certainly a man who needed help.

He was extraordinarily tense, gripping the wheel so tightly his knuckles showed white. He talked ceaselessly in a nervous manner, complaining about all the other drivers thronging the avenue. Pushing through the maelstrom of traffic, listening to him, I got the naïve idea that he alone, of all the drivers on Madison Avenue, knew how to drive. He leaned out of the window and instructed the others vociferously. In fact, he communicated with them in theological terminology.

He created a very tense atmosphere despite the fact that a sign in the cab urged his passengers to "Sit back, enjoy the ride." I really felt very sorry for this high-strung, nervous man and employed a spiritual technique I have often used of sending out quieting prayers toward him. I tried to surround him with God's peace as we pushed on down the jam-packed thoroughfare.

Then I noticed something that explained much. It was a printed sign, not hand-lettered, but apparently done by a printer. It was appended with Scotch tape to the instrument panel at eye level where one could easily see it. I became quite amused by this sign which read: "If you can keep your head amidst all this confusion—you don't understand the situation."

I asked the taxi-driver what it meant and he said he didn't know but it comforted him. Well, of course, we are not likely to escape from the confusion of this world. We have to live in it and we must understand the situation. And that is just the point; we *can* understand and adjust to outward tension, living in it successfully, because we have the secret of peace of mind.

When we reached our destination I said to the driver that I was sorry he was so nervous, that unless he conquered it he might become ill. He assumed from my remarks that I might be a physician and anxiously asked me how a nervous, tense condition might be cured.

I told him that I was not a medical doctor, but could recommend a Doctor who could heal him. In fact, I knew that Doctor's methods, and could give him a prescription. It would not be a liquid in a bottle or a pill, but a healing thought which, lodged in his mind, could fill him with peace and strength. Whereupon, I took a sheet of paper and lettered the following words; "The peace of God, which passeth all understanding." (Philippians 4:7)

"Put that up alongside your other sign," I said. "Keep looking at it until those eight words are printed upon your mind so deeply that they sink into your consciousness. They have healing power. They can draw off your tension."

The man looked long and intently at what I had written. That the words impressed him was evident. "Guess that's what I need," he said. "I'll try taking your prescription."

I could have given him other tension-healing words, but this seemed sufficient for the time.

But for you who may work with the teaching of this book, I shall add others. The procedure is to cancel out your tension thoughts by the systematic and deliberate use of more powerful thoughts of peace. Inject into the mass of tension thinking which fills your mind with some really potent and healing thoughts that have the power to change the condition. Physicians tell us that certain thoughts can make you sick, actually physically sick. Such thoughts are hate, fear and tension, to mention only three. Alexis Carrel says: "Envy, hate, fear, when these sentiments are habitual, are capable of starting organic changes and genuine diseases." And other thoughts can make you well; such long-held thoughts as love, faith and peace.

But they must be directed and systematic thoughts, taken regularly into the thought stream. In due time they will change its essential character. Then the tension which has agitated you, which has perhaps even affected your blood pressure, your heart and certainly your disposition, will subside and you will return to a normal and satisfying condition of mental, emotional and physical well-being.

For one week "take" the following thoughts daily. Read each one thoughtfully several times to perceive its deeper meaning and to get the feel of the words. Then commit each to memory. Keep saying it until it is firmly lodged in your conscious mind. Then conceive of it as sinking steadily and deeply into your subconscious, there to do its healing work.

Proceed similarly each day with each one. After these seven have been fully integrated into the thought stream, go through the Bible on your own, culling out the many texts that are especially designed for tension curing. Saturate your mind with them, "soak" them deeply into the inner consciousness.

This may seem a strange and curious method, but it will work miracles, so what else matters? Hundreds, maybe thousands of people tell me the great things this procedure has done for them; how finally it has freed them from tension. It is truly one of the most amazing results of positive thinking.

Here follows a one-week prescription of tension-healing thoughts:

| | |
|---|---|
| *Monday* | "Peace I leave with you, my peace I give unto you . . . Let not your heart be troubled, neither let it be afraid." (John 14:27) (Where it says you or your, use your own name.) |
| *Tuesday* | "Thou wilt keep him in perfect peace, whose mind is stayed on thee; because he trusteth in thee." (Isaiah 26:3) |
| *Wednesday* | "My presence shall go with thee, and I will give thee rest." (Exodus 33:14) |
| *Thursday* | "Rest in the Lord, and wait patiently for him; fret not thyself." (Psalm 37:7) |
| *Friday* | "Come unto me, all ye that labour and are heavy laden, and I will give you rest." (Matthew 11:28) |
| *Saturday* | "Let the peace of God rule in your hearts." (Colossians 3:15) |

*Sunday* "He maketh me to lie down in green pastures: he leadeth me beside the still waters. He restoreth my soul." (Psalm 23:2,3)

Another point at which to attack tension is in your conversation or talk. Actually, you can easily talk yourself into being tense. A verbal statement is simply an articulated thought. So, when you talk tension you are thinking tension; and as you think tension you develop a tense state which results in high-tempo talk. Manifestly then, if you stop making tense and nervous remarks you will in time starve the thought that produces tense talking. The process can be encouraged by speaking calmly and by reducing the tempo of speech, using quiet, composed tones and words.

Take it slow and easy when you speak. Watch the elevation of the voice, keep a curb on its intensity. If someone breaks in before you are finished, just realize that maybe they are tense, so let them break in. If you want to resume your line of thought later, very well. But maybe you'll just let it slide. It's a kind of nervous habit nowadays just to jabber, whether anything is said or not.

Easy does it in speech as in all human activity.

There is one final technique that I would like to tell you about. It is a technique that is always used by the men and women who have learned to live successfully with pressure. Sometimes it is used instinctively; sometimes, as in the case of the business executive I am about to tell you of, it is used with planned deliberation.

I met this man on a railroad train and he taught me a good technique for reducing tension. A distinguished looking gentleman, he was headed for a business convention in the South. He settled down in his roomette across from me, pulled out a small briefcase and proceeded to surround himself with various stacks of paper. He had brought his office with him, and he was getting ready to go to work right there on the train.

But before starting, he did a strange thing. From his briefcase he pulled a black enamel plaque about the size of a postcard. Written on the plaque in large white letters were two words: PLAN BACKWARD. The man propped these words on the table before him and went to work.

Curiosity finally got the better of me, and I leaned across the aisle and said, "Pardon me, I hope you don't mind if I ask you a question?"

The gentleman took off his glasses and looked at me and said that he didn't mind at all: what could he do for me?

"Well," I continued, "I've seen a lot of these signs that say PLAN AHEAD. But I've never seen one that says PLAN BACKWARD."

He laughed. "All it is," he said, "is a reminder to myself that I've got to organize my time."

"But why the backward? Why not ahead?"

"Because," he said, "planning backward contains the idea of a specific goal. You choose a goal, picture yourself accomplishing it, then plan backward until you know exactly where and when you must start."

What a clever idea that is, really. Plan backward! I have tried it and it works. The big thing it helps you do is to organize yourself so that you start a project in time. I am a firm believer in the idea that every program has an ideal, intrinsic time-value of its own. To allow less time produces tension; to allow more time produces waste.

Try to discover this intrinsic time-value for the tasks that make up your day. How long does it really take you to handle your correspondence thoughtfully? How long does it really take you to prepare breakfast, walk to the bus stop, get the children off to school? Plan backward from these goals, and you will know when you have to *start* in order to reach them effortlessly, efficiently and without rush. This really cuts down tension. Simply start in time.

Of course, as previously suggested, the basic cure of tension and pressure is through God's peace. "Peace I give unto you: not as the world giveth, give I unto you. Let not your heart be troubled . . ." (John 14:27)

Knowing that modern people need the peace of God, I introduced a period of creative spiritual quietness into the services of worship in Marble Collegiate Church. Everyone is urged to let the body relax and to think only of God and Jesus Christ. A deep, a very deep silence settles over the large congregation. The only sounds are those on Fifth Avenue, but they are muffled by the thick marble walls of the ancient church.

When all is still I suggest quietly that everyone "drop" his problems, fears, tensions into the "deep pool of quietness" which has been created. The effect is deeply moving. The peace of God does indeed move over the people, taking life's fitful fever from minds and hearts.

And, as an illustration of how we all need the peace of God, I want to close this chapter with a touching letter from a young woman:

> First of all, I'll tell you that I'm twenty years old and a Roman Catholic. I've been brought up to practice my religion faithfully, and I have always done so. But lately, I had begun noticing that my faith in God, and His powers, was leaving my thinking more and more. I knew my faith was slipping away, and so I prayed that my faith and belief in God be renewed and strengthened. God, through your book, has done just that for me.
>
> I cannot tell you how much happier I am . . . how much peace of mind I now have, and how much more I love life. As I read your book, I practiced every suggestion you gave with all my heart, and so I will continue practicing those sugges-

tions until they become so much a part of me that I will do them naturally.

The other day, I had a rather upsetting experience. I have, for about a year, lived with an acute guilt complex about something I did. This feeling kept me from being happy, and in fact, kept me constantly nervous and miserable. I have confessed this sin to God many months ago, and have received absolution. Yet, in my mind, this wasn't enough. I let it eat at me, and imagined all sorts of terrible things that could result from it. Just the other day, reminders of this sin, and memories were brought back to me, and my guilt feeling kept telling me that I might some day do these things again, thus falling back into sin. The whole day I was a case of nerves, and even though I kept trying to apply your suggestions of relaxation, etc., to myself, I was still very upset. That night, in bed, I couldn't sleep, but suddenly I thought that by my talking it over with God, He would give me peace and relief. I told Him I knew He had forgiven me, and that He knew how sincere I now was to better myself. I asked Him to let the guilt feelings leave me. Instantly they did, and I fell into a peaceful sleep. These feelings have never again haunted me, and I know that they never will.

In your book, I felt, as I read it, that you were sincerely trying to help me personally. And so you have.

Take a vacation from tension when you can. Throw away your watch temporarily; build little islands of peace into your day; learn the art of storing up relaxed power. But for those times when you must live with tension, learn the art of saying, "Just a minute, please . . ." Cram the mind full of peace producing thoughts. Keep the speech tempo down. And avoid getting tense in reaching objectives. Plan backward; allow yourself enough time for the jobs you have to do. And, finally, and most important of all, practice the peace of God every day.

Follow these simple rules regularly, and there is no reason

why your life cannot become one of peace, tranquility and poise. You don't need to allow pressures to pressure you.

## XI

# Better Health Through Positive Thinking

IN MY OFFICE at Marble Collegiate Church is a small, toy coal bucket containing miniature lumps of real coal. I think I shall always keep that bucket, because it symbolizes an effective secret of health through positive thinking.

It happened in this way. A well known political personality asked me to call upon his wife's aunt who was in the hospital. This woman proved to be an amazingly interesting and able person. "I'm already getting better," she said. "It's my coal bucket that's doing it."

"Your coal bucket," I repeated. "I never knew coal buckets had healing properties. Besides, who has coal buckets in this era of better heating."

Then I saw it. There she was, propped up in her hospital bed, surrounded by the usual bottles and buzzers and vases of flowers; and on her bedside table, right in the middle of it all, was a miniature coal bucket, an exact replica of the black, old-fashioned kind our grandparents used.

"Well," I said, "this is certainly the most unusual piece of hospital equipment I've ever seen. Does it have something to do with how well you're looking?" And she did look very well, sitting straight up in bed, her eyes sparkling.

"It does indeed," she said. "It is my symbol of victory. Let me tell you about it. Here I was in the hospital, sick in body and despondent in mind. One dark trouble after another went through my thoughts. Then someone gave me a copy of your book about positive thinking. I was particularly struck with the idea that negative thoughts can do damage to our bodies. So I decided I would get all the old, black thoughts out of my mind and put bright, hopeful thoughts in their place.

"I started praying and reading the Bible as you suggested, but the black thoughts continued. Then one day I got to thinking that a black thought was something like an ugly black lump of coal. Strange the ideas we get, but I believe God gave me this one. So I sent out and got this little bucket of coal. Now, when a black thought comes, I pick up a lump of coal and say, 'With the help of God I now cast this thought out of my mind and I toss the coal into that receptacle over there. I'm sure my nurse thought I was going daft; but then she saw how much my spirits were improving. This simple technique has helped me no end, and I thank God for the bright thoughts that have come to take the place of the dark old thoughts which had so much to do with making me ill. You have no idea, Dr. Peale, how much this silly, little coal bucket has had to do with my recovery."

When she left the hospital she sent the miniature coal bucket to me and there it stands atop a bookshelf to remind me of an important truth about well being—get rid of black thoughts.

I have been impressed many times by the effect of positive thinking on health and how dark negative thoughts tend to induce illness. Holding negative thoughts is very dangerous. Job said, "The thing I greatly feared is come upon me." (Job 3:35) And Job was not the last to find that you can bring catastrophe upon yourself by unhealthy thinking.

Occasionally one comes across some dramatically clear-cut example of this fact. In England I read a story in the

*London Daily Mail* describing the curious death of Gem Gilbert, a British tennis star. She had died as a dentist was about to extract a tooth.

Years before, when Gem Gilbert was a small girl, she had gone to the dentist where her mother was to have a tooth pulled. And a most unusual and tragic thing happened. The little girl, terrified, watched her mother die in the dentist's chair. So what happened? Her mind painted an indelible picture of herself dying in the same way. The picture became a mental reality. Gem Gilbert carried it in her mind for thirty years. This fear was so real that she would never go to a dentist, no matter how badly she needed treatment.

But finally there came a time when she was suffering such acute pain that she agreed to have a dentist come to her house at a seacoast place in Sussex to extract a tooth. She had her medical doctor and her pastor with her. She sat in the chair. The dentist put a bib around her. He took out his instruments and at the sight of them—she died.

The writer in the *Daily Mail* remarked that Gem Gilbert had been killed by "thirty years of thought." It is an extreme case, of course, but everywhere there are people who are doing great damage to themselves just as surely, if more slowly, by sickness-producing attitudes compounded of defeat, hate, fear, guilt. Obviously, then, a most important technique of good health is ridding the mind of all unhealthy thoughts. It is important to have regular mind cleansings. We must get rid of mental infection in order to have healthy bodies.

It is astounding how often the pattern of resentment causing illness is repeated. Bernard Baruch says, "Two things are bad for the heart: running up stairs and running down people." It's true not only of the heart but of the entire physical being. And forgiveness has an amazingly therapeutic effect. I received a letter from a woman who had suffered an accident, while hunting with her husband, which bears this out:

> I had an accident in 1946, when a gun I was firing gave a hard recoil and injured my right shoulder. Great pain ensued, and some time later I went to an orthopedic specialist. X-rays revealed a bony spur, with a great amount of calcium, and a nerve spasm was also present over the site of injury.
>
> I was given an injection of procane into the nerve spasm and put on cortisone. But the pain came back again and I was unable to lift the arm beyond a certain degree in motion. I had made an appointment with my orthopedic surgeon to begin X-ray treatments when he returned from a trip.
>
> Then I started reading *The Power of Positive Thinking.* After reading about resentments and their effect on physical conditions, I put the book down and did some thinking. I had had some trouble over family affairs with my only sister, and we were not on good terms, though we observed the amenities when meeting. We had not visited nor made personal calls for over four months, and had not been truly friendly for a number of years.
>
> After a great deal of thinking I called her on the phone, had a pleasant talk with her, which was a great surprise, and I found myself offering to help her, if I could, in any way. When I laid down the phone I was weeping silently.
>
> Then, much to my astonishment, I had a burning sensation on the inside of my forearm. It's hard to explain the sensation only to say it felt as if the glands were secreting backwards, with a warm burning sensation. So intense was this sensation that I just looked at the spot on my forearm expecting to see it break out in some rash. It lasted for a few seconds only, and the pain went.
>
> I then, gingerly at first, began putting my arm through motions and found I could move it freely, in flexion, extension, supination. Since then I have had complete free motion of the arm without soreness or pain.

Resentment! What is this powerful emotion that wreaks so much havoc with our bodies? Apparently what happens is that we make ourselves feel painful experiences over and over again. "Resent" is an interesting word: it comes from the Latin words meaning "to feel again." It operates in the following manner. We have an experience that is full of hurt to the personality. We resent it and so make ourselves miserable and sick by constantly re-feeling it. But finally the conscious mind may refuse to relive the actual painful memory. However, instead of forgiving and forgetting, it forces the memory down into the subconscious and then the smothered, emotional reaction may break out in the form of physical pain or sickness.

A physician told me about a woman of fifty who kept coming to him with various kinds of sores on her body. He would cure the sores with local applications, but sooner or later they would reappear and so would she. Finally, the doctor began to suspect that his patient's trouble was more spiritual than physical, and he decided to make an experiment.

"Do you know," he told her the next time she came for treatment, "I believe you are terribly afraid of something or else you are holding some deep resentment. I don't know what it is, and unless I do know I'm not going to be of much help to you."

There followed a prolonged counseling session in which it became obvious that the doctor's suspicion was well founded. This patient, as a child, had suffered a shocking traumatic experience. She had a beautiful sister, while she herself was always considered a homely child. When they were both still very young, the pretty sister died. Alongside the casket, the mother stood weeping. Suddenly she whirled around on the homely daughter and cried, "Why wasn't it you!"

This was such an extremely painful experience for the

girl that her mind tried to avoid accepting it. How incredible that her own mother did not love her! But she did not want to remember that. So she managed to bury it in the unconscious, but still it remained very active in total consciousness. She developed a hatred for her mother and this, too, was an emotion that she could not accept and would not admit. She also buried that in the subconscious. So these unhealthy emotions were driven deep underground and there they festered, sending off ill health.

Things would go all right until for some reason (perhaps it was a telephone call from her mother, or maybe she saw someone on the street who reminded her vividly of her mother) the old resentments were stimulated again. She resisted the painful, remembered emotions, but they came out anyhow, in the form of another *kind* of pain. But once she recognized the real source of her physical troubles, she was able to empty out her resentments to her doctor. When she utilized the therapy of forgiveness she finally was rid of hate. The spiritual health she achieved led to mental and physical health. Thereafter she was also rid of the constantly recurring sores.

This patient had buried her feelings of ill will for many years before they erupted into ill health, but sometimes the effects of such feelings are much more immediate. Just the normal frictions of day-to-day life can result in headaches, back troubles, aching joints, and that "gray sickness." A case of this kind came to my attention recently in a rather amusing way. An old friend blurted out that he was "feeling lousy" and that he "hated his mother-in-law." He, himself, saw the connection between the unwell feeling and the cause.

"Let me tell you about her, Norman," he said. "If you want to hear about witches, listen to this one. I have to get up early each morning, earlier than my wife; and while I'm getting breakfast in comes the mother-in-law. She's a hag. Underneath a frayed kimono she wears a sloppy old nightgown that's dragging along the floor, and she shuffles along in dirty carpet slippers that keep kicking off and on. Her hair is never combed and it falls down in front of her eyes. But the thing that I hate worst of all is the way she grinds her toast. She puts it between her false teeth and grinds it back and forth like a horse. I sit there every morning, just waiting for her to start grinding the toast."

Well, it's no wonder my friend was having stomach troubles, starting his day off with such emotions. I suggested a simple solution. "You're not distinguishing between your mother-in-law as a mother-in-law and as a woman," I said.

"She's no woman," my friend said firmly. "That's all she is, a mother-in-law."

"Well now, that just isn't so. She was a woman before she was a mother-in-law; and if you want to find a solution to your problem, I suggest you start treating her like a woman. Some morning soon, when she comes to breakfast, why not invite her out to lunch. That will surprise her. She won't know what to do with that one, and she'll at least be so surprised she'll stop grinding her toast for a couple of minutes.

"Invite her to lunch in a nice place. Say to her, 'I'm going to take you to a swank spot that I know, so you'll want to dress your best.' And when she meets you at the restaurant, usher her in like you were proud of her. Buy her a corsage, and pin it on her. Compliment her on her hair-do, and on her dress. And then, say this: 'I never realized how pretty you were, just seeing you at breakfast and all. My, but you are really a pretty woman.' Then drop it. Have a good meal, be full of fun, give her a good time and see what happens."

It worked like a charm. The morning after that luncheon the mother-in-law came down with her hair combed and as soon as she had the opportunity she purchased some new slippers and a bright, pretty housecoat to replace the shabby old kimono. In time the two became as thick as thieves, and all the old symptoms of tension and stomach distress disappeared.

But you may say, "Dr. Peale, your ideas are all very well for the person who has an emotionally induced illness. But not all illness is caused by the emotions."

This is very true. But in one important way, it makes no difference whether the disability is functional or organic. In either case, the patient's spirit can be healed. And that is a large element in healing, even if the physical disability remains.

In fact I believe that, whatever your problem—it can be solved. I make that statement with complete awareness of all the terrible, heartrending problems to which human nature is subject.

I preach no easy philosophy because we do not live in an easy world. But neither do we live in an impossible world. Never forget that fact. We have available the help of Almighty God in the problems of this life. And underscore that word *Almighty*. The help we get from God is tremendous help. We all know of the astonishing victories which are achieved in the lives of human beings through that vast Power. For example, take this letter from a woman in Wisconsin:

> My husband was a strong, healthy man until, in his early forties, he was stricken with arthritis. Many days of suffering extreme pain followed, but after the first bout was over he continued to travel his sixteen states as a salesman.
>
> Finally he had to use a cane. The joints on his feet and fingers became horrible knobs. I was with him on one of his trips. It was so pathetic to see this once strong man hobbling along the streets, complaining about his inability to take a step without pain.

Suddenly a young man in his thirties passed us, whistling merrily. As he went by, to my dismay, I noticed that he had only hooks for hands. I called this to my husband's attention. It suddenly presented a picture of a young man with a lifetime ahead of him, having hooks for hands. And yet he was happy.

So my husband braced himself and said, "I'll never complain again." He never has. He has had phlebitis, gangrene, and lost the sight of one eye. Three weeks ago he had an operation for a ruptured gall bladder, has an eneurysm of the lower aorta, and the liver growing around the gall bladder. His fingers are so bent he cannot button his shirt.

But he is happy, victorious. He never complains. He is grateful for all small or large favors. When the ambulance man deposited him in his chair, he turned to me and said, "I've come through this just great. God has been so good to me."

This man's problem was not removed from him, but he solved it. There are many situations like this, where problems are not eliminated, no matter what one does. But the person who has faith in God, even though his problem remains unchanged, shall indeed gain victory over it. This arthritic man emptied himself of his negative and self-pity thoughts, and while his arthritis was not cured, his spirit was healed. He is not an unhappy man today. He is not victimized by his condition. And as a result, he has the blessings of mental and spiritual health despite his physical handicaps. So it is possible for us to improve our spirits even though, occasionally, we may not be able to improve our physical condition. Many times our physical condition is beyond control. We inherit our health from our parents and from our grandparents. Frequently, fortunately, it is good health we inherit. Sometime ago I had a letter from President Harry S. Truman in which he pointed out this fact:

> I have always been of the opinion that to live a long, healthy and happy life, you must be careful to pick the right grandparents on both sides of the house. Apparently, that is what I did. Of course, I have obeyed the rules the best I could about the forms of exercise best suited to my age and about eating habits. I eat what I want when I want it, but not as much as I would like.

Mr. Truman, however, does go on to say that living by spiritual principles has effected his health:

> One of the principal contributions to good health is a moral code that considers the welfare of the people around you as well as your own. I have found the 20th Chapter of Exodus and the 5th, 6th and 7th Chapters of the Gospel according to St. Matthew to be nearly perfect guides by which to live. The 10th Chapter of St. Luke also has a wonderful effect upon people who are trying to find the true definition of a good neighbor.

Dr. George W. Crane says, "In modern medicine we are beginning to realize that positive thinking seems to exert a beneficial tonic to many of the internal organs. On the other hand, negative thinking can throw a monkey wrench into the smooth functioning of those inner organs and glands. Drugs and chemicals can influence glands, but the mind can do so too."

Ronald J. Smith discovered that fact. The S.S. *Homeric* was moving slowly up the St. Lawrence River and Ronald Smith, who had long been plagued with a nervous disorder that affected his stomach bringing the chances of an ulcer within distance, was standing in his cabin looking at a large jar of stomach tablets in one hand and a copy of *The Power of Positive Thinking* in the other.

Ronald Smith's cabin companion ventured: "You have

been reading that book for five days now. Are you going to ignore what you have learned from it? Go ahead and throw the tablets out the porthole." After a brief hesitation, Smith gave one throw and the jar of stomach tablets splashed out of sight.

Smith has never again had need to revert to the habit of taking tablets. He learned the amazing power of positive thinking to heal. Let me repeat. The technique is to believe that you are going to be better, believe that positive thinking is going to work for you, and remedial forces actually will tend to be set in motion.

The newspapers carried a story about a man who was hit by a truck while crossing a street and was killed. An autopsy established that he had lesions from tuberculosis, ulcers, bad kidneys and heart trouble. Yet he had lived a vigorous life to the age of 84. The doctor performing the autopsy said, "This man should have been dead thirty years ago." The widow, when she was asked how he had lived so long, answered, "My husband always *believed* he would feel better tomorrow."

One definite step that some have found helpful in applying positive attitudes to physical well-being is that of affirmation or the use of definite positive statements. Words are dynamite. If you constantly use negative words concerning your health, you may stimulate negative forces that can adversely affect you. Words, habitually used, are reflections of strongly held thought, and thoughts can affect internal organs negatively or positively. But this fact also works to your advantage in that forces favorable to well-being may be stimulated by the constant use of positive words or affirmations. And it is a fact that positive thinking is stronger than negative thinking as faith is stronger than fear.

Alfred J. Cantor, M.D., former President of the Academy of Psychosomatic Medicine, in speaking of the effect of affirmations on health cautions against even such qualified statements as, "I am not going to be ill today." That is a half-positive assertion. Use instead, "I am going to be better today," which is a wholly positive statement and therefore much healthier. "Affirmations," says Dr. Cantor, "are based upon proved, scientific facts—the facts of biology, chemistry and medicine. Properly employed, such affirmations will improve your health, lengthen your life, rejuvenate your body, increase your happiness, give you success and guarantee for you the most important gift of all—peace of mind."

Here are some examples of health affirmations which have been used successfully by many persons. Try them for yourself, but be sure to use them daily, thus training the mind to think in positive concepts.

> I see myself as whole—every organ of my body operating perfectly in harmony with God's perfect laws.
>
> My whole being is fulfilled with health, I think health, feel health, practice health.
>
> The healing grace of the great physician Jesus Christ is flooding my life. In Him was life. His life is in me.
>
> I am a child of God. In Him I live and move and have my being. I am strong, vital, joyous. The kingdom of God is within me and I am grateful to God.

Here is a prominent medical doctor who recognizes the role of affirmed belief in health and who recommends affirmation as a road to well-being.

Actually, making affirmative statements and holding affirmative thoughts is a major first step toward causing the affirmed belief to be actualized. A second step is to put the affirmations into action. And to do that, act as if the thing affirmed is already true. As you think, affirm and act; just so will you strongly tend to feel. Act vigorously and energetically and you will be amazed at the new energy and vigor you will enjoy.

Recently I sat beside James A. Farley at a luncheon. I marveled at his obvious good health and vigor. He seemed to be in the very best of condition and didn't appear any older than he had twenty years ago when I first knew him.

"Jim, don't you ever intend to get old?" I asked admiringly.

"No, sir!" he answered, smiling at me broadly, "not on your life."

"Well, I can believe it," I said. "But what's your secret?"

"I never think any old thoughts," he declared.

Jim Farley by thinking and living on that positive basis is actually demonstrating the power of positive affirmations.

Sessue Hayakawa, the Japanese actor who played the role of the prison camp commander in the film "Bridge on the River Kwai," is often mistaken for a man in his forties, although he is seventy. How does he accomplish this? By acting quietly and sincerely as though he were in his forties. "I stopped counting the years when I became 45," he said recently. "Aging is often a matter of the spirit. It exists in the imagination before it exists in the body. It is in the mind. It does not matter how long I sleep or what I eat. When a person gets little sleep one night, he usually says to himself, 'I didn't get enough sleep last night, I must be tired.' And so he is tired. His body did not need the sleep. Only his imagination did."

What sound insight! Our bodies do not need to become tired, sick, exhausted and old. Change your "image" of yourself; see yourself well, of course observing and practicing all the rules of health, and you will tend to be that which you visualize and practice.

This has long been a personal theory of mine, one that I

have applied to myself through actual personal demonstration. I am humbly grateful to God that through the practice of His mental, physical and spiritual laws I have, in sixty years, been inside a hospital, as a patient, exactly twice. Once was when I was still a youngster and had a slight ear operation. The second time was when I was twenty and had my tonsils and adenoids out.

I am not a strapping athlete but have been fortunate in having good health. In twenty-eight years at the Marble Collegiate Church I have missed just one Sunday due to illness, and that was because of a cold that settled in my vocal cords and I couldn't speak. Since then I have discovered principles of relaxation and right thinking that would have overcome such a voice difficulty. What are the principles I use? Simply those I have advocated in previous books which many have applied effectively.

They are all sound principles, adapted from a lifetime of observation and experiment, not merely by myself, but in the "laboratory" demonstration of thousands of people who have shared their practice with me. They will work. I know that they will work because they have worked for me, and for the many others with whom I have shared them. They are part of the amazing results of positive thinking.

1. Affirm that you are healthy. Say to yourself, "I feel well today. God created my body, mind and soul; so today, I feel as God intended, healthy and vigorous."

2. Hold constantly before your mind a clear picture of yourself as a well person.

3. Thank God frequently, every day, for the wonderful feeling of vitality. I asked Dr. John Riley who, at 91, was the oldest practicing physician in the state of New York the secret of his good health to ninety plus. He said, "Every day I thank God for the amazing organs of my body. I name them over and say, 'Thank you God, for my excellent

stomach; thank you God, for my wonderful heart; thank you God for my marvelous blood stream.' "

That this rather unique procedure added to his life of health and longevity Dr. Riley had no doubt. In daily thanksgiving he was firmly establishing the image of good health in consciousness and it demonstrated itself in fact.

4. Make every effort to keep your mind free of unhealthy thoughts. Flush out negative thoughts such as antagonisms, regrets, mean or vindictive images, disappointments. Replace them with healthy, kindly, positive thoughts. Did you ever hear the Balinese proverb, "If you get angry you will quickly get old"? I am told that in Bali there is less heart trouble than anywhere in the world.

5. Take nothing into the system that debilitates.

6. Keep your weight down. Find out what the doctors think your weight should be and keep it there. The solution of the weight problem requires a kind of strength that is essentially spiritual in nature. Control of extreme appetite whether for drink, for power, or for food is a problem of character. And character, of course, is spiritually conditioned.

A few years ago I became increasingly concerned about my own weight. It was far beyond the point at which I should have tipped the scales. Still, I kept on eating. I wasn't cutting down and realized that fact all too well. I began to wonder if I really could. It became an issue with me, actually a moral problem; was I defeated by a food appetite?

So I went on a diet that took off thirty-five pounds. Several years later, having re-added some fifteen of the lost poundage, I repeated the process—thirty pounds this time—to reduce to a level that has seemingly become a permanent weight. To accomplish this desired weight reduction, I employed certain spiritual and mental procedures which are described in *Live Longer and Better* which I wrote jointly with my brother, Dr. Robert Clifford Peale, a practicing physician.

7. Regular daily exercise is essential to good health. I prefer push-ups, calisthenics and swimming, sometimes a little golf, and hiking. It is important to choose a form of exercise that you enjoy enough to keep up regularly without its becoming a bore.

Personally I walk at least a mile every day, usually just before retiring. And when I am at my farm, I follow Dr. Paul Dudley White's advice to ride a bicycle.

Dr. White says, "A long brisk walk in the evening may help more to induce sleep than any medication. Nervous stress and strain can be counteracted and even prevented by regular, vigorous exercise. It is the best antidote I know."

Dr. White further points out that "good muscle tone in the arms and particularly in the legs resulting from regular exercise maintains an improved circulation in the veins. Since the veins have valves which, when in good condition prevent the blood from going the wrong way, the compression of the veins by the skeletal muscles helps to pump the blood back to the heart. Soft unused muscles do not accomplish the job as well and also make clotting in the veins more likely. And," adds Dr. White, "deep breathing exercises several times a day are of definite value." I have added this latter to my own exercise program with excellent results.

8. Have regular examinations by a doctor. Prompt attention to any imbalance helps restore the proper health conditions.

9. The greatest point of all, in my opinion, and this is based on personal experience, is to open one's life to the inflow of God's renewing power. The words "meditate" and "medicate" are almost identical in root meaning. Right thinking is medicinal. God creates good health, and He re-

creates it as well. The word health comes from the Anglo-Saxon word "wholth," which is also the root of the word "wholeness," and of the word "holy." Thus health is directly related to the idea of wholeness, and to the idea of holiness. In fact, holiness means to be a whole person, not a disorganized one; more than it means to be pious.

This brings to mind Plato's famous statement, "So neither ought you to attempt to cure the body without the soul." Indeed the whole man must be well, body and soul, if health is to be sound. So I keep in mind always that to be a healthy person it is important to be spiritually vital. When one becomes filled with positive thoughts and God thoughts there is no room for negative, unhealthy thoughts that are so often at the root of ill health.

XII

# How to Be Married and Enjoy It

Do you want a successful and happy marriage? Of course, everyone does. And many couples have learned through positive thinking how to be married and enjoy it.

Take, for example, that cynical young man who sneered, "Me marry—nothing doing. I'm too smart for that." He began attending the Young Adult activities at our church shortly after the last war. He went out on dates, but made it clear that he wasn't going to marry. That was that!

Eventually we discovered the reason for his cynicism about marriage. In the first place he had come from a broken home. Then, he had seen too many unhappy marriages among the couples he knew. When he was overseas with the Navy as a pharmacist's mate on a small ship, he got the idea that "not one of the married men aboard was faithful to his wife." As soon as the ship pulled into port, the married men, it seemed, were the first ashore, "running to cavort" with whatever women they could find.

The result of such negative experiences was that this young man firmly decided that marriage was not for him. He had kept his eyes open. He knew the score and he was going to steer clear of it. That was for sure.

Well, it happens that in our church there is a wonderful couple, the Merle Wicks. The Wicks are happily married. It was arranged for the young man to visit the Wicks in their home. He spent several days with them. He watched them laugh and play and pray, and even argue, disagree and make up. He saw them in a variety of moods and situations, handling a variety of problems; and what he observed proved to be a revelation.

"Do you know," he said later, his face animated with a new discovery, "these people actually know how to be married and enjoy it!"

I've always liked that phrase: "How to be married and enjoy it!" This is a vitally important factor in successful living. When people know how to "enjoy" such a close relationship it means that they have a healthy, creative marriage in which both partners are encouraged, helped, built up. Each bolsters the other. It is a relationship in which the children know genuine warmth and affection. It produces a home that radiates happiness and emanates well-being.

The National Education Association held a meeting at which the presidents of practically every important university in the country were present. The purpose of the meeting was to discuss what education could do about the country's most pressing need. And what was the most pressing need? More scientific education to compete with the Russians? More space education? Better training in economics? Not at all; these educators felt that the most pressing need of today is happy and substantial home and family life. The happy, healthy home is the cornerstone of a healthy society. Create health in the home and that health will radiate outward, touching business, industry, education, government, all phases of society.

So, how to have a successful marriage is a vital matter, a top concern of our time.

In collecting material for this book, I have separated my correspondence according to categories, and one of the thickest folders is marked "Marriage Problems." Week after week the letters pour in:

I have been married fourteen years and not at all happily, though I do have three wonderful healthy daughters for whom I thank the good Lord. My husband, age forty-nine, treats me shabbily. Sometimes he strikes me so hard with his fists. I think the real trouble is that he needs rest and relaxation. He doesn't take his vacation. He'd rather have double pay, though we don't need it. He makes good money. He owns his home. And we have never been in debt. Well, I wonder what should be done tactfully about him. Can you give me any suggestions?

We have a daughter who is married to a man who does not work steadily and is otherwise very irresponsible. They have three young children. She has made regular trips for a long time to a guidance center, as the pressures were affecting her nerves and mind. Her condition is better, but she has been advised that her only hope of complete recovery is divorce.

There is always a lot of talk and advice about the "little woman" keeping herself attractive, not to let herself show the effects of child bearing, housework and worry; keep herself as pretty as the office secretary. How about the husband; a paunchy, bald male is no longer a jaunty Romeo. How about a bit of advice to him?

I have a problem in my marriage, and I don't know what to do. I left my husband nine months ago, one month before our wonderful little son was born to us. I haven't been happy since I left him. The reason for leaving my husband was that he started running around with single men and drank an awful lot. Also, he would never let me have any money in my purse. Just enough to pay the rent and get groceries with. You see my real problem is that I live with my parents and they want me to get a divorce and they are planning on it very much. I'm afraid of losing their love if I go back to him, and I still love him very much. He has told me of the mistake he has done and wishes me to come back to him. What should I do?

It seems the thing that disturbs me most of the time is my relationship with my wife. I never know how to take her. We have been married eighteen years and I love her very much, but she, being the type she is, quiet, self-sufficient, and satisfied to be by herself, I find it difficult to feel that she needs me for anything. Sometimes she volunteers some affection, but seldom cares for me to go any further. When I try to tell her how I feel she simply won't listen. Can you help me?

And so it goes, on and on, week after week the letters pouring in, giving intimate glimpses into problems people face in their married life.

One of the outstanding results of positive thinking has been its effectiveness in difficult marital situations. When people who are having trouble with their marriages begin to apply positive attitudes to their situation, the marriage almost always strengthens. New appreciation, esteem and regard come into the relationship. When two people begin to think constructively about marriage they get constructive results.

Not long ago I was making a speech on the West Coast. When the talk was over a man came up to me and said he wanted to tell me how positive thinking had affected his life.

He said that he had been married for nine years. Two weeks after his wedding he began to realize that he had not chosen his mate wisely.

"That marriage was a mistake," he said. "Right away both of us knew it. It had been a case of physical attraction, but my wife turned out to be just plain dumb. She was selfish, too. I had to face the fact that I wasn't ever going to get along with her, and I had to make up my mind whether or not to stick it out."

This man chose to stay with his wife. He told me that he decided to make the best of a bad situation and endure the marriage. He said that as soon as he made this decision he stopped griping and tried to get along as well as he could with a woman he did not love.

Things went along this unhappy course for five years and then this man read *The Power of Positive Thinking*. He began to use the principles outlined in this book in his business life. They worked very well. One day it occurred to him that if the principles of positive thinking worked in business, perhaps they would also work in his personal life.

"What would happen," he asked himself, "if I applied *The Power of Positive Thinking*, chapter by chapter, idea by idea, to my own home situation."

He began to do this. He began to analyze his wife, asking himself why she was selfish and why she appeared to be stupid. The thought came that perhaps his marriage had been a form of guidance. He started to picture his wife as an entirely different sort of person: as a stimulating, attractive life partner. He began to pray for her and eventually even out loud with her. Simultaneously he examined his own personality objectively and honestly for the flaws which were making his wife unhappy. This was important to the process for he, too, had not a little selfishness and self-centeredness, as he readily admitted.

This process lasted for four years, but "the results were very good," he declared. And it was evident how sincerely he meant that. From a marriage which was simply endured, the relationship between these two people became a warm partnership in which each tried to give more than he received.

"Positive thinking," this man told me, "was directly responsible for the remaking of our marriage."

Now the fact of the matter is that the married relationship is one of the most touchy and difficult of all human relationships requiring, as it does, the adjustment of two different personalities in intimate association. Making a marriage succeed cannot be left up to chance, or even to hope. A definite, practical program needs to be established so that each party to the marriage may grow and mature; so that the children may have full, rounded, happy, creative lives. These are the purposes of marriage and should always be held firmly in mind. A happy marriage, let me repeat, is one in which all parties concerned—husband, wife and children—are fulfilled to the maximum.

Let us examine a few of the problems that arise in marriage and see how they have been met successfully.

One of the most common complaints about marriage is that couples do not have common interests. Admittedly, it is sometimes difficult for a husband and wife to develop common interests. The husband leaves on the 8:10 train every morning and returns on the 6:57. His day has been filled with active business interests, but these he never explains to his wife because he has learned that she is not interested, or else he is too tired to talk. On the other hand, the wife has perhaps filled her day with Town Hall or club lectures, and when she tries to regale him with the details of the lectures he is bored to distraction. The result is that these two people never really communicate. Their interests become more and more divergent.

Some years ago I had a rather amusing example of conflicting interests when a member of our church told me that he and his wife had begun to argue over who was going to watch television. This was back in the days when TV was new and most people could afford only one set. So there they were sitting in the living room each night, the husband wanting to watch fights, sports programs and westerns, and the wife wanting to see programs on the cultural side. They began to argue over the television. They said cutting, mean things to each other, and while the marriage never came close to divorce, things definitely were not smooth.

This problem may seem too petty to bring to a pastor, but what seems petty can be a symptom of a deeper problem, or it can work up into a major cleavage. The husband could not understand his wife's dumb interests, and the wife could not understand her husband's stupid interests. Well, this went on for quite a while until both husband and wife decided they would have to do something about the situation, so they came to see me. After talking with them I decided upon a little strategy. Privately I made an arrangement with the husband, then later with the wife, on the basis of the principle of ". . . in honor preferring one another." (Romans 12:10)

"Now what this means," I said, "is that you should prefer each other: by that I mean that you insist that the *other* party shall have the preferred treatment. I want you to apply this Bible principle to your problem with the television. When you get back home tonight," I said to the husband, "you insist that you both see her cultural program, and really get something out of it." A little later the same day, I said to the wife, "When you go home, you insist that you and your husband watch the ball game. See if you can't enjoy it yourself."

At first this had a rather unhappy turn. That night the wife turned on the TV—to the ball game.

"Oh no you don't!" said the husband. "I *insist* that you listen to the Philharmonic tonight."

"Not at all," said the wife. "We are going to watch the ball game, whether you like it or not."

So that first night, believe it, they got into a terrific argument trying to follow the Biblical injunction, ". . . in honor preferring one another."

Later, when they came back to my office to complain, they saw the humor of the situation, and after that we got down to the more serious question involved. Actually, their problem was only a lack of common interest. Their lives were too narrow. They were living by themselves, for themselves. They needed to find outside activities which would take them, together, away from their television set into the great world outside.

Since then this couple has become so active in community and church activities that they seldom watch television. Together they have achieved the goal of finding mutual interests. They are one of the happiest married couples of my acquaintance.

The matter of common interest raises the question of marriage with a member of another faith. I have received hundreds of questions dealing with the problem of whether a Protestant should marry a Catholic, or a Christian marry a Jew. Few questions so agitate families as this one.

If people truly practice positive thinking they can work out an interfaith marriage successfully. But it involves complete mutual respect of each other's faith, and an equal balance of every factor relating to the marriage. However, on the basis of considerable experience, I strongely urge young people to marry within their own religious group: Protestants with Protestants, Catholics with Catholics, Jews with Jews. Many hazards are eliminated by selecting a life partner from your own background. Marriage has many problems of adjustment as it is, and it's wiser not to add a difference of religion.

But a mixed marriage, as indeed any marriage, can rise to high levels of happiness if the home is packed full of love and faith and esteem for personality. Fill any household full of a love of God and of each other that transcends theological differences, and men and women and children can dwell together in peace and joy.

Another pesky problem that keeps coming up is the holdover of the ancient concept of the husband's role in marriage; that he is lord and master of the home. He handles the money, doling out an allowance, while the wife supposedly has the business sense of a babe in the woods.

Paralleling this is another anachronism: that many women, consciously or unconsciously, regard themselves as objects of art, to be taken care of by a father substitute in the form of a husband. This immature, infantile, ungrown-up state of mind assumes as the wifely right that the woman is to be made happy. In her thought, apparently, the whole purpose of marriage is to provide happiness for her; meaning, of course, that she shall receive all she wants from this kind "Papa" husband whom she has taken as a spouse.

But it often happens that the "Papa" husband becomes disinclined to act out the father figure. He indicates that he expects a real contribution from the supposedly mature woman whom he has taken as his life partner. Then she is likely to react emotionally according to the immaturity on which her concepts are based; and the marriage starts to disintegrate.

So one of the really major steps that a couple needs to take in developing a successful marriage is to become mature individuals. Perhaps this is the most difficult assignment that life gives us. Dr. Smiley Blanton, the psychiatrist who heads The American Foundation of Religion and Psychiatry, with the assistance of Dr. Irwin Smalheiser, psychologist, has worked out a Maturity Score. This simple test will give some clues as to whether or not you need to work on the question of maturity in your own married life or in your life generally, for that matter.

*Maturity Score*

*Yes* *No*

1. Do you lose your temper, stamp your feet, throw or kick things?
2. Do you always give the other person equal consideration with yourself?
3. Do you criticize your wife or husband in the presence of other people?
4. Are you insistent upon always having your own way, and sulk if you don't get it?
5. Are you a chronic worrier?
6. Do you put your trust in God and then just do your best?
7. Do you accept the ups and downs, and things that are inevitable, with serenity of spirit?
8. Do you have a positive conviction that you can meet and solve your problems?

Yes to questions one, three, four and five indicates immaturity.

Yes to questions two, six, seven and eight is a sign of a mature personality.

With the results of this test as a guide you will be able to know whether you need development of your emotional maturity. Certainly a major difficulty is that many people have an immature concept of love. A great deal of damage has been done to marriage by our Hollywoodish ideas of love. We seem to feel that "love" has got to be one prolonged moonlight and roses thrill.

Just the other day a young wife came to my office complaining that there was no thrill left in her marriage. She had been married nine months and now her husband's touch ceased to start her heart pounding. She had, however, found another boy who did give her this Hollywoodish sense of excitement. She wanted my advice about divorcing her husband to find married happiness with the second boy. She "simply must recapture the thrill of romance," she said.

"Well, young lady," I said, "suppose this new excitement lasts, as did the first, for only nine months; then what? In fact, the next might last only five months, for thrills tend to diminish with repetition. By the time you are forty you could be nothing but an old hag desperately looking for this so-called glamour that forever eludes you. You need to realize that this thrill you seek is something special that belongs to a certain stage in your development, but to expect it to last at high intensity is pure Hollywood hokum. It won't do that and it should not. It is against all the facts of human psychology that it should."

This young lady had never been apprised of the fact that sexual excitement is only one facet of a successful and enjoyable marriage. My father, who was first a physician and later a minister, and always a wise man, used to say that thrill-love was nothing but a biological trick on the part of nature for the simple purpose of perpetuating the race.

Far too many young couples think that as soon as sexual excitement begins to wear thin, they are falling out of love. They haven't adjusted to each other on any other basis than sex, and in their immaturity they do not want to work at marriage in all of its many aspects. The physical, while it is important, is certainly not the whole by any means.

In a newspaper I saw the results of a survey in which some four hundred happily married couples were interviewed. This survey indicated that the *average* time needed for two people to adjust to each other was six years! Note the fact that this is the average length of time; for many people it must have taken considerably longer. So when a young couple tries marriage for a few months, or even for a few years, and finds that the sense of excitement has abated somewhat, they should not become discouraged. Learning to be happily married takes time and patience. It is a mistake, indeed it is preposterous to think that as soon as the first flush of romance passes, it is time to seek another partner.

Now I do not want to indicate that sexual enjoyment should be confined to the first, few, pink-cloud months. Sexual adjustment is vital to a mature marriage. And in the overwhelming majority of successful marriages, sexual interest and capacity lasts into old age. Certainly sexual maladjustment can cause deep problems as many letters indicate:

> You have said many wise things about sex, so I turn to you with a serious problem.
>
> I have a perfectly good relationship with my wife in everything but the sexual area. She is about one-third as needful as I am. What should I do with my psycho-sexual difference? I don't want to express myself with another woman, yet my wife, whom I love, does not fulfill me.

> My wife is a dream girl, very attractive. She has the personality that attracts friends, especially children, who love her. It is her dream to have a child. I love her very much, and she is everything in the world to me. My problem is that we have been married two years and I have not been able to have sexual intercourse with my wife.
>
> I have been to one doctor after another, and all they tell me is that there is nothing wrong with me physically. Finally, one doctor told me that it was a combination of emotions, nerves and subsconscious mind that was blocking off any successful attempts.
>
> Do you think I have the right to ask her to spend the rest

of her life with me when I cannot fulfill the part of the husband and man to make a happy home and marriage? Is there anything you could suggest that might help me?

My husband and I have been married a year and one month. I haven't enjoyed our sexual relations at all, don't get any pleasure in love making, and dread even kissing him for fear it will lead to intercourse. I have never actually wanted intercourse and my life would be perfectly happy without it. I've explained this to my husband. It disgusts him, which I suppose, is normal. Should I divorce my husband and let him have another chance at happiness, or should we go through life like this?

My daughter was married last July. I tried to prepare her adequately for the physical side of marriage. I felt that she was quite mature and ready. She seems to be having trouble adjusting—wonders if, after all, she is "frigid." I wonder sometimes if we read too much and become completely confused. Would you have a word of some sort that might help her?

I have been married eighteen years and have a wonderful husband and four children. But, Dr. Peale, I still have an indifferent attitude toward sex relations. Possibly it is because I was led as a child to look at it as a vulgar act. Does the Lord look at it that way? Is it to be entered into only for conception's sake and the bringing of babies into the world?

So very often this question of vulgarity comes up. Apparently our Puritan backgrounds have left an indelible mark on our attitudes toward sex. I think it is important to state firmly that a full, natural enjoyment of sex is normal and right, else God would never have created people as He did. Love is both physical and spiritual. Therefore, a complete enjoyment of the physical senses within a spiritual marriage is never an expression of vulgarity.

The sexual act is a sacred expression of love between two people who have spiritually become one through marriage. "The twain shall be one flesh," the Bible says. While sexual union itself is physical in nature, it is also a fundamental expression of the highest and purest emotions in love. To regard it as vulgar indicates a warped concept, probably originating in childhood when, to make you moral, a dirty connotation was put upon God's principle.

Notice, however, that while we have been talking about the physical aspects of love, we have consistently brought the spiritual side of married life into focus. The spiritual element is where its real strength lies, and this is one of the areas where positive thinking becomes most important. Positive thinking says that through the proper mental and spiritual attitudes we are able to overcome our difficulties, whether they are marital or otherwise.

One of the most effective aspects of positive thinking is positive prayer. I am a firm believer in a statement originally made, I believe, by Father Patrick J. Peyton, "The family that prays together stays together."

A young couple told me they happened to be walking on Fifth Avenue in New York City at the moment the boy asked the girl if she would marry him. She said, "Yes." These two youngsters were both religiously inclined. Their first impulse was to drop into church and dedicate their engagement to God.

The nearest church happened to be St. Patrick's Cathedral, and although they were both Protestants, they entered the church, knelt, and prayed together. They felt that their forthcoming marriage was thus spiritually consecrated to God long before it was officially sanctified at the altar. It isn't surprising that their marriage turned out to be highly successful. That is really a valuable thought; consecrate your engagement to God. Thus, from the very beginning the relationship is based on an enduring spiritual foundation.

Far too many young people actually leave God at the marriage altar. They do not take Him into their homes. I was talking recently with one very troubled woman named Sally whose marriage, she said, was about to dissolve. In the course of our conversation, I spoke about my belief that a praying family will stay together. "Is God ever mentioned in your home?" I asked her.

"Oh yes," she said, "but not in the way you mean."

"Have you ever considered praying aloud with your husband?" I asked, and to this the woman gave a short but conclusive little laugh. "You just don't know my husband!" said Sally.

"Well now," I said, "I have known many men who give that impression. They say they will never pray. But that's an act, I've found, in a great many cases. I want you to try something tonight. At the table before dinner is served tell your husband that you would like to say a blessing. Use that as an opening wedge to bring a spiritual note and then, bit by bit, see if you can't bring additional prayer into your home."

I could see that this lady felt it was a useless experiment, but she agreed to try it, even so. As she reported later the experiment worked. That evening when her husband came home even more morose and grumpy than usual, he buried himself behind his newspaper and refused to talk, except to mumble, "About time!" when the wife finally announced that dinner was ready.

When they were seated at the table she said, "It may surprise you, but I feel like saying a blessing. Do you mind?"

"Well, go on," growled the husband. "It's a free country."

So a little embarrassed, the wife did say the blessing. And at breakfast she said one again. She kept this up for several days until one evening, still in a rough manner, the husband said, "Hold your horses, Sally. You've been saying the blessing at every meal. Who's the head of this house? I'll say the blessing around here." With that he searched his memory and drew out one of the old family blessings that he had heard as a child and, stumbling, he got it off successfully.

This couple had never before heard each other's voice in prayer. As time went on, it became easier to pray together. Eventually they began to say a prayer at bedtime. The last time I spoke with Sally she was able to report that a remarkable new spirit of cooperation and affection had come into their marriage.

Having a prayer centered home is one of the best of all techniques for a happy marriage. I have known couples who have made God central in their home life in a variety of very interesting ways. One woman was having a great deal of trouble with her housekeeping. In my contacts I often hear poor housekeeping mentioned in marital difficulty. This wife did not like housekeeping and as a consequence her home was always untidy and messy. This rankled with her husband who was an orderly and fastidious person.

"I decided that the only way for me to handle my attitude toward my house," she told me, "was to dedicate my housekeeping to God. The Bible says, 'Let all things be done decently and in order.' (I Corinthians 14:40) This became my housekeeping motto, and the results were really quite pleasing."

Another wife who has tried this technique successfully gets up earlier than her family and "fills her house full of positive affirmations." She stands in the middle of her living room and faces, in sequence, every corner of her house. As she does this she affirms aloud that "this house is a place where God dwells; it is a home full of peace, love and joy." She declares, "The result is really marvelous." Such affirmations become a reality; any home can become a happy place;

the toilsome part of housekeeping can be transformed into meaningful purpose. A husband-providing and a wife-keeping house—these are two of the most basic functions of life, and in them, when done in love and harmony, is true happiness.

My own mother had a remarkable ability to turn the chores of housekeeping into creative family experiences. Our house was always full of fun and happy excitement. Mother was a real strategist. No one was aware, for instance, of the fact that the dishes were being washed. Mother's trick was to start a discussion on some lively subject just at the moment that the unpleasant job of dish washing had to be done. Automatic dish washers were away off in the future. We were the dish washers of that generation, and we were not automatic.

When the meal was over, my mother would throw some highly controversial subject into the conversation. In no time, we would all take sides. As soon as the argument had reached a certain crescendo, mother would quietly hand a dish to my father, another one to me, and others to my brothers. She herself would rise and walk out into the kitchen carrying some dishes, all the while constantly stimulating the discussion. Before we knew what was happening we were all out there with her, washing and wiping dishes, and still arguing at full tilt, and having a wonderful time.

In any chapter on successful married life, a discussion of the selection of your mate is important. This is, of course, one of the most single decisions that a person will have to make in his life. Sometimes the decision is wrong, and a lifetime of misery follows. Therefore, I am a firm believer in an engagement of adequate length. A couple has so much to learn about each other. Can they really communicate with each other? Are they interested in many of the same things? Do their family backgrounds mesh gears?

A good friend of mine, Mr. M., a very prominent man, told me that his son Jim came home with the announcement that he was in love. He had fallen head over heels for a "fabulous" girl and was going to marry her right off, just as soon as commencement was over. The boy's family met this young girl and immediately sensed that she was not right for Jim. But to say so would have been wasted energy.

Wisely, the M's decided to let their son discover for himself how he really felt; so at the first opportunity they invited the girl to spend a week with them in their home. Almost immediately it became clear that the girl was not fitting in. She was quite a bit on the sloppy side. She did not get up when the rest of the family did. She would not help with the household chores. She obviously considered herself intellectually superior to the rest of the family, and in general succeeded in keeping herself apart from the rest of the group.

The boy was somewhat disillusioned, but was not ready to admit that he had made a mistake. Then, at Christmas time, Jim's parents strategically insisted that he spend the whole vacation at this young lady's home. They packed him off to her home, not expecting to see him until New Year's Day. But three days later he was back. Bit by bit the story came out. Jim was particularly disturbed by the way his fiancée yelled at her parents. She was difficult around the house and refused to participate in normal household activities. She acted sullen and spoiled.

The parents themselves seemed "neurotic" and were slovenly. Jim said the bathroom soap dish looked as if it had not been cleaned since Hector was a pup. The result of these two visits was that Jim's ardor cooled off entirely. Suppose, however, that Jim had not discovered these facts about his "true love" until after they had been married. Suppose he had insisted upon haste in marrying the girl, only to have his education in her qualities when it was too late to retreat. Love at first sight may have its place, but that doesn't go for marriage at first sight. There are far too many problems to be ironed out before marriage to risk a hasty wedding.

I am going to end this chapter with a "Marriage Mirror" arranged by Dr. Smiley Blanton and Dr. Irwin Smalheiser.

"How well do you know your spouse?" One of the saddest facts about many marriages is that two people will share the most intimate relationship, yet know next to nothing about each other's outlook on life.

One measure of emotional maturity in marriage is the degree to which you understand your spouse. The following test compares your viewpoints on a number of critical areas.

Part I is to be filled out by husbands. Part II is for wives. After both have completed the test, compare answers to each question and count the number on which you agree.

### PART I—*For Husbands Only*

1. Are you as romantic now as you were on your honeymoon? .............. Yes___No___
2. Do you get along amicably with in-laws? .......................... Yes___No___
3. Are you sympathetic to your wife's household problems? ............. Yes___No___
4. Do you put family needs first in budgeting money? .............. Yes___No___
5. Do you believe American women are too domineering? ................ Yes___No___
6. Do you surprise your wife with occasional gifts ..................... Yes___No___
7. Do you put your work or career ahead of your family? ............ Yes___No___

8. If your wife wanted to work, even though it might not be financially necessary, would you agree? ...... Yes____No____

9. Should a husband and wife take separate vacations? ................ Yes____No____

10. Do you make the major decisions in your family? .................... Yes____No____

11. Are you and your wife sexually compatible? ........................ Yes____No____

12. Would you resent it if your wife had friends and interests outside the home? .......................... Yes____No____

13. Do you and your wife agree on how to raise the children? ............. Yes____No____

14. Is planning for the future a family project? ........................ Yes____No____

15. Does your wife strive to keep herself attractive as she was when you were first married? ................... Yes____No____

16. Does your wife show an interest in your work? ...................... Yes____No____

17. Does your wife greet you with a recital of household problems as soon as you come home? ............... Yes____No____

18. Does your wife try to run the house as economically as possible? ....... Yes____No____

19. Do you feel the children take first place in your wife's affections? ..... Yes____No____

20. Does your family take time to renew its spiritual faith? ................ Yes____No____

## Part II—*For Wives Only*

1. Is your husband as romantic as he was during your honeymoon? ...... Yes____No____
2. Does your husband get along amicably with in-laws? .................. Yes____No____
3. Is your husband sympathetic to your problems in running the house? .... Yes____No____
4. Does your husband put family needs first in budgeting money? ......... Yes____No____
5. Does your husband believe American women are too domineering? ...... Yes____No____
6. Does he surprise you with occasional gifts? ......................... Yes____No____
7. Does he put his work or career ahead of the family? .................. Yes____No____
8. If you wanted to go to work, even though it might not be financially necessary, would your husband agree? ......................... Yes____No____
9. Should a wife and husband take separate vacations? ................. Yes____No____
10. Does your husband make the major decisions in the family? .......... Yes____No____
11. Are you and your husband sexually compatible? ................... Yes____No____
12. Would your husband resent it if you had friends and interests outside the family? ........................ Yes____No____
13. Do you agree on how to raise the children? ........................ Yes____No____

14. Is planning for the future a family project? ........................ Yes____No____
15. Do you strive to keep yourself as attractive as you were when you were first married? ........................ Yes____No____
16. Do you show an interest in your husband's work? ........................ Yes____No____
17. Do you greet your husband with a recital of household problems as soon as he comes home? .................. Yes____No____
18. Do you try to run your household as economically as possible? ......... Yes____No____
19. Do the children, rather than your husband, take first place in your affections? ........................ Yes____No____
20. Does your family take time to renew its spiritual faith? ................ Yes____No____

Agreement on fifteen or more indicates that you understand each other's viewpoint remarkably well.

Agreement on ten to fifteen questions suggests that differences of viewpoint exist, but they are likely to be minor.

Agreement on less than ten questions indicates that many major questions in your marriage have been avoided. A frank, calm discussion of these issues can prevent such misconceptions from developing into more serious problems.

## XIII

# Learn to Live with the Spiritual Forces Around You

WHAT WONDERS there are in your mind!

A woman says, "I saw in the paper that so-and-so died of a heart attack."

"What paper?" she is asked.

"I don't know just what paper, but I saw it in the paper." She quotes the item verbatim.

A search of the files of newspapers discloses no such item. Inquiry establishes that the person in question has not had a heart attack. But, three days later, that person dies of heart failure and the newspaper story reads exactly as the woman had quoted it in advance.

And what is this strange power? Precognition.

A little four-year-old girl, during World War I, calls to her mother: "Mommy, Daddy is choking to death! He is down a deep hole!"

Later investigation ascertains that the child's father, at that exact moment, had been down in a cellar under gas attack.

And this is an equally strange power—clairvoyance.

A middle-aged man is driving his car along a New Jersey highway when he feels a terrible pain in his chest. It is so excruciating that he stops his car, thinking he is suffering a heart attack, but eventually it passes.

A few hours later, he learns that his son, driving in Colorado, had been killed at that exact moment, his chest crushed by the wheel of his car.

And this mystic force? Telepathy.

Such phenomena as the foregoing are being investigated by Dr. J. B. Rhine of Duke University, leader in the science of parapsychology, the systematic study of mental activity by means other than the physical senses. What are these things that he describes as precognition, clairvoyance, telepathy? What could they prove? Well, Dr. Rhine believes that these are only some of the powers of the human mind ranging the universe without obstruction of space and time. We mention them here as further evidence of greater capacity within yourself, a capacity that can aid you in living a stronger more effective life.

Now, of course, there are always people who will respond to such phenomena with the flat assertion, "It's impossible." Yet their only reason for saying so is that they have never heard of it before. I met the man who developed the automobile radio. The banker he asked for a loan to finance production told him: "I never heard of such a preposterous idea! There will never be radios in automobiles!" That is how an unimaginative mind often responds to anything that is new.

This author is convinced there is something very great in man that is beyond the physical, beyond the material. We need to see ourselves in vaster relationships in God's great plan. A prominent scientist told me that in higher mathematics if they introduce infinity into the formula it works.

This emphasis on infinity will bring you into closer contact with great forces around you and within you. As you tap these deeper powers you will gain greater victories over the defeated elements in your life.

For example, I have before me a remarkable letter which

illustrates graphically what happens to some people when, through positive thinking, they make contact with the spiritual forces around them.

I was forty-four years old in June. I have been a professional jockey since 1930. The reason for this letter is an incident that happened to me in October, 1956.

I had been a heavy drinker since 1934. In April, 1955, a copy of your book, *The Power of Positive Thinking*, came into my possession. Incidentally, the man who owned the bar where I drank gave the book to me.

I had practically lost my power of concentration, though I had always been able to keep in shape fairly well physically —had to, to ride. It took me three weeks to memorize the 23rd Psalm—so you can see I was pretty far gone.

I bought a Bible and put your theories to work. It was slow work. I couldn't remember what I read, but I kept on reading and praying. Even memorized a few short psalms.

In the meantime, I had practically cut out hard liquor, but hit the beer pretty hard. I didn't get drunk as often, but I still got drunk, and I kept on reading my Bible, drunk, or sober, and praying, too.

By fall of 1956 I had made some progress—nothing startling, but noticeable. This brings me up to the point.

I was riding in a race meeting at Spokane, Washington at the time. I lived in a motel a few miles from the track. One night I went to sleep early. I was awakened by a strange feeling starting in the vicinity of my heart, gradually spreading over my entire body. First, all the tension that had accumulated inside me over the years passed, and was replaced by a great feeling of love. My whole body was aglow. I could see my father and mother beside me. They faded away, and I saw many things. I shed tears of joy and tears of sorrow. I prayed for many people who floated through my mind one after another.

I got up and turned on the light so I could look in the mirror. My skin felt like smooth warm satin. I was shedding tears of ecstasy and then of great sorrow.

When we went to work at the track next morning, people would look at me real puzzled. A few said, "What in the world happened to you?" Most of them were good friends of mine so they didn't say anything more. I felt that I could heal any crippled or lame person by touching them. I stayed in this state of illumination about two weeks, then it diminished and would come and go for short periods at a time. It has never gone away altogether.

Now, here's where you come in. The next day I didn't ride any races, so I stayed at the boss's house and mowed the lawn. Everyone had gone to the races. I went by the side of the garage and sat in the sun. A donkey they had there that I could never get close to at all, walked right up to me and stood there and looked at me a long time. I began to cry, and after awhile I got up and cranked the mower and went to work.

All the time I was in this condition there was great emphasis on the most minute details. After I had finished the lawn, I went in the house and took a bath, and lay down on the sofa. I didn't sleep, but seemed to be in a sort of trance of prayer. There were running through my mind many things. Finally your name came to me. It hit me with great force, not once, but many times, one right after the other, with great emphasis upon each one of your names.

Then a little later I was reciting the 23rd Psalm, and when I would come to the last verse, "Surely goodness and mercy shall follow me all the days of my life; and I shall dwell in the house of the Lord forever," a wondrous burst of happiness came over me, with great emphasis on each and every word. I quit smoking in about ten days. By the first of January I had lost all desire to drink. I haven't smoked or taken a drink of any kind since.

I have met this man personally and found him a quiet and intelligent person. He shows a strong desire to help people and seems to go about doing so in a sensible and creative manner.

What a fabulous world we live in! We are surrounded by strange mystic forces which we have only barely begun to understand, let alone use. This jockey was privileged to know a mystical force, the like of which few experience, especially in such a dramatic form, and his life was remade thereby.

But to some degree, everyone of us may identify ourselves with these tremendous forces. In this chapter I am going to share with you some of the remarkable letters I have received dealing with these great matters. I shall not attempt to interpret these letters, but quote them for you to reflect upon. Those who have had these mystical powers touch their lives have many times found an amazing remedy for frustration, hates, weaknesses, sin, even physical ills. Perhaps the experience of others will be of comfort and strength to you.

The following experience was sent me by a professor at a famous New England College:

> In my student days, I was bothered by occasional headaches which were always relieved when my grandmother, who made her home with my parents, would place her hand on my forehead. Later, when I began teaching at Amherst College, these peculiar headaches continued to trouble me.
>
> One night, in December of my first year there, the pain obliged me to retire earlier than usual. Toward midnight I suddenly felt my grandmother standing beside my bed. She placed her hand on my head and the pain ceased, *never to return.*
>
> There had been no recent letter from my parents so I had not been told of grandmother's sudden illness. It was not until the following day that word was received saying that she had passed on at the very hour when I felt her hand on my

head. I am sure that she thus took the first opportunity to bring me the relief she alone could give.

In a letter written by a reader who lives in Inman, Kansas we are told of an experience that tended to diminish the fear of death.

> This past November 18th, I was stricken by an illness and was taken to the hospital in an unconscious state.
>
> The ambulance driver, afterwards, told me it was a miracle I was still alive as he thought that he hadn't gotten me to the hospital in time.
>
> I experienced a wondrous thing. I saw a bright light and as I came nearer and nearer to it, it was like a beautiful sunrise close by, and as I advanced I saw a wide expanse of water and I stood by the edge of the water, finally just looking across at this beautiful light. Then I turned and saw it was such a long way back to the place where I had started.

Is this type of experience unique? By no means. In my files are scores of similar accounts, all pointing to the possibility that death is not the dread terror we think it is. It, too, is surely governed by the amazing forces all around us.

A national magazine ran a remarkable article called, "How Does it Feel to Die?" The article consists of a series of nine statements by eminent doctors on the nature of death. Sir William Osler, the famous physician, once made the statement, "Most human beings not only die like heroes, but in my wide clinical experience, die really without pain or fear. There is as much oblivion about the last hours as about the first and therefore people fill their minds with spectres that have no reality."

Kate Holliday, the author of this article, asked the nine doctors whether they agreed with Sir William's statement and the amazing thing is that not one of the doctors disagreed. "Nature is good to the human race," said Dr. Frank Adair, Associate Professor of Clinical surgery, Cornell University Medical College. "The haunting fear which the average person carries all through life is dissipated by the approach of death."

And Dr. H. D. Van Fleet, President of the Los Angeles Academy of Medicine, says, "I have sat with dying men of every race and creed—Hindus, Shintoists, Catholics, Protestants, Jews and Mohammedans. They die in peace and I have found that the sweetness of death is intensified in all men by a childlike faith in their religion. Except for their own interpretation of religion, what men cling to is the same throughout the world."

Dr. Johannes Neilsen, Associate Clinical Professor of Medicine at the University of Southern California says, "People who dread death do so because they imagine they're going to be snuffed out of life suddenly. That isn't the way it is at all. As you become more and more ill, whether it is from anemia or cancer or even accident, you become more and more absorbed with the problem of the moment, the condition of your own body. Even doctors who are dying experience this. Their circle of interest grows smaller until they are concerned only with the immediate challenge, until life at last is merely a question of whether or not they will breathe again. And when the circle becomes too small, they go to heaven . . . The circle, in other words, has drawn in to such a degree that even fear is shut out. When you meet eternity all trivialities, even fear, fade into nothing."

So, it would seem from Kate Holliday's research that the fear of death is not as realistic as we have supposed. It is acute to us in the fullness of life, but in sickness and disability the world recedes and God provides a blessed anesthetic for the mind and spirit. The final end is not a painful experience, nor a frightening one, though the illnesses preceding death may be painful indeed. The fears which we attach to death are strongest while we are still very much alive and healthy. But when people approach the experience itself and are weak and ill, it seems that life constricts, ordinary concerns lose their value and death itself becomes so natural that it no longer frightens.

Who knows how near those on the other side may be to us. Readers almost shyly tell how departed loved ones seem to brush their lives for what reason we cannot know. But it does suggest that great and good forces are around us. Some years ago I was driving with my wife from Asbury Park, New Jersey to New York City. At Asbury Park I had attended an auction of household furnishings from an estate called Shadow Lawn, made famous as the summer White House of President Woodrow Wilson. I purchased a pair of beautiful hurricane lamps. While I got them at a bargain price, still I paid a rather good sum for them and perhaps felt a bit guilty. But since they were intended as a birthday gift for my wife, Ruth, I thought the expenditure justified. They were packed and put into the luggage compartment of the car and we started for home.

Midway on the trip we stopped at a Howard Johnson roadside restaurant for lunch. The place was crowded but we got two stools at the counter. I finished first and to give someone else a seat, I told Ruth I would wait for her at the car.

As I stepped into the brilliant sunshine outside, I suddenly had an overwhelming sense of my mother's presence. She had crossed to the other side several years before. I felt rather than saw her smile, and sensed her warm loving personality as distinctly as any feeling I have ever had. Then came the sound of her voice with all the old time familiarity and strength. She said something about Ruth being a wonderful girl and that she deserved those beautiful hurricane lamps and not to worry about things, but be happy and keep on doing good. Then it all faded but I was stirred and moved to the depths of my being. I stood speechless and totally unconscious of surroundings except for a sharp clear beauty in everything.

I wept and believe me I am not the weeping kind. I hurried to the car and when Ruth found me, she was shocked to find me weeping and unable to talk. We drove for several miles before I recovered myself and told her the story. Why should my mother have contacted me at such a time and place and about a seemingly trivial matter? Who knows the logic of the amazing forces around us. That we were together in that vibrant moment, personally I have no doubt, and from this meeting I have drawn a strange peace and strength.

Such things are not uncommon and there is certainly no need to be reticent about relating these experiences. I had a letter from Mrs. Mark Clark, the wife of the famous World War II general. In part it read:

> On many occasions I have heard my grandmother and mother relate the story of the death of the former's twenty-five year old son, Elmer.
>
> Elmer had typhoid fever and in 1900 that was often fatal. A twin sister, Eva, to whom Elmer was devoted, had died two years previously with the same disease.
>
> For many days my uncle had been in a coma, too weak to move. Suddenly he sat up straight in bed with arms extended to the heavens, his face radiant with happiness and cried out in a firm clear voice, "Eva"—then he died.

Cecil B. DeMille told a wonderful little story of an experience which gave him insight into the nature of life and death and life again. "I was up on a lake in the Maine woods. The canoe was drifting. I was reading, resting, searching for an idea. I looked down in the water, for my little craft had drifted where the lake was only about four-inches deep. There in a world of mud and wet, were water beetles.

"One crawled up on the gunwale, stuck the talons on his legs into the woodwork and died. I let it alone and turned to my reading. The sun was hot. In about three hours I noticed my water beetle again. He was parched. His back was cracking open. I watched, and out of the back of that dead beetle I saw crawling a new form—a moist head—then wings. A most beautiful dragonfly. It scintillated all the colors of the rainbow. As I sat watching, it flew. It flew farther in a second than the water beetle had crawled in days. It hovered above the surface, just a few inches from the water beetles beneath. They did not know it was there.

"I took my fingertips and moved the shriveled water beetle husk from the canoe's gunwale. It fell back into the lake and sank down to the mud-covered bottom.

"The other water beetles crawled awkwardly to see what it was.

"It was a dead body. They backed away from it.

"If God does that for a water beetle, don't you believe He will do it for me?" asked Cecil B. DeMille,

This is a sound description, to my way of thinking, of the nature of death. Death is simply a change, not an ending, and that we shall emerge into a better form of life it seems logical to assume.

All of the experiences related to me, dealing with extra sensory phenomena, seem to stress continuity.

On May 2, 1914, our beloved mother was dying. She was in a weakened physical condition due to diabetes. She had not gotten up since May 1st and gradually sank into a coma.

Father was sitting at the head of the bed, holding his

opened-face watch in one hand, his fingers on mother's pulse with the other. I was gone from the room for a few minutes, leaving my sister standing at the foot of mother's bed. As I came from the hallway to the open doorway, facing the foot of the bed, I stopped suddenly, in astonishment at what I saw —then I slowly walked to the bed and stood silently beside my sister at its foot—to the end. I never mentioned to her what I had seen lest she imagine she saw the same thing. I wanted her to tell *me*.

Two weeks after mother was buried, my sister and I were quietly sitting on the porch, occasionally speaking. After some time she spoke, saying: "I saw the strangest, most unusual thing as we stood at the foot of mother's bed shortly before the end came." I did not interrupt her. When she had finished I said: "Yes, I saw the same. I have waited for you to tell me." The following is what we saw:

Directly over and about nine or so inches above mother was a thin sheet of grayish-blue mist, the color one sometimes sees at twilight in the mountains. This mist, side edges blending into the air like a water color painting, was very slowly moving from foot to head; as it moved upward, the bottom edge was even—straight as this paper's edge.

Mother's gown was open carelessly at the neck to several inches on her chest. The flesh seen *through* the mist was the color of life, but as the mist passed upward, over her flesh, the color was of death, both colors visible in passing.

Just as the mist passed over her head, father, eyes never raised from his watch, fingers yet on her pulse, said sadly: "Mother has gone." The mist vanished immediately into the atmosphere of the room. No outside door nor window was open. We two saw her life pass from her visibly.

These two women believe that they "saw her life pass from her visibly," as if the life itself were a separate entity that continued outside of the body. The incident seems to indicate that death is a passing of the personality or soul from one state into another.

The scores of experiences which have been told to me indicate further that the change in life called death is not without beauty. Always the spiritual forces around us seem to be concerned for us.

A reader from Stratford, Connecticut, wrote me about an incident related by a medical doctor. A woman had been hit by a car and lay by the roadside. Those who gathered thought she was dead. When the ambulance came bringing the doctor, he knelt and lifted the woman's head. She opened her eyes and asked if he was the doctor. When he replied that he was she said, "Well, I want to tell you to tell all my friends; if this is dying, it is the most beautiful experience I ever went through," and with that she dropped her head back and she died.

God has built into us the will to live and the love of life. It is our nature to resist the death of the body to the very last. But can we not believe that God has also arranged our lives so that when they are finished in this world, they shall pass into a better place. Those who live with God in this life need have no fear of the next one. This is the testimony of the hundreds of sincere people who have described their experiences, in one form or another, as to the spiritual forces around us.

Such experiences are related to me with great frequency and they invariably are reported as having aspects of beauty. For instance here is a letter from a lady who lives in Hamilton, Ohio.

> When I was twelve, a simple tonsil operation touched off terrible hemorrhages. In those days transfusions were seldom given and I was already home from the clinic. My mind was clear; and since children seem singularly unafraid of such occasions, I only wished the ordeal were over.
>
> I saw that my mother's face was gray as she brought more basins; the doors of my bedroom were filling up with people,

even Grandma had managed to get up the stairs. . . . Suddenly they were all gone, and I was alone. I was standing in a dark corridor, unafraid, just hesitating. In the darkness of it, at times, people would brush against me, rushing forward, together, to the end of the corridor, where shone a wondrous light, more bright than any I had ever known. They were all happy people.

I went forward a little, until I could see "outside." No crowds, only a beautiful field of great white daisies, shining under a radiant sky, and in the field a little girl, smaller than I, was sitting and picking the flowers.

All my short life, since a visit to an uncle's farm, I, a city girl, had always thought a field of daisies shimmering on a breeze-swept hill under a bright sky was the most beautiful thing I had ever seen. I knew for certain the daisies were for me; and the brightness of all that lay beyond that corridor, beyond that hill, was mine.

Then, like a curtain dropped against the light, the words came: "Mama needs me." I shall not trouble you with why I believed this, but it was so. . . . I woke, to find my head cradled on my mother's breast; she was softly calling me, over and over again. In the ensuing days, I alone was sure that I would get well.

Such experiences may offer some hint of the nature of life on the other side. And note that they are vivid and bright and joyous experiences without exception. Do they provide a glimpse of reality that is usually known only after death?

Extra-sensory perception must be another of God's kindly gifts supplying occasional glimpses into the true nature of reality. There is something extra wonderful that is just beyond our usual mortal reach but which can effect our lives even so. It is given to us only in flashes and in fragments of insight to remind us that while we are physical beings in a mortal world, we are also part of a greater world.

Do we understand these mystic laws? Not as yet. We do

not even understand to any great extent the physical laws which surround us, much less these profounder spiritual laws. C. B. Colby writing in the White Plains *Reporter Dispatch* posed the following question:

> Have you ever wondered what ultimately becomes of the waves that radio and TV stations send out into space twenty-four hours a day? Do they fade and vanish, or do they keep going forever? We do know that sometimes pictures appear mysteriously, long after a program has finished. One of the most famous of all such weird happenings was in England in September, 1953.
>
> Suddenly in many parts of England television screens blossomed out with the identification card and call letters of TV station KLEE in Houston, Texas. Even today transatlantic programming is but a dream, so several viewers took pictures of the image to prove the happening.
>
> What really startled the TV world was the fact that when British broadcasting engineers advised KLEE in Houston of the unusual event, they were told that the station had been off the air since 1950. No KLEE identification card had been shown for the past three years.
>
> Where had that picture been for three years? Why did it appear only in England and how did it get back from wherever it had been? Does make you wonder, doesn't it?

We are surrounded by phenomena—even physical phenomena—which we cannot easily explain. And strange happenings give hints of a fantastic world of spirit in which we are doubtless nearer to the true realities of our universe and which also defy explanation. What, for example, is the relationship of those on the other side to our lives? Do they sometimes draw near in strange and wonderful ways to help us?

Over the years many instances have been reported which

suggest the protecting and supporting aid of the strange forces about us. From a practical point of view it bears out our conviction that the broader life in which we dwell will undergird us with extra power if we go confidently about our duty.

Dr. Smiley Blanton gave me a letter from an enthusiastic reader of his fascinating new book *Now or Never.* This reader tells of a controversy in a community meeting years ago in which the local Episcopal minister opposed an action which was violently advocated by a rough sort of man named Sam ——. When the vote was taken the minister's position was sustained. Enraged, Sam shouted, "I'll kill you for this!"

Since this man's character was known to be violent, some men said to the minister, "We will walk home with you for you have to pass that lonely wood lot and we aren't too sure Sam won't try to carry out his threat."

But the minister said no, he would go without them as he was never alone . . . there was Someone who would watch over him.

A number of years later the minister was called to Sam's deathbed. He said, "Reverend, there is something I must confess before I die. You remember the night I swore I'd kill you? Well, I intended to and I waited for you in the wood lot with a bar in my hand."

The minister asked, "Why didn't you, Sam?"

Sam looked at the pastor in surprise, "How could I with those two big men on each side of you?"

There is no magic in the universe. But God is there and His powers are vast indeed. We have long since learned and accepted that fact in the world of materiality. What men once called "miracles" are now everyday facts. No wonders of any kind astonish us, for so many wonders occur almost daily in the realm of science.

Why, then, should we doubt the workings of a whole world of phenomena in the psychic sphere? That isn't miraculous either, for without doubt it will be found to be operating according to law. This is a law abiding universe. We call a phenomenon a miracle until we understand its relationship to law. Instances such as I cite are not presented as bizarre curiosities but are given to indicate that, as spiritual beings in a spiritual universe, we are related to immense forces which we do not comprehend. Their meaning is that, if we live normal humble lives, walking by faith, living in unbroken contact with God, we shall be strangely supported all our days.

Then, by the same forces, we shall enter into that even larger life, which impinges on this one so closely, which we call the eternal. We cannot separate mortal life from eternal life. Eternity means all of time. We are in eternity now. When mortality ends, immortality begins; but there is no break in the flow of time.

The mortal is only an aspect of the spiritual. The body is but a temporary tool of the real person, who is spirit.

Dr. J. B. Rhine cites many cases of psychical phenomena bearing on this matter, for example, this from a school teacher:

It occurred in the first school where I taught. I was then just eighteen and doing my practice teaching. There was a young lad (he was fourteen) who insisted on knowing where I was going to teach. I didn't know at the time. He made it very emphatic on several occasions that no matter where I taught, he was going to my school and no other.

I was seated at my desk shortly after our afternoon studies began when a voice said "Hello, Miss Long." Glancing up, I saw him standing there, smiling at me, hat in hand, holding onto the door. "I told you that no matter where you taught I was going to your school and here I am." Pleased as well as startled I smiled back, exclaiming, "Truman, how did you get here?" He replied, "Oh, I just came. Where can I sit?"

I was aware of the dead silence in the room and every pupil seemed frozen in their places, mingled emotions stamped on their faces, all eyes watching me. Ready to reply I noticed that instead of a solid substance, as he had first appeared, the figure was fading and I could see the details of the room through him. Shaken, I, who hadn't thought of him before, couldn't get this out of my mind.

A few days later a letter from my mother telling of Truman's sudden death made me have the creeps. He had been only slightly ill for a few days and his mother was planning on sending him to school the next day. He had been downstairs eating his noon lunch. At 1:30, the time I saw his apparition, as he started to go back upstairs he collapsed and died, hanging on the stair post.

Such phenomena are remarkable in that they are repeated with frequency and similarity of detail. That they indicate a world beyond our senses seems not unreasonable. And since every phenomenon in God's created universe is intelligent and purposive we cannot but feel that we are related to these amazing powers, that their values may contribute to man's well-being.

Dr. Rhine, in his collection of experiences of pre-recognition, tells the startling story of a Los Angeles streetcar motorman who dreamed one night that he was driving over a new route. As he passed a streetcar coming from the opposite direction, a green truck shot across the tracks. In his dream, his streetcar struck the truck; two men were killed instantly and a woman was badly injured. "You could have prevented it!" the woman screamed at him. He saw that her eyes were bright blue.

The next morning the motorman reported for work, still musing over his dream. "I'm giving you Jim's route this morning," the dispatcher said to him. "He's just phoned in sick." As the motorman drove over the new route he suddenly became aware that it was the very route of his dream. He broke out in a cold sweat. Then he saw a streetcar coming toward him. Instinctively, he slammed on his brakes. At that moment a green truck shot from a side street and darted across the tracks. The streetcar squealed to a halt, missing the truck by inches. In it were two men and a woman. As they passed close to him, the woman's bright blue eyes caught his. She said nothing, but slowly closed her thumb and forefinger in the familiar gesture of "okay."

These experiences would seem to indicate that our usual concepts of time and place are not based on total reality. There are, apparently, other ways of receiving knowledge than through ordinary sensory reactions. One of the top technical experts in the United States, Charles F. Kettering, said that a great mistake of education today is that it does not place sufficient emphasis upon intuitive knowledge. He cited the case of a professor of organic chemistry at Darmstadt about one hundred years ago. This professor had a dream or vision in which he saw the complete atomic structure of a molecule of hexametabenzene. He wrote it down, but he died with people still ridiculing it.

In a research laboratory only recently, a scientist took a picture of a molecule of hexametabenzene. And there, precisely as the professor had seen it by pre-cognitive insight one hundred years ago, to the exact detail, was the outline of its atomic structure!

We seem to be part of some immense spiritual mechanism which, occasionally, in spite of ourselves, we grapple with. A practicing neuropsychiatrist in New York City, Dr. Russell G. MacRobert, wrote an article called, "Science Studies Intuition," for *Tomorrow* magazine. In it Dr. MacRobert said:

The following experience occurred to a woman in April, 1949, while she was being given gas anesthesia in the office of a prominent New York dentist. The patient had a dream under the anesthetic and when she awakened she was very upset. In her dream she saw her friend, Mrs. Manuel Quezon, widow of the first President of the Philippines, ambushed and murdered on a lonely mountain road near Manila, half-way around the world. Allowing for the difference in time between New York and Manila, the dream occurred ten hours before the same crime was actually committed—a very ample margin of knowing beforehand as well as seeing something true at a distance without the eyes.

Weird [concluded the dentist's report to me] especially coming from a very intelligent, two-feet-on-the-ground type of person.

That's the kind of report that makes one pause. And note, these experiences do not necessarily come to the spiritualist; often as not they are experienced by the most conservative personalities. And sometimes they are extremely well documented. One of the editors of our own *Guideposts* magazine happened to be in Boston a few hours after the occurrence of an amazing example of mental telepathy. This editor himself interviewed the people involved, cross-examining them carefully for any possibility of intentional or accidental "exaggeration," and came away convinced that he had just seen a genuine illustration of the fact that the human mind is capable of mysterious extensions of itself. This is the story:

On the afternoon of June 14, 1955, Thomas Whittaker, a welder from Boston, got a sudden and strong hunch. He had the feeling that something was wrong. He didn't know what it was, but he sensed it so strongly that he quit work and got into his car and just started driving. At various stop-lights along the way, he tried to turn his car toward his own home, but the intuition kept him from doing so. Time after time instead of turning toward home, he turned toward Washington Street where his company was also doing some work.

"This is ridiculous," he kept telling himself. "That Washington Street job has been suspended." But he kept edging toward the area just the same.

It's a good thing that he did. When he finally got there, he looked down into a fourteen-foot deep trench that had been dug down the center of the street, and there in the bottom, he saw a cave-in. The sides of the trench had collapsed. And projecting out of the tons of dirt, sand and debris, was a human hand!

Whittaker jumped down into the trench and tried to claw away the dirt with his own hands. He dug down deep enough to uncover a wrist watch, and immediately he recognized it as belonging to his best friend and boss, John H. Sullivan, owner of the Stoneham Welding Service. The hand moved. Frantic now, Whittaker scrambled to the top of the trench and called for the fire and police to help dig Sullivan out of the hole.

Several hours later, safe, if not entirely sound after his ordeal of being buried alive, John Sullivan told the *Guidepost* editor how he had decided to go, alone, to the Washington Street job to finish up some work, and how the sides of the trench had suddenly given way. He was buried. The only thing that saved him from immediate suffocation was the fact that he had on his welder's mask, and inside of it there had been captured enough air to keep him alive until help came.

Had he called for help? Indeed he had. At first he called out loud, and then, when it became clear that that would do no good, he began sending out mental distress signals like an S.O.S. "God send someone," he prayed. "God send someone. God send someone." Over and over again he said these words. And it was while he was thus praying that Tommy Whittaker began to get his strong urge to visit the Washington Street scene. It seems logical to assume that John Sullivan called Tommy Whittaker to his aid by means that are not usually available.

What has all this got to do with everyday life?

Perhaps some day it will be possible for us to bring these spiritual processes under control for the use of mankind, just as we have controlled natural processes the very thought of which our forefathers regarded as miraculous, even ridiculous. Whoever thought that man would fly or send pictures through the air? The Creator placed these powers in the world for man to find and use for his betterment.

Apparently these strange forces around us have been known and used for centuries. For example, in the writings of the early Spanish explorers and adventurers who fought the South American Inca Indians, there are strange reports that indicate the Incas knew the secret of controlling mental telepathy. The Spanish armies would move out on a secret expedition only to discover that the Incas knew exactly when they were leaving, with how many troops, and with what intent. It drove the Spanish mad. There was no evidence of drums, or smoke signaling or of any other form of physical transmission of information. The Spanish concluded that the Incas had the secret of passing information to each other through a form of telepathy.

But even if the day of our practical use of such phenomena should be far off, we cannot avoid the belief that man will become ultimately master of forces in the psychic realm as he is in the material. This is an amazing world God has set us in. It is a world that is ruled by physical laws which are being used in ways almost incredible, as for example outer space exploration. But also around us and within us are spiritual laws which are hardly being used at all in comparison with potential possibility.

We are part of an alive, vibrant universe where the true reality is spirit. When we learn to live in harmony with this spirit, and catch its rhythm, then we will be in tune with power as never before. The end result will be to bring us closer to God and to the exciting knowledge that our existence with Him is not tied to the physical world but to a far greater spiritual world. We shall find that we are part of His immortal spirit and thus are greater and more important than we think. It will make us know that the Lord does not intend us to be weak or little or defeated but to walk the earth in the power of God's great spirit.

You and I have the power to live truly great lives. The strange and powerful forces all about us and within us were surely designed by God to enable His children to master life rather than to be mastered by it. And these forces are infinitely greater than all our weaknesses and sins, our fears, hates and inferiorities.

The power to live with joy and victory is available to you and to me. This power can lead you to a solution of your problems, help you to meet your difficulties successfully and fill your mind and heart with peace and contentment.

The life which the Good God created for us is not little and mean and limited. It is big and beautiful and unlimited. Its possibilities are boundless.

XIV

# You Can Become Strongest in Your Weakest Place

You can become strongest in your weakest place. That is a fact of vast importance to you, to me, to everyone. Repeat that amazing statement aloud, allowing it to sink deeply into consciousness. It is absolutely true—you can become strongest in your weakest place.

That people can become altogether different—strong where they were weak, right where they were wrong, is demonstrated by the experience of a twenty-year-old boy. From his letter it seems he had been a "delinquent," but he is certainly that no longer. Read his letter:

> I have just read your book *The Power of Positive Thinking*. It has made a new man out of me. I am only twenty years old, but I never realized how badly I have wasted those years. All I have ever done with my life is try to be bad, such as fighting, drinking and swearing, because all my friends did it. But I see now how mistaken I have been and I have really been trying your ideas. They have done wonders for me. I have quit smoking and drinking and looking for fights. I have stopped hanging around with people that do those things. I have turned to sports which I greatly enjoy, but best of all I have started going to church again because I have learned to believe in God.

> I have found a girl friend that really loves me and we believe in the same things. She is a good girl, not like the girls I have known before. I have learned love and respect with her help, which is something I never had much of, for anyone but myself, before. And I am making more and more friends because I am using your ideas. Truly I have never been happier in my whole life than I have been since reading your book.

Many people have demonstrated in various ways how you can become strongest in your weakest place. There was Glenn Cunningham, whose legs were so badly burned as a child that he was told he would not walk again. But he became one of the fastest Olympic milers in history.

Glenn Cunningham told me that faith and positive thinking are 85 per cent of an athlete's success; in other words, believing that you can do it. "You have to perform on three levels," he explained, "physical, mental and spiritual. And the spiritual helps you to draw on power from the Master to help pull you through. And," he added, "I don't believe there is such a thing as an impossibility."

Paul Anderson was a sickly, puny weakling. In back of his house in Tacoma, Georgia, he constructed a homemade weight-lifting outfit. It consisted of blacksmith weights tied on the end of a stick. Paul Anderson became the strongest man in the world, breaking strength records that had stood for decades.

Positive thinking looks upon weak places in people as challenging opportunities. You can turn them into your strongest points. The process of so doing is somewhat like that of welding. If a piece of metal breaks and is welded together, the weld is stronger than the metal which surrounds it. At the point of intense heat the molecular structure of the metal flows together.

A cabinet maker once told me that when two pieces of

wood are reversed and glued together under heat, the wood will crack elsewhere before it will break at the glued point. This same process can, and often does, take place in personality. Through the intense application of right thinking and strong faith, a weakness can actually become one's strongest point.

Well then, how do we go about turning a weak point into a strong point? The following six-point formula has been used most successfully.

1. Isolate your weakness; then study and know it thoroughly. Plan a real campaign against it.
2. Precisely specify the strength results you wish to attain.
3. Picture or visualize yourself as becoming strongest at your weakest point.
4. Immediately start *becoming* the strong person you wish to be.
5. Act as though you are strongest where you have been weakest.
6. Ask God to help you and believe that He does.

This formula was developed by H. C. Mattern, one of the most thoroughgoing positive thinkers I have known. H. C. Mattern himself is an example of how a man can change a serious weakness into real strength. He was thoroughly negative, in fact so negative that on a balmy night some years ago he walked into a lonely meadow on Long Island and tried to commit suicide. Life was worthless. There was no hope left. He had with him a vial of poison. He lifted it to his lips, drank it and slumped to the ground.

The next thing he knew he was opening his eyes and staring with astonishment into a moonlit sky. At first he wondered whether he were dead. He never did know why he did not die. He always believed, simply, that God wanted him to do a job in life. When he realized that he was still alive, suddenly he wanted very much to live. He thanked God for having spared him and dedicated himself to a life of helping other people.

Mattern became a unique positive thinker. He made it his whole mission in life to encourage others.

What weakness do *you* want to conquer? Is it fear? Anger? Hurt feelings? Inferiority? Disappointment? Is liquor your weakness? Or women? Whatever it may be, one thing is sure, it does not need to keep on defeating you. Remember this powerful fact; you can become strongest in your weakest place.

Let us look at some examples of people who have turned weakness into strength.

This letter is from a young man who lives in New Mexico.

Dear Dr. Peale:

I don't know how to start this letter. I live on a ranch here in New Mex. For the last ten years I have spent most of my time in bars and night spots. And I was getting in bad shape. I have tried three times to kill myself. I had no friends of my own. And no girl would have anything to do with me. And I don't blame them. I have no one to blame but myself.

But things have changed for me now. I was in Lubbock, Texas, to see my brother. Him and his wife left me there one night to take care of their kids so they could go to the show.

While the kids were asleep, I went into the bedroom to see how they were. On the floor was two of your books about positive thinking. I picked them up and looked at them. I went back in the living room and sat down.

Began reading them. I had found what I was looking for. A new life. I have been without God for a long time. I have now been going to church every Sunday and Bible Class every Wednesday night. The people here in town sure have changed toward me now. I have lots of friends, new ones. But I lost a lot of my old bar buddies. They think I've lost my mind. I just wish and pray that they could follow me and find what I have—a new life. Without God's help I could not have done it. And I have you to thank, too.

I still don't have a girl friend, but I understand that now. Because here in the Southwest a ranch hand or cowboy isn't too well liked. I don't have too much school, but I am not going to let it get me down. If I live by God's way, which I will, there will be a home for me up there if I cannot have it here on earth—because I have faith and believe and have confidence in myself and God. Be content with what you have, for he has said, "I will never fail you nor forsake you." I carry these books with me all the time. Never a day goes by that I do not learn a verse from one of them.

I am thirty-two years old. I am sending a picture of me taken here on the ranch last summer. I am so happy I had to write this letter to let you know what your books have done for me. I will close this letter. And pray for me.

P.S. Please overlook my writing. I don't know how to spell very good. I have to write with pencil. I make mistakes. I have to cross out a lot.

The life of this young man was transformed by a sudden exposure of his mind to the power of God through positive, creative ideas. If a person has a weakness which he wants to get under control and seemingly cannot, but is willing to take into his mind the best positive ideas, he will find that the power of such ideas to affect his life is amazing indeed. This explains many of the dramatic changes that happen to people through religious faith. A new and powerful thought has burst into the mind, shattering old weaknesses, breaking them to bits. It is in the mental processes that all motivation changes take place. The phrase "a change of heart" really means a profound change of mind. The heart is only a muscle to pump blood. It is the mind that accepts the new concept that changes. And faith is an idea so powerful that it can set the entire life going in a new direction with new and amazingly increased strength.

This is why you should read the Bible, the most powerful accumulation of life changing thoughts ever assembled. This is why you should go regularly to church and hear the great words, the words of God which, if received deeply into your mind, have the power to change your life. Dynamic, powerful, positive thoughts take a bold step forward in the conquering of an individual weakness.

Some time ago I was lecturing in Los Angeles when I ran across a most interesting example of a young lady who was ruining her life by the use of the wrong kind of words—words as symbols of a destructive idea. If you constantly use negative or deprecatory words about yourself, you are implanting equivalent destructive concepts in your mind.

On this particular day, after my lecture, I was at the front of the auditorium greeting quite a number of people. In this line was an attractive young lady who took my hand with a timid little shake and greeted me with this shocking sentence.

"I so much wanted to speak to you," she said. "But of course I'm a nobody. You wouldn't know me. I don't amount to anything, but I have read your books and I just wanted to shake your hand."

I say this statement was shocking, for it minimized and depreciated God's highest form of creation, a human being.

I was a little tired of hearing so many people say they were "nobodies." It happens time and again across the country that people speak this way of themselves. So I stopped this young lady and said, "Miss Nobody, will you do me a favor? Will you please wait until I am through here . . . I'd like to talk with you." A little later I turned and found that sure enough she was there waiting.

"Now, Miss Nobody," I said. "I'd like a few words with you."

The girl laughed. "What did you call me?" she asked.

"Miss Nobody," I said. "Because that is what you called yourself. Do you have some other name?"

She said yes and gave me her proper name.

"Just why did you tell me you are a Nobody?" I continued. "You say you've read about positive thinking, but you evidently haven't gotten very much out of it, else you'd never think of yourself as Miss Nobody. These books are designed to make people realize who and what they really are. Now, obviously, you have been telling not only others, but what is more serious, you tell yourself that you do not amount to much of anything. But I can see that you are wrong for, obviously, you have many qualities which are admirable. Certainly you are attractive. You have a good, clear eye. You know how to dress well. You have a charming smile. I think you are a very fine person and I don't think you should be carrying around a 'nobody' complex."

This young lady and I talked for some time about her ambitions and hopes and about the fact that it is very important not to weight these hopes down with negative thoughts. Her weak spot was a deep-seated "nobody complex" and she was compounding the difficulty with negative words. The cure for her situation was a reversal of the concept of herself.

I gave her the formula for overcoming her weakness and told her how to apply. I also suggested that she use the following affirmation: "I am the temple of God. In God I live and move and have my being. I am a child of God. I will think and act like a child of God."

She agreed to say this affirmation a dozen times every day and at the same time to visualize herself as being as the words describe. Months later, when I was again in California on a speaking engagement, an attractive young lady appeared before me and said, "You used to know me, but you don't now." That was an unusual thing to say and I turned to look carefully. To my astonishment who should it be but "Miss Nobody." "I have found that I can do things," she continued. "I have gotten out of that awful habit of thinking of myself as a Nobody and I just wanted to thank you for helping me change my identity."

As we talked it became very clear that she had, indeed, changed noticeably. Here was a girl who overcame a weakness through the use of positive ideas. She had become strongest in her weakest place; she had had a depreciatory and inferior attitude toward herself.

This self-depreciatory weakness is one that a great many face under the name of inferiority. Such feelings of inferiority can be extremely painful and self-defeating. Believe me, I know from hard, personal experience. When I was a boy I was what they used to call "bashful." That word isn't used much any more, but under whatever name, the feeling of being abashed by life is certainly painful. And the trouble is very widepsread judging from the number of letters I receive on this subject. Here is one, for example:

Dear Dr. Peale,

I have been wanting to write to you for a long time. I surely do need help, but do not know if anyone can help me or not.

This is my problem. My husband is custodian of our church and I assist him, but I do not feel accepted among the women. Many times when I go to church I sit alone. The women will come in and sit in front of me or behind, but not in the pew with me unless all the others are filled up.

We do not dress as well as they do and I think the main reason is because I am not as bright as they are. I am quiet and sometimes say things that I should not and I do not mean it the way it sounded.

The women do not have me work with them in sewing or anything they do in groups. I have volunteered my services, but they say they are saving me for a time when I am needed. Still I hear them asking others to help.

My relatives seem to be ashamed of me or something. They do not introduce me to their friends or do not care to have me go to church with them. We have lived here in this community for a year and only one neighbor has been in.

I surely would appreciate it if I could learn how to be accepted among the women and have friends.

This is a typical letter showing tragic glimpses into the suffering of men and women who have become victims of the feelings of inadequacy. Very often (and I think this was true of the custodian's wife) these painful weaknesses are self-imposed. Notice in the above letter that this woman puts herself into a position where she asks to be hurt. She deliberately arrives in the church early, sits in the pew where people will either have to say to her, symbolically, "I like you" or "I do not like you." Now, the mathematics of the situation are very much against her. If one hundred people came to the church, only two can sit next to her and ninety-eight have to sit somewhere else. But she interprets the action of each of the ninety-eight as being against her.

Why is it that so many people actually seek out this feeling of inferiority? Psychologists tell me that one of the most common weaknesses of personality is that people often *do not want to succeed!* Somewhere along the line they have learned that it is a dangerous thing to succeed as it imposes upon them the burden of responsibility to live up to a success status. So they deliberately, though unconsciously, seek ways to keep themselves inferior by emphasizing their weaknesses.

Now it is a fact of life that each person is made up of stronger and weaker areas of personality. The question is, which are you going to dwell on? Which are you going to emphasize? If you specialize on the weaker areas in your personality you will become weak; if you stress the stronger areas you will become strong. It is as simple and certain as that.

But we must be careful not to confuse real weaknesses with self-assumed ones. Learning to accept ourselves is the first step in overcoming the weakness of inadequacy. Most of us, at least those of us who are troubled with the inferiority complex, pay far too much attention to ourselves, to our self-assumed weaknesses and drawbacks. We become self-conscious about things which are not important. We feel that everyone is noticing them when in reality they are not.

Not long ago I had an unusual opportunity to test this theory. I had been receiving a great deal of mail from people all saying the same, pathetically inferior thing: "No one likes me because of this or that."

One girl was ashamed because she was too fat; another because she was too thin. One boy felt that his ears were too big; another that his ears hugged his head too closely. Still another boy was self-conscious because he was too tall and another had painful inferiority feelings because he was short. I even recall one letter from a young girl who complained that she was too pretty. Nobody liked her for herself, but only for her body.

Now it happened that one of these typical complaints came to me from a young boy in our city. "Dr. Peale," he said, "nobody likes me because my nose is too big."

I had heard so much of this sort of thing that I decided then and there to make an experiment. "Name six of your acquaintances who do not like you because your nose is too big," I said to this boy. He gave me six names and a little later I took the time to place a call to each of these young people. As soon as I got them on the phone I asked them to name the outstanding characteristic of this young man's personality. Each one had to think a while, but this was the result of my inquiry. One told me it was his friendliness; another that he was unusually good in arithmetic. A girl said he was a marvelous dancer. And so it went. Not *one* of these people signaled out this boy's nose as his outstanding characteristic. Apparently no one but he himself had any consciousness of that nose.

So it is true that many of us pick out some little characteristic which we consider to be a weakness and spend a great deal of effort convincing ourselves that *because of this weakness we cannot succeed.* The solution of the problem lies in realizing that God intends you to be a happy, successful, strong person. You must decide whether you will emphasize your weak points or your strong points, for you have both. The choice is up to you. Just as soon as you start emphasizing your strengths, your inferiority will diminish and a new sense of capacity will replace your old weakness and inadequacy.

Let us take a look at another common weakness and at solutions that were found; and this weakness is that of discouragement. So many times discouragement spells the difference between success and failure. If only you had carried on a little bit longer! Or harder! But discouragement made you give up just short of something really great. How tragic to quit when one more extra push would have brought success.

The fact of ups and downs is something we have to deal with in life. But positive thinking handles that problem. My friend Frank W. Kridel, General Manager of the great Manhattan and Astor hotels in New York, is a good example of the power of positive thinking in meeting potential discouragement. Referring to the helpfulness of prayer and guidance in practical problems, he said, "It is terrific how the whole pattern has worked out. And we've had some tough problems too, but it's a fact that when you trust God and keep plugging, while you have your ups and downs, with positive thinking you can turn your downs into ups." What a tremendous truth: "You can turn your downs into ups." That is to say, we must know how to turn our negatives into positives.

It is in problems of difficulty and discouragement that positive thinking has had some of its most amazing results. Another friend of mine, Ruth Hardy, also a hotel proprietor, runs the Ingleside Inn in Palm Springs, California. This is a little gem of a place set amidst lush gardens of bougainvillea, orchid bushes, palm and orange trees. Nestling in the lee of towering San Jacinto, it basks in the golden sun and balmy desert air. At night, when a silvery moon rises over the mountains, the place is almost etherial in charm and peacefulness. It is one of my favorite spots.

But there has been struggle here as well as beauty. Indeed, how can there be any real beauty without struggle?

This charming Inn came into being through faith and positive thinking. Mrs. Hardy had plenty of troubles before making a success of her enterprise. She knew that she needed spiritual strength to do it and searched everywhere for guidance. She found help through Ernest Holmes and others.

To a friend, who passed the letter along to me, she writes:

> It is strange how Norman's teachings came to me. Away back in 1942, when I was left alone, I decided I had to have some plan of living or something to go by. I have read everything that I could find in metaphysics that seemed to have some of the answers. Then along in the 40's someone sent me some of the literature from the Marble Collegiate Church. To me it made sense, and I thought that if this theory that I believed in really works than I should depend on it. And from that time on I have attempted as near as possible to run Ingleside along the plan for living that Norman advocates. Norman has told me many times that his theory is in the proving stage. He believes it and he knows it works, and he is always looking for evidence and proof that it *is* the way of life.

You know, by all the rules of aerodynamics, the bumblebee cannot fly! But the bumblebee doesn't know it and just keeps on flying! He is too fat, too big, and his wings are too short, but he just keeps going. In all the hotel books it says that any American Plan hotel under fifty rooms cannot exist, as there is not enough income to make it survive, as it is too small an operation with a dining room. Yet for twenty-six years I have run a small American Plan hotel, and it has worked. And the more I go along the lines of Norman's teachings, the better it works. I find I don't have to hurry and strain and be tense—I find that it is a very relaxing, happy life, all because I ask God for guidance and get it. I read my Bible and my books and apply the theory. The greatest thing that ever happened to me was to have Norman's literature fall into my hands.

Positive thinking has been responsible for many a successful battle against failure by turning another prevalent kind of weakness into strength. One man, today a successful and respected executive, had to battle a dull sense of inferiority. When I first met him he seemed an extremely retiring young man. In fact, he was retiring to the point of shrinking. It was a real weakness which hampered him greatly. By it he minimized himself and gave the impression that he lacked force and ability.

He was with a large business organization in the personnel department. One day he was notified that his services were no longer required—this after eight years with the company. He was crushed and dazed. He had accumulated very little money, the future was dark, he was keenly discouraged. But then a strange thing happened; now that he had to depend upon himself, now that he was faced by a real crisis, he turned his weakness into strength. He remembered some of the things we had been saying about positive thinking, and he resolved to put these theories to work.

I heard of his difficulty and said, "I want to help you. I have some contacts and maybe we can do something."

But to my surprise he replied, "I do not want you to do a thing, not a thing. I am going to put your principles of positive thinking into effect. You just forget me except to pray for me; that is all. If these principles are workable, they will work whether you help me or not, and if they will not work, then your help will not do me much good." I liked that as it showed strength coming up.

A few months later he told me of the results of his experiment. He said, "For the first time in my life I was forced to do some real creative thinking. Here I was, no job, none in sight and a family to support. But I visualized that somewhere was a future for me. Indeed, I intended to find it. I had to use my brain and my faith to do it."

So what did he do? Simply this; he secured the names of the presidents of one hundred firms. He read *Who's Who* and other types of directories in order to form an insight into the thinking of each executive whom he wanted to contact. He studied what type of businessmen they were. He investigated their personal attitudes, their likes and dislikes. He developed a comprehensive analysis of the mental slant of each man.

To each of them he then wrote a personal letter saying that he was trained for personnel work and outlining his experience. He told the prospective employer, modestly but specifically, what he had to offer. He outlined how he felt he could help that employer. He slanted his sales presentation of his own services to the employer's self-interest. He was not bold, but neither was he shrinking. He presented his qualifications objectively. And he received a number of replies expressing interest.

He held on to his mental picture of the work he wanted, continuing to think positively, and his contacts produced a choice between two good positions. He accepted a job at twelve hundred dollars more a year than he had received in the business he had left. After he started his new job I said to him, "It is really a miracle, the thing that happened to you."

"Miracle, not at all. It's merely a demonstration of the power of positive thinking which you teach. I've discovered by the acid test of personal experience that positive thinking is practically and scientifically sound. I know now why the Bible tells us to have faith, for when you believe, really believe, your mind becomes clear and then you can think your way through your difficulties. And besides," he added, "an experience like this isn't all bad. Maybe I needed something to shake me out of the mouse-like, half-scared rabbit that I was. I feel more self-confidence now." He had, in fact, become strongest where previously he had been weakest.

The most effective way for developing strength from weakness is through the life changing process of a positive faith. Evidences of this fact are multiplied daily; so much so, that selection among illustrations is most difficult. Dramatic demonstrations of people who out of weakness were made strong seem to be without limit.

Oftentimes I have mentioned this process of change to people struggling with a weakness and they say to me, "But I go to church, I contribute to charities and read my Bible. It seems to me that I am living with an active faith and it doesn't help at all." But, you see, the really important thing is a spiritual experience of God's power. It requires much more than religious formality to do the powerful job necessary in building real strength out of weakness.

Take the case of Bill Carter. I will call him that though Carter is not his name. Bill was having a great deal of trouble with alcohol. He tried every known method of curing himself of this weakness, with no results at all. One day his physician told him rather bluntly, "Bill, I am sorry but there is nothing more that I can do for you."

"You mean my case is hopeless?"

"Yes, unless you get top expert help."

"But, Doctor, who knows more about alcoholism than you?"

"Well," said the doctor, "I know of one specialist who might be able to help you. He is very high priced, however, and you'll have to be willing to pay. He takes everything you've got, but He can cure you for sure."

Bill sat straight up in his chair. "Who is this specialist? I will pay whatever is necessary if I can just get a hold on myself and solve this drinking problem."

"Bill," said the physician, "this specialist I'm talking about keeps office in the New Testament. You know who He is. And I doubt very much that you are willing to pay the price He asks. I know that you go to church, say your prayers; you even read your Bible, but you are not paying the price required for change. And what does this Doctor charge? Yourself, your whole self. You're holding out, that's why we can't get a cure in your case. You won't let go of that last 5 per cent of yourself. I've got the alcohol boiled out of you, but that area of 5 per cent of your brain, that I cannot reach. Only the Great Physician can get in there and cure the weakness that licks you and will continue to lick you.

"You see, you have to go all out, give all of yourself. Do that and you will really get strength."

What a doctor! He was a doctor of the mind and soul as well as body. It is true that a great many of us actually are giving just a part of ourselves to our faith. It takes the whole man, the whole heart and soul, to make religious faith effective in this deeper sense. Bill Carter finally took his doctor's advice. He said a simple prayer which, however, was a prayer he had never before been able to say. Here is what he said —and meant:

"Lord, I am no longer going to hold on to this 5 per cent of resistance. I am going to give You the whole of myself. You take charge. I no longer belong to me. Do with me what You will. Amen."

As a result, spiritual power began to come. In time Bill's ability to cope with the problem of alcohol strengthened. Today he is a sober and effective person because he learned how to give all of himself to God's will. "When I let God take over," he said, "I could actually feel that old weakness being burned out of me." It is a basic fact about faith that it will work with power when you give *all* of yourself to what you believe. Withhold nothing. Have no reservations. Believe *positively* with all your heart, all your mind, all your spirit and no weakness can be too great for you to master.

In this chapter we have been looking at the methods used by actual people to transform weakness into strength through positive thinking. We have paid particular attention to anger, inferiority, discouragement, moral defeat.

The same principles can be applied to any weakness, whatever it is. Bring your own particular problem into the patterns suggested by this chapter. First, get your problem into a clear focus so that you know specifically what weakness it is you are trying to combat. Then focus on the results you wish to attain; specifically, what is it that you wish to accomplish? Start right away to become the person you wish to be. Practice expecting to be strongest in your weakest place. And you will be. Always persevere in your efforts to attain this goal. Don't give up. Continue—continue—continue.

If you feel your energies flagging, reread this chapter; notice in particular how others who have faced similar weaknesses have carried on to victory. And, finally, keep forever before you the firm belief that God does not intend you to be victimized by weaknesses. Believe this, for it is true. Believe that the natural way for you to face life is with courage and strength. Believe that God built potential strength into you which you have not been using. But now you are going to start using it.

Isolate your weak spot, specify the results you wish to attain, picture yourself becoming strong, start being the strong person you wish to be. Act as though you are now changing into strength, believe you can attain the results you seek, humbly trusting in God to help you. This is the pattern, the tremendous pattern of deep personality change. Apply it to your own particular problem and you, too, can become strongest in your weakest place.

In fact your whole life can become stronger and happier in every particular. As you study and apply the teachings of this book, great things will happen to you because something great will have happened within you. Your stronger faith, deeper understanding and greater dedications will open up a wonderful new life for you. You will become a vital personality well able to handle all your own problems. And you will have enough extra strength and insight to be a creative influence in the lives of many others.

No more defeat, no more failure, no more dull hopelessness. Life won't suddenly become easy or superficial—not at all. Life is real. Life is earnest and it is full of problems. But thank God it now becomes full of the overcoming of problems. Through the formulas of thinking and acting outlined in this book you need no longer be mastered by your difficulties. You can now master them. The difference is due to that Master who has entered into your life to make you a very different person. So to you, as to the others will come the amazing results of positive thinking.

# Epilogue

I COULD GO ON and on telling of the amazing results of positive thinking. So many others than those mentioned in this book have experienced great personal victories. And I would like to tell you about all of them. But there is a limit to the length of a book. And we must close.

But before doing so there is just one final thing I want to say: Never become discouraged with yourself or with your life. Never give in to defeat, never lose heart.

There is a way out, there is a way around, there is a way through any problem, any difficulty. And that way is by positive thinking and positive action. It is accomplished by spiritual motivation.

What others have done—with the help of God—you also can do. And how to do it has been stated with sincerity, and, I hope, with clarity in this book. On page after page are formulas and techniques used by others to turn defeat into victory.

Now that you have read the book go back and practice it. This, unlike most books, is not merely a reading book. It's a practicing manual. It will work, but only when you work it. For best results disciplined and prayerful perseverance is required.

I dedicated this book in sincere prayer. I dedicated it to God with a prayer that it might help you. And the book *can* help you as others have been helped. Faithfully practice its teachings as suggested and you too can have the amazing results of positive thinking.

With friendly good wishes and a sincere God bless you, I am

Cordially yours,
NORMAN VINCENT PEALE